To my longtime
colleague, friend,
and supporter, John Shoven,
with deep admiration

Ralph Landau

~ 26, 1994

Uncaging Animal Spirits

Uncaging Animal Spirits

Essays on Engineering,
Entrepreneurship,
and Economics

Ralph Landau

edited by
Martha V. Gottron

The MIT Press
Cambridge, Massachusetts
London, England

This book was set in Palatino by Asco Trade Typesetting Ltd., Hong Kong, and was printed and bound in the United States of America.

Library of Congress Cataloging-in-Publication Data

Landau, Ralph.
  Uncaging animal spirits: essays on engineering, entrepreneurship, and economics / Ralph Landau; edited by Martha V. Gottron.
    p.   cm.
  Includes bibliographical references (p.   ) and index.
  ISBN 0-262-12183-2
  1. Chemical industry. 2. Chemical engineering. I. Title.
HD9560.5.L233   1994
338.4'766—dc20   94-817
                                                                    CIP

"Most, probably, of our decisions to do something positive, the full consequences of which will be drawn out over many days to come, can only be taken as a result of animal spirits—of a spontaneous urge to action rather than inaction, and not as the outcome of a weighted average of quantitative benefits multiplied by quantitative probabilities.

"Enterprise only pretends to itself to be mainly actuated by the statements in its own prospectus, however candid and sincere. Only a little more than an expedition to the South Pole, is it based on an exact calculation of benefits to come. Thus if the animal spirits are dimmed and the spontaneous optimism falters, leaving us to depend on nothing but a mathematical expectation, enterprise will fade and die;—though fears of loss may have a basis no more reasonable than hopes of profit had before. . . .

"This means, unfortunately, not only that slumps and depressions are exaggerated in degree, but that economic prosperity is excessively dependent on a political and social atmosphere which is congenial to the average business man."

John Maynard Keynes
General Theory of Employment, Interest, and Money

Contents

Foreword:
The Endless Career

This book is about an individual in search of understanding about technology and society and about how the world of theory and practice interact. It is about wealth creation triggered by intellectual curiosity and realized by dogged entrepreneurial spirit. It is also about a human being and the way he saw the world—his view of how he could contribute to the world's well-being while enriching himself intellectually and materially. It is about a lesson to all that careers do not have an end but are only pathways to new modes of personal enrichment and service to society. This book is about Ralph Landau and his work and ideas; about his intellectual drive, his managerial styles, and his philanthropic deeds that continue to enrich the education of students and all others who can benefit by example.

This book goes to the heart of the poorly understood process of the interaction between technology and economics, and the way that the power of technology to improve mankind's lot can be released by wise economic policies. As Ralph Landau points out, technology is the source of wealth creation in the modern world. It is the product of the resources of the mind. In modern times it is the resource that confers the comparative economic advantage that arises from intellectual achievement tempered in the furnace of daily competition among firms and countries. Wealth creation is the key to higher standards of living, a quality environment, and good health care. It is also the touchstone of economic and military influence in world affairs.

In microcosm this book illustrates the opportunities, the obstacles, and the satisfaction of a career of a single individual in the field of chemical engineering. Multiply Ralph Landau's career a thousand times and you have the greatness of America.

Robert White
President, National Academy of Engineering

Introduction

Ralph Landau defines an entrepreneur as one who brings together people, money, markets, production facilities, and knowledge to create a profitable commercial enterprise. He is, of course, defining his own experience. As cofounder and chief executive of what was one of the most successful chemical engineering design firms in the world, Landau was instrumental in developing and commercializing nearly a dozen innovative chemical products and processes in use today—a remarkable record for any company and especially for a small entrepreneurial company operating in an intensely competitive field.

Landau's creativity extended well beyond the design and construction of process technology. The involvement of chemical engineers in all phases of the business, from the bench to the sales office to the front office, was itself an innovation that helped to establish the relatively new profession as an integral part of the chemical industry. So, too, were many of the financial arrangements that Landau and his partner, Harry Rehnberg, put together. In a capital-intensive industry, they were able to finance their company's operations for nearly forty years without turning to outside investors. Close attention to the realities of the marketplace and opportunities for commercialization, combined with astute business and management skills and one of the best chemical research and management teams ever assembled, earned the company and Landau an outstanding reputation and ultimately substantial financial reward.

Others also benefited from the company's creativity and success. Two American chemical companies, Amoco Chemical and Arco Chemical, were built on processes developed by Landau's engineers and chemists. Through licensing agreements, plant construction, and manufacturing arrangements with chemical companies on nearly every continent, Landau and his company helped spur the growth of the petrochemical industry after World War II. This is now one of the largest global industries, employing tens of thousands of workers and providing thousands of everyday products to consumers around the world.

In 1982 Landau sold his company and embarked on a new career as an academic economist. This shift was motivated in large part by a strong sense that the economic policies of the U.S. federal government were adversely affecting incentives for investment and innovation and that neither politicians nor many economists fully understood the vital role technology plays in promoting economic growth. Landau decided that only concentrated study of the relationship between technology and growth could give him the grounding he needed to draw others to his viewpoint.

Now able to converse comfortably in the language of both the entrepreneur and the economist, and to see issues from both perspectives, Landau uses a variety of forums—meetings, seminars, papers, and books—to move academic economists, politicians, technologists, and business executives toward a more comprehensive view of the issues involved in growth. He argues that the factors affecting the commercialization of technology, not the development of the technology itself, determine the level and often the rate of economic growth. His hope is that a broader understanding of these basic issues will lead to public policies that foster a climate in which innovation, risk-taking, competition, and thus economic growth can flourish.

Landau's crusade has already shown some signs of success. David Warsh of the *Boston Globe* noted just before the 1988 presidential election that "Landau has for much of a decade brokered a dialogue between engineers, economists, and high-tech businessmen. In the last few months, the talk has paid off by achieving a surprisingly widespread consensus among professionals about the nature of the problems facing the next president of the United States."

The Chemical Engineer

"Luck," Landau is fond of saying, "beats brains every time. And I've been a very lucky man." No doubt Landau was lucky, but he gave the luck a powerful boost. Creative intelligence, focused persistence, flexibility, an uncanny ability to recognize and seize opportunities, a willingness to take risks, and a clear vision of the goals he was pursuing all combined to make Landau one of the foremost entrepreneurs of post-World War II America. His achievement is all the more remarkable because Landau devoted his energies to an industry in which many niche and specialty companies are dominated by large transnational firms.

In a very real sense, Landau, the petrochemical industry, and the chemical engineering profession grew up together and nurtured each other. When Landau was born on May 19, 1916, the petroleum-based chemical industry and the chemical engineering profession were also in their infancy. Until World War I, organic chemicals were derived primarily from coal tars, and Germany was the undisputed industry leader. When German exports of coal-based chemicals to the United States were cut off during the war, U.S. chemical companies were forced to develop their own sources for raw materials. Coal was, of course, a possibility. The most attractive alternative, however, was oil, which the country had in abundance and which could fuel the new mass-produced automobiles that clearly would be in high demand when the war ended. The chemical companies therefore began to develop both continuous and automatic processes for refining petroleum into gasoline and also the processes that would eventually produce petroleum-based raw and intermediate materials for other uses.

Coincidentally, 1916 was also the year in which William H. Walker and Warren K. Lewis established the School of Chemical Engineering Practice at the Massachusetts Institute of Technology. The "practice school," as it soon became known, consisted of several small installations, known as "stations," set up by MIT at chemical companies and supervised by MIT faculty members. Graduate students rotated through these stations, working in operating plants on solutions to real research, engineering, and design problems encountered by the host company. The experience benefited both the companies, which in those days seldom had research laboratories of their own, and the students, for whom the experience added a practical dimension to their more theoretical classroom work. As one observer wrote, "these industrial plants became [the students'] laboratories, where making a profit was an essential criterion for success and chemical engineering was practiced on a scale impossible in an academic environment."

Growing up in Philadelphia, Landau knew little of these developments until his sophomore year of high school (1930), when he began to think about possible careers. A story in the *Philadelphia Evening Bulletin* about the new "glamour field" of chemical engineering captured his attention. In the Depression era, "glamour" was an enticing word. "I made up my mind, tentatively, to be a chemical engineer, not knowing a damn thing about it," he has said.

Gifted in math and science and well read in English and German, Landau at age 16 graduated first in his high school class and won a full scholarship to the University of Pennsylvania, where he majored in chemical engineering and, fortunately for his career plans, "loved it." One professor tried to persuade him to become a physicist. Quantum physics and electron diffraction had both recently been invented, and if it was soon to be a golden age for the chemical industry, that era had already arrived for physicists. Landau agreed to take a graduate-level physics course during his junior year at Penn. He finished first in the class (ahead of a few professors who were also taking the course) but concluded that this was not the career for him. "Physics was too theoretical," he has said. "I wanted to deal with real things, to make things happen."

Landau ranked first in his engineering class at Penn, where he received his degree in 1937. He decided to take a doctorate in chemical engineering for the simple reason that 1937 was a dismal year for a job search, and he chose MIT for graduate work "because it was without question the leading university in chemical engineering." A national Tau Beta Pi fellowship helped him finance his first year, while jobs as a teaching assistant and then as a research assistant supported his later years at MIT.

During his practice school work at a steel mill in Buffalo, a paper mill in Bangor, and a chemical plant in Parlin, New Jersey, Landau discovered that he had a zest for problem-solving. "I never worked so hard in my life, but I learned how to concentrate and get a job done under forced draft," Landau told John Matill, the author of a book about the practice school experience. Here he also began to learn the art of interacting with others—in this case, describing the work of his team to faculty and fellow students.

Although his advisers told him he would be good at research, Landau was still not sure what career path to follow. Doctorates in chemical engineering were rare in the 1930s, and because the profession itself was still so new, few companies fully understood the services that chemical engineers might offer. Many of his classmates went on to work for the oil companies, where several made their reputations and their fortunes, among them Jerry McAfee, who became chairman of Gulf Oil, Maurice F. "Butch" Granville, who became chairman of Texaco, and Robert C. Gunness, who became president of Standard Oil of Indiana.

Landau's future began to crystallize in the summer of 1939, when he helped design petroleum refining plants for M. W. Kellogg, one of the first of the specialized engineering firms that were beginning to undertake the design and development work necessary for full-scale processing, primarily for oil companies. That was when he "began to pick up what design companies really know how to do," to understand the full potential of the systems approach of chemical engineering.

When Landau returned to Kellogg after receiving his doctorate in 1941, the company placed him in its design unit as a process development engineer working primarily on chemical plants. In 1943 Landau was transferred to the Kellex Corporation, a Kellogg subsidiary, and was assigned to work on the Manhattan District Project. Warren Lewis, Landau's mentor at MIT, had earlier recommended him for a war research assignment as someone who had "a head on his shoulders." "Coming from Doc Lewis," Landau has said, "that's the greatest compliment I ever had." The young engineer soon headed the chemical department. Working both in Oak Ridge, Tennessee, and New York, he took charge of designing the equipment to produce and dispose of fluorine, a highly corrosive and toxic substance that was used to manufacture uranium hexafluoride, from which uranium 235 and uranium 238 were derived. He was also responsible for the production of all fluorinated compounds, such as plastics and lubricating oils that could resist the fluorine and uranium hexafluoride.

To accomplish all this, Landau coordinated research and manufacturing on various aspects of fluorine conducted by several companies and universities. The experience, he later wrote, taught him "that bringing together the very best talent from many different sources was a powerful process development tool." It also demonstrated that the systems approach could be applied to a larger sphere than that in which the chemical engineer normally functioned, namely problems of war and peace and the larger economy. (See chapter 13, "The Chemical Engineer and the CPI.")

It was at Oak Ridge that Landau met Harry Rehnberg, a construction engineer who was in charge of building the fluorine unit Landau had designed. Rehnberg was not eager to return to the machine shop he had left in Seattle and kept urging Landau to go into business with him. Landau has described Rehnberg as "fearless—not always sure what he was going to find but absolutely sure that something good would come of it." The two men tossed several different ideas around over daytime coffee and evening poker games. "I'd say, 'What are we going to do?'" Landau recounted, "and Harry would say, 'I don't know. You tell me.'" As the war drew to a close and work at Oak Ridge began to wind down, the two seemed no closer to an answer.

Then one day it dawned on Landau that he and Rehnberg could set up an engineering design company, applying to chemical plants the same systems approach that Kellogg employed to design petroleum refineries. Landau and Rehnberg would provide everything from the process design to the actual construction and start-up of the plant. "We had dabbled with petrochemicals at Kellogg," Landau has said, "but it was obvious that wasn't their main interest. And I had a hunch that petrochemicals were coming in. So I suggested this to Harry, and he said, 'Fine, let's do it.'"

All the two men needed was a job to get them started. Landau decided to call on his former boss at Kellogg, who had become the vice president of research for Stauffer Chemical. As luck would have it, Stauffer was looking for someone to help design a full-scale plant for a new process the company had developed for making monochloracetic acid. While Rehnberg negotiated the details of the contract, Landau returned temporarily to Kellogg. In June 1946, with a contract in hand, Scientific Design Company, Inc., was born, with Rehnberg serving as president and Landau as executive vice president. "At this point there were only the two of us and not a hell of a lot of money," Landau has said. (The two had pooled $700 to capitalize the new company.) Several excellent engineers joined the company early on and made important contributions, but by 1957, when the shape of the enterprise truly emerged, these engineers had been bought out or left the company.

Scientific Design completed the Stauffer project, but the materials used in construction—the only ones available within the project's economic constraints—could not withstand the acid's corrosivity, and the plant was eventually converted to other uses. By then, however, Landau and Rehnberg had bought a laboratory on 32nd Street off Park Avenue in New York City. Realizing that innovative and proprietary research had been the key to Kellogg's success, Landau believed that Scientific Design's fortunes lay in researching and developing original chemical processing technology that it could ultimately use in its own manufacturing operations. Until the company had sufficient capital to engage in manufacturing, it would license its processes to others and construct production plants incorporating those processes; but eventually the company would also manufacture many of the catalysts these plants used.

The Start-Up Years

Landau has said on more than one occasion that he and Rehnberg made up Scientific Design as they went along. Although that may be true in the details, they began with several key principles in place. The two men were adamant that they would retain control of the company. They wanted the flexibility to move quickly to take advantage of market opportunities and to take longer-term risks. During the company's first decade, Landau and Rehnberg occasionally financed some portion of their operation with company shares; their first laboratory, for example, was paid for with stock, which the two men bought back as soon as possible. Although after 1957 they occasionally offered modest stock sales or participation in executive compensation packages to key executives and technologists, they were always the dominant stockholders.

The two men would also seek out the ablest associates they could find and would offer them long-term incentives to induce them to join the company. Landau says he always saw himself as the conductor of the orchestra who gave overall direction to the technologists who were already masters of their individual jobs.

Furthermore, all research would have to have a practical application. The demands of the marketplace would determine the research to be undertaken, and research that could not be commercialized or competitive would be abandoned. Because technology was their capital, Landau and Rehnberg would seek and enforce patents on any original processes the company developed.

Accordingly, Landau and Rehnberg aimed their first effort at one of the fastest-growing and most widely used chemical compounds, ethylene oxide. The compound is a key component of both antifreeze and polyester fiber, which was just beginning to be exploited in 1946. At the time, the industry was using large quantities of expensive oxidants, such as nitric acid, chlorine, and pure oxygen for organic oxidations. "We decided ... our work should concentrate on air as the cheapest of all oxidants," Landau and a colleague wrote in 1965. (See chapter 5, "Making Research Pay.")

Scientific Design's first major development—and the company's first significant patent—was a direct air oxidation process for producing ethylene oxide. Although SD was not the first to use direct air oxidation, it used a more efficient catalyst that made the process cheaper to install and operate than the chlorohydrin process typically used to produce the chemical. (See chapter 1, "Ethylene Oxide by Direct Oxidation.") Scientific Design now needed to scale up the design to resolve some remaining problems, and the company soon made an arrangement with an innovative British oil company, Petrochemicals Ltd., to build a pilot plant in England in exchange for an exclusive license in the United Kingdom.

With the pilot plant up and running in 1948, Landau and Rehnberg thought they might be able to realize their ambition to participate in a manufacturing arrangement. Within a year they were negotiating with Sears Roebuck, which had an obvious market for antifreeze, and Shell Chemical, which had surplus ethylene, about joint ownership of a plant to produce ethylene oxide with the SD process. Sears approved the venture, but the talks collapsed when Shell withdrew. Scientific Design, which went on to license its process to customers throughout the world, later found itself in a head-to-head competition with Shell that was to last for decades. A few years after developing its ethylene oxide process, Scientific Design came up with its first original process, the bromine-assisted oxidation of paraxylene to terephthalic acid, which is the main raw ingredient in polyester fiber. (See chapter 2, "Development of the M-C Process.") Again, Landau and Rehnberg thought they might be able to interest another company in a manufacturing venture. Through the networking that successful entrepreneurial companies tirelessly nurture, they learned that Standard Oil of Indiana (Amoco) was interested in their process, and in 1956 the smaller company proposed a partnership to the large oil company. Standard Oil viewed this proposal as "the mating of an elephant and a mouse" and instead offered to buy the worldwide rights to the process. Landau and Rehnberg agreed to the sale, which brought the two men their first substantial personal financial gains in ten years of partnership. The process became the foundation on which Standard's subsidiary, Amoco Chemicals Corp., grew, and the company remains the leading manufacturer of terephthalic acid in the world today.

In these first years, royalties and engineering fees from licensing and design, primarily to foreign manufacturers, were Scientific Design's bread and butter. The company's first ventures in foreign markets were born of a combination of opportunity and necessity. In the years immediately after the war, few of the major American chemical companies were willing to buy technology from outside companies. Indeed, aside from its work for Stauffer, Scientific Design did not perform any work for companies in the United States until 1954, when Allied Chemical gave it some engineering contracts.

At the same time, European oil and chemical companies were struggling to get their petrochemical programs off the ground. Many had some of the money and feedstocks necessary but lacked the technology. Nascent chemical companies in some of the more advanced developing countries also began to seek out special engineering firms like Scientific Design, which could provide process technology and could also construct the production facilities and transmit the know-how learned from replicating a particular process many times over. (See chapter 14, "Role of American Engineering Design Companies in the Chemical Process Industry" and chapter 15, "Technology and Obsolescence in the Petrochemical Industries for Developing Countries.")

Scientific Design built its first commercial ethylene oxide plant in France in 1953 for Naphtachimie, a subsidiary of the French firm Pechiney and the

British Petroleum Company. In the next few years, the company had licensed technology to major chemical companies in Britain, France, Holland, Germany, and the United States. By 1960 the company had offices in London, Paris, and Tokyo. Landau traveled extensively, seeking new business and new ideas, while keeping tabs on work in progress. Scientific Design and its successor companies, Halcon International and the Halcon-SD Group, eventually worked in thirty countries in the Americas, Europe, the Soviet Union, Asia, Australia, and the Middle East. It was in many ways a forerunner in the globalization of industry. Indeed, when Landau was elected to the National Academy of Engineering in 1972, his citation was for his activities in chemical process licensing.

As gratifying as it was to play a key role in building the global chemical industry and spreading its benefits to consumers throughout the world, Landau, like others, eventually began to question the wisdom of selling technologies to companies that would then compete against American firms. He also knew that licensing alone could not sustain Scientific Design. To be sure, licensing had its advantages. Selling the same or a variation of a process to many different companies allowed SD to spread the costs of research and development among many clients, and the valuable know-how the company gained each time it designed a new plant for a particular process helped it to stay ahead of its competition.

But royalty income was unlikely to be sufficient to finance the increasingly expensive research and development of new technology. "Licensees prefer to pay only for your research successes and leave the failures to you," Landau observed on more than one occasion. Furthermore, a service company such as Scientific Design was unlikely ever to have a large capital value. Only through manufacturing could the company and its owners realize a full return on its innovative technology.

The Breakthrough Years

The late 1950s and early 1960s were especially creative years for Scientific Design. The sale of the M-C process to one of the large oil companies gained the company recognition as one of the leading innovators in the field. Although some of the big companies still refused to buy technology from engineering design firms, the prejudice against technology "not invented here" was in decline. American companies figured increasingly among SD's licensees.

Other discoveries and developments added to the luster of the company's reputation. In 1955 SD began to license an improved catalyst for oxidizing benzene to produce maleic anhydride, used in malathion insecticide and fiberglass resins. Some years later, the company developed an alternative process that used butane as the oxidizing agent. By the late 1970s, more than half of the world's maleic anhydride was produced with one of these processes.

In 1959 Scientific Design announced another breakthrough: the development of air oxidation technology to convert cyclic aliphatics into a variety of alcohols (with some acids and ketones), including the key intermediates used in making nylon. (See chapter 3, "Boron-Promoted Oxidation of Paraffins and Cycloparaffins.") Monsanto eventually acquired an exclusive license for the process in the United States; Scientific Design also licensed the process to Rhone-Poulenc, ICI, Bayer, and Mitsubishi, among others.

During this same period, in collaboration with the Goodyear Tire and Rubber Company, Scientific Design developed a new method for producing isoprene based on the dimerization of propylene. SD then designed an isoprene plant as part of a $30 million synthetic rubber complex that Goodyear built. The isoprene was used to produce an array of rubber products. (Goodyear was forced to close this plant after the 1973–74 shock made it uneconomic to operate.)

Throughout this period the company continued to patent and license its processes, engineer and construct plants, and manufacture proprietary catalysts. Ultimately the company built more than 300 plants throughout the world and held more than 1,400 patents, worldwide.

The Oxirane Venture

It was in 1962 that Scientific Design discovered the original process that gave Landau and Rehnberg the manufacturing opportunity they had long sought. The discovery was a process for producing high yields of propylene oxide, a major constituent in polyurethane foams and rigid polymers widely used in mattresses, furniture, automobiles, and insulation. The process produces two important co-products: tertiary butyl alcohol (TBA), which is used to improve gasoline octane numbers and to produce high-purity isobutylene for butyl rubber, and styrene, which is used in a variety of plastics applications and as a component of synthetic rubber. (See chapter 4, Epoxidation of Olefins.")

"There was never any doubt in my mind that this technology would be our ticket to chemical manufacturing," Landau has written. To exploit the discovery, the company reorganized in 1963, forming Halcon International Inc., with Rehnberg as chairman and Landau as president. (Upon

Rehnberg's death in 1975, Landau became chairman and chief executive officer as well as the major stockholder.) Scientific Design became a wholly owned subsidiary of Halcon, engaged in design and construction. Four other subsidiary companies were eventually formed: Halcon Chemical Company, Inc.; Halcon Computer Technologies, Inc., which engaged in computerized engineering services; Halcon Research and Development Corp., which became the R&D entity; and Catalyst Development Corp., which manufactured proprietary catalysts.

The newly formed company embarked on the search for a partner. The Atlantic Richfield Company was not an immediately obvious choice, but the two companies soon found they had many mutual interests. Robert O. Anderson, ARCO's board chairman, and Robert D. Bent, the head of ARCO's newly formed chemical company, wanted to enlarge the company but did not have all the people or technology they needed. Furthermore, ARCO was conducting oxidation research along similar lines but recognized that Halcon was likely to hold the crucial patents. The agreement to set up the separate Oxirane Corporation, with ownership shared 50–50, took only six months to negotiate. This wholly new field of activity required executives with quite different experience from that of the managers in the Halcon organization. Landau therefore recruited a number of key officers who helped materially in running both Halcon and Oxirane. Many of the financial and management aspects of this unusual partnership are described in chapter 8, "Corporate Partnering Can Spur Innovation."

By 1978 the partnership had built and was operating five plants in Texas, one in the Netherlands, one in Spain, and one in Japan, all based on new technology. These plants had a combined capacity of 7 billion pounds, and sales exceeded $1 billion a year. The Oxirane venture also brought Halcon—and ultimately its stockholders—the first large sums of money in the company's history, "far, far more than we ever could have made in licensing," Landau says.

The Meaning of Risk

Meanwhile, research continued in Halcon's laboratory, which had moved from 32nd Street in Manhattan to Port Washington and then to Little Ferry, New Jersey. In the late 1960s, while looking for a way to make ethylene oxide through liquid phase oxidation, Halcon researchers hit on a method for producing high yields of ethylene glycol directly from ethylene. Ethylene glycol is used in a wide variety of products, including antifreeze, polyester fiber, plastics, and fiberglass. When the Organization of Petroleum Exporting States imposed its oil embargo in 1973, causing a shortage and raising the price of petroleum-based ethylene, the Halcon process, which produced substantially more than a pound of glycol from a pound of ethylene, seemed particularly promising.

Once again Halcon appeared to have a manufacturing opportunity. DuPont, which used glycol to produce Dacron polyester fiber, was an obvious potential partner. A demonstration of the new process for DuPont officials was successful, but DuPont ultimately decided it did not want to get involved in producing a commodity chemical.

Then ARCO Chemical Company decided to build a second cracking plant and suggested that the Halcon glycol process might be a good outlet for some of the ethylene produced. The initial Oxirane agreement did not cover new processes, and so the two companies negotiated a new financing arrangement that involved construction of two new plants at Channelview, Texas, one a propylene oxide-styrene plant, which used a thoroughly tested and commercially established Halcon process, and the second, an ethylene glycol plant, using the new Halcon process. The glycol plant would come on line nine months after the styrene plant, so that the cash flow from the styrene plant would carry the cost of the glycol start-up. To finance construction of the project, the company borrowed $230 million from a bank syndicate at the prime rate, which was then 11 percent.

At first, the project went more or less according to plan; but almost as soon as the glycol plant was started up, corrosion problems appeared that had not been apparent during the pilot demonstrations. By the time Halcon engineers were able to coax full yields from the plant, it was 1979 and the second energy crisis had hit. The glycol process used a great quantity of energy to recycle the many intermediate products. "The energy costs, which had been calculated in the early 1970s, had become an enormous burden on the process by the late 1970s," Landau said. "We had to shut it down. Halcon and ARCO both agreed there was no point in maintaining a process that simply would not pay for itself."

By the winter of 1979, Landau had yet another problem: The $230 million loan taken out to help finance the Channelview plant was tied to the prime interest rate, which was rising steadily as inflation accelerated in the late 1970s. When the prime rate hit 21 percent in late 1979 and early 1980, "all our cash flow was going to the banks," Landau wrote in "The CEO and the Technologist" chapter 25 in this volume. "Technological strategy was no longer my concern—it was sheer survival." Thus, when ARCO offered to buy Halcon's share in Oxirane for what Landau considered to be a fair price, he agreed. After the sale, in June 1980, ARCO

Chemical continued to expand; in 1990 it was the largest producer of propylene oxide and tertiary-butanol in the world, and one of the largest styrene producers.

Without its Oxirane connection, Halcon, now formally the Halcon SD Group, was once again a licensing company with a large research department—by many accounts the best in the industry. One process it had been working on—and the last to be licensed—was technology to convert carbon monoxide derived from coal into acetic anhydride, which is used to produce rayon and films. The Tennessee Eastman division of Eastman Kodak had discovered a similar process at about the same time, and in 1980 the two companies decided to merge their technology. Tennessee Eastman would own the process, while Halcon would retain worldwide licensing rights. Tennessee Eastman built a plant incorporating the technology, which began operation in 1983. This was the first commercial process based on coal to be developed since petroleum-based chemicals began to dominate the industry.

Another process was also showing some promise, and Landau thought that Halcon might be able to stand on its own, but he was soon forced to reconsider. "Everything fell apart in 1981," he said, as a consequence of the deflationary, tight-money policies of the Federal Reserve Bank, and in November he decided to sell the company. Landau and his executive team searched the world for a buyer, finally finding one in the Texas Eastern Corporation, a pipeline company that wanted to diversify its holdings. The sale was finalized in July 1982. In 1985 Landau sold his remaining manufacturing interest, a share in the Brazilian firm Oxiteno, which manufactured ethylene oxide and derivatives.

Unable to carry the considerable costs of operating Halcon's research division, Texas Eastern eventually closed it down and sold off the remaining part of the company to American Denka, which itself had recently emerged as a management buyout of a Japanese venture. Denka soon sold itself to the German company Bayer. Bayer was interested only in the facilities and processes for producing maleic anhydride and chloroprene rubber and so sold the remaining licensing and catalyst business (once again named Scientific Design) to Linde, a German producer of liquefied air products that was looking for an opening in the United States. Texas Eastern itself became vulnerable to takeover, especially after its acquisition of Petrolane Co. (which was later sold and went into bankruptcy), and was absorbed into the Panhandle Eastern Corp. This extraordinary series of corporate changes in just the latter years of the 1980s serve as powerful examples of the turmoil and corporate merger mania that preceded the recession years of the early 1990s.

Professional Interests

To be successful in any field, Landau says, "you must bathe in the industry, immerse yourself in the stream, and really know everything about it and all the people in it." From the very beginning, Landau practiced his own advice, closely tracking trends in the chemical industry throughout the world and sharing his analysis with others in speeches and articles in professional journals. His first nonscientific articles, for example, were assessments of the rise of the chemical industry and chemical engineering profession in Europe and Japan. (See chapter 9, "Chemical Engineering in West Germany.")

Through his companies, Landau helped to define the role of the chemical engineer both in the United States and abroad. The company's systems approach to solving problems, together with its emphasis on finding cheaper and more efficient production techniques, set a pattern that many other companies imitated. The responsibility and independence that Landau and Rehnberg gave their engineers and scientists produced a creative atmosphere that few others could match.

Indeed, much of Halcon's success was attributable to Landau's innovative use of chemical engineers in all facets of the business. (See chapter 5, "Making Research Pay," chapter 6, "Industrial Innovation: Yesterday and Today," and chapter 7, "Halcon International Inc.—An Entrepreneurial Chemical Company.") Whether they were in the sales office, the legal department, or the front office, Landau believed that chemical engineers were more likely than nontechnical employees to understand and take advantage of opportunities in the marketplace and the laboratory. A chemical engineer was usually in charge of seeing a project through from the laboratory to construction and start-up. Landau himself oversaw the research operation and coordinated its work with the company's other activities.

Landau encouraged open communication among all departments. The SD management hierarchy was relatively flat, which allowed for more direct communication, as did the comparatively small size of the company. The small size also made individual performance easier to recognize and reward. To stimulate creativity, research was often divided among task forces, sometimes with different groups working on various aspects of the same process. Independence was also encouraged. The company had many brilliant scientists and engineers who undertook initiatives on their own, within generally defined strategic goals. All of these management policies anticipated the actions of later entrepreneurs in other high-tech industries.

Landau has maintained an abiding interest in the quality of training that chemical engineering students receive and has been an active alumnus at both Penn, where he is a life trustee emeritus and former chairman of the board of overseers of the engineering school, and MIT, where he is a life member emeritus of the MIT Corporation and the visiting committees to the departments of chemical engineering and economics.

From those positions and in papers, articles, and speeches, Landau has adjured the academic community to relate the intellectual life to the practical world, to match theory to reality. He has expressed concern that engineering professors do not have the practical experience in industry that was more prevalent in earlier decades. He has urged that engineering curricula be broadly drawn so that graduates are equipped with basic business and management skills in addition to their engineering skills. (See chapter 10, "The Chemical Engineer—Today and Tomorrow.")

At Penn, Landau initiated and funded the Landau Chair in Management and Technology to ground students in the skills needed to manage technology-based companies. The four-year undergraduate program gives graduates a B.S. in applied science from the engineering school and a B.S. in economics from the Wharton School. Still the only such curriculum in the country, it is always oversubscribed. Landau also sponsors four Landau fellows in the MIT Practice School as well as three chemical engineering fellows at the California Institute of Technology, where he is also a senior trustee (the only trustee to sit on both the CalTech and MIT boards).

Landau has long contended that substantial benefits can be gained from applying the principles of chemical process engineering to other engineering disciplines. "[P]erhaps the United States needs to invent a really new discipline, a science of modern manufacturing, using the chemical-engineering model," Landau and Nathan Rosenberg wrote in a 1990 article in *American Heritage of Innovation and Technology*. This discipline, which would have a strong computer-science orientation, "should strive to bring together manufacturing with research, design, and development as did chemical engineering long ago." To that end, Landau has recently helped the engineering and business schools at Stanford obtain a grant from the Sloan Foundation to create a manufacturing engineering curriculum embodying concepts similar to those that underlay the founding of chemical engineering by "Doc" Lewis and his colleagues and followers.

Others have since noted this need. "For obscure reasons," MIT's Nobel economist Robert Solow told a congressional committee in 1992, "U.S. industry seems to devote too little of its engineering skill to making continuous routine improvements in the manufacturing process: reducing wasteful movement of people and parts, simplifying designs so that they are easier to manufacture and assemble without defects, adapting existing machines to odd tasks, and so on. Correspondingly, process engineering is looked down upon and neglected in many engineering schools (except in chemical engineering apparently, so maybe it is not surprising that the U.S. chemical industry has preserved its world leadership)."

One of the signal events in Landau's life was the dedication in 1976 of the Landau Chemical Engineering Building at MIT. (See chapter 11, "From Chemical Engineering to Moral Philosophy," and chapter 12, "The Chemical Engineering Trilemma.") When he was first asked to sit on MIT's Visiting Committee to the Department of Chemical Engineering in 1966, the reputation of the department had slipped badly. Among other problems, the department was housed in a building that had been designed as temporary quarters for the Chemical Warfare Service in World War II. The committee strongly recommended construction of a new building to provide modern facilities, raise morale, and attract new students and faculty; it also recommended the appointment of a new department chairman. Landau agreed to fund a large portion of the costs, and the remaining funding for the building, designed by I. M. Pei, was secured in less than a year. Landau was also instrumental in reviving the Practice School and creating an endowment for it, since it too had fallen on hard financial times. It is now the David H. Koch School of Chemical Engineering Practice, named after the final major donor (who had once worked at Scientific Design).

A Wealth of Recognition

Every major honor that the chemical industry and the chemical engineering profession bestow has been awarded to Landau, who quickly acknowledges that his honors also belong to all of his colleagues as well. Among the awards was the Chemical Industry Medal, given by the Society of Chemical Industry, American Section, in 1973 for "conspicuous service to applied chemistry." For Landau this medal was an "exceptional event," signifying that he was no longer viewed as "a peddler of processes" but "a figure of the industry."

In 1981 Landau was awarded the Perkin Medal, making him the first person since 1946 and only the fifth in the history of the awards to receive the two most prestigious medals given by the chemical industry. In 1982 the American Institute of Chemical Engineers gave him its Founder's Award, as did the National Academy of Engineering in 1994. In 1986 the chemical engineering profession (together with the four other founding engineering societies) honored Landau with the John Fritz medal.

In 1985 Landau was among the first group to be awarded a National Medal of Technology. Presented by President Ronald Reagan, the medal cited Landau for his "technical, leadership, and entrepreneurial roles in the development of commercially successful petrochemical processes which have been licensed or jointly developed and have helped maintain U.S. leadership in petrochemical processing." Other honorees in this prestigious initial group included the designer of Boeing's 747 jet airplane, the developers of communications satellites, the team that produced the 360 line of computers as well as the personal computer, and the Bell Telephone Laboratories.

"It was a great thrill to be in this august company, indeed a humbling one," Landau said afterward. Perhaps, he felt, his award represented the nation's appreciation of the key role that the chemical industry played in America's postwar growth and competitiveness. Others, too, have noted the contributions the chemical industry has made to American wealth. (For example, Alfred Chandler, Harvard's preeminent historian of business, chose it as the prototypical high-tech industry in his account of postwar business enterprise development.)

The Economist: A Search for Understanding

Not until he began his own economic studies did Landau run across the term "animal spirits," the phrase John Maynard Keynes coined to describe what motivates men and women to invest time and money in an endeavor for which the return is uncertain. For Landau, Keynes's thesis held much that applied to his own experience. As an innovator and entrepreneur, Landau had exhibited the urge to action and instinctual optimism that Keynes said was necessary to supplement and support "reasonable calculation ... so that the thought of ultimate loss which often overtakes pioneers ... is put aside."

Keynes's observation that economic prosperity is dependent on a congenial political atmosphere held even more resonance for the man who had decided to sell a successful company because he could no longer operate it profitably in the environment of high inflation and high interest rates that prevailed at the beginning of the 1980s. But at the time Landau had only a layman's understanding of economics and economic policy. "I turned to academic economics to try to understand what happened to us at the height of our success," he has written.

Landau's interest in economic policy was not new. For more than a decade, he had been thinking, writing, and talking about the economic

policies and financial problems affecting his and other businesses, general-
izing from the particulars of his experience to the broader and more general
environment. Landau's first realization that government policy might not
always support American business occurred in the late 1960s, when he was
unable to persuade the Johnson administration to help him with a foreign
licensee who had misappropriated some of Halcon's technology and resold
it. (See chapter 16, "The Chemical Process Industries in International Investment and Trade.")

After that experience Landau began to pay more attention to economic
and political policies that affected industry in general and his business in
particular. He didn't like much of what he saw. In his view, tax policy was
changed too frequently and too often penalized innovators and investors.
Well-intentioned government regulations too often imposed unnecessary
costs on companies. At the same time, U.S. productivity was declining,
American companies were beginning to face increasing competition from
foreign companies, inflation and interest rates reached intolerable levels,
and capital markets shrank markedly.

In speeches, journal articles, testimony to congressional committees, and
private conversation, Landau warned that a continuation of policies that
discouraged investment and risk-taking would further erode technological
innovation and economic growth and ultimately undermine the uniquely
successful American entrepreneurial system. Landau once described his
message in those years as "the worm's eye view—how the fellow in
the trenches feels when he gets contradictory and frequently changing
orders from his commanding officers, and what he tends to do about it."
(See chapter 17, "Financial and Capacity Needs," chapter 18, "Innovation
for Fun and Profit," chapter 19, "Taxes—Their Impact on Innovation
Decision-Making," chapter 20, "Technology, Economics, and Public Policy," chapter 22, "Capital Formation in the United States and Japan," chapter 23, "Capital Investment: Key to Competitiveness and Growth," and
chapter 24, "U.S. Economic Growth.)

During this period Landau began his long association with the National
Academy of Engineering. Elected to the NAE in 1972, he was named to its
council the following year and served as vice president from 1981 until his
retirement in 1990. Through his activities with the NAE, Landau met engineers and executives from other industries, economists, and policymakers.
In 1976, while he was working on an NAE project on technology and
trade, Landau began to realize just how little economists and economic
policymakers knew about technology. "They understood that technology
had a big influence on economic growth, but they considered it exogenous,
outside the economic system—'manna from heaven,'" Landau says. It was

then that he decided that he would get involved in economics whenever it became feasible.

That opportunity arose just a few months after the sale of Halcon, when Landau became a consulting professor of economics and of chemical engineering at Stanford University, where he was instrumental in establishing the Technology and Economic Growth Program within the Center for Economic Policy Research. Directed by Nathan Rosenberg, an economic historian, and co-directed by Landau, the program conducts research on the connections between technology and economic growth at both the macroeconomic and microeconomic levels. In appreciation of the importance of the new understanding of growth that Stanford's economists are developing, Landau has contributed the naming gift to build a new Ralph Landau Center for Economics and Policy Research.

Landau has a similar association at Harvard's Kennedy School of Government, where he co-directs the Technology and Economic Policy program with Dale Jorgenson. He is also a member of the National Research Council's Science, Technology, and Economic Policy Board, which he helped organize while he was vice president of the NAE.

In all three forums, Landau—aided by his unique ability to speak the languages of the economist and the technologist—has worked to clarify the links between technology and economic growth. In so doing he has helped to stimulate an ongoing intellectual discussion that is pushing economists, policymakers, and technologists beyond the normal—some would say artificial—bounds of their individual disciplines to see how policy, technology, and economic growth interact. Landau still believes that technology is capital and that technology and physical capital, which complement each other, are the major determinants of economic growth. His hope, as he and his co-editors wrote in *Technology and the Wealth of Nations*, is that this integrated approach will result not only in an end to the conceptual division between innovation and capital formation but also to the adoption of public policies that consistently support investment in physical, human, and intangible (technical) capital.

Since 1982 Landau has co-edited five books dealing with technology and economic growth. *The Positive Sum Strategy: Harnessing Technology for Economic Growth*, co-edited with Rosenberg and published in 1986, was intended to initiate a dialogue between engineers and economists: "Specialization has been not only the source of well-known benefits in economic activity but also the source of spectacular advances in the production of knowledge," the two men wrote in their introduction (see chapter 21 in this volume). "However, increased specialization of disciplines has fostered compartmentalization and fragmentation of knowledge about particular subjects that can, in some instances, prove to be dysfunctional and there-fore costly. This occurs when one group of specialists no longer has even minimal comprehension of bodies of information that are highly relevant to the successful performance of some of its responsibilities.... We believe that we are now at such a juncture in our understanding of the determi-nants of successful technological innovation. We believe that engineers and economists can benefit from a dialogue in which each group of specialists acquires a deeper understanding of the concerns, priorities, insights, and methods of the other."

Technology and Economic Policy, co-edited with Jorgenson, is a collection of essays on the relationships between economic policies, primarily taxa-tion, and technological innovation. A follow-up collection, *Technology and Capital Formation*, examined the relationship between capital formation and technological change. *Technology and the Wealth of Nations*, co-edited with Rosenberg and David Mowery of the University of California, Berkeley, examines issues surrounding the commercialization of technology. The fifth, *Tax Reform and the Cost of Capital: An International Comparison*, co-edited with Jorgenson, compares the effects of tax reforms on investment incentives in nine countries.

In addition, Landau has continued to churn out papers and magazine articles. Three in particular are notable because they synthesize his thinking on three important topics. "The CEO and the Technologist" (chapter 25) discusses the responsibilities of the technologist from management's view-point. "Economic Growth and the Chemical Industry" (chapter 27) uses the chemical industry to illustrate the policies necessary for economic growth in other industries. And "Risk-Taking and Entrepreneurship" (chapter 26) discusses policy alternatives to stimulate innovation and growth.

Landau makes a unique contribution to theoretical economic discussions because he can bring to bear his considerable practical experiences as an engineer, manager, and entrepreneur. Just as he believed that his engineers and scientists would create better processes if they had some understand-ing of all phases of the business, so too does he believe that economists and policymakers will devise better policies if they have some understanding of the real, everyday concerns of the technologist.

The Papers

In his academic endeavors, Landau is still very much the integrating engi-neer that he saw himself to be when he set out on his own in 1946. But he is something more as well. Throughout his career, he has been a witness and analyst of his own company, his profession and his industry, and the political and social context in which they operated. Landau views each stage of his career as the learning process for the next, and that progression is reflected in his papers.

Initially, Landau's writings announced new or improved process developments, discussed the contributions that chemical engineering design firms could make to the chemical industry both at home and abroad, and examined trends in the chemical industry and chemical engineering profession around the world. Appearing in magazines written by and for the chemical industries, these articles proved to be an important marketing venue for the new company and its chief technical officer.

As Scientific Design and then Halcon grew more successful and the company's reputation for innovative approaches to engineering and management spread, Landau was frequently invited to speak and write about those elements that made his company unique. Those invitations, combined with his academic training and his natural inclination to look for underlying connections, led Landau to begin writing about the development and workings of the chemical and chemical engineering industries and their contributions to the domestic and world economies. In the 1970s Landau's writings began to focus on the external economic conditions and policies that were affecting the health of American technology. In the 1980s Landau's writings started to concentrate on the links between technology and economic growth.

Only a small number of the more than 130 papers and books that Landau has written, co-written, or edited could be excerpted in this volume. Those that appear were selected as representative of the progression in Landau's thinking as he moved through his careers as an engineer, entrepreneur, and economist. The resulting record holds many lessons for those in other fields who would seek to emulate Landau's success. Perhaps more important, it offers valuable insights into the conditions necessary for technological innovation, international competitiveness, and continuing economic growth.

Discoveries and
Developments

Over the course of thirty-six years, Scientific Design and its successor companies developed and commercialized nearly a dozen major innovative or improved chemical processes—roughly one every four years. This is a remarkable record for any company, and particularly so for a small organization working from a small financial base in competition with the giants of the industry. The British company ICI, for example, discovered the equivalent to SD's process for making terephthalic acid, only to find that Scientific Design had filed for patents on the process a few weeks earlier.

That this small company produced so many new and improved processes is in large part attributable to the innovative atmosphere in which the chemists and engineers worked. Landau sought out talented chemists and design engineers who would thrive in an entrepreneurial setting. He has noted that the people attracted to Scientific Design were likely to be independent and individualistic: "Many of our employees, in fact, had left large companies precisely because they wanted the relative freedom and excitement which they hoped to find with us; and we had a very good record of keeping most of our able people."

Joel J. Kirman, who joined Scientific Design in 1962, captured that sense of excitement in a speech in which he described the company as a "veritable anthill of activity. The laboratory and pilot plant would be working on perhaps ten processes. There would be continuous interaction with the process engineers and sales people to determine the best routes to redirect investigations. Judgments were constantly required on where to accelerate activity and where to reduce it; at what sales or managerial level to notify industry of either pending or completed results; how to deal with the discovery of weaknesses in any process as it then stood, how readily and with what factors of safety could huge scale-ups be performed, and so forth."

As one of the process engineers, Kirman was often present at discussions of what to do about results that did not meet earlier expectations. "These results were often negative. New directions of research or changes in the process had to be assigned and costs of production reevaluated. In all these meetings, the one characteristic that I most recall was the intrinsic optimism of Dr. Landau that a way can be found out of a dilemma.... His insight proved to be right so often."

The following papers describe the discovery and development of four of the company's most commercially successful processes. Although they are technical in nature, they are included in this volume to give readers a fuller sense of the context in which Ralph Landau worked. Readers lacking a grounding in chemistry will find the discovery and development of these processes discussed in lay terms in the papers included in the next section on innovation and entrepreneurship.

1   Ethylene Oxide by Direct Oxidation

Ethylene oxide and glycol (the latter readily made from oxide) are among the largest volume organic chemicals manufactured in the United States. By 1955, the Defense Production Administration goals have projected a production of about 900,000,000 pounds per year of ethylene oxide.

At present, more than half of the ethylene oxide made is produced by the older chlorohydrin process, which consumes about two pounds of chlorine per pound of ethylene oxide. As such, it represents the second largest single use for chlorine.

In the past fifteen years, ethylene oxide has been produced commercially by direct oxidation of ethylene by only a single producer in the world. This article describes briefly the direct oxidation process developed and licensed, and engineered by Scientific Design Company, Inc., over nearly seven years, and now in the course of commercialization in a number of countries—the only such plants outside the domain of the aforesaid original single producer.

Chlorohydrin Process

In the chlorohydrin process, ethylene is bubbled through a solution of chlorine in water. A dilute solution of chlorohydrin in water is obtained. The acid solution is neutralized, and then saponified with lime; ethylene oxide is distilled off and purified, while the solution of calcium chloride, too dilute for recovery, is discarded.

Normally, the efficiency (on a molal basis) of conversion of ethylene directly to ethylene oxide by this process is 75–80 percent. The balance is either lost in the tail gas, or converted into by-products (ethylene dichloride, dichlorethyl ether, etc.), or lost as glycol in the waste calcium chloride

Reprinted by permission from *Petroleum Refiner* 32, no. 9 (September 1953). Copyright 1953 by Gulf Publishing Co., all rights reserved.

water. Per pound of ethylene oxide, the ethylene consumption is therefore 0.79–0.84 pound, while the chlorine consumption is roughly 2.0 pounds per pound oxide. The lime consumption (possibly substituted for in part by limestone) is about 2.0 pounds per pound oxide.

Direct Oxidation of Ethylene

In contrast to the chlorohydrin process, which uses chlorine to oxidize the ethylene molecule, the Scientific Design Company process oxidizes ethylene with oxygen (such as in air, etc.) with the aid of a catalyst, and absorbs the oxide in a simple scrubbing system, followed by distillation and purification. The reaction was first discovered by Lefort, a Frenchman, and has since been studied by Twigg who suggested a reaction mechanism. The only by-products of the reaction are carbon dioxide and water and almost *no* acetaldehyde is found in the product, which is thereby quite pure in contrast to that made from chlorohydrin. The reasons for this lie in the fact that all other intermediate reaction products, such as acetaldehyde, are extremely rapidly oxidized under the conditions of the reaction to carbon dioxide.

With these two advantages, it is hardly surprising that considerable attention has been given to the commercial development of such a process. Many substantial industrial groups in the United States and Europe have conducted research looking toward the attainment of a feasible method. Nevertheless, it has not been an easy task, as is evidenced by the relatively large proportion of world oxide production still being made by the chlorohydrin route.

The Scientific Design Company process was successfully developed by careful attention to all of the factors which are necessary for commercial success. A brief account of the principal accomplishments follows:

(1) Yields have been raised, on a satisfactory commercial basis, until they begin to approach those of the chlorohydrin process. Actually, within certain limits, yields are not inflexible, but can be varied to permit forced operation which, under some circumstances, is advantageous. In general, yields of pure ethylene oxide in the range of 55–65 percent of theory (on a molal basis) are readily attained, and even 70 percent is possible under certain special conditions. These yields are equivalent to ethylene consumptions of 0.92–1.16 pounds per pound of ethylene oxide. From another point of view, the efficiency of the process, under commercial conditions, is nearly the maximum which it is believed can theoretically be

obtained, and the most that could be expected of further refinements would be the possible increase of a few points in this efficiency. However, as long as the fundamental reaction kinetics prevail (and these are now very well established as authentic), the area for such improvements is very narrow.

(2) Capital costs have been reduced substantially by careful engineering at every point, and a thorough analysis of all the process variables. The current designs have given cost estimates of high precision, based on purchasing and erection, either completed or nearly so, and these show that the capital costs are now, within the precision of calculation and estimation, practically the same as those of a chlorohydrin plant of the same capacity.

Earlier developments, and published accounts thereof, have suggested much higher figures, and help explain the lack of success of some of the previous work.

It should be noted that a chlorohydrin plant is an order of magnitude more difficult with regard to corrosion than is direct oxidation, which is a relatively non-corrosive system on the whole.

(3) Rugged new catalysts have been developed which have long life, and remarkably steady efficiency throughout their life.

(4) Careful attention to sparing of equipment, and automatic control, have produced designs which feature smooth operability and rapid recovery from upsetting conditions.

(5) Careful study has been given to avoidance of fire and explosion hazards. Experience shows that these are genuine, and must be avoided by both design and operational safeguards.

(6) Like the chlorohydrin process, the SD direct oxidation process is also capable of producing substantially all its product as oxide in pure form, which can then be converted at will into the various derivatives of oxide, including glycol. The system is, therefore, 100 percent flexible, a feature not always found in prior work on direct oxidation.

While the catalyst plays an essential role in the process, engineering and operating factors are perhaps just as important, in every step, in order to arrive at a truly commercial process.

Comparison of Direct Oxidation With Chlorohydrin

To the advantages of the SD process given above must also be added the basic economic advantage offered by the direct oxidation process. There are obviously two economic factors to consider—capital investment and operating costs. A capital cost comparison is somewhat difficult to make because it depends upon whether one makes or purchases ethylene, and makes or purchases chlorine. If neither ethylene nor chlorine is made, the capital investment is about the same for both processes. If one makes ethylene as well, the capital investment required is somewhat greater for the direct oxidation process, due to the slightly larger ethylene plant required. If one must make chlorine in addition to ethylene, the capital investment required for the chlorohydrin process is considerably greater. Perhaps the best simplification of this process is to forget the investment in either ethylene or chlorine plants, but use current market prices for both these commodities in making an operating cost comparison, since normally these prices reflect a return on the investment satisfactory to the owners of the plants producing them.

In making a comparison of operating costs, one must consider raw materials, utilities, direct labor, maintenance, overheads, and fixed charges.

(1) Utilities charges in the United States form a small part of the total cost and are nearly the same for both processes. Thus, they are not a significant item in any cost comparison.

(2) Labor costs for the direct oxidation process are somewhat less because the process is basically simpler than the chlorohydrin process. However, in terms of proportionate costs, the differences are small and not a compelling advantage of the direct oxidation process.

(3) Maintenance costs for the direct oxidation plant are lower (obviously corrosion problems and lime-handling equipment result in higher maintenance charges for the chlorohydrin process), but if one adds to maintenance the cost of replacing the catalyst required by direct oxidation, then again there is little difference between the two processes.

(4) Also, since investments within battery limits are about the same, no appreciable difference exists in the resulting fixed charges for the two processes.

Thus, it is seen that the prime difference between the two processes lies in the consumption of raw materials. The chlorohydrin process requires about 2.0 pounds of chlorine and about 0.80 pound of ethylene, and produces 0.22 pound of ethylene dichloride *per pound of ethylene oxide*. If one allows for the chlorine and ethylene contained in the by-products, the net consumptions are about 1.8 pounds of chlorine and 0.74 pound of ethylene. The direct oxidation process may require about 1.04 pounds of ethylene and no chlorine. Thus, it is seen that 1.8 pounds of chlorine are used to save

1.04 pounds minus 0.74 pound, or 0.30 pound of ethylene. Hence, it is obvious that since 6 pounds of chlorine must be consumed to save 1 pound of ethylene, the chlorohydrin process is only economic when the price of ethylene is greater than six times that of the chlorine price. Parallel with the development of the direct oxidation process, there has come the general availability of several good processes for cheap and abundant ethylene, and at the current writing ethylene prices are figured at about 4.5–5.0 cents, and chlorine prices at 3.0 cents. Thus, there is a strong advantage in favor of direct oxidation. The prices of lime and limestone have been neglected as these costs are minor, but they are, nevertheless, and additional penalty against chlorohydrin.

At present prices for ethylene and chlorine, the difference in cost for ethylene oxide produced by the two alternate processes is, for typical situations, about 3.0 cents per pound. For a plant producing 40 million pounds per year, this means a savings of $1.2 million per year on raw materials alone.

The question of the ethylene dichloride by-product deserves one further mention. It has been excluded from the foregoing calculation by correcting the chemical consumptions for the ethylene and chlorine converted into dichloride, which amounts to crediting the process for the by-product at raw material cost. This may seem unfair, but is almost valid, because ethylene dichloride is so readily made in a separate, small installation directly from ethylene and chlorine, that it could easily be appended to a direct oxidation plant and thus put the two processes on the same basis. In such a case, the only difference would be the extra cost of making the dichloride directly, and this is very small—being, rather, balanced out by the lime consumption of the chlorohydrin process. The principal point of difference under these circumstances would be that dichloride must always be made in the chlorohydrin process, regardless of market conditions, but not so in the direct oxidation case.

Technical Considerations in Direct Oxidation

A.   Mechanism

Twigg developed kinetic data to establish the relative reaction rates and, in general, has reasonably good results from his simple bulb studies. However, a study of his rate constants showed considerable fluctuation. The Scientific Design Company studies his data, and found that a modification of his kinetics resulted in a better correlation of his own data. This modified mechanism was then applied to laboratory data in flowing tube experiments for widely different conditions, and resulted in re-evaluation of the Twigg constants, with modifications particularly for his less accurate constants. The kinetic equations thus obtained were arranged to express the selectivity as a function of conversion, at any given point. Selectivity is defined as the percent of ethylene reacting which goes to ethylene oxide, and is, therefore, a measure of catalyst efficiency. These differential equations could be applied to a commercial reactor in one of two ways:

(1) For a stirred pot reactor, in which the conditions at all points are those of the exit gases, the point conditions are also the actual conditions, and the mathematical curve selectivity vs. conversion is readily obtained for any particular set of initial boundary conditions. Such a case would be found in a conventional fluidized dense bed reactor, which has been shown to have such good back-mixing as to render it nearly a perfect stirred pot reactor.

(2) For a packed or fixed bed reactor, with piston-type flow, the equations would have to be integrated from the initial boundary conditions to the desired final state.

A number of different cases were set up and solved, still using the constants obtained in small laboratory reactors. The curves for the two types of reactors were obtained for each case. Then, suitably corrected for the different conditions, the data were compared with larger-scale evidence. The agreement found was excellent, despite very widely differing circumstances.... Data on a fluidized reactor were also obtained, and confirmed these findings. Further study showed that there was a limit to the applicability of these equations over a wide range of conditions. Additional reactions enter into the mechanism, and account for changes in the correlations obtained. As a result of this theoretical work, the correlation of data has been put on a sound basis, and lends confidence to the results gained, and to the designs derived therefrom.

B.   Effect of Major Variables

Many variables influence the direct oxidation reaction. Some of the most important are: (1) ethylene concentration, (2) hydrocarbon concentration, (3) oxygen concentration, (4) carbon dioxide concentration, (5) flow rates, (6) pressure, (7) pressure drop, (8) temperature, (9) catalyst composition and age, (10) poisons, (11) materials of construction, (12) type of bed, and, (13) bed height.

The proper combination of these variables into the economic optimum required a great many engineering and pilot plant studies, and the complexity of these factors helps account for the scarcity of direct oxidation plants to date.

From the above list, a few items are particularly noteworthy:

The oxygen, hydrocarbon, inert, and ethylene oxide concentrations are limited to certain values if operation in an explosive range is to be avoided. Actually, most previously disclosed work has involved operation at some point of the process within an explosive range. Operation within the explosive region is possible in laboratory and small-scale pilot plants but is not advisable in commercial plants where serious explosions can occur. It is, accordingly, essential that plants be operated under very carefully controlled conditions outside the explosion limits, otherwise serious risks are inevitable not only in the reactors but elsewhere in the system. This limitation profoundly affects the choice of operating conditions, including the question of whether recycle or single-pass conversions are preferable for any particular set of conditions.

The proper design of a fixed bed plant, which particularly involves a choice within certain limits of temperature, pressure, flow rate, catalyst, etc., makes it possible to avoid any significant temperature gradients, and to remove heat very smoothly. In fact, selectivity, within certain ranges, is relatively independent of temperature. Hence, such a fixed bed design produces substantially the maximum selectivities attainable, ... that is, highest selectivity at a given conversion level.

C.   Fixed vs. Fluidized Beds

Scientific Design Company, Inc., originally studied both types of beds, including pilot plant results. However, the fixed bed development was ultimately chosen for several principal reasons. The fluidized bed is a valuable tool in certain cases, but as the investigation developed, it appeared strongly that the ethylene oxide reaction would not benefit from it, but actually showed some disadvantages, viz:

(1) The effect of back-mixing and channeling inherent to fluidized beds is deleterious to yield in large plants. This is true even in fluid beds or tubes of very small diameter, as shown in a recent article.

(2) Commercial experience in the application of the dense bed fluidized reactors to chemical reactions (not petroleum) is very limited, and has had a history of substantial difficulties in initial operation. It is well known that commercial plants of this type are difficult to extrapolate from pilot units.

The real pilot plant for catalytic cracking was PCLA of about 100 barrels per day capacity—a size which is equivalent to a commercial chemical plant. Fixed bed oxidations of all types, on the other hand, have a large background of experience.

(3) Catalyst attrition, life, and recovery problems, become particularly serious for a catalyst as expensive as this one when in the finely divided fluidized state.

(4) Reactor design and distribution of flow, in the effort to partially overcome these defects, become complex and costly.

(5) Fluidized beds, being hydrodynamically unstable systems, can operate successfully only over a narrow range of flow conditions and particle size distributions. Departure from these conditions leads to severe channeling or excessive catalyst carry-over.

In addition, it was found that the expected advantages usually associated with a fluidized bed have not materialized in the specific case of the ethylene oxide reaction, namely:

(1) There is no regeneration of catalyst involved, which has been an important advantage in catalytic cracking.

(2) Because of the specific nature of this reaction and the equipment employed, a fixed bed unit provides most satisfactory heat transfer, including substantially theoretical selectivities, so that the usual temperature uniformity of a fluidized bed offers no appreciable advantage in this respect, but rather suffers from the disadvantages inherent in such a system.

(3) The cost of reactors (which are very few in number) in a typical commercial plant using the Scientific Design Company process, is only about 6–8 percent of the capital investment, so that it can be considered as of rather minor influence on the economics of the process; no saving in reactor cost, even in a very large plant, is therefore afforded by a fluidized bed.

It is felt that these factors may be of interest to others attempting to resolve the advantages of each type of bed for their own interests, as applied to chemical reactions. For this reaction, it appears clear that higher yields, lower investment, and greater simplicity of design and operation are provided by a fixed bed, if properly designed.

Commercial Development

... The first plant using the Scientific Design Company process, has just been completed for Societe Naphtachimie at Etang-de-Berre, in France, thereby concluding the cycle which began with the discovery of the basic process in France. Another oxide-glycol plant of similar design is under construction for Allied Chemical & Dye Corporation, at Orange, Texas, as previously announced, and will soon be in operation. These two are the first direct oxidation plants by new producers, aside from the original manufacturer, to be built anywhere in the world, and are the only such new units now in the construction phase. Other projects utilizing the Scientific Design Company process are in various stages of commercialization. Ultimately, the reduced costs made possible by this process will bring ever wider applications for ethylene oxide to the chemical industry.

2　　　　　　　　　　　　Development of the
　　　　　　　　　　　　　M-C Process

The technical paths traversed to develop new processes can be complex and challenging. Such was the case with the M-C Process, which provides for the high efficiency oxidation of alkyl side chains attached to an aromatic nucleus to [produce] carboxylic groups. This technology is widely employed throughout the world to manufacture terephthalic acid from para-xylene, and its progression from laboratory developments to current practices is traced in the pages which follow. The basic discoveries were made in the authors' laboratory commencing in the early 1950s. The Standard Oil Company (Ind.), the owner of the world's rights to the process, constructed the first commercial plant in the United States under its subsidiary, Amoco Chemicals Corp., and has continued the development program, which has led to further process improvements during the last ten years.

Before relating the pertinent details of the laboratory and pilot plant phases of this research program, it is perhaps of interest to emphasize two unusual sidelights:

1. This technological breakthrough had the additional attractiveness of taking place just at the point when the worldwide interest in polyester fibers was beginning to skyrocket. Currently, more than half of the Free World production of terephthalic acid is based on this process.

2. This development is one of the infrequent examples of how a small research and development organization with limited facilities, personnel and financial support succeeds in discovering a basic chemical reaction actively sought by many of the giant chemical and petroleum research laboratories in the world.

With Alfred Saffer, Halcon senior vice president for manufacturing. Published in *Chemical Engineering Progress* 64, no.10 (October 1968): 20–26. Reproduced with permission of the American Institute of Chemical Engineers. © 1968 AIChE. All rights reserved.

The Story Began in 1952

The technical story began in 1952 when our company [then Scientific Design] was asked if we had a process available for the recovery of aluminum chloride catalyst from an alkylation reaction. Further discussion brought out that (a) the aluminum chloride was being used in a development program wherein the Gattermann-Koch reaction (addition of carbon monoxide to the ring of a mono alkyl benzene) was being studied for the manufacture of para-tolualdehyde, (b) a commercial process for the manufacture of terephthalic acid was the goal of the program, and (c) this route was under study since the para-xylene supply in the United States was pretty much tied up by DuPont for Dacron.

While we expressed a willingness to assist in the recovery of spent aluminum chloride, it did not appear to be very economical, and as an alternative we proposed to the company in question that [it] consider our trying to develop a para-substituted aromatic compound other than para-tolualdehyde which [the company] might use in another process which [it] had acquired rights to very recently, namely, what was then known as the Imhausen process and now called the Witten process. The Witten process is based on the discovery that the air oxidation of para-xylene to para-toluic acid is easily achieved in the presence of a metal salt catalyst in the liquid phase, but the rate of oxidation of the second methyl group can be enhanced considerably by first esterifying (with methanol) the carboxylic group in para-toluic acid.

The company in question readily agreed that this might be a useful contribution, and pointed out that at that time most of the large-scale production of terephthalic acid in the world was based on nitric acid oxidation of para-xylene.

The Most Likely Material

Immediately after the discussion described above, it became our conclusion that the most likely prospect for a compound to meet the specifications required was para-diisopropylbenzene. This was based primarily on the fact that we had already had experience in the design of a cumene plant for Allied Chemical involving the Friedel-Crafts reaction of propylene and benzene, and we could imagine that with some assumptions and a few inventions this process might be adapted to making para-diisopropylbenzene. This seemed a particularly attractive possibility, because para-xylene production was even less readily visualizable outside the United States where mixed xylene streams were much fewer in number. On the other hand, low-cost propylene and benzene were available in large amounts in most of the industrially developed countries, and it had seemed to us that para-diisopropylbenzene might have substantial economic advantages. For example, with benzene and propylene selling in the early 1950s for about 5 and 3 cents per pound, respectively, at theoretical yields the hydrocarbon cost per pound of terephthalic acid would be about 3.9 cents per pound as compared with 12.8 cents per pound from para-xylene valued near 20 cents per pound.

On study of the literature we discovered that there was confusion with regard to the physical properties of the diisopropylbenzene isomers and in particular regarding the boiling points. Since our concept of making diiso-propylbenzene involved separation of the para-isomer and recycling of all of the other products made to extinction, a relatively simple separation was mandatory. In order to resolved the confusion we in fact had to obtain experimental data, and the fractionation work proved that the data contained in an Atlantic Refining Co. article were correct, that there was a significant boiling point difference of 6.6°C., sufficient for separation.

Two Obstacles Were Faced

It did not take us long to develop a para-diisopropylbenzene process based on these findings, but when the time came to present the successful results to the company which had initiated our interest in the matter, we discovered two obstacles: (1) the impossibility of disclosing the identity of our compound without also tipping our hand as to the method we proposed, and (2) para-xylene had suddenly become available. We were able to solve the first obstacle, but not the second. Since the company in question had received technology which was solely based on para-xylene, they were most reluctant to undertake a new development program with a new starting material even though there was a potential raw material saving of considerable magnitude. We were thus left with a fine para-diisopropyl-benzene process but no market for it. It was then that we decided that, having gone this far, we might still pursue the matter further, and the decision was taken to attempt oxidation studies on para-diisopropylbenzene. The theory of this was simply that we were reasonably sure we were among the very few people in the world who made relatively pure para-diisopropylbenzene and therefore it was most unlikely that its oxidation characteristics were well known. As a result, after extensive literature study we commenced experiments in air oxidation of para-diisopropylbenzene in liquid phase system and in the presence of catalysts. We soon discovered that, unlike para-xylene, the isopropyl groups were much more readily oxidized and therefore both groups could be attacked instead of stopping at the first one as had been the case in all the reported work on xylenes.

With this decision, we immediately put our full research staff of two chemists and one laboratory technician on the simultaneous programs of (1) purchasing samples of diisopropylbenzene for oxidation experiments, (2) further studies of the propylation of benzene in the presence of aluminum chloride to develop operating skills, additional process design data, and to provide samples for separation and oxidation studies and (3) starting investigations in laboratory glassware of the oxidation of the isomeric mixture of diisopropylbenzene. We purchased a few gallons of diisopropylbenzene from a commercial cumene plant using another process, but initially failed in separating a pure enough para-diisopropylbenzene fraction. In the first series of diisopropylbenzene oxidations using a variety of catalysts in the liquid phase at atmospheric pressure, we did not obtain any terephthalic acid.

Feedstock Problems Were Faced

We encountered some delay in our isomer separation program because, as was established somewhat later, the purchased, commercial diisopropylbenzene mixture contained some trimethyl-indane, which boils between the meta-and para-diisopropylbenzene isomers. We learned that some of the cumene made in the plant from which we obtained the diisopropylbenzene mixture was fed to a dehydrogenation unit to produce alpha-methylstyrene and it was likely that trimethyl-indane was formed from small amounts of alpha-methyl-styrene recycled to the alkylation reaction. Once this situation was understood, the laboratory column was operated thereafter to produce feedstock for oxidation from our own propylation of benzene, which did not form trimethyl-indane.

The studies of the oxidation of para-diisopropylbenzene in agitated laboratory flasks did not produce any significant amount of terephthalic acid for a large number of runs at the reflux temperature just above 200°C. Most of the experiments led to the formation of black, tacky, polymeric masses. It was apparent that the isopropyl side chain was being oxidized to a variety of intermediate oxidation products—such as alcohols, aldehydes, etc. It was then hypothesized that when a hydroxyl group appeared on the side chain, dehydration could lead to an olefinic group which would polymerize. Starting with this idea, it was suggested that an acid solvent might quickly esterify the hydroxyl group when formed and this could in turn alter the course of the oxidation to the desired carboxylic group.

Since at that time we only studied oxidations in glassware and we were very anxious to try out the acid medium idea promptly, we next looked in a handbook for the boiling points of the aliphatic acids and selected caproic acid, which has a listed boiling point of about 205°C. This medium would provide an atmospheric reflux temperature somewhat higher than we had established in earlier experiments as the minimum temperature to start the oxidation of para-diisopropylbenzene. Caproic acid was added to the next oxidation of para-diisopropylbenzene in the presence of manganese cumate catalyst and we obtained the first reasonable yield of terephthalic acid. Analyses were made of the reaction product, which was also converted to the dimethyl ester for further identification. We established that the reaction product had a high concentration of terephthalic acid. As expected, the caproic acid itself did not show very much stability under the conditions of this reaction, but because of its convenience, many more successful oxidations to terephthalic acid were conducted using caproic acid with a variety of metal salt catalysts. Meanwhile, since we anticipated that acetic acid would be much less subject to oxidation than caproic acid, we rushed the construction of a stainless steel reactor tube, one inch in diameter by three feet long, topped by a reflux condenser of identical dimensions, so that we could extend the studies of the reaction to the elevated pressures needed for a reaction temperature of about 200°C with acetic acid.

Disappointments and Frustrations

Initial experiments in the pressure oxidizer were made with para-diisopropylbenzene, a manganese salt and acetic acid. To our great disappointment, little or no terephthalic acid was produced. After about a dozen frustrating experiments, it was decided to go back to the basic successful experiment. We operated the pressure reactor at atmospheric pressure with an open top and with caproic acid in place of acetic acid. The result was a yield of terephthalic acid comparable to that obtained in the stirred glass reactors. The next pressure oxidation was again made with acetic acid and to our great satisfaction we obtained a good yield of terephthalic acid. At this point, and with a bit of hindsight, an explanation was suggested for the apparently peculiar sequence of results in the pressure reactor. It was known that caproic acid is used to clean metal surfaces and it was thought that the atmospheric pressure oxidation experiment with caproic acid must have simultaneously removed unidentified inhibitors from the reactor walls and flanges. Thereafter, for hundreds of experiments, we never had any problems duplicating the results with acetic acid under "standard conditions" in the pressure reactor.

The best single-pass yield obtained from para-diisopropylbenzene in the pressure reactor with acetic acid was about 35 weight percent. (Weight yields and theoretical yields are practically the same for this reaction.) However, it was observed that, in addition to terephthalic acid, the reactor effluent, following evaporation of acetic acid from the filtered reactor effluent, contained a mixture of intermediate oxidation products. These partial oxidation products, after separation of terephthalic acid, were returned to the pressure reactor with makeup para-diisopropylbenzene and fresh acetic acid and catalyst. Such recycle operations demonstrated that an overall yield of para-diisopropylbenzene to terephthalic acid of about 60 percent could be obtained in a multistep series of batch runs.

The Elements of a Commercial Process

At this yield level, it was felt we had the elements of a commercial process, but it was necessary to move to a larger scale operation to fix plant design parameters, to establish the efficiency of acetic acid recovery, to produce terephthalic acid samples for evaluation, etc. This program required a new research and pilot plant laboratory at another site, additional operating personnel, a substantially larger research budget, etc. We coordinated our activities carefully so that only a few days research time was lost in transferring all the operations to the new location. Before this transfer was made, we already had obtained the interest of a prospective licensee and we had made a contractual commitment to perform a demonstration series of pilot plant runs within three months after we were established in our new quarters. In addition to the pilot plant to carry out the oxidation program, we had to construct large-scale equipment to supply the para-diisopropylbenzene feedstock. A rapid program was initiated to construct the required alkylation system and a fractionating tower ten feet long and four inches in diameter. In the interim, before the feedstock preparation equipment was in operation, we made para-diisopropylbenzene by propylating benzene in ordinary, lined 55-gallon drums and used a rented, high efficiency fractionating column available in the laboratory of an equipment supplier. With all these construction and startup programs underway simultaneously, we were very fortunate to meet the pilot plant demonstration schedule. The process yield was successfully demonstrated to the representatives of the interested company.

In the pilot plant demonstration first stage reaction, para-diisopropyl-benzene was oxidized in the presence of acetic acid and manganese acetate catalyst. In the second stage of this series, we began to recycle the re-covered intermediate oxidation products and, after several stages, the equi-librium yield per pass reached 60 weight percent terephthalic acid.

Hundreds of oxidation experiments had been made by this time in the laboratory pressure oxidizer in an attempt to increase the oxidation effi-ciency of para-diisopropylbenzene. These studies included all kinds of met-al catalysts (single and in mixtures), solvent media, oxidation initiators, pressures, temperatures, etc. Nevertheless, about 60 percent overall weight yield remained the maximum attainable. Our estimates of the capital in-vestment and production costs of a commercial plant based on a 60 weight percent yield of terephthalic acid from para-diisopropylbenzene appeared quite attractive when compared with the then utilized higher yield technol-ogies which started with para-xylene valued at about 20 cents per pound. At this point, we began to design a commercial plant with a capacity of about 5,000 tons per year of terephthalic acid to be constructed outside the United States.

A Catalyst Breakthrough

Our efforts to improve the oxidation yield continued after the successful pilot plant demonstration. Since we had made no progress by investigating most of the metals in the periodic table, usually in the form of organic salts such as acetates, terephthalates, octoates, etc., we felt more attention should be given to the accompanying anion. It is interesting to note that we had not uncovered in any of the chemical or patent literature we had reviewed any highlighting of this particular feature. Accordingly, we pro-ceeded to study in the pressure oxidizer various salts of manganese and of cobalt, since these metals seemed to provide the best catalytic properties for oxidizing para-diisopropylbenzene. The first indication that something different had occurred was when manganese bromide was used as the catalyst. Manganese bromide in the reaction medium of para-diisopropyl-benzene and acetic acid permitted the attainment of about 60 weight per-cent yield terephthalic acid in a single oxidation step, as compared with about two-thirds of this yield for the corresponding reaction utilizing man-ganese acetate or terephthalate. While there was the expected excitement after so many unsuccessful experiments that something new had been uncovered with manganese bromide, we soon found practically no inter-mediate oxidation products in the reactor effluent. Hence, the overall yield in para-diisopropylbenzene oxidation utilizing manganese bromide in a recycle series turned out to be no better than using other salts of manganese. However, the important property discovered for manganese bromide was its ability to increase markedly the rate of oxidation.

It was then decided to study metal bromides in less complicated systems. Our earlier experiments confirmed that an isopropyl group is more easily oxidized than a methyl side chain. It was also known that it was relatively simple to oxidize one methyl group in para-xylene and that the second methyl group was almost refractory. We therefore selected para-cymene as the model feedstock and we expected to form para-toluic acid as the principal product in such oxidations. This line of thinking led us to the critical experiment—the oxidation of para-cymene in acetic acid in the presence of manganese bromide. By outlet gas analysis, we first noted a very rapid rate of consumption of oxygen and then a sudden breakthrough of air feed through the liquid phase. Rather surprisingly, in place of the expected para-toluic acid, we found a 73 weight percent yield of terephthalic acid, which is about 60 percent of theory. Since the same experiment with manganese acetate in place of manganese bromide only produced one-tenth the yield of terephthalic acid, it was obvious that we had discovered a unique oxidation catalyst.

New Direction: Full Emphasis

The next part of the program was easily set. We side-tracked all other parts of the planned oxidation study and went directly to the oxidation of para-xylene with manganese bromide in acetic acid. This experiment, which was conducted at 400 pounds/square inch gauge pressure and 200° C, resulted in the plugging of the reactor with solids. After careful collection, washing, and drying of the light colored solids, we measured a terephthalic acid yield of 120 weight percent (77 percent of theory). We quickly confirmed that the product was indeed terephthalic acid and there was practically no para-toluic acid. We rapidly followed these experiments with (1) a para-xylene oxidation with manganese acetate in place of the bromide and obtained a very low yield of terephthalic acid, (2) a manganese bromide oxidation of para-xylene with benzene in place of acetic acid solvent and obtained no terephthalic acid whatsoever, and (3) the oxidation of para-xylene in acetic acid with cobalt bromide in place of manganese bromide and obtained 123 weight percent yield of terephthalic acid (79 percent of theory). We concluded that the critical combination of reaction ingredients required for high efficiency oxidation of para-xylene to terephthalic acid

was a source of bromine, a metal catalyst, preferably in the form of manganese or cobalt or mixtures thereof, and acetic acid. This discovery was
quickly confirmed on a much larger scale in the pilot plant. Another interesting observation was the very high efficiency of reaction of the oxygen
in the air feed. A pilot of the outlet oxygen concentration versus time
showed that better than 95 percent of the oxygen was reacted during the
first thirty minutes with a typical batch oxidation of para-xylene. In an
interval of less than two minutes thereafter, the oxygen in the outlet gas
reached 21 percent. The curve looked like the classical pH curve when
titrating a strong acid with a strong base. Further optimization experiments
ultimately raised the yield of terephthalic acid above 140 weight percent
(about 90 percent theoretical yield) in a one-pass batch oxidation.

These studies demonstrated that great economies could be achieved in a
commercial plant reactor design with a relatively small reactor volume per
annual ton of terephthalic acid, efficient use of high pressure air, and a
simplified reaction scheme not requiring the recycle of intermediate oxidation products.

It is significant to note that other halide salts of manganese and cobalt
showed little or no activity in this reaction. Further, it was observed that
there was a synergistic effect by using a mixture of cobalt bromide and
manganese bromide. It was observed that the metal catalyst could be added
in the form of an organic salt such as the acetate, naphthenate, octoate and
the bromide could be added as elemental bromine or as inorganic or organic derivatives, such as hydrogen bromide, sodium bromide, tetrabro-
moethane, etc. Acetic acid appeared to be the desired medium, since it was
the most stable to oxidation of all the alternatives investigated.

Commercial Acceptability Was Next

Since the major market for terephthalic acid is in the manufacture of polyester fibers and film, we had the burden next of establishing that the product
from this process could meet the stringent requirements of the industrial
consumers. During the time the studies of this unique reaction were in
progress, all polyester manufacturing techniques were based upon reacting
dimethylterephthalate [DMT] and a glycol. The concept of feeding pure
terephthalic acid from any process was inhibited in those days by difficulty
in purifying the acid. While the industry had chemical specifications for
DMT, it was made clear to us that the only certain way to establish that
the DMT from the newly discovered reaction could be used in existing
polyester production facilities was to produce a DMT sample of several

thousand pounds so that a full-scale commercial test could be made, permitting an actual study of the resultant fiber in the spinning operation. Such a program was impractical for us since our pilot plant was only capable of producing about 25 pounds per day of terephthalic acid. We did learn, however, that an unpublished specification for DMT was a freezing point measurement wherein the freezing point had to be measured accurately to the third decimal on the Centigrade scale. We estimated it would likely take us six months to build and calibrate the equipment necessary for making such measurements, so we decided to investigate how such determinations could be made quickly. We were fortunate in working out arrangements with the cryogenic laboratory at Pennsylvania State University, where the necessary freezing point apparatus was available for immediate use. Within a fortnight after we first learned of the freezing point specification for DMT, we had received the first results on the samples we had made from the new process. It was confirmed that we had made a high purity DMT with the necessary freezing point.

Once the basic discovery was made of the unique properties in this type of oxidation reaction of a metal catalyst in the conjoint presence of bromine, we pursued the commercial application of the technology. The Standard Oil Company (Ind.) ultimately purchased the world rights to the process and constructed the first commercial plant in Joliet, Ill., under its subsidiary, Amoco Chemicals Corp. It is interesting to note that the Amoco plant made the first commercial production of terephthalic acid four and one-half years after the discovery of the unique catalyst system. Since the Joliet plant commenced production in 1958, Amoco has authorized several expansions, and plants are currently under construction or are in operation for Montecatini Edison S.p.A., Imperial Chemical Industries, Ltd., Maruzen Oil Company, Ltd., Mitsui Petrochemical Industries, Ltd., Kuraray Yuka (a joint venture of Mitsubishi Petrochemical Company, Ltd. and Kurashiki Rayon) and Algemene Kunstzijde Unie, N. V. More than half of the Free World production of terephthalic acid is now based on this technology.

Other Feedstocks Respond

The fundamental discovery has been extended to other feedstocks. Generally, it can be stated that with this catalyst system, all of the alkyl side chains on a benzene nucleus can be converted at high yield to the corresponding carboxylic acid group. It is of interest that the first commercial plant built by Amoco was designed to oxidize a mixed xylene feed containing ethylbenzene in addition to the three xylene isomers. After oxidation, the reactor effluent was composed of a mixture of benzoic acid, orthophthalic acid, isophthalic acid, and terephthalic acid, and all of these were separated to yield individual products (including phthalic anhydride from orthophthalic acid) meeting commercial specifications. More recently commercial production has been extended to the oxidation of pseudocumene to trimellitic anhydride, a very interesting trifunctional molecule. It is fully anticipated that future commercial applications will be the manufacture of trimesic acid from mesitylene and pyromellitic dianhydride from durene. Further, we expect that phthalic anhydride will be manufacturd in the 1970s from ortho-xylene oxidized in liquid phase by this process since it has been established that almost 90 percent of theoretical yield (over 120 weight percent) of phthalic anhydride can be made with this catalyst system.

In any fundamental discovery of commercial importance, considerably effort must be devoted to the patent position. Our company was attentive to this matter from the beginning and large portions of the later laboratory and pilot plant programs were used to reinforce our patent position. It was quite apparent that other laboratories were active in studies similar to our own. We found our basic U.S. patent on para-diisopropylbenzene oxidation without bromine in an interference action with Shell. Our earlier date of invention coupled with our prompt patent filing enabled us to win the interference.

In the early 1950s, Imperial Chemical Industries, Ltd. was well established in terephthalic acid manufacture for its Terylene program. ICI became interested in acquiring rights to our technology to replace its own nitric acid oxidation process. In the midst of the business discussion, ICI terminated negotiations when its own laboratory reported "a new development." Later, when our first foreign patents were published, ICI learned that the bromine/metal catalyst system, which it had recently discovered in its own laboratory, was already patented by us. We believe we were about two years ahead of ICI in this discovery. ICI soon thereafter became a licensee of the M-C Process.

As we look back at this program now, it is apparent that para-diisopropylbenzene would not have been competitive with para-xylene as a terephthalic acid precursor in the middle 1960s. The benzene price today is only a little cheaper than it was ten years ago and propylene is essentially valued the same as when our research program commenced. On the other hand, the price of para-xylene has dropped more than half during the same time period.

Standard Oil Company (Ind.) and ourselves have attempted to gain a better understanding of the mechanism by which this catalyst system operates. While some progress has been made and Indiana Standard has published some of its ideas on this subject, the mechanism of the reaction is not fully understood more than ten years after the basic discovery. In the interim, a number of publications from both sides of the Iron Curtain report studies based on reactions catalyzed by the conjoint presence of a metal and bromine. This unique system has widened the scope of academic chemistry in addition to its substantial commercial importance.

3 Boron-Promoted Oxidation of Paraffins and Cycloparaffins

Process Research

The oxidation of cyclohexane has long been used for the production of the adipic acid intermediate usually called KA Oil. KA Oil, as ordinarily produced, contains 65–75 percent of a mixture of cyclohexanol (A; OL) and cyclohexanone (K; ONE) and 35–25 percent of a miscellany of other oxidation products. OL and ONE are the main precursors of adipic acid made by nitric acid oxidation of KA Oil, although some adipic acid is produced from the 35 percent portion of miscellaneous oxidation products. The nonprecursors of adipic acid present in the KA Oil are, for practical purposes, oxidized to extinction. There is, furthermore, a residue of nonadipic acid by-products, including shorter chain dibasic acids, which must be subsequently removed from the adipic acid by elaborate and costly recrystallization procedures. The quality of the KA Oil affects the cost of the final adipic acid in three ways: A low OL-ONE content gives a low yield of adipic acid, which directly increases cost; relatively expensive nitric acid is consumed while destroying impurities; and the resulting impurity of the crude adipic acid product requires expensive multiple recrystallization.

Attempts to improve the selectivity or efficiency, to OL-ONE, of the cyclohexane oxidation processes has been a continuing one; and published data relating to the oxidation of other hydrocarbons seemed, at first, to offer several courses of action. Several very old patents suggested that a variety of adjuvants, such as arsenous acid, silicic acid, phosphorous pentoxide, or even boric acid, might be used to enhance the yields of alcohols obtained in the air oxidation of long-chain paraffinic hydrocarbons. Russian

With David Brown, Halcon senior vice president, and J. L. Russell, Halcon vice president for research and development. Paper presented before the 158th national meeting of the American Chemical Society, New York, New York, September 7–12, 1969.

publications, within the last decade, showed significantly augmented production of alcohols from high molecular weight straight chain paraffins when the oxidation was effected in the presence of boric acid with oxygen at concentrations substantially below its concentration in air. The Russian investigators and almost all others who examined this work assumed that the significant factor in the production of the enhanced yield of alcohols lay in the use of an oxygen-containing gas less rich in oxygen than air. They assumed that the boric acid functioned only to esterify the alcohol produced by the oxidation in the belief that the alcohol when bound as an ester was thus protected from progressive oxidative degradation.

Efforts to apply the heavy paraffin work with boric acid to enhance reaction yields of light hydrocarbons were, when first attempted, altogether unsuccessful. The reasons for the failure were not clear; but one explanation was that, if the boric acid functions to esterify cyclohexanol, it might be necessary to maintain liquid-phase water levels in the oxidation mixture lower than was normally the case. In fact, the inability to remove water was suggested several years earlier by one of the conferees at the Fifth World Petroleum Congress Symposium as a reason for the lack of success in applying the heavy hydrocarbon procedures to light hydrocarbons. In its initial work, SD had established conditions which insured that no liquid-phase water was at any time present in the reacting mixture. Nonetheless, reduced oxygen concentration and the presence of boric acid worked no significant improvement.

SD patents confirm what previously had been only suspected; it has been discovered how to use boric acid significantly to increase the yield of OL-ONE in KA Oil from cyclohexane oxidations. Under some circumstances, it can bring the content of these two substances in the unrefined oil to a value in excess of 90 percent. Moreover, while increasing selectivity, it simultaneously shifts the traditional ratio between these two compounds from the classical value of about 1 to 1 to a ratio of 9 or 10 to 1 in favor of cyclohexanol. Surprisingly, what SD found and broadly claimed is that the essential factor in producing these results is the control of water vapor pressure in the cyclohexane oxidizer during the course of the reaction.

The SD researchers began to suspect that what had previously been written about reactions of this type failed to explain their intricacies. Perhaps the boric acid was having some effect in addition to that of simply esterifying the produced alcohol. It was at this point that the SD workers began to consider what they had heretofore dismissed as an interesting but not significant observation. Boric acid normally used was relatively available in the laboratory. This type of boric acid is the so-called ortho-boric acid having the formula H_3BO_3. This material can lose water when heated and form meta-boric acid HBO_2. At the temperature and under the conditions of the cyclohexane oxidations being attempted, the first observable event was the dehydration of the boric acid to meta-boric acid. Interestingly enough, the reaction mixture did not begin to consume oxygen until most of the added ortho acid had been dehydrated to meta acid. This being so, the reagent involved in SD's oxidation mixture was not ortho- but meta-boric acid. Meta-boric acid itself can exist in several thermodynamically stable states. Did this have significance? If it did, it might mean that lower concentrations of water might be required in the reaction mixture than had ever previously been assumed. In short, perhaps what was needed was not simply the elimination of water in the liquid phase from the reaction mixture but reduction of the water dissolved in the cyclohexane undergoing oxidation. If this were the case, control of water vapor partial pressure might be needed.

Any attempt to control water partial pressure in the vapor phase makes it necessary to understand the factors which determine the water partial pressure in the system. The vapor system involved has essentially five components: oxygen in the oxidant gas stream, the inerts in the oxygen gas stream, water vapor, cyclohexane vapor, and, to a minor extent, by-products of the reaction.

The concentration of cyclohexane in the gas phase is set by the reaction system temperature and pressure. Most of the water of consequence in the system is that formed as a by-product of the oxidation reaction. Its amount is related to the amount of oxygen consumed and the efficiency of oxidation. In consequence, the idea that a boric acid-assisted oxidation requires control of water vapor pressure for good results can be tested by further increase in the inerts and cyclohexane in equilibrium with the reactor.

As a matter of fact, further reduction in the concentration of water in equilibrium in the reactor did enhance OL-ONE selectivity—but the degree of improvement obtained varied widely from run to run. These initial experiments looking to the control of water partial pressure suggested that either control was less satisfactory than expected or that other factors, as yet unrecognized, might be involved. Moreover, if the results of these early experiments were any guide, the water vapor pressures seemingly required for satisfactory selectivity increases were so low that no economic process seemed possible.

Detailed analyses, both by experiment and by calculation, were made to explain this variability and to improve the optimum operating conditions. Painstaking laboratory work eventually showed where the problems lay.

In any cyclohexane oxidation reactor, the gaseous effluent is largely cyclohexane vapor, which must be condensed from the vapor phase, separated from the noncondensable inert gases and returned to the reactor. In such a system, it is impossible to avoid condensing much of the water content of the gaseous effluent along with the cyclohexane. As is normal chemical engineering practice, the condensed liquids were separated in a decanter prior to returning the cyclohexane to the reactor. This method of separation, it turns out, is not adequate. Enough of the condensed water is present in droplets of such small size that they do not separate from the cyclohexane; as a result, an uncontrolled water recycle is established which renders fruitless all normal attempts to control water vapor partial pressure. Once this fact was discovered, the reason for earlier fluctuation even with very low oxygen concentrations in the input gases became clear.

At this juncture the unexpected occurred. It appeared that SD had undertaken a classical exercise in futility. On one hand, it was now known what was required to produce OL-ONE in high selectivity by cyclohexane oxidation. On the other hand, because of the need to control water partial pressure, it was soon observed that the utility requirements of the reaction in the boron-aided oxidations were considerably higher than in the conventional processes. The operation hardly seemed commercially feasible. The reason for the increase in utilities is as follows: The conventional processes normally use air as the oxidant and are unconcerned with water either as liquid or vapor. Sufficient degrees of freedom exist to allow the rate of the oxidation to be varied. Consequently, at one condition it could be adiabatic and produce enough heat to maintain the reaction temperature, to bring the cyclohexane coming into the reactor to the reactor temperature, and to provide the heat of vaporization required to enable evaporation of cyclohexane into the air stream without reducing reaction temperature. Operations at another condition could even generate enough heat to use in subsequent distillation operations.

Unfortunately, in the new SD process, in which the partial pressure of water vapor in the vapor phase is controlled, a degree of freedom is lost compared to the conventional process—the next concentration in the inlet gas and the total pressure cannot be independently fixed. The air must be diluted with nitrogen in order to reduce water concentration, or else the system pressure must be reduced in order to increase cyclohexane concentration in the vapor phase. As partial pressure of water is lowered, the heat requirements of the systems increase. Two main factors cause this increased heat requirement over the classical process: the heat of reaction is lowered because of increased selectivity, and the quantity of cyclohexane distilled from the reactor per unit of oxygen reacted is greatly increased. As a side factor, the rate of reaction differed from the classical route which affects reactor design. With the limited degrees of freedom in this system, it is impossible to operate adiabatically at a low water pressure, much less to generate heat for distillation.

Two factors, water recycle with the condensed cyclohexanes and the high heat requirements, made the process appear uneconomical. Surprisingly enough, SD found the solution to both problems in a single concept —direct heat exchange between the liquid cyclohexane entering the reactor and the effluent gases from the reactor. This technique, which has been patented, insures that all significant amounts of water are removed from the returning cyclohexane. Conditions in the reactor are fixed so that it is not saturated with water; consequently, in a direct contact heat exchanger, the effluent gas has sufficient driving force to strip water from the recycle cyclohexane. Heat is conserved by simultaneous heat and mass transfer from gas to liquid. The effluent gas is cooled and cyclohexane is condensed from the gaseous phase into the liquid phase. As a result, cyclohexane is returned to the reactor both bone-dry and preheated. Condensation of cyclohexane decreased many times the heat lost to the condenser water.

At this point, the development of a commercial economic process seemed more hopeful. There were still scale-up problems to be solved, but there was confidence that solutions would ultimately be worked out.

What is the role of boric acid in this new process? SD chemists have not proven its role but have made some observations. First, it is clearly not enough to say that the boric acid prevents further oxidation of cyclohexanol by reacting with it to form an ester. For one thing, the chemists observed, as with the earlier processes, that the new process exhibits a decrease in selectivity with increasing conversion. Cyclohexanol in the form of its ester may not be oxidized at the same rate or by the same mechanism as is free cyclohexanol; but it seems evident that the ester is subjected to oxidative attack. Our chemists point, too, to the fact that this new process drastically alters the usual ratio of OL to ONE, increasing the former and greatly reducing the latter, from the classical 1-to-1 ratio to a 20-to-1 ratio. This must, they think, point to a basic change in the reaction sequence following the initial production of cyclohexyl hydroperoxide....

Water, if present in sufficient quantity, hydrolyzes the boric ester back to alcohol and boric acid. It should be noted that boric acid is not a catalyst. It does not permit a lowering of reaction temperature. It is required in substantially stoichiometric or greater than stoichiometric amounts, and it leaves the reaction system as the cyclohexanol ester. Fortunately, the SD staff was able, after much inventive effort, to work out procedures for recovery of the boric acid and its recycle to the reactor system so efficient that its use does not unduly increase process cost. Such cost increase as it may impose is largely due to handling rather than consumption.

Development of Commercial Process

Through SD's technological advancements, the molar yields of cyclohexanol and cyclohexanone were raised from 65–75 percent in the classical process to 90–95 percent with boron. At the present time, plants using the SD process have a combined capacity to oxidize more than a billion-and-a-half pounds of cyclohexane per year. SD licensees are the only commercial plants using this revised technology. The development of this process, from the discoveries described above to the commercial plant, involved much more than the usual scale-up problems and taxed the ingenuity of the SD chemical engineers. The process is not only a research but an engineering success.

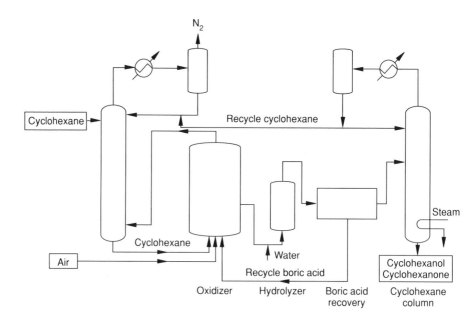

Figure 3.1
Schematic KA Oil production flowsheet.

A schematic diagram of the cyclohexane process is shown in figure 3.1. Fresh plus recycled cyclohexane is fed to the top of the direct heat contacter and preheated by the off gases from the oxidizer system. Noncondensables are bled from the top of this heat economizer. The preheated cyclohexane is charged to the oxidizer system along with the recycled boric acid and air. Three considerations dictated to the operating temperatures, pressures, and flow rates in this system were to maximize the yield of high cyclohexanol and cyclohexanone, to minimize deleterious byproducts, and to obtain long on-stream time. The reactor effluent containing primarily the borate esters, cyclohexanone and cyclohexane, is brought into contact with water and caustic. The ester reacts to release cyclohexanol. Boric acid is recovered and the ortho-boric acid recycled to the oxidation section. The cyclohexane is separated from the cyclohexanol-cyclohexanol product and recycled back to the reactors.

The engineering of the process required more than normal experience and ingenuity. Three phases—solid, liquid, and vapor—are handled simultaneously throughout most of the process. Although to a much lesser extent than in the classical process, polymeric materials, so-called "coffee grounds," are formed, which makes handling of solids even more critical. SD research discovered the critical conditions that minimized "coffee ground" formation. Another engineering success was the design of separation and recycle systems for boric acid. The success of the engineering is measured in the long on-stream times achieved in commercial plants.

Commercial Cyclohexane Oxidation

By virtue of its strong patent position, SD has designed and engineered and started up eight commercial plants, all of which are operating successfully. They range in size from relatively small to what can be called gigantic product capacities of several hundred million pounds a year of KA Oil, producing both adipic acid and caprolactum. These plants are: The Monsanto Company, in the United States; Imperial Chemical Industries, Ltd., in England and Scotland; LaPorte Industries in England; Rhone-Poulenc in France; Farben Fabriken Bayer, A. G., in Germany and Belgium; and the Mitsubishi Chemical Industries, Ltd., in Japan. Additional plants have been licensed but have not been announced. SD is the only company who has built a commercial plant for cyclohexane oxidation which uses boron as a mediator.

The reason the process has been so successful, of course, is the economic advantages over the earlier process. The molar yield of cyclohexanol and cyclohexanone is, as was mentioned above, 90–95 molar percent, compared to 65–75 molar percent in the conventional process. On a U.S. basis, the cost of utilities plus catalyst and chemical in a plant producing one hundred million pounds per year using the boron technologies is only half of the corresponding costs in plants using the older process. The extremely large savings in raw materials and the operating costs are achieved in plants requiring only slightly higher capital than in the conventional process.

The success of this process does not depend on the obvious saving of money above. The higher yield of KA Oil from cyclohexane means fewer raw materials; but perhaps even more important, it means fewer by-products to remove. The caprolactam producer benefits because the distilled cyclohexanol and cyclohexanone produce a purer caprolactum. The adipic acid producer benefits because the crude oxidation oil contains a higher concentration of cyclohexanol and cyclohexanone than the oil from the conventional process. Hence, this oil yields more adipic acid per pound, and as an added benefit, less nitric acid is consumed during the oxidation of by-products. Also, as a consequence of fewer by-products, the purification of the adipic acid is simplified and less adipic acid is produced during the purification. The advantages of the boron-mediated process are clearly amplified in subsequent processes—both to caprolactam and adipic acid.

Figure 3.2 is a typical cost curve showing the advantages of the boron-mediated process. As the trend to larger capacity plants continues, the advantages of the boron process over the nonboron process do too.

Cost curves ... are only a part of the picture for a company calculating the profitability of a new process. Pragmatically, the cash flows when the products flow to the market. Delays in start-up can completely upset the most precise cash flow evaluations of a new process. Figure 3.3 illustrates this effect. This is a plot for the discounted cash flow relative to the break-even point as a function of the time required for start-up. The steepness of this curve has been tempered because it is assumed that the only loss of income is due to inability to sell the product. Need the manufacturer purchase KA Oil for his own nylon production or else pay penalties as a result of failing to deliver the product on schedule, the discounted cash flow is very low. It is clearly seen that even under optimistic assumptions, a profitable situation could become unattractive if start-up were delayed for as little as two months.

Start-up experience is critical in a process as sophisticated as the boron-mediated oxidation process, a process which necessarily handles many

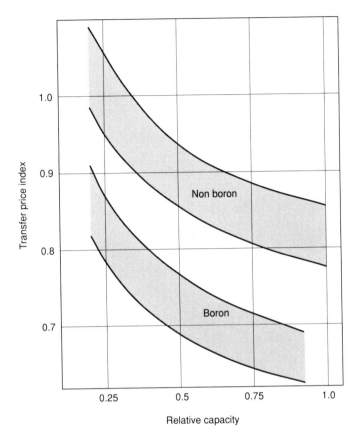

Figure 3.2
Relative KA Oil production costs according to Scientific Design data.

phases of matter and has many by-products. SD's experience could be essential to the profitability of the process. The most recent plant to come on-stream has been the Mitsubishi Chemical Industries, Ltd., plant, which was started up within two days of the time originally projected at the beginning of the fourteen-month construction schedule.

Commercial Oxidation Plants for Other Paraffins and Cycloparaffins

SD has developed plant designs for other uses of the boron technology, and one plant is now operating. Processes of particular interest are the oxidation of paraffins to secondary alcohols for the detergent industry and

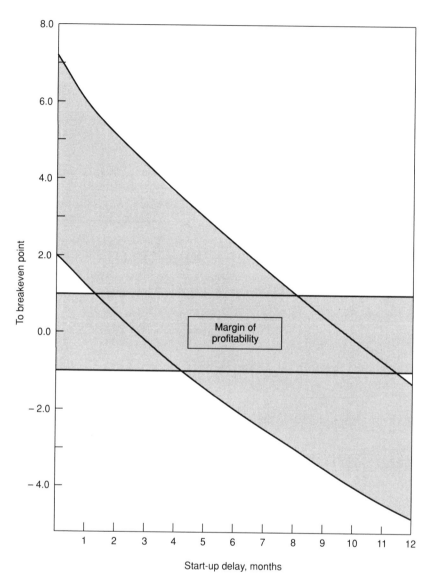

Figure 3.3
Effect of start-up delay on return for a typical KA Oil plant.

the oxidation of cyclodecane to produce cyclododecanol and cyclododeca-none. Phenol and cresols can be produced from products of the oxidation of cyclohexane and methyl cyclohexane.

SD had researched these and other processes thoroughly in its labora-tory. This research background plus the invaluable experience in cyclohex-ane oxidation has enabled SD confidently to design commercial plants, which will operate at a high profitability.

4   Epoxidation of Olefins

Ethylene oxide and propylene oxide account for substantially all of the epoxides produced today. The non-Communist world ethylene oxide production alone amounts to about two million metric tons per year. At present about 500,000 metric tons of propylene oxide are produced annually and production capacity is increasing at a rapid rate.[1]

The impetus for the tremendous growth in ethylene oxide and propylene oxide production in recent years has been due not only to the expansion of the established uses of these materials in the manufacture of solvents, plasticizers, humectants, explosives, and antifreezes, but also to the development of new uses, primarily in the manufacture of polyesters and polyurethanes. Still newer uses, for example, in the manufacture of epoxide homopolymers,[2] promise substantial further increases in demands for propylene oxide and other miscellaneous polyfunctional epoxide compounds.

The most direct method for the formation of epoxides is suggested by their structures, that is, the direct union of an atom of oxygen with an olefin.

Historically, however, the first commercial production of ethylene oxide employed the chlorohydrin process, which utilized the oxidative power of chlorine as hypochlorous acid to attack the olefin.

With David Brown, Halcon senior vice president; J. L. Russell, Halcon vice president for research and development; and J. Kollar, a Halcon research chemist. The paper was originally presented at the Symposium on New Concepts and Techniques in Oxidation of Hydrocarbons, Seventh World Petroleum Congress, Mexico City, April 1967. Printed in *Proceedings* of the Congress, *Petrochemistry* 5 (1967): 67–72. Reprinted with permission of Elsevier Publishing Co., Essex, England. All rights reserved.

$$Cl_2 + H_2O \rightarrow HCl + HOCl$$

$$\overset{\displaystyle OH \quad Cl}{\underset{\displaystyle C\text{---}C}{C{=}C + HOCl \rightarrow}}$$

$$\overset{\displaystyle OH \quad Cl}{C\text{---}C} + \tfrac{1}{2}Ca(OH)_2 \rightarrow \overset{\displaystyle O}{C\text{---}C} + \tfrac{1}{2}CaCl_2 + H_2O$$

Currently the chlorohydrin process accounts for essentially all of the existing propylene oxide capacity. Many of the present plants were originally designed for the production of ethylene oxide.

The basic chlorohydrin process technology was developed by the 1920s. While there have been, since that time, extensive efforts to develop a commercially useful direct oxidation process for propylene oxide manufacture to supplant the chlorohydrin process, the [solution] remains as elusive as ever.

Catalytic vapor phase oxidations of propylene to propylene oxide have reportedly achieved propylene oxide in low yield under special laboratory conditions. These have not so far led to a feasible process for manufacture. Even with silver catalysts, which are so effective for ethylene oxide manufacture, the direct oxidation of propylene, under process conditions appears to yield only CO_2 and H_2O.[4]

The non-catalytic vapor phase oxidation of propylene can yield propylene oxide in molar selectivities up to a maximum of 25 percent in a very narrow range of conditions.[5] Selectivity is defined as the moles of product obtained per mole of initial reactant consumed and is thus equivalent to what is sometimes designated yield under actual operating conditions. Selectivity suffers from the complications encountered in recovering propylene oxide from the multitude of co-produced substances.

Liquid phase oxidations of propylene using molecular oxygen as an oxidant have also been extensively studied. Both catalytic and non-catalytic liquid phase oxidations of propylene have given selectivities of up to 30–50 mol percent. Many patents have issued claiming one or another type of inert solvent employed in the liquid phase oxidation, but none of these have significantly modified the chemical reaction efficiency.[6] All such processes produce substantial quantities of formic and acetic acid and a multitude of other degradation products; these contribute to product recovery complexity and [corrosion], which creates a need for expensive materials of construction.

Another epoxidation system which has recently been investigated employs in essence the classic organic peracid reaction with olefins. One modification involves the telescoping of two reactions, oxidation of acetaldehyde to peracetic acid and concomitant use of the latter for the immediate epoxidation of an olefin; a co-oxidation of acetaldehyde and propylene thus performed is reported to yield acetic acid in about 75–80 mol percent based on acetaldehyde and propylene oxide in about 70 mol percent based on propylene.[7] Among other difficulties, this process suffers the disadvantage of a large acid by-product stream.

Halcon's New Process

Halcon's new process is based on its original discovery that hydroperoxides can be made to react with olefins in the presence of selected catalysts to give high yields of both alcohols and epoxides. With propylene as the olefin, selectivities of propylene to propylene oxide can be made better than 95 percent (molar basis).

$$\text{ROOH} + \quad \overset{H_3C}{\underset{H}{}}\!\!>\!\!C\!=\!C\!<\!\!\overset{H}{\underset{H}{}} \quad \rightarrow \text{ROH} + \quad \overset{H_3C}{\underset{H}{}}\!\!>\!\!C\!\!\overset{O}{\frown}\!\!C\!<\!\!\overset{H}{\underset{H}{}}$$

Aside from the novelty of the reaction, the most essential aspect of this invention lies in the discovery of the catalysts that promote the reaction. Indeed, the basic reaction can be forced to proceed in the absence of catalysts, but the rate and specificity of reaction is so poor that one might be tempted to explain the formation of the epoxide as a minor side reaction, which is formed via a radical mechanism similar to that proposed by Twigg.[8] A variety of catalysts have some degree of effectiveness for the epoxidation; these include compounds of molybdenum, vanadium, titanium, niobium, tantalum, tungsten, rhenium, and the like. These catalysts exhibit a remarkably high degree of reactivity at low concentrations. In table 4.1 are presented typical data obtained with propylene and with butene-2 using number of these catalysts.

The selectivities cited are hydroperoxide utilization selectivities (moles of epoxide produced per mole of ROOH consumed). The olefin to olefin oxide selectivities (moles of epoxide produced per mol of olefin consumed) for propylene are generally about 95 mol percent and with butene-2 are still higher.

Table 4.1
Catalyst effectiveness

With butene-2		
Reactor feed:	Butene-2 + ethylbenzene hydroperoxide + ethylbenzene	
Catalysts:	All as naphthenates	
Conc.:	.002 Mol of metal/Mol of ROOH	
Conditions:	One hour at 70°C.	
Catalyst	ROOH % conversion	% selectivity Mol epoxide formed/Mol ROOH converted
Mo	100	95
W	99	95
Ti	99	95
V	98	95
Nb	76	95
Ta	68	95
Re	100	50

With propylene		
Reactor feed:	Propylene + ethylbenzene hydroperoxide + ethylbenzene	
Catalysts:	All as naphthenates	
Conc.:	.002 Mol. of metal/Mol of ROOH	
Conditions:	One hour at 110°C.	
Catalyst	ROOH % conversion	% selectivity Mol epoxide formed/Mol ROOH converted
Mo	97	71
W	83	65
Ti	54	55
Nb	22	20
Ta	25	23
Re	100	10

During our studies of the epoxidation reaction, the various compounds of a given metal were added to the reaction mixture in a number of different valence states and found to have at least some degree of effectiveness. For example, we have employed molybdenum compounds as catalysts in which the molybdenum was initially in valence states of zero, plus four, plus five, and plus six with good results.

We prefer to operate with readily soluble forms of catalysts such as the naphthenates, the acetyl acetonates, etc., although forms of the metals which are less soluble can be employed. Listed in table 4.2 is a variety of very soluble forms of molybdenum that have been tested in the epoxidation of propylene. Less soluble forms of molybdenum, such as the trioxide or the disulfide have been utilized and have been shown to be highly effective in promoting the epoxidation.

Table 4.2
Influence of catalyst compound on hydroperoxide conversion

Reactor feed:	Cumene hydroperoxide + t-butyl alcohol + propylene
Catalyst:	.006 Mol of molybdenum/Mol of ROOH
Conditions:	15 minutes at 100°C.

Catalyst	ROOH % *conv.*
None	About 1%
Molybdenum citrate	81
Molybdenum naphthenate	79
Molybdenum acetylacetonate	73
Molybdenum oxalate	65

Reactor feed:	t-butyl hydroperoxide + t-butyl alcohol + propylene
Catalyst:	.006 Mol of molybdenum/Mol of ROOH
Conditions:	One hour at 130°C.

Catalyst	ROOH % *conv.*
None	About 2%
Molybdenum naphthenate	97
Permolybdic acid	88
Phosphomolybdic acid	67
Lithium phosphomolybdate	45
Sodium phosphomolybdate	32

Table 4.3
Reaction rates of olefins with peracetic acid

Comparative rates (generalized)		Comparative rates (specific)	
$CH_2\!=\!CH_2$	1	$CH_2\!=\!CH_2$	1
$RCH\!=\!CH_2$	24	$CH_3\!-\!CH\!=\!CH_2$	21
		$CH_3\!-\!(CH_2)_4\!-\!CH\!=\!CH_2$	27
		$\phi\!-\!CH\!=\!CH_2$	
$RCH\!=\!CHR$	500	$CH_3\!-\!CH\!=\!CHCH_3$	450
		Cyclopentene	925
$R_2C\!=\!CH_2$	500		
$R_2C\!=\!CHR$	6500	$(CH_3)_2C\!=\!CHCH_3$	5600
$R_2C\!=\!CR_2$	Very great		

Table 4.4

Reactor feed:	ROOH + *t*-butyl alcohol + propylene
Catalyst:	.006 Mol of molybdenum as naphthenate/Mol of ROOH
Conditions:	15 minutes at 100°C.

Hydroperoxide	ROOH % conversion	% selectivity Mol epoxide formed/Mol ROOH converted
Ethylbenzene	92	83
Cumene	79	85
t-Pentyl	29	92

Reactor feed:	ROOH + *t*-butyl alcohol + propylene
Catalyst:	.006 Mol of molybdenum as naphthenate/Mol of ROOH
Conditions:	One hour at 100°C.

	ROOH % conversion	% selectivity Mol epoxide formed/Mol ROOH converted
Cyclooctyl	92	87
Methylcyclohexyl	80	84
Dimethylcyclohexyl	76	88
t-Pentyl	71	91

While the catalyst is the most important factor contributing to rate and specificity in the hydroperoxide epoxidation of olefins, the reacting hydroperoxide, the olefin, and the solvent also affect either or both the rate and the efficiency of the reaction. The reactivity of the olefins parallels the reactivity observed with organic peracids although the absolute reactivity is lower. This can be seen from table 4.3.

The contributing effect of the hydroperoxide structure on the epoxidation is basically one of reaction rate enhancement or retardation, while the effect on the hydroperoxide utilization selectivity is minor. In addition to the hydroperoxides listed in table 4.4, we have successfully employed, among others, the hydroperoxides of the following hydrocarbons: tetralin, *p*-ethyltoluene, *p*-cymene, and mixed diethylbenzenes, and the like.

In essence, every hydroperoxide which was tested could be made to epoxidize the relatively inactive propylene in an efficient manner. As the list might suggest, our emphasis was placed on hydrocarbons readily obtained by air oxidation of inexpensive hydrocarbons.

The solvent or reaction medium could also influence the epoxidation. For economic reasons we generally prefer to operate with a solvent indigenous to the system. In general, this will be the parent hydrocarbon of the hydroperoxide or the corresponding product alcohol formed from the hydroperoxide or both. The olefin to olefin oxide selectivity is generally not affected by such solvents and generally remains 96 mol percent. There is no appreciable degradation of such reaction solvents. The loss of hydroperoxide to side reactions is due to oxygen liberation or the result of a small amount of oxidation of the solvent components.

Operating conditions for the hydroperoxide epoxidations of olefins can vary enormously, primarily due to vast differences in reactivity of the olefins. Based on Swern's relative reactivities of olefins,[9] over a six-thousandfold reactivity difference can be anticipated in going from ethylene to trisubstituted ethylenes. Successful operations have been conducted with various olefins and hydroperoxides over the following ranges of conditions: temperature—25 to 175°C; reaction time—four minutes to sixteen hours; pressure—from atmospheric to two-thousand pounds per square inch gauge (psig), olefin; concentration—one to thirty moles per mol of hydroperoxide; and catalyst concentration—0.00001 to 0.2 mol per mol of hydroperoxide.

With propylene, conditions are generally chosen so that hydroperoxide conversion is essentially complete and catalyst costs are kept to a minimum consistent with overall efficient operations. The range of conditions most appropriate for the epoxidation of propylene include the temperature range of 80–130°C, reaction times of 0.3–2 hours, pressures of 250–1000 psig, olefin concentrations of 2–6 moles per mol of hydroperoxide, and catalyst concentrations of 0.001 to 0.006 mol per mol of hydroperoxide.

The chemistry on which this radically new technology is based is novel, and thus it is useful to briefly consider the state of our understanding of reaction mechanisms.

It has not previously been suggested that a hydroperoxide might react with an olefin such as propylene to form alcohol and epoxide in nearly quantitative yields. Twigg has postulated a radical mechanism to account for epoxide formation in liquid phase olefin oxidations using peroxy radicals. But again, this is not quite the same as establishing the possibility for such reaction between an olefin and a stable hydroperoxide.

Studies to date indicate that the class of reaction is ionic in nature and is not of a free radical type. It is known that the performance in epoxidation can vary markedly, depending upon the specific catalyst and the specific system employed. This and other evidence indicate that it is possible to encounter distinctly different mechanisms in effecting the class reaction. It is anticipated that there will be continuing speculation on this reaction in chemical publications in the coming years.

This new technology lends itself to many modifications. Halcon has, of course, covered the novel technology with a broad program of patent filings throughout the world. Its flexibility with respect to feedstocks can lead to many combinations of product epoxides and alcohols or olefins, or to the production of epoxides with no co-products. It is, of course, not feasible here to review all of these possible process variations; let us instead consider in reasonable detail a commercial embodiment of this technology which leads to the manufacture of propylene oxide with styrene as the co-product. The process in a broad sense is analogous to the cumene process for manufacture of phenol and acetone. Both utilize hydroperoxides as intermediates and result in two products of commerce.

Figure 4.1 shows a simplified schematic flow diagram of such a process, which employs ethylbenzene and propylene as the feedstock materials. Basically, three chemical steps are involved:

(a) Peroxidation of ethylbenzene to the hydroperoxide.

$$\phi - CH_2CH_3 + O_2 \rightarrow \overset{\overset{\textstyle OOH}{\textstyle |}}{CH} - CH_3$$
$$\diagdown$$
$$\phi$$

(b) Epoxidation of propylene with the hydroperoxide to form propylene oxide and methyl benzyl alcohol.

$$\phi - \overset{\overset{\textstyle OOH}{\textstyle |}}{CH} - CH_3 + CH_3 - CH = CH_2 \rightarrow \phi - \overset{\overset{\textstyle OH}{\textstyle |}}{CH} - CH_3 + CH_3 - \overset{\overset{\textstyle O}{\diagup\diagdown}}{CH} \overline{} CH_2$$

(c) Dehydration of methyl benzyl alcohol to styrene.

$$\phi - \overset{\overset{\textstyle OH}{\textstyle |}}{CH} - CH_3 \rightarrow \phi - CH = CH_2 + H_2O$$

The peroxidation step of the Halcon process, in which the organic hydroperoxide is prepared, employs basically conventional technology and, therefore, requires relatively little discussion, although it should be noted that it has been possible significantly to improve the previously reported peroxidations of ethylbenzene. In this first step there are two factors of importance to the overall process. The first is the ratio of hydroperoxide to alcohol and ketone; this largely governs the ratio of propylene oxide to styrene eventually made. The second is the total selectivity to products having the skeletal structure of ethylbenzene; this selectivity controls the ultimate ethylbenzene to styrene selectivity. This selectivity can be easily maintained very high.

In the epoxidation reaction, the peroxidation effluent is mixed with propylene and the catalyst at 100–130°C for one to three hours, until reaction is essentially complete, that is, until 99 mol percent of the hydroperoxide has reacted. This reaction is simple and straightforward. Typical selectivities obtained are:

(a) Ethylbenzene hydroperoxide (EBHP) → methyl benzene alcohol + C_8 (styrene precursors) = 98 mol percent.

(b) Propylene → propylene oxide (P.O.) = 95 + mol percent.

(c) Hydroperoxide utilization, i.e.,

$$\frac{\text{Mol P.O.}}{\text{Mol EBHP}} = 80\text{–}90 \text{ mol percent}$$

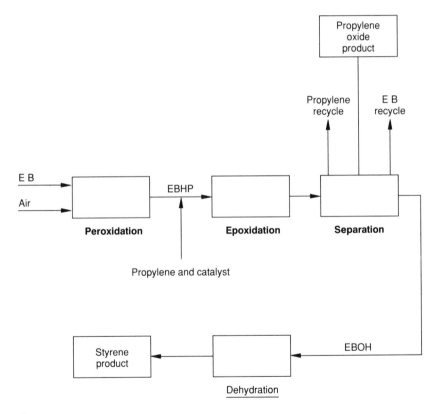

Figure 4.1
EB = Ethylbenzene. EBHP = Ethylbenzene hydroperoxide. EBOH = Methyl benzyl alcohol.

The relatively lower hydroperoxide utilization selectivity is accounted for by release of molecular oxygen or by side reactions of ethylbenzene hydroperoxide with ethylbenzene or the methyl benzyl alcohol formed in situ. Conditions can be chosen to minimize these side reactions, but economic considerations control the actual method of operation. The absence of any significant amount of high boiling materials facilitates the removal of methyl benzyl alcohol.

Propylene oxide is highly stable under the epoxidation conditions and is readily separated by distillation to yield a high quality product.

Dehydration of methyl benzyl alcohol to styrene is not a new process; it is carried out over a supported titania catalyst at 200–250°C. The dehydration is carried out with a high boiling cut of methyl benzyl alcohol and acetophenone totally free of ethylbenzene so that the final separation of styrene by distillation is clean and uncomplicated. The bottoms from the styrene distillation, unconverted methyl benzyl alcohol and acetophenone are hydrogenated to convert the acetophenone to methyl benzyl alcohol for subsequent recycle to the dehydrator, thus increasing the styrene yield. The overall selectivity of alcohol and ketone to styrene is well over 95 mol percent. The ethylbenzene to styrene portion of this system is in some ways similar to a route that has been reported to be employed by a large company for the production of styrene. That route proceeds along the lines: ethylbenzene oxidation to acetophenone, hydrogenation of acetophenone to methyl benzyl alcohol and finally dehydration of the alcohol to styrene. There are two major important differences between Halcon's new route and that previously used considering the manufacture of styrene alone. They lie in:

(a) A higher ethylbenzene to styrene selectivity, at least as high as that attainable via conventional dehydrogenation; the new peroxidation and epoxidation steps cause considerably less degradation of the C_8 structure,

(b) The hydrogen consumption is minimal since acetophenone production is small by comparison to alcohol production.

This epoxidation system enjoys a number of significant commercial advantages over peracid systems or direct oxidation routes. The hydroperoxides employed are more stable than the organic peracids, and the fact that they are essentially noncorrosive avoids the necessity for special equipment or exotic materials of construction. The absence of acids, such as acetic acid, which are present in all other oxidation systems and the economically useful peracid system, insures that the selectivity of propylene to propylene oxide, once the latter is formed, can be preserved, and that the oxide can ultimately be isolated, without fear of its disappearance in subsequent undesired reactions.

Process Versatility

The potential range of products that might be made by employment of this new technology is vast. A new field of commercializable chemistry has been opened.

Our emphasis has been placed on propylene oxide because it is a large volume chemical having great economic significance. Manufacture by the chlorohydrin process necessarily retards the natural growth rate since raw material costs, as a result of chlorine use, are high.

Since the new process is so general, the means are now at hand inexpensively to produce other epoxides which, until now, were not readily available. The peracid systems, by contrast, are inherently costly, and the chlorohydrin process loses utility because selectivity drops markedly when attempts are made to add hypochlorous acid to higher molecular weight or more branched olefins than propylene. On the other hand, the new hydroperoxide technology offers a future opportunity for sharply reduced manufacturing costs to produce epoxides from olefins.

References

1. *Chemical Economics Handbook*, Section 654. 5030, Stanford Research Institute (1965); *Ibid.*, 691.7020 (1964).

2. C & EN, May 11, 1964, page 57; C & EN, Oct. 29, 1962, page 32.

3. Kent, V. A. (Editor) Reigels Industrial Chemistry, New York, Reinhold Publishing company, 1962, page 900.

4. Garakhovatskii and Robinak, *Ukrain. Khin. Zhur*, 24, 63–67 (1958).

5. British Patent No. 960, 332 (50 Farbenfabriken Bayer).

6. Sharp & Reid, U.S. Patent No. 3,210,380 (to Monsanto).

7. Coffey and Lowley British Patent No. 963,430 (to Imperial Chemical Industries Ltd.)

8. Twigg, Proceedings of the Conference on Oxidation Processes, page 5, Special Supplement to Chemical Engineering Science, 3, 5, (1954).

9. Swern, D., *J. Amer. Chem. Soc.*, 69, 1692 (1947).

Innovation and Entrepreneurship

A report prepared by the National Academy of Sciences in 1967 referred to innovators like Ralph Landau as technological leaders, people who match "the world of science to the world of society, with a foot in management and a foot in science." Whenever Landau repeats this quotation, he hastens to add that because his company's only source of revenue was what it earned, both of his feet were always planted firmly on the ground.

This quip explains a great deal of Landau's success. From the beginning, he understood that inventions were valuable only if they could be commercialized, and that rapid commercialization was the one sure way to gain a competitive edge. As he and David Brown, a senior vice president at Halcon, explain in "Making Research Pay," the company's strategy was to research the market thoroughly before undertaking any new process research and to abandon a particular line of research if the market changed or if the developing technology did not match the existing market. The successful entrepreneur, Landau says, "listens to the market and shapes his strategy accordingly."

He also understood that if a small company is to stay competitive, it needs to be able to make decisions quickly. Consequently, Landau and Rehnberg insisted on owning and managing the company with no other major stockholders. This control allowed them to compete with larger, more bureaucratic organizations that had to answer to shareholders; this is illustrated by Landau's three-decades-long competition with the Royal Dutch Shell group of companies.

The competition began in the late 1940s when Shell dropped out of talks with Scientific Design and Sears on forming a joint venture that would use SD's new ethylene oxide process to make antifreeze. A few years later Shell announced that it had developed an ethylene oxide process that used oxygen instead of air and began to approach SD's actual and potential clients to find someone willing to build a plant using the Shell process.

At about the same time Shell acquired Petrochemicals Limited, which was the exclusive licensee of the SD process in the United Kingdom. Realizing the potential conflict of interest, Rehnberg and Landau proposed that the two companies negotiate a worldwide deal under which the two technologies would be pooled. After several meetings, Shell turned down the offer and continued to search for clients for its process, which the company was willing to license for virtually no royalty.

Several plants using the Shell technology were eventually licensed; Scientific Design countered by developing its own oxygen oxidation process, becoming the only company to offer its clients a choice of processes; and the two companies continued to compete. Years later Landau had an opportunity to ask why Shell virtually gave away its process. He was told it was the only successful chemical process the Shell research labs had produced for some years and that its "commercialization" justified the research expense.

Landau and Shell tangled again in 1974 when Shell announced that it would not renew its contract to buy propylene oxide from Oxirane's Rotterdam plant but would instead build its own plants using a process it was developing. Believing that the Shell process was an infringement on the Halcon patents, Landau sought validation of Halcon's Dutch patent. The initial ruling went against Halcon, but upon appeal Halcon was granted a patent that covered the process Shell was working on. Shell eventually paid Halcon a sizable royalty. About the same time, Shell and SD encountered each other again, in Brazil, where the government was choosing one exclusive licensee to manufacture enthylene oxide in the country. SD's client eventually won the license, and SD became a 10 percent stock owner of a very successful business, Oxiteno.

In a speech delivered in the late 1970s, E. G. G. Werner, the managing director of Shell in charge of chemicals, grouped Landau with Karl Ziegler and Giulio Natta, the Nobel prize-winning inventors of low-pressure processes for making polyethylene and polypropylene, as the three outstanding individuals in the postwar petrochemical industry. Landau takes that compliment not only as a tribute to his company's technological innovations but also to its tenacity in competing successfully against one of the largest companies in the world. These incidents, Landau says, show that "a small, flexible, energetic company can compete with the giants in many areas and more than hold its own. This is a major justification for the support of entrepreneurship in this country as an ongoing public policy." He hastens to point out, however, that few entrepreneurial companies can endure in the face of adverse macroeconomic and institutional policies.

5   Making Research Pay

For the Scientific Design Company, Inc., with whom the authors have long been associated, research and development is an integral part of its business, not merely a department. An interesting characteristic of the authors' work is that the chemical engineer is heavily featured in all aspects of the research and development program. Their business is to originate and develop new organic chemical processes that can be licensed to chemical producers. If they can also design and construct the plant using the process, so much the better (because it assures successful translation to commercial reality), but the main goal is the commercialization of research. For SD, the company's livelihood depends on profitable research—research must pay. This is indeed a unique position to be in. Chemical manufacturing companies have other sources of income and usually many different products for sale. This dependence on research has made us aware from the beginning of the difficult problems of assessing research. For us, research must generate the income needed to perform additional research to keep the company in being.

In the nineteen years that we have managed to maintain our organization based on research, we have faced all of the problems and developed our own philosophy of the hows, whys, and wherefores of making research pay.

The Role of the Engineering Construction Company

The background of the engineering construction company and the part it has played in the chemical process industry provides an interesting story.[1]

With David Brown, senior vice president of Halcon. Published in *Symposium Series No. 7* (London: Institution of Chemical Engineers, 1965), 7:35–7:43. Reprinted with permission of the Institution of Chemical Engineers, London, England. All rights reserved.

Of American origin, the first engineering companies were formed about the time of the first World War as research-minded, process-development firms to assist in furthering the wide technological exchanges then beginning in the petroleum industry. As the oil companies spent their efforts searching for crude oil and establishing retail market facilities, the engineering organizations led in the development of processes and manufacturing techniques that were needed in the refining industry.

The field of chemicals developed more slowly in this regard, and there was little interchange of information between manufacturing companies in the chemical process industry themselves or by the manufacturing companies and engineering contractors. A chemical-producing company would expand by doing its own process design, and contractors would be called in to handle construction, piping and mechanical work, electrical work, and other separated facets of the project.

Gradually, contracting firms grew that were capable of handling the more sophisticated engineering and construction requirements of the chemical as well as the oil companies. The formation of this type of company was an important step forward, with all responsibility placed in one organization.

As the chemical and refinery processing industries forged ahead, other types of engineering firms found that an important job was still not being done adequately—that of providing interchanges of know-how among companies in the chemical industries and of the development of processes universally available for licensing. Companies with strong chemical engineering background emerged—some limiting themselves solely to research and development—others doing research, development, licensing, engineering, and construction. Table 5.1 lists the important United States research and development engineering companies.

In Great Britain there is no direct equivalent to this type of company. However, there are English companies which do licensing in certain fields and which derive at least a portion of their income from process sales. Included among these companies are Power Gas Corporation Ltd., British Oxygen Co. Ltd., Humphreys and Glasgow Ltd., Constructors John Brown, Ltd., Simon-Carves Ltd., and others. There are, of course, similar types of companies in the U.S.A., Germany, France, Italy, Japan, and other countries.

The growth and importance of process research and licensing firms specializing in the design and construction of chemical plants is dependent on several factors. To begin with, not all chemical-producing companies are large enough or diversified enough to support their own research pro-

Table 5.1
U.S. research, development, and contracting firms (providing proprietary licensed processes in addition to engineering and construction)

Air Products (low temperature processes)

Chemical Construction Corporation (heavy inorganic chemicals)

Chemical and Industrial Corporation (heavy inorganic chemicals and gas processes)

Houdry Process Corporation (petroleum and selected petrochemical processes such as butadiene)

M. W. Kellogg Company (petroleum, metallurgical, and selected petrochemical processes such as ethylene)

Scientific Design Company, Inc. (organic and petrochemical processes)

Universal Oil Products Company (petroleum and selected petrochemical processes such as aromatics manufacture and recovery)

grams. Also, in the course of their work, engineering companies have made widespread contacts with chemical producers all over the world, and they have gained knowledge in all phases of engineering and in many different processes and industrial trends. One of the most important roles played by the engineering company has been in acquiring, trading, and disseminating know-how. Immediately after the end of World War II, the flow of chemical and petrochemical technology was from the United States to Europe and the Far East. Today there is considerable and ever increasing flow of technology in both directions.[2]

This is the picture of the industry—it is with this background that we discuss research based on our experience. The results, however, could be applicable to other types of companies.

Research Today in Manufacturing Companies

In the United States the chemical and allied process industries continue to lead all industries in research expenditures by company management—almost 78 percent of the $1.1 billion spent in 1962 was supported by industry. Actually, research expenditures are growing at the rate of about 10 percent per year and are increasing at a greater rate than either sales or profits. In the past seven years, sales have increased at 6 percent per year, and profits at $5\frac{3}{4}$ percent per year. This does not represent an outstanding performance and the profitability of stockholders' investment in the chemical industry shows a declining trend over the same period.[3]

The decrease in productivity has been shown in a different way.[4] Data presented for the years 1953 to 1962 were based on the relation of the number of patents, volume of scientific literature, and capital investment to research expenditure. The figures, based on research dollars spent during the preceding third year, show that:

(1) U.S. patents issued per million dollars of research declined from 12.9 in 1956 to 5.8 in 1962.

(2) Plant and equipment investment ratio to research expenditure declined from 13.1 in 1956 to 4.8 in 1962.

(3) U.S. scientific publications (based on U.S. papers in *Chemical Abstracts*) declined from 6.1 in 1956 to 3.7 in 1960.

That these factors have caused considerable concern is evidenced by the thought being given to the subject of creativity and productivity of research in the United States and in Great Britain. The business press in both countries has had numerous research-based stories, and it is interesting to note that all roads lead in the same direction. Thus, a report on the Manufacturing Chemists Association meeting in the United States revealed that the traditional research approach of many chemical firms to develop new products and then look for applications for them was being replaced by a policy of finding out what customers need and then planning research to meet these needs.

Business Week[5] reported that a quiet but intense revolution was sweeping through U.S. laboratories as industrial chemical producers reconsidered their organization and aims of their costly research programs. Unidentified (for obvious reasons) research heads are reported as saying that they and their management knew that they weren't getting a good return on the research dollar and the stockholders were beginning to realize it. One went so far as to state that many companies including his own had no business doing research just for the sheer pleasure and prestige that it brought. They really should be thinking in terms of their customers' needs, then doing something about developing new chemicals to meet those needs.

In an excellent article "Winds of Change in Industrial Chemical Research," Dr. Richard Gordon,[6] head of central research activities of Monsanto, is quoted—"One of the great myths of industrial research has been that if you spend enough money, something wonderful will happen. Management is beginning to realize this isn't so. But now there seems to be a trend to over-program research efforts. This doesn't work, either, if you lose sight of what you're trying to do in the process."

There is, therefore, increasing agreement that productivity can be improved; and a lot of waste still exists in research and development programs. It is being increasingly recognised that there is too much duplication of research in the chemical industry. Imitative research too often adds to the overall size of the industry's research and development budgets without really developing much new technology. Many companies do not take full advantage of existing technical know-how that is offered either outright or under a license arrangement. One of the failings in the chemical process industries is the strong determination of many companies to favour internal development against technology which can be bought outside. Although originally rising from wholly creditable motives, such policies are obsolete today and they stand in the way of the forward march of progress in the face of fierce competition.

More effective use can be made of money and manpower by concentrating a company's resources on new and novel items in process and product development. These items should be restricted to specific areas in which the company is particularly fitted.

If one takes a very long-range view of developments in this field, it would appear that the chemical processing industries are slowly recognizing that their true forte may be to concentrate their research more and more on new products, with closer consumer-orientation, leaving an increasing amount of the process development activity to outsiders, whether they be engineering licensing firms of the types described herein, or other manufacturing companies. In a sense, this trend is the same as that which occurred some years ago that led to most chemical companies' abandoning the development of new types of equipment, For example, when Imperial Chemical Industries Ltd. first developed its high-pressure polyethylene process, it found it essential to design and arrange for the manufacture itself of the high-pressure compressors as these were not available from any equipment manufacturer. Now, however, the very large build-up of high-pressure polyethylene plants throughout the world has been due in no small measure to the increasing availability of very well-developed compressors which are reasonably priced because the cost of their development is spread out over a number of companies who buy the machinery. Today, for instance, very few chemical or oil companies are still conducting significant research in the field of ammonia manufacture. A number of processes of excellent quality are available from licensing companies of the type listed in Table 1 and also from other companies of various kinds, so that it would be unjustified to conduct research inside a chemical company solely for this purpose. An apparent exception, namely the development by Texaco of its partial combustion process for the manufacture of synthesis gas, and the more recent development by ICI of its new pressure reforming process, is in fact probably only justified by virtue of the spreading of the development cost over the licensing of such technology to a large number of companies. Since, in general, the more sophisticated organic chemical processes are not licensed freely by manufacturing companies to other potential competitors, the shifting away from manufacturing companies doing their own process development work in this field will be slower, but the widespread activities of the authors' company and the others in the same category have demonstrated that where such process technology can be developed for sale to a wide number of customers, the industry will eventually recognise that it is cheaper to buy than to develop for their own internal use. This has also been amply demonstrated in the field of hydrocarbon and naphtha cracking for the production of ethylene and propylene, in which several major American contractors like Lummus, Kellogg, Stone & Webster, etc. have made important contributions to the world petrochemical industry.

Sir Ronald Holroyd of Imperial Chemical Industries Ltd. summed up ICI's position in research.[7] We concur with his following opinions on productivity in research:—"Purely academic research should be free to follow its own line irrespective of immediate 'productivity' in the shape of worthwhile applications. At the same time, academic research like any other activity comprises work which is outstandingly brilliant, some which is only average, some which is downright poor and, as more and more money and effort goes into this field, there is a growing need to find some form of quality or 'productivity' measurement which is more effective than simply counting the number of publications.... With industrial research and particularly research inside industrial organisations there is no doubt that productivity is vitally important."

Sir Ronald also reports that return from research is of the same order as that of other worthwhile industrial activities, and not as high as is often imagined. For every £million spent on research of all kinds, the yield averages £200,000 a year, for ten years, representing a doubling of the original investment in ten years. This is not a particularly handsome interest rate of return, when we consider how far in the future the money is paid back. We would say that in our corporate experience the returns are better. This suggests that the type of business has a good deal to do with the productivity of its research.

Of the total research and development expenditures of the chemical industry, only a small portion (about 15–20 percent) represents industrial basic research. The rest goes to technical service improvements, plant improvements, etc. While these are important indeed, it is necessary to separate out the fundamental research expense, if a company's real progress is to be gauged. Although presenting many difficulties in some ways, such expenses for technical service and development should not figure in the research budget at all, but be applied to the departments they aid—manufacturing, sales etc. A study of such real and segregated research costs might evaluate companies quite differently from present day yardsticks. E. I. du Pont de Nemours, Inc. has recognized the importance of this, and segregates its fundamental research expenditures in its financial reports.

The research "facts of life" have been presented—increasing expenditure, lower productivity, need for evaluation, etc.—as well as many of the contributing factors. Against this background, companies must still make research pay. It is assumed, of course, that privately held companies must ipso facto hold these aims. Social, scientific, or other very long range non-profit research may possibly be the responsibility of private industry, if the overall society decides it is in its interest to do it in this way, but then no part of this paper is applicable to such situations.

SD Makes Research Pay

Since most chemical research is performed by large industrial organizations, SD starts with an advantage—the company is relatively small. We have long maintained that the efficiency of a research body drops as the size of that body increases. This was recently emphasized in an article "R&D is more Efficient in Small Companies—in the sense of getting more results per dollar of expenditure".[8] Evidence collected from interviews with research and development managers with various classes of companies in the electronics and chemical industry suggested that large companies tend to spend substantially more to develop particular products than do small firms, with the large firm typically spending three to ten times as much as a small one to develop a similar product.

The three major factors cited as giving the small company an advantage are the ability of chemists and engineers, the attitude towards costs, and communication and coordination. In a small firm the average capabilities of technical people can often be higher. This is attributed to the small firm offering a more powerful appeal to the individual who has the opportunity to exert more influence and who may attain more independence. The larger firms also hire a substantial number of new graduates while small firms typically hire men who have already demonstrated their technical competence: it is also easier to evaluate the performance of an individual in a small company and to advance the responsibilities of the more competent.

Where costs are concerned, the employee of a small company is more sensitive to the business prospects of the company and is less likely to spend money unnecessarily. Communication and coordination are simplified because there is greater contact within and between departments as well as directly with top executives, and there is a shorter chain of command: it is sometimes surprising how much these factors alone can improve the motivation of individuals.

A deliberate effort is made in this size of company not to keep increasing research budgets. We have a great preoccupation in getting maximum dollar results from expenditures by avoiding uneconomic experiments. There are several ways of accomplishing this. One is to study the trends in industry carefully and thoroughly before spending research dollars. This system of premarketing goes a long way toward making sure that a market really will exist for the fruits of the research. Although market research is a most important and useful tool if used correctly, there are growing records of failures where companies have misread or misjudged the information gathered. Even sophisticated nontechnical industries with a huge background in marketing have misread product demand and acceptance. The sales department often has an essential role to play in market forecasting, more than it has been vouchsafed, because it may well be able to sell a new product when forecasts based on existing situations will be more conservative. On the other hand, ... a product ... which might otherwise be expected to sell easily [might not sell because of competitive factors]. It is also important to note changing raw material situations—many products and processes are obsolete when developed because the required raw materials are depleted or have been superseded by cheaper raw materials which come from other processes. It is hard to give enough emphasis to the immense importance of immediate knowledge in great depth of the actual operations of the chemical industry in regard to planning one's research program. Up-to-date acquaintance with the chemical literature is by no means enough, nor are communications with the market development and planning personnel alone. Good insight must also be attained into what top management is doing in planning in the chemical industrial field. This entire picture can only be attained by close personal ties in depth throughout the industry, combined with active practice in the field.

Uneconomic experiments can also be avoided by staying within the field with which a company is most familiar; at the same time not being afraid of something new if the prospects are reasonable. This too, was brought out by Sir Ronald Holroyd in his conclusion that ICI's most profitable programs are those in which the ideas of the company's own speculative research are exploited and that a much higher proportion of projects originating from ideas external to the company fail than of projects originating from within. This supports our thesis that in every case where adequate technology can be bought, it should be, and a company's staff restricted to developments not elsewhere available.

Another method of getting maximum dollar results is the avoidance of putting up large, automated, integrated pilot plants. The use of modern computer techniques, the improvement in chemical engineering disciplines, and the development of techniques for studying "miniature" experimental sections of plants have made it possible to bypass the conventional large pilot plant in an increasing number of cases. The finest technical judgment is needed to make this system work, but it can be done, and more of it will be done. A number of large companies already have decided on this route for themselves.

At Scientific Design we recognize the importance of intense participation in communications between people of varied skills in the research program. This admittedly works best in the smaller organization. Research must be directed by a high officer of the company—with both authority and knowledge. The almost immediate results are wiser decisions and stimulation of research and research workers through proving their importance. One of the failings in the American chemical process industries is the still common tendency to restrict promotion of its top scientific and technical men into the highest administrative posts.[9]

There is no dearth of projects that could lead to successful pay-off in research. However, a company must be ready, willing, and able to apply the results of research to commercial applications. David Kiefer[6] sums it up by saying that, "... unless operating groups put new technology to use, research has no economic value. In fact, some observers believe that one of the biggest wastes in research and development stems from new technology that is never commercialized because the production or sales people cannot or do not want to put it to work."

This cannot and does not happen at Scientific Design. Our ability to commercialize the results of research is a large contributing factor toward making research pay. The fact that we have a world-wide clientele in all industrial countries has led to a high rate of commercialization of processes; incentives vary so greatly from area to area and client to client that usually some use can be found somewhere for any interesting technology. However, our work is not primarily directed at very limited markets. In one sense, every manufacturing company doing its own research has a comparably limited market within its own ranks.

We have also found that research is better conducted in small groups, often in parallel, with simultaneous attack on several parts of a process, than in large groups. Competition as to projects between some of these research groups in the same company would not be unhealthy if properly coordinated at the administrative level. Unfortunately, the trend in the industry today is not in this direction, particularly due to the necessity of applying an ever-expanding spectrum of specialized disciplines to the project; large numbers of people, therefore, become involved inevitably in most projects which brings increased problems in control and coordination (application of specialized disciplines has an almost infinite capacity for expending man-hours).

Research and research people should be encouraged to come down from what is often their "ivory tower." Dr. Alfred E. Brown of Harris Research Laboratories,[10] said, "I personally believe that a sense of urgency, dither, or pressure in a laboratory can greatly spur research creativity and productivity." Scientific Design's method is to put pressure on research from the first idea onward, and particularly on terminating of the project in a viable industrial scheme. We search early for companies, anywhere in the world, who might have such an adequately strong incentive that they would be prepared, in the right circumstances, to take the risk of being the first producer under the new process. As soon as this has been done, we try to conclude the research and reduce the period from test tube to tank car to the shortest time (and lowest cost) possible consistent with an economical plant startup. No research chemist or engineer will ever admit he has enough data for design of a plant, and if left alone may well be tempted to research the project "to death." Our company is privately owned, and has no subsidies from anyone—we have to work for our living. Hence, we pay close attention to the profitability of our work to the chemical industry at all stages. We can't afford an "ivory tower."

The Role of the Chemical Engineer

In a successful research and development project the use of many specialized skills is essential—chemists, design engineers, statisticians, computer group, theoreticians, patent department, etc. Except in preliminary exploratory work, which is properly the domain of imaginative and skilled chemists, we believe that close control of a project should be exerted by the design people who will be responsible for assuring the ultimate success of the commercial process, and all reporting (on technical matters) should be to a single head of research and development. We believe strongly in the importance of the role the trained chemical engineer plays in coordinating these activities and in minimizing the expense of the total development-design-startup operation.

To show the utility and importance of the chemical engineer in the research and development chain leading to commercialization, we have listed ten positions he occupies in the Scientific Design organization:

(1) *Heterogeneous catalyst research.* It is invaluable for the chemical engineer to work with organic chemists because his training in kinetics and in heat and mass transfer leads to proper design of experiments and interpretation of results. He often helps in the "engineering" of the catalyst.

(2) *Patent and legal work.* The combination chemical engineer and patent attorney is uniquely able to work creatively with research and development people in preparing and prosecuting viable patent applications and to help guide research work away from areas where patents of others might be infringed. We find that many research people are inadequately able to understand the workings of the various patent systems and the importance of patents to industry. Part of our attorneys' job is to provide this education and even to overcome the bias toward patents which seems to prevail in some academic circles. The combination of chemical engineer and attorney is also a most effective developer of the complicated technical and legal details that go into a modern plant design contract and licensing agreement.

(3) *Experimental process development.* The chemical engineer is used, as he has been historically, in obtaining scale-up data for design of commercial plants.

(4) *Statisticians.* Rather than pure statisticians, chemical engineers with statistical training are preferred because of their ability to plan and interpret experiments aided by the insight due to their understanding of process problems.

(5) *Unit operations engineer.* The chemical engineer has specific skills and is disciplined in the specialized calculations in kinetics and heat and mass transfer required for the design of processes and equipment.

(6) *Process evaluation engineer.* In estimating capital and operating costs, the chemical engineer is particularly skilled in recognizing and developing relationships between process variables and costs. We make estimates before, during, and after research—innumerable estimates with flowsheets in varying amount of detail, and in this area particularly the chemical engineer

provides a viewpoint seldom found among research chemists, and can "feed back" to research important information regarding further process optimisations and shortcutting.

(7) *Sales executives.* Almost all sales executives at SD are chemical engineers because they have the skills most suitable for explaining our technology in economic terms to clients, helping the process engineers to tailor processes for the client's specific requirements, and negotiating technical matters for contracts.

(8) *Project managers.* Chemical engineers are particularly suited to form the key link in the highly specialized plant design procedure which involves extensive communication between research and development people, client and engineering staff in order to optimize and expedite plant design.

(9) *Start-up technical direction.* Chemical engineers are widely used in SD because they understand processes and have the ability to diagnose and cure operating problems.

(10) *Administration.* Most of SD's officers are chemical engineers because of their understanding of the company's and the industry's technical as well as business problems.

Most, if not all, of the foregoing types of chemical engineers are experts in what we call "process engineering." Yet, little formal education in process engineering is given in any United States university. Our process engineers are trained in industry. Perhaps our chemical engineering curricula will eventually recognise this major lacuna.

Profitable Research Strategies—Generalities and Examples

Generalities

Our research and development work can be broken down into three fairly definable stages, although very naturally there can often be some blending between the stages. The nature of these stages, their targets, and the general operations conducted within each stage are as follows:

(1) *Exploratory stage.* The target is to discover and prove out new chemistry which will reduce costs of a known large-scale manufactured product. The operations in this stage include literature and patent searches and preliminary economic evaluations; exploratory laboratory work is done for

the purpose of studying the reaction, performing patent screening experiments and developing preliminary analytical methods.

(2) *Process development stage.* The target is to develop reliable economics for a commercializable process. The operations of this stage include a great many economic evaluations and studies of basic process alternates, rough optimization of yields, utilities, and capital, screening of materials of construction, development of the most essential basic physical data, preliminary tests for estimating catalyst life, development of catalyst manufacturing methods, development of the patent structure surrounding the entire process, and a complete experimental run-through of the entire process on any scale which is sufficiently representative and experimentally convenient (including all recycles).

(3) *Process design stage.* The target is to provide all necessary data for a commercial plant design; this stage, therefore, would *only* be entered if there was a firm commitment to build a commercial plant based on the economics developed in Stage 2. The operations of Stage 3 include specific optimizations, testing of client's feed samples, provision of product samples for evaluation, comprehensive corrosion testing, confirmatory tests on equipment design and scale-up problems, operating tests of commercial equipment (for example, centrifuges), testing the life of catalysts on catalysts manufactured by commercial techniques, completion of basic physical data, and completion of analytical methods.

In planning an overall research program, management's basic decision is whether to start or to *not* start any of the above stages. This decision will be based upon a study of all available information surrounding the following factors:

(1) Are the projected economics noticeably *better than* (note: not *equal to*) anything known to be commercially available?

(2) Are the chances good of achieving the technical success necessary to get the desired economics?

(3) Is the estimated future market size and price realistic for the product to be made?

Examples

Some interesting examples of the six basic decisions regarding not starting or starting each of the above stages have been culled from our research and development history and are discussed below.

1. Decision to Not Enter Exploratory Stage 1

One example of this particular decision concerns a suggestion by one of our experienced technical people for a process for the preparation of acetylene from hydrocarbons. The employee was quite enthusiastic about this suggestion and, as is generally the case, considerable pressure was put on management to include it in the research program. An assessment was made of the expected chances for technical feasibility of the proposal and it was considered to be reasonable good, although the costs of development of a process of the expected technical complexity would be high. The competitive picture, however, did not look favorable; there were readily available many advanced technologies for the manufacture of acetylene, all highly competitive, and there were indications of new developments under way which might be even more favorable. The future market for acetylene was then examined and was deemed to be somewhat insecure; for example, the conversion of vinyl chloride manufacturing processes from an acetylene base to an ethylene base was proceeding at a rapid rate (vinyl chloride today still represents one of the principal uses of acetylene); a similar trend was also noted towards the manufacture of vinyl acetate from ethylene rather than acetylene; relatively slow growth was also noted for neoprene, which is also a major user of acetylene. A study was also made of the true costs of commercially operating acetylene plants, taking into account scale factor, location, depreciation status, etc. In light of all these considerations, it was decided that investing money even in the relatively low-cost exploratory research of Stage 1 was not a good gamble.

A second example can be cited in the field of a conversion catalyst for automobile exhaust gases. This has been a field of growing interest in the U.S. as a suggested partial answer to the air pollution problem. It was thought that SD's broad background in the development of oxidation catalysts could somehow be applied to advantage in this field. A deeper assessment of the opportunities indicated, however, that the competitive and market situations were most unfavorable; there would be arbitrary governmental control with regard to performance specifications and prices, and there were, during our period of consideration of this matter, a large number of announcements of hot competition in this field. Furthermore, it was recognized that this problem might be solvable without the use of *any* catalyst. We decided, accordingly, not to enter the fray.

2. Decision to Enter Exploratory Stage 1

Our successful work in *cyclo*-hexane oxidation (discussed later) led us to consider the general techniques as applied to the oxidation of other hydrocarbons. At one point in our study in this field there appeared a flurry of commercial interest in methyl ethyl ketone. Preliminary economic calculations indicated that there was a likelihood that our already-developed air oxidation techniques could lead to a process which might be considerably cheaper than the (at that time) only commercially-available one, based on the sulfation of butenes. As the commercial market, the projected competitive economics, and the chances of technical success seemed good, the decision was made to engage in this exploratory program. This positive decision was further implemented by the fact that suitable experimental equipment was already installed, thus reducing the ante on this gamble.

Interestingly enough, this program led us, in the course of our exploratory techniques, to some results which justified an exploratory program on the conversion of butane to acetic acid.

3. Decision to Not Enter Process Development Stage 2
The decision not to enter Process Development Stage 2 is generally made if there is some change in the picture as it was seen when it was decided to enter Stage 1. An example of this decision could be found in the case of manufacture of fresh water from sea water. Many years ago we had had some interesting concepts regarding the preparation of fresh water by refrigeration and crystallization techniques. After some exploratory money had been spent in this field, it became painfully obvious that while the expected technical success could probably be achieved, there was now a tremendous amount of competition from various similar processes or dissimilar processes having competitive economics, mostly developed by organizations which had been lavishly endowed with federal funds. Furthermore, the actual cash return to anyone licensing such a process (other than government payments for research and development programs) seemed very far in the future if, indeed, there would be any at all. It was, therefore, decided to discontinue experimental work in this field.

Another example is found in the oxychlorination of ethylene to produce ethylene dichloride. We had discerned a growing need for processes which would limit the coproduction of hydrochloric acid by producers of vinyl chloride based on ethylene. We had, therefore, undertaken exploratory work (Stage 1). In the course of our work it became apparent that there were being developed a number of competitive processes, perhaps to become available on very reasonable terms. We therefore felt that we would be at a time disadvantage with regard to the industry's immediate needs. Also the pay-out on the costs of our research and development would be poor in view of the potentially low royalty schedules and the relatively small proportion of the total market we could expect to have, considering the large number of potential process competitors. Yields were already high for the process and there did not seem much chance of a technological break-through. We also felt that we would be at a tremendous disadvantage in trying to sell an experimentally-developed process in the face of competition of at least one process which had had a long and successful history of proven commercial operation; this process had been developed and put into commercial practice by the Monsanto Company. We were able to make arrangements to act as exclusive licensing agents for the Monsanto process and, consequently, discontinued our research program before entering Stage 2.

A third example lies in the ozonolysis of *cyclo*-hexene to oxygenated products. Although screening tests indicated that the chances of high yields of desired product were easily achievable, an extensive review of the commercial costs of ozone preparation indicated that such a process would be unlikely to be competitive economically with air oxidation techniques for preparation of the product from *cyclo*-hexane, which in itself is cheaper and more available than *cyclo*-hexene.

4. Decision to Enter Process Development Stage 2
As the Process Development Stage is an expensive one, and as it involves further extensive participation by engineering, patent, legal, and sales personnel, all the favorable factors expected when entering Stage 1 must still obtain.

A good example of this lies in our propylene oxidation work. The hoped-for technical success had been achieved in Stage 1, the supply and price of propylene continued to be favorable, and there was growth in expected markets at a satisfactory price for propylene oxide. Preliminary evaluation of the economics of the new technology, based on our exploratory data, indicated that it could be most attractive economically in comparison with all other new or old technologies. It was obviously necessary, now, to firm up our data in all areas so that reliable capital and operating costs could be developed for study in connection with real projects. The decision was therefore made to place this project in the hands of an experimental group staffed mainly by chemical engineers, which could, with as great rapidity as possible, develop the necessary data for the preparation of reliable alternate designs for economic estimates by our engineers.

5. Decision to Not Enter Process Design Stage 3
The decision not to enter Process Design Stage 3 is probably one of the most painful of all decisions to make as at this point a considerable invest-

ment has been made, often in the hundreds of thousands of dollars. Our internal efforts are very great to try and minimize the necessity of making such a decision. Sometimes the handwriting on the wall can be seen early in Stage 2 and the project can be stopped before too much money has been committed. Such a decision would be based on lack of achievement of the technical aims promised by Stage 2 (for example, it might be found that the only way in which one could obtain desired yields would be by using uneconomical recycle rates or product concentration), on deterioration of the market for the product, or on the appearance of unexpected competition.

Without going into technical details, a good example of this decision in our development program is provided by a caprolactam process which had initially appeared attractive to us even in the face of a number of commercially available competitive processes. During the course of our Stage 2 work on this process, two things occurred. Firstly, serious unexpected technical difficulties made their appearance and were not easily bypassed without adversely affecting the economics of the process. Secondly, Stage 1 development on *another* route to caprolactam within our own exploratory organization showed great promise of a considerably improved process for this chemical. After some agonizing reappraisals we decided to halt the original project. Fortunately, we cannot provide many examples of this sort of unremunerative expenditure.

6.   Decision to Enter Process Design Stage 3
The decision to enter Process Design Stage 3, in our company, would only be made if there were overwhelming evidence of a planned commitment to build a commercial plant. Very often the design of such a plant will proceed concurrently with the development and completion of the necessary design data. Very obviously there is no room for technical surprises at this point although one cannot protect oneself from economic surprises provided by competition.

Examples of this stage are provided by all of our internally-developed processes practiced commercially or abuilding....

The foregoing simple examples are fairly obvious to anyone active in these fields, but for the organic chemicals industry as a whole (including fibers, plastics, detergents, solvents, and rubbers) it is indeed difficult to select rewarding chemical processes or products for research and development. It need hardly be said that even after selection has been successfully accomplished, it is equally important to be merciless when the process or product that seems to be promising turns out to be less so. It should be jettisoned promptly after revelation of serious weaknesses....

Future Research Trends at SD

The trend at Scientific Design is to consider the process direction of the future at the research level. As we see it, to remain profitable our work may well be in the following directions:

(1) Improving existing operations through development of new catalysts and new processes to reduce cost of manufacture of present products—no increase in the number of chemicals, but increase in competitive position for producers. Examples of successful accomplishments by SD in this category ... are o-xylene catalyst for phthalic anhydride, improved ethylene oxide catalyst, and precursors for adipic acid, terephthalic acid, isoprene, cyclo-hexanol, and cyclo-hexanone.

(2) Trend to multi-reaction processes. More sophisticated, more complex schemes can still be cheaper than some current methods. Most of the easy things have been done—more complicated areas remain to be attacked. A good example is given by the processes for synthetic glycerol by several different routes.

(3) Abundance of petroleum raw materials will spur development of processes to fully utilize these inexpensive sources.

(4) Continuous improvements in technology, spurred in part by competition, will lower prices and therefore encourage development of uses for common raw materials and monomers. For example, low-cost cyclo-hexane and p-xylene, can lead to new processes and intermediates for fibers.

(5) The synthetic organic chemical industry today is based fundamentally on the utilization of aromatic hydrocarbons (benzene, toluene, xylene, naphthalenes) and the low molecular weight, largely olefinic, aliphatic hydrocarbons (ethylene, propylene, butene). These materials are being used wisely and well, but there is little room left for improvement in their present cost to expect startling new developments which will increase their use. Probably the one important area in which cost reductions will take place for these basic raw materials is in the scale factor; sizes of plants are continuously increasing. As an example, a decade ago ethylene plants of 150 million pounds per year were considered very large whereas today there are known plans for plants approximately five times as large.

When the extent to which materials like ethylene and propylene are transformed to widely used products is compared with corresponding figures for utilization of butylene (excluding of course the fuel markets) or, even more surprisingly, the pentenes and hexenes, it is clear that one of the next big steps to be expected in the chemical process industries is utilization of these latter as basic raw materials. Direct conversion of paraffinic hydrocarbons to useful chemicals is a further area of interest and profitable research.

(6) The chemistry of the six-ring materials, whether benzene or cyclohexane, is not new. What about the chemistry of the eight-and twelve-ring materials, the C_8s and $C_{12}s$? These materials can be obtained from acetylene or butadiene. It will be the task of the chemical process industries to sufficiently improve the processes for generating these raw materials and transforming them so that the newer chemistry now being developed around their transformation products will find places in commerce.

(7) Nuclear energy is still only to be considered as another way of producing heat, but an important aspect is that it makes available enormous amounts of "radioactive energy," that is, ionizing radiation, free radical producing radiation, etc., with which in the future it will be both necessary and profitable to deal.

As an example, ionizing radiation was not long ago announced to be used by Dow Chemical Company for carrying out an anti-Markownikoff addition of hydrogen bromide to an olefin.

(8) Use of large amounts of acoustic energy both in subsonic and supersonic range will ultimately be economical. It can be anticipated that energy in these forms, and particularly supersonic energy, will more efficiently bring about some kinds of chemical reactions than do present processing methods.

(9) Processing with heat and pressure are not new but the peculiar combination of heat and pressure which we have come to know as shock waves has clear applications to chemical synthesis for production of substances which require both pressure and high temperature for their manufacture or which are too unstable to survive the required conditions when applied conventionally.

(10) Equal consideration must be given to plasma technology, the new device for economical and practical production of extremely high temperatures which has yet to exert full impact on the chemical processing industries.

(11) Light has long been known as a desirable activator for certain kinds of chemical reactions. In the past, small size and relatively poor efficiency of suitable light sources has limited industrial use. Reactions of this kind were

limited to those cases in which a reaction once initiated would proceed by means of a chain reaction to the transformation of many thousands of molecular substrates for each active photon initiating such a chain. Only recently have we seen the commercial application of radiant energy to a process in which one photon is required for each molecule transformed, namely, in the manufacture of caprolactam.

Conclusions

Our experiences as outlined herein are not directly applicable to any other company. Nevertheless, we believe there may be some useful suggestions of a wider significance. If we were to summarize certain basic factors, we would say they are:

(1) The pre-eminent role of the chemical engineer, from top management on down.

(2) The vital necessity for understanding of worldwide industrial, technological and business trends in selection and supervision of research projects, and minimization of duplication of effort.

(3) The development of a long *tradition* and staff skilled in a company's philosophy and goals, exploiting its strong points of technological and business skills—in short, the acquisition of *momentum*. For us, the momentum really took fifteen years to acquire, including the financial return to permit long term sustenance of a major research program; perhaps today it would be very much more difficult to attain such momentum if one were to start again.

(4) A strong profit motive with incentives for all.

(5) A strong sense of urgency on all development projects, with the stress on rapid commercialization and avoidance of "researching the project to death."

References

1. Landau, R. *Chem. Age, India,* 1962, 13, 9.

2. Landau, R. *World Petrol,* 1962, 33, 47: *Idem ibid,* 53: *Idem ibid* 73.

3. Hammesfahr, F. W. *Chem. Engng Progr.,* 1964, 60, June, p. 20.

4. Croxton, F. C. in Rottenberg, P. A. (Ed.). *"Productivity in Research",* p. 8. I. Chem. E. Symposium Series No. 13, 1963.

5. Anon. *Business Week,* 1964, 4 April, No. 1805, p. 92.

6. Kiefer, D. M. *Chem. Engng News*, 1964, 42, 88.

7. Holroyd, R. in Rottenberg, P. A. (Ed.). *"Productivity in Research"*, p. 4. I. Chem. E. Symposium Series No. 13, 1963.

8. Cooper, A. C. *Harvard Business Review*, 1964, May/June.

9. Landau, R. *Industr. Engng Chem.*, 1959, 51, July, 47A.

10. Brown, A. E. *Chem. Engng News*, 1960, 102, Oct. 24, p. 100.

6   Industrial Innovation: Yesterday and Today

As one who has participated directly in creating an industrial enterprise primarily devoted to innovation, I stand before you in a somewhat different category from many of the distinguished past recipients of your prestigious award, which I am so deeply honored to accept tonight, on behalf particularly of the wonderful people who make up the Halcon group of companies. The last such technological entrepreneur medalist (Bradley Dewey) received his award from you almost thirty years ago. The suggestion has been made to me, therefore, that I spend a short while tonight on observations based on our own experiences, which might have some pertinence for conditions today, and this is the reason for my choice of title.

Before I do, however, let me quote from a particularly relevant treatise, which seems to have been written with great insight into organizations such as ours. Professor Peter Drucker says in his remarkable book, *The Age of Discontinuity*:

> ... the fifty years before the outbreak of World War I have been called the "Heroic age of invention." They might equally be called the "Heroic age of the entrepreneur." The inventors of this period had to know how to convert their technical work into economic performance, and their invention into a business. It was then that the big businesses of today were founded.... In the ... years since World War I, the premium has been on management. Not that entrepreneurship has been lacking.... Since the end of World War II, more new businesses have been founded ... than in any similar period before.... More of these businesses have grown ... into worldwide giants, such as IBM, Xerox, and some of the pharmaceutical companies, yet the great need has been for the productive organization of large numbers of people ... for doing something that was already reasonably well known. Now we are entering again into an era in which emphasis will be on entrepreneurship.... It will not be ... the ability of a single man to organize a business he

Chemical Industry Medal Address to the American Section of the Society of Chemical Industry, New York, October 3, 1973. Published in *Chemistry and Industry*, no. 3 (February 2, 1974): 96–100. Reprinted with permission.

himself could run, control, embrace.... It will rather be the ability to create and direct an organization for the *new*. We need men who can build a new structure of entrepreneurship on the managerial foundations laid these last ... years ... and who ask: Where are the opportunities for a new industry, or at least for a new major process [or product]? ... In an age of rapid change, a technological *strategy* is essential for the success and indeed for the survival of a business and perhaps even of an industrial nation. The market is the most potent source of ideas for innovation....[1]

Thus, Professor Drucker says what I am convinced is deeply true: *Innovation geared to market demands is vital to the solution of man's many problems of the future.*[2]

History and Growth of Halcon International

Time will permit only a very "high-spot" description of our evolution as an entrepreneurial innovative organization. Actually, our history could be conveniently seen as a series of five-year periods, included in each of which was the commercialization of at least one successful and important new organic chemical process. This is a rate considerably better than that of most companies in our industry, I believe.

Our first fifteen years were devoted primarily to forging an independent existence. The first prerequisite, after the basic idea, was money. No capital was available for an unconventional business such as we aimed at, that is, a research-oriented company in the organic chemical field. Therefore, we were able to get started only by providing services. Initially, this was consultation abroad, and the management of the design and construction of a chemical plant in the United States based on a client's new process (Stauffer Chemical Co). We purchased a research laboratory in Manhattan in 1947, and began the work on our first commercial proprietary process, that for the direct oxidation of ethylene to ethylene oxide. Only one commercial installation of this kind existed, based on a French chemist's discovery; everyone else used the World War I–invented chlorhydrin process. Our first pilot plant was erected in England with an innovative firm (Petrochemicals Ltd.) seeking to establish Europe's first petrochemical plant, but the initial commercial version was installed by Naphtachimie in France. Thus, we discovered very early that Europe, exhausted by war, was eager for new ideas flowing from the United States, with few reservations about a struggling young enterprise without credit or reputation, and that technology was international in outlook and opportunity. We also proved that mission-oriented research, closely associated with top management, was the prescription for successful growth.

It took us some years before we could get additional work in the United States, because continued competition from the larger engineering companies made it very hard for us to break in. Finally, Allied Chemical gave us some significant engineering contracts back home. We subsequently were able to enter the construction field, commence the manufacture of catalysts, and undertake substantial lump-sum turnkey projects, all under the name of Scientific Design.

Undoubtedly, a substantial boost for this diversification came from the enhancement of our reputation by the development of our first wholly novel industrial chemical technology, the Mid-Century Process for terephthalic acid.[3] Even though we were persuaded to sell this technology to Standard Oil Company (Indiana) in 1956, despite our hopes for a joint manufacturing venture, we were "put on the map" as an important international designer and builder of new chemical plants, and as a truly innovative organization.

Standard Oil has carried this invention very far in the seventeen years since then, through its subsidiary, Amoco Chemicals Corp. In the recent words of H. Cudd, Amoco's President, "the process constitutes our major area of growth without qualification." The worldwide production capacity for terephthalic acid using this process, built or building, is 5.3 billion pounds per year, and it provides a majority of this free world's basic raw materials for polyester fibers.

This particular invention of ours also illuminates a larger truth. Twenty years ago, when we started on the search for a better way to made terephthalic acid, no government plan or prodding put us up to it—we did it because we thought we could make money if we succeeded. Simultaneously, Du Pont was working hard to build a market for Dacron fiber (invented in England) which was still expensive and a luxury, and other companies (like Chevron) were studying how to make p-xylene more cheaply. What government plan could have produced the result of all these and other efforts as seen in 1973—that polyester fiber has become substantially cheaper than cotton, and remains the principal hope for [expanding] the inexpensive clothing market now supplied by cotton? While cotton acreage diminishes as food production needs preempt the land,[4] the functioning of a private international incentive system has produced a workable and improved product at lower cost, not dependent on slave or sharecropper labor. And we derive a good deal of satisfaction from the fact that, as we have developed higher yield technology, we have also been working in the direction of pollution reduction, because the more efficient and direct a process is, the less it generally pollutes.

This is what innovation at the grass-roots and private levels is all about —and it can not be made to order by government fiat. And now this kind of strategy needs to be applied to government science also, as W. O. Baker, President of Bell Telephone Laboratories, has recently said.[5] The era of large government research projects in performance systems of national and strategic importance is drawing to a close and the challenge is to serve mankind in economic systems.

Our work in the later part of this primary period led to projects in Japan, as well as the United States and Europe. We formed strong ties in the Far East, and it is interesting to note that the first terephthalic acid plant in the world to use the Mid-Century Process actually started up in Japan at Mitsui Petrochemical. More processes were discovered, including especially our cyclohexane oxidation process for the production of cyclohexanone-ol mixtures, the building block for nylon manufacture. It has been licensed to Monsanto, Bayer, ICI, Mitsubishi, Rhône Poulenc, and others.

Thus, by the end of these fifteen years, we finally began to create enough cash flow through royalties and fees to permit us to dream once again of going into the manufacturing of chemicals. This was not a new thought, but now we felt we were on the threshold. The reasons for this desire on our part were complex, but included:

1. recognition that royalty income alone could not pay for the increasingly greater costs of research and development for new technology;

2. recognition that pure service organizations would never have great capital value;

3. realization that the return on really creative new technology would be greater by participation in the manufacture of the products under the exclusive protection features of the free world's patent system, in large units, rather than by nonexclusive licensing for modest royalty to many smaller plants (often uneconomical in size). We are gratified to note that spokesmen for such successful companies as DuPont and Dow have recently expressed similar conclusions.[6, 7]

At the beginning of our second phase of existence (the last twelve years), we discovered the third of our truly original chemical processes, the epoxidation of propylene, and other chemicals, to propylene oxide [PO] with oxygen or air. This tool gave us the opportunity at last to enter the chemical manufacturing field ourselves. The prevailing industrial situation was like that in ethylene oxide manufacture fifteen years earlier—all industry was still using the World War I–developed chlorhydrin process. We really geared up to exploit this technology, organized Halcon as the parent company with primary emphasis on its own research and development to be utilized in operating subsidiaries in a variety of ways, and came to an agreement in 1966 with the Atlantic Richfield Company which also was doing innovative work in the same area. From this was born the Oxirane group of companies, which are owned equally by [ARCO and Halcon]. We also have formed with Calvo Sotelo S.A. in Spain the firm of Montoro, which is now in successful operation, and are, in association with Sumitomo Chemical Company and Showa Denko, also building as Nihon Oxirane Co, a large propylene oxidestyrene plant in Japan.

In the seven years since then, as Professor R. Stobaugh of the Harvard Business School has put it last year, "the Oxirane family has resembled that of a family of rabbits.... Beyond the rapid announcement of over one billion pounds per year of worldwide PO capacity, the Oxirane entry into the PO field is notable for choice of different by-products at different locations." Since the Oxirane technology produces roughly twice as many other chemical co-products as PO itself, this means that in this short period of time, the total productive capacity of the Oxirane group for organic chemicals, built or building, has achieved the order of 4–5 billion pounds per year (new capacity having been announced by Oxirane after Professor R. Stobaugh's article).

Again I want to emphasise: the work done by Atlantic and ourselves paralleled work being done independently by many other innovative organizations in other aspects of this broad field of polyurethane chemistry— Bayer, Du Pont, Upjohn, and other companies in isocyanates, Wyandotte and C. C. Price in polyethers, Carbide, Mobay, and Houdry in one-shot urethane foam technology, and many others. The combined results of the efforts of all these organizations, guided by market and competitive forces, is the great urethane polymer industry of today.

Now, in furtherance of our new existence as an R&D oriented manufacturing entrepreneurial company, we have hit upon our fourth fundamental discovery, a new way of converting ethylene to ethylene glycol with unusually high yields, well suited to these days of rising ethylene costs and scarcity. Plans are well along to exploit this advance in the other part of the polyester fiber molecule. Other even newer technology is in the offing, and we believe our fifth major discovery is on its way. We are confident that many new opportunities for our type of approach and in our fields of specialization lie ahead.[8]

Recently, we participated as a stockholder in an ethylene oxide-glycol-amine-ethers complex (Oxiteno S.A.) in Brazil, the country which is growing economically at the fastest rate, and which has some lessons to teach us, too.

But we are not neglecting the engineering business which got us started. Just today, Scientific Design signed an agreement with the well-known French engineering firm of Technip, to sell them an interest in our subsidiary, SD Plants, Inc, which will broaden its services into many new areas of technology such as cryogenics, petroleum and gas processing, fertilizers, pharmaceuticals, foods and others. In addition, we are going to put Scientific Design's innovative chemical engineering skills to good use in new fields such as synthetic fuels, coal processing, and so on. The demand for chemical (and other) engineers in the future will strain all of our resources, for they hold many keys to the solution of society's problems, as I have written recently in another paper.[9]

In this account of our evolution, you may have noticed that I omitted any reference to our frustrations, heartaches, setbacks and failures, of which we have had plenty!

Government Intervention

If there are any lessons in our history, they perhaps come into focus a bit more sharply if we ask the question, "Could we do this over again if we were starting today?" I hope so, but I have some doubts. The reasons for my caution are based on the different climate existing today, as compared with 1946. Of course, the non-American worldwide technological and industrial vacuum resulting from the World War is happily no longer in existence, although large gaps exist between the industrial powers and the rest of the world. But the really basic difference is that we have too much government today. To paraphrase Wordsworth: "*Government* is too much with us; late and soon, Getting and spending, *it* lays waster *our* powers." It is unbelievable how many obstacles to the international technological entrepreneurial enterprise (and to industry generally) now exist because of the heightened role of nationalist governments. Except for the excess profits tax, all the obstacles (some reasonable, many not) we encountered are still here, and being added to year by year: greater restrictions on currency transfers; foreign investment controls; higher taxation in many areas; price, wage and profit controls; increased reporting and bureaucratic procedures; increasing ecological restraints; antitrust and consumerist legislation; political restrictions on imports and exports; laws favoring restrictive trade union power; and others. It takes many more lawyers and accountants to stay out of trouble, and litigation consciousness is much greater than ever. Inflation has risen at unprecedented rates. Resources and energy limitations are becoming very restrictive of economic growth. Non-governmental organizations of all sizes, all over the world, are increasingly subject to governmental regulations, frequently changing, and politically unpredictable. Incentives are increasingly chipped away, including raising capital gains taxes, reducing the attractiveness of stock options, reducing depletion allowances in many areas—in short, the formation of capital is constantly undergoing erosion while government's spending increases steadily.[10] As a result of these and other forces, profitability of industry has declined materially since World War II,[11] and the willingness and ability to take risks has been reduced accordingly. Why take risks if the rewards are less than the penalties? With this has come the unwillingness of the securities markets to take similar risks.[12,13]

So I say that concentration of power in government and its misuse are the primary obstacles that we face in improving the environment for technological and economic innovation, which alone can really solve the many problems of our rapidly increasing world population.

But the will to create new enterprises (and new ideas) is still very strong in the United States and abroad. What is signally lacking today is the risk capital to start and help sustain in the early years many of these ventures. We were able to accumulate capital by long years of service work, before we could generate enough to enter the capital intensive chemical industry; today, it would be much more difficult. Hence, new approaches are needed to help spawn the enterprises of the future. But this does not mean that the great companies of today are anything other than indispensable for the future as well. Their role, as before, is essential in helping new ideas enter the marketplace, and our organization could never have grown beyond a small consulting group without the simultaneous growth of a healthy worldwide chemical and petroleum industry, who became our clients, customers, and partners.

Size and Innovation

In addition to the adverse influence of big government, we must, however, recognize that big, highly structured organizations in general do not have any strong incentives to engage in far-out innovation. The risks usually outweigh the likely rewards. This appears to have been true of the great chemical companies, which could grow in the post–World War II period largely on the basis of proven technology and an apparently insatiable worldwide demand for their products. Hence, many of the great discoveries of this period in our organic chemical industry did not originate in such major companies, for example:

1. Polyester fiber—discovered by R. Whinfield working at the most unlikely research laboratory of the small Calico Printers Association in England.

2. Ziegler-Natta chemistry—this single most important post-World War II chemical discovery, resulting in a rare Nobel prize for industrial innovation, came from a German independent researcher in a small laboratory, and an Italian university professor. We owe high density polyethylene, polypropylene, polybutadiene and polyisoprene rubbers, among many others, to their work.

3. Acrylonitrile from propylene and ammonia, a base building block for many plastic and fiber products, was discovered in the small chemical research laboratory of a smallish oil company, Standard Oil company of Ohio.

4. The great evolution in manufacture of olefins, aromatics, and other chemicals from light and heavy hydrocarbons was provided by contracting organizations such as Kellogg, Lummus, Stone & Webster, and UOP [Universal Oil Products].

There are other examples, but the above illustrate a fundamental point, that basic invention is often done outside "establishments."[14] But these discoveries, like many of our own, could never have been industrialized (and the innovation completed) without the subsequent participation of the major oil, chemical, and rubber companies, who had the marketing skills, people, and capital. The aforementioned inventors were pursuing their own path, which they hoped would lead to fame and fortune, but they needed the big fellows to accomplish these goals.

There are, of course, exceptions even to this pattern. One that comes immediately to mind is the Du Pont Company, with such internally discovered innovations as Qiana, Fiber B (Kevral), Delrin, and its new Hexamethylene Diamine process from butadiene, for nylon manufacture. The Bell Telephone Laboratories can be mentioned in another field. An even bigger exception may appear to be the United Sates Government achievements for the atom bomb and the space program—here, the scale required was so enormous that only government funds liberally applied could provide a solution. Nevertheless, most of the real innovations in both these projects were made by private companies or universities working on government contracts. When the stakes are big enough, and the rewards (monetary or otherwise) large enough, big organizations can be innovative indeed! Another example is the American oil industry, which has developed major innovations in finding gas and oil by scientific prospecting, and where the rewards of success outweigh the risks. Our pharmaceutical industry provides other examples. How long will governments permit these successes as things are going today? They seem to want to reduce the rewards, and collaborate constantly at increasing the risks.

One can see the full consequences to innovation of government control in a country such as the Soviet Union, where it becomes very hard to find. Even its space program was inherited (as was ours at the beginning) from German World War II work, and pioneering work by Goddard in the United States. I have found no evidence of any creative innovations at all in their chemical industry; and no appreciable record of Russian contributions to the competitive international chemical scene exists, despite the fact that there are many brilliant Russian chemists. It is difficult to escape the conclusion that no incentives exist for risk taking in such a top-heavy society.[15] An excellent account of this was given in a recent article from the London *Economist*:

Managers in industry are given little opportunity, or incentive, to do more than stick to the task of fulfilling the production plans handed down to them by remote bureaucratic bodies. A story in the Soviet *Builder's Gazette* illustrates the pitfalls of the single-minded concentration on crudely defined targets. Russia apparently produces twice as much glass as the United States, although it builds only half as many houses. Where does it all go? Well, 46 percent of it gets broken before or during installation. Why? Because glass production plans are set in terms of square meters, which tempts managers to concentrate on producing thin glass, which then breaks easily.

It is not surprising that innovation, that essential part of technological progress, does not flourish. Many inventions emerge but few are applied, because, as Soviet economists themselves admit, it is safer and more profitable for the managers to churn out the same old items than to expose themselves to the risks and uncertainties of new production. According to a *Pravda* report last year, more than six hundred standard processes and blueprints in the petrochemical industry were twenty—thirty years old, and only about eighty were being revised.[16]

Is it any wonder that this society still cannot feed itself, fifty-five years after its Revolution? I am convinced that for Russian industrial society to develop as far as it has, it would have had to invent a capitalist industrial system to model itself on; fortunately, such a system already existed! In fact, Chairman Brezhnev's recent visit to the United States in search of our capital and technology shows how important these really are. In this part of the world also we feel, as do others, that the day of licensing really modern technology for royalty is over: it is simply too valuable. As I said earlier, the invention must be exploited by investing in a plant in order to get a fair return, because such technology *is* capital. If the Soviet philosophy bars the actual embodiment of a joint venture, ways should be found to provide the equivalent of a manufacturing return. As to capital *per se*, I think we can rely on prudent investors to decide what degree of risk they wish to take in any given foreign country. The same will no doubt apply to trading practices. In all this, we must not forget the Japanese experience. Japan's extraordinary growth from a defeated country to a major competitor in world markets shows how little time it takes if advanced technology is made available cheaply, as was the case in most instances.

Needs and Conditions for Innovation

From the foregoing historical analysis there emerges the paradox of today: the increasing difficulty of entrepreneurial innovation, and the increasing need for it. The challenges for innovation are immense, and we are all aware of them: the public desires greater amenities, better education and knowledge, improved communications and transportation, better attention to ecology and pollution problems, more complete medical and health care, relief from job boredom, more leisure, compassionate help for the unfortunate of the world, better nutrition—and more. We see, as a consequence of the explosive growth in world population, the great shortage and high price of foodstuffs on a world scale, which will persist for a long time and create great inflation.[17,18] What better area for technological innovation is there than in agriculture and food science, where America has always led the world? Taiwan's experience also shows the value of innovation in agriculture. The same is true for energy requirements, for job creation in all countries, particularly the less developed ones.

Our balance of payments problems also underline that a technologically advanced industry can make real contributions to society. The chemical trade surplus of the United States jumped 41.5 percent in the first half of 1973 over the first half of 1972, and even more in August; but for years we have had a healthy surplus.[19] This is certainly not the case for many less technologically oriented American industries.

Finally, one fact is crystal clear: the idea, propagated by some ill-informed (and, yes, immoral) ecologists and others, that zero economic growth is the only hope for mankind is a stillborn idea. No one can hope to freeze the status quo of mankind today. Redistribution of existing wealth, which such misguided spokesmen advocate as an answer to this critique, means sharing the poverty by enforced totalitarianism—something which all of Western civilization for over two thousand years has been painfully trying to escape. The failure of this concept in Chile, and the contrasting successes in Brazil, Iran, Japan, Taiwan, and others, point to one clear conclusion: the only decent hope for mankind is for more and better innovation—technological, educational, economic, and, social—but in the direction of less government, less oppression, more freedom, more decentralization of decision and judgment making, and especially of risk taking.[20–22]

We must all accept that each society has the basic political right to set the ground rules and establish the priorities under which its citizens can work, but it must be, as I plead herein, based on a greater historical and practical understanding of the limits within which successful results can be obtained. And I would dare to suggest that industry should be less defensive, and take positive initiatives to work out with government and the consumer better balances between society's needs, the consequences of fulfilling them, and the critical necessity for economic growth.[23]

Suggestions for Innovation

In this address, no panacea for the problems we all perceive comes readily to mind. But I can offer some suggestions of my own, in addition to my broad theme of the basic need to encourage innovation and reduce bureaucratic restraints. These would include:

1. Recognition by governments that capital formation and profits are essential to maintain the climate for the innovative society.[24] Big companies and large pools of capital as well as new types of venture capital and changes in investment practices by our large financial institutions are essential to provide the tools for the entrepreneurial growth of the future.[25] The current hearings by Senator Bentsen's committee on these subjects are of extraordinary importance to the healthy growth of our society.[26] Examples being considered by that committee include suggestions of radically reducing the capital gains tax, especially in connection with property held for longer periods of time, and changes in the whole structure of financing equity issues of American corporations and maintenance of suitable markets for them. These are essential to encourage risk-taking investment.

2. Governments must stop changing so rapidly the ground rules under which business operates, as has been the practice during these last fifteen years.[27] The innovative programs I have described take years to accomplish; businessmen cannot take risks if the rules change frequently in

midstream. Economics as a profession must evolve further in the direction of less governmental intervention, fewer stop-start programs, more long-range climate creation.

3. For many years, education for the élite was grounded in the classics and humanities, which were preparation for the callings of the law, medicine, religion, and teaching. The twentieth century has shown that our present liberal arts curriculum is no longer able to prepare the educated citizenry of the future.[28] A recent article in New York said, "Mass higher education has created a new problem: a growing liberal arts proletariat that is only marginally employable."[29] In my opinion, the future education of the public (a large percentage of which now goes to college) should be grounded on science as the basic liberal education for all. This is not meant to exclude other cultural subjects from the curriculum. From such preparation the student can proceed to specialized schools for any further training he wishes. I know this is expecting a great deal of our educational system, and certainly it will have to develop much better and different methods for teaching science universally. But if the general public (including economists, lawyers, politicians, and journalists) cannot acquire a scientific understanding of the world, it will become increasingly frustrated by decisions made (or not made) by a small élite of technologically trained people, and this bodes ill for our society.[30] Toward the same end, the large gap that exists today between the real worlds of economic behavior and the university must be narrowed significantly.

4. Large corporations can develop even better ways to work with the technological entrepreneur, not necessarily by taking his enterprise over or seeking to control it (as often occurred in the past), but by various imaginative means which can preserve the best features of both types. I must in this regard pay tribute to the entrepreneurial spirit and imagination of our distinguished partners, the Atlantic Richfield Company. They helped find a way to marry a modestly sized technological enterprise with a great international oil major to produce the Oxirane group as an offspring, and I do not think either parent can do anything less than take great pride in what is probably the most successful internally generated growth staged by any chemical company in recent years.

References

1. Drucker, P. F., 'The age of discontinuity', 1969, New York: Harper & Row

2. Science and Government Report, 1973, 15 Oct., p. 5

3. Landau, R. and Suffer, A., Chem. Engng. Prog., 1968, 64 (10), 20

4. *Bus. Week.*, 1973, 11 Aug., p. 41

5. *Chem. & Eng. News*, 1973, 30 July, p. 9

6. *Chem. Week*, 1973, 29 Aug., p. 28

7. *Petrochem. News*, 1973, 17 Sept., p. 3

8. Landau, R. and Brown, D., A.I. Ch.E.—I. Chem.E. Symposium Series, 1965, No. 7, p. 35, London: *Institution of Chemical Engineers*

9. Landau, R., *Chem. Engng. Prog.*, 1972, 68 (6), 9

10. Silk, L., *N.Y. Times*, 1973, 19 Oct., p. 18

11. *Forbes.* 1973, 15 Sept., p. 39

12. Metz. R., *N.Y. Times*, 1973, 31 July

13. *Wall St. J.*, 1973, 25 July, p. 3

14. *Technology Review*, 1973, July/Aug., p. 67

15. Astrachan, A., *The New Yorker*, 1973, 24 Sept., p. 117

16. *The Economist*, 1973, 28 July, p. 36

17. *N.Y. Times*, 1973, 29 July, Section 3, p. 1

18. *Science*, 1973, 181, 17 Aug., p. 634

19. *Chem. Week*, 1973, 15 Aug., p. 12; Wyss, A., *J. of Comm.* 1973, 28 Sept.

20. Kristol, I., *Wall St. J.*, 1973, 20 July

21. Medawar, P., *Smithsonian Magazine*, 1973, May

22. Diebold, J., *Foreign Affairs*, 1973, April, p. 555

23. Bliven, N., *The New Yorker*, 1973, 17 Sept., p. 154

24. Davenport, J. A., *Wall St. J.*, 1973, 27 July

25. Metz, R., *N.Y. Times*, 1973, 20 July

26. *Bus. Week*, 1973, 22 Sept., p. 42

27. Melloan, G., *Wall St. J.*, 1973, 22 May

28. Plumb. J. H., *Horizon*, 1972, summer, p. 4

29. Bird, C., *New York*, 1973, 27 Aug., p. 35

30. Janeway, E., *N. Y. Times*, 1973, 29 July, Book Review Section p. 17

7

Halcon International, Inc.—An Entrepreneurial Company

My fellow members of Newcomen:

… We are proud that our successes to date have been the result, in our opinion, of simply being better at our chosen field of endeavor than our competition, and, where possible, we have sought to find markets and niches where our special talents would permit us to enjoy a lead over others, often very large companies.

And now, since this is a momentous occasion in our thirty-two years of existence (almost to the day), Newcomen tradition leads us first to looking backward, although we consider we still have "miles to go before we sleep." Let us count a few ways in which we might see the history of the Halcon Group.

The Key Accomplishments

Our first look is the distant perspective: factually, what have we achieved, and how does it compare with others? We were entrepreneurs, which means bringing people, money, concepts, skills and markets together to create something that did not exist before, and is profitable; that was essentially our role from our inception as a "systems," "multinational," "high-technology" company, specializing in the field of organic (now mostly "petrochemical") chemistry.

However, the concepts of "systems," "multinational" and "high-technology" used today to describe our company's early beginnings had not yet been invented at our inception. They evolved from experience and the needs of the marketplace. No ideology or preconceived philosophy has led

Address to the New York dinner meeting of the Newcomen Society of the United States in honor of Halcon International Inc., June 21, 1978. Published by the Newcomen Society, October 1978. Reprinted with permission.

to the wide usage of these terms, since in other entrepreneurial companies, too, they were responses to market needs. And this is the hallmark of the entrepreneur—he listens to the market, and shapes his strategy accordingly. Following is a brief account of how we evolved, leaving out many of the setbacks, frustrations, failures and heartaches that are the lot of the entrepreneur!

Our corporation, initially called Scientific Design Company, provided the "systems" approach to design of chemical plants, adapting ideas from the pre-war period as applied to petroleum refining. We perceived a need for organic and "petrochemical" technology as a result of World War II. The greatest areas of devastation (Europe, then Japan) offered us broader market opportunities than a more prosperous U. S.; hence, the early introduction of the "multinational" aspect of our work. And, because we knew that innovation and proprietary "high technology" had been the keys to the successful development of roughly comparable companies like UOP and M. W. Kellogg in the petroleum field, we started our own original research early in our career. Our direct oxidation ethylene oxide research was commenced in 1947 (ethylene oxide and its derivatives are widely used for polyester fibers, detergents, fiberglass resins, antifreeze, and many other valuable products). We realized that the chlorhydrin process used since World War I to make this valuable chemical would have to become too expensive; furthermore, chlorine as an oxidant is very wasteful of energy and contributes to excessive pollution when the resulting chlorine salts are discharged into bodies of water. We considered this a challenge to our technical skills, although the discovery that ethylene could be oxidized with molecular oxygen over a silver catalyst had been made in the 1930s by Lefort in France and commercialized shortly thereafter by Union Carbide. We felt that other companies might like to license our version of such a process, if we could develop it.

Our first pilot plant was erected in England with an innovative oil firm (Petrochemicals Ltd.), seeking to establish Europe's first petrochemical plant, but their money ran out and they were eventually acquired by the Royal Dutch Shell group. Thus, our initial commercial version had to be constructed elsewhere, because Shell by this time had decided to develop their own ethylene oxide process. We succeeded at Naphtachimie, a subsidiary of the French firm Pechiney and the British Petroleum Company, near Marseilles. These were some of our early experiences with oil companies, who had the feedstocks and the money, but not the technology for the construction of the major petrochemical complexes of the modern era. They therefore were willing to buy technology from companies like ours, whereas the big chemical companies felt less need to do so at that time. Also, the latter were slower to realize that the possession of large quantities of petroleum hydrocarbons would lead to the prominent role oil companies would ultimately play in the petrochemical industry.

Since then we have licensed thirty companies, designed sixty-six plants in twenty-four countries, and they provide more than one-third of the world's installed capacity for ethylene oxide (and related products). Evidently our understanding of the requirements of the market was not mistaken. Our experiences confirmed our initial view that mission-oriented research, closely associated with top management, was the prescription for successful growth.

Nevertheless, in the first five years of our existence, we hung on literally by our eyeteeth. Without any capital resources of our own (so typical of young technological companies, but especially for an unconventional research-oriented business like ours), we could sell only services and ideas. Finally there came our first U. S. engineering work, and a bit later (1954) our first really original chemical discovery—the bromine-assisted air oxidation of p-xylene to terephthalic acid (the main ingredient of polyester fibers), replacing the previously utilized nitric acid oxidant (also polluting and energy intensive). DuPont then held the patents for Dacron polyester fiber, and seemed like the natural outlet for product to be made by us; we wanted very much to use this process as a basis for entering the manufacturing area ourselves. However, here too we learned that what seems obvious to the entrepreneur is not a view always shared by large companies who have interests to protect, and develop a "Not Invented Here" resistance to external change or ideas. *The Technology Review*, published by MIT, in its May 1978 section on innovation, treats this same problem in an article by Louis Soltanoff:

If you believe that companies early support the development of new products, you will discover a far different reality. Despite your [the inventor's] credentials, you will find that most companies will not jump at your offer to discuss how you could help them meet new product objectives. You disturb them. They prefer their immutable picture of the world in which there is a perpetual demand for their existing product lines, a satisfactory share of the market and a healthy growth in sales and profits. It is a fantasy world in which technical obsolescence never occurs and the competition prices their products fairly. While most companies cannot be described as being innovative, a few are.... Your problem, of course, will be to locate them.

The history of technology is replete with such examples. After extensive efforts of this kind, however, we realized that we couldn't quite muster the muscle.

As an alternative, therefore, we sold the whole technology to Standard Oil Company (Indiana), where it now forms one of the principal businesses of Amoco Chemicals Corporation. Something like six billion pounds per year [of terephthalic acid] are currently made by Amoco and its licensees (one of which, interestingly enough, is DuPont!). So, by 1956 (the end of our first ten years), we were moderately well known, and had some capital and new annual income—we were "on the map."

It was in this era also that we formed strong ties in the Far East, particularly Japan, and it is interesting to note that the first terephthalic acid plant in the world to use the bromine-assisted oxidation of p-xylene was actually started up in Japan at Mitsui Petrochemical Industries, followed shortly by Amoco's first plant.

Most of the income thus generated by us was invested in more research, which produced in 1959—among others—our second piece of original chemistry, the oxidation of cyclohexane in the presence of boric acid to make the basic intermediates for nylon, in much higher yield than had previously been attainable. We now have 1.6 billion pounds per year of capacity licensed to ICI, Monsanto, Rhone Poulenc, Farbenfabriken Bayer and Mitsubishi Chemical, among others. Also flowing from the research in this period came our maleic anhydride process, which accounts for approximately 60 percent of the world's capacity of the important chemical intermediate, widely used in resins, insecticides, etc. While this technology was not invented by us, radical improvement in the catalyst and the modernization of processing methods have led to the establishment of our widespread dominance in this product. We have licensed about forty plants for twenty-five companies in fifteen countries under this process. These two major developments assisted us significantly in establishing closer relations with the chemical companies of the world.

We had, a little earlier (1957), also formed a catalyst manufacturing company and entered the chemical plant construction field as well. The flow of royalties and other income thus building up permitted us to think once again about entering the chemical manufacturing business ourselves.

Our ticket of entry to manufacturing appeared when we invented a third piece of original chemistry (in 1962), the direct oxidation of propylene to propylene oxide, again in lieu of the older and universally employed chlorhydrin process, but by very different technology than that involved in ethylene oxide. This led to our reorganization to exploit it, by forming Halcon International, Inc. in 1963 (seventeen years after we started). Within three years, our changed mode of organization had successfully identified the best commercial opportunity for us, and led to the formation in

1966 of the Oxirane Group with the Atlantic Richfield Company. Thus, twenty long years after our founding, we had at last created enough capital and technology to accomplish what we had hoped for since at least 1948, namely, the establishment of our own chemical manufacturing, without surrendering control of our enterprise to outside financial sources, via a 50:50 joint venture. Much has been written elsewhere of the extraordinary success of this effort in its first twelve years. Suffice it to say that it has, so far, three plants in Bayport, Texas, two in Channelview, Texas, one in Rotterdam, one in Spain, and one in Japan. The capacities of these plants for organic chemicals production add up to over seven billion pounds per year! And Oxirane is unique in that it is a large chemical company built *entirely* on new technology.

Since then our fourth major discovery has occurred (1968) in the form of our new high-yield direct ethylene glycol process, which is in the throes of startup at Oxirane. But we are also developing our fifth, sixth and seventh pieces of original chemistry, which we believe offer us opportunities for further diversification. We recently announced the organization of Halcon Chemical Company to focus the efforts of the Halcon Group on continuing to explore various forms of investment in our manufacturing. We are working on many aspects of the initial endeavors of this company, as well as other joint ventures (we have had one for several years in Brazil), and possible acquisitions, but we are confident that our original work to develop new processes for such products as vinyl acetate, methacrylic acid, methyl methacrylate, ethylene oxide, phenol, aniline and other important chemicals will lead to commercialization in a variety of forms in the future.

This is an outline of our thirty-two years of technical and commercial accomplishment so far.... Most companies produced only one or two major discoveries during the last quarter century, and only a few had as many as four. The industry as a whole averaged perhaps a little over one a year.... Halcon is conspicuous by having contributed to or originated nine of these, an average of a major discovery commercialized approximately every four years, and constituting over *one quarter* of all the significant developments in our industry during this period. Of course not all of these are of equal worth, but perhaps it is not immodest to consider that our record, overall, is the best—certainly the most unusual, in that it was created by an entrepreneurial struggle lasting all through our history, and involved pitting ourselves against the majors. An example is cited by Dr. J. D. Rose, late research director of Britain's Imperial Chemical Industries, in an article back in 1970. Therein he described the near simultaneous invention by ICI and ourselves, with us in the lead, of the bromine-assisted air-oxidation of p-xylene to terephthalic acid, as follows: (it was) "one of our ... that is, ICI's ... great tragedies which cost ICI millions in royalties." But, continued Dr. Rose, "that is the luck of the game." Luck will beat brains anytime, but it pays to move rapidly, because someone may be gaining on you!

We truly feel that in over thirty years we have evolved a particularly effective system for creativity which has real commercial value, and we consider that our best years still lie ahead of us. In addition, we have acquired a tremendous reservoir of know-how and skilled people; while we are certainly the world leaders in innovative vapor and liquid phase oxidations, we have built plants and licensed technology for chlorination, alkylation, dehydrogenation, fermentation, polymerization, esterification, dehydration, ammoxidation, isomerization and many other reactions: altogether, more than 275 plants in thirty countries. This is a lot of organic chemical technology and international experience to have under one roof —it will match the best of the biggest companies!

Some Anecdotes to Illustrate the History of an Entrepreneurial Company

Another way of seeing our history is from the anecdotal point of view, which illustrates the continuing nature of the entrepreneurial struggle to achieve. Here are some memories that bob to the surface:

(1) Harry Rehnberg talked me into going into business for ourselves over many a coffee break or poker game in New York and Oak Ridge, Tennessee, during our Kellex days together for the Manhattan District project. Harry was a born pioneer and adventurer; he never knew fear (probably a characteristic of his Viking forebears). I was an ScD chemical engineer who thought research was my destiny. It proved to be so, but in an unexpected sort of way—by guiding the research of brilliant scientists and engineers, most of whom in the earlier years were persuaded by me to throw in their lot with a struggling young company.

Throughout our long career together of almost thirty years until his untimely death, Harry was always willing to take on the really difficult negotiation or confrontation. Naturally, I had quite a few myself, but never with him: we had no harsh words for each other, and our initial handshake was all we ever needed to accommodate ourselves to changing circumstances. Because he had young children, I took no money from the company for some time, living off my wife's earnings. Here I find one lesson for the would-be entrepreneur: consider carefully the family situation before embarking on the great adventure. We had other business partners at different times, but for one reason or another none survived the ultimate rigors of such a life and career. We have of course sold some stock to employees, but we have not been willing to bring outside financial shareholders into so independent and complex a business. . . .

(3) As I intimated earlier, we had started to think about going into manufacturing chemicals as early as 1948. With the apparently successful outcome of our ethylene oxide research becoming more visible, we considered a venture using this exciting new technology. We approached Sears Roebuck, who had a market for antifreeze, and Shell Chemical, who had surplus ethylene. Our proposal was simple: a three-way venture, with us contributing our new technology. Sears was in favor, and so was Shell initially, but somewhere in the vast recesses of that giant organization resistance developed, and the plan never came off. Instead, Shell subsequently set out to develop its own ethylene oxide process, and we have between us licensed since then most of the free world capacity except for Union Carbide's plants. Subsequently, as I mentioned, we attempted a joint venture with Standard of Indiana in terephthalic acid, but that too failed. Other attempts were also made. Why were we so interested in chemical manufacture, when we had a good licensing and engineering business going? The reasons for this desire on our part were complex, but included: (1) recognition that royalty income alone could not pay for the increasingly greater costs of research and development for new technology; (2) recognition that pure service organizations would never have great capital value; and (3) realization that the return on really creative new technology would be greater by participation in the manufacture of the products under the exclusive protection features of the free world's patent system, in large units, rather than by nonexclusive licensing for modest royalty to many smaller plants (often uneconomical in size).

We are gratified to note that spokesmen for such successful companies as DuPont and Dow have expressed conclusions similar to my last point, which was our principal reason. James Affleck, Chairman of the Manufacturing Chemists Association (and Chairman of American Cyanamid), recently testified to the same effect in Congress, and I have written an extensive paper on the general views of the chemical industry on this vital matter. Technology *is* capital, and should be invested in equity participation in the plants that utilize it: this is our hard-won conclusion after over three decades of developing new technology.

(4) Apropos of the foregoing considerations, one of our concerns has been the growing insecurity of proprietary technology in a world where (in

many countries) appropriating someone else's property or money or abro-
gating international agreements unilaterally is not considered immoral. We
had a convincing demonstration of this when we discovered that a subsidiary of the Italian State Oil Company ENI, although a licensee of ours, had
apparently used our data in designing an ethylene oxide plant for Czechoslovakia (and later Poland). We were unwilling to acquiesce in this, and
devoted four years of our time and money to obtain evidence that our
suspicions were correct, and to pursue them both in court and with our
government. Part of the extensive time consumption was due to the fact
that the then Democratic government really did not want to help American
business, even if in the right, and even if American technology was, in our
opinion, illegally being reexported despite the Export Control Act provisions. This attitude is part of the adversary position that our government
is increasingly adopting toward all private organizations and groups, including universities, probably as a consequence of the major influence of
lawyers on our system of government—both in writing the laws and
administering them. Law is one of the great growth industries!

Finally, after convincing victories in the courts, and with a little help
from the new Republican administration, we were able to prevail. We got
a very large cash settlement, and the government got a cease-and-desist
order. I do not, however, believe that this matter was a partisan issue, but
rather one of differences of style and personnel among administrations. The
labels could be different next time. Indeed, the first government official to
give us a sympathetic hearing was Secretary of Commerce John T. Connor,
of the Johnson Administration, but he left soon thereafter to become Chairman of Allied Chemical. The important point is that eternal vigilance is
necessary, and new technology must be protected. But, as technology ages,
licensing may become justified, and we have done so in a number of other
Communist countries with the approval of the American licensing authorities. Of course we also have some non-American competition in this area!

This episode was our first experience in extensive litigation, but unfortunately our world is much more litigious today, and this makes creativity,
productivity, and entrepreneurship even more difficult than ever before.

(5) And no backward look at dramatic moments in our history would
be complete without an affectionate greeting to our "godfather," Hans
Stauffer. He gave us our very first commission, to engineer and build a
plant for monochloracetic acid, based on a Stauffer-developed process. We
completed it, and it ran for a while, but the materials of construction
available in those days (within economic limits) were not able to withstand
the ravages of this most corrosive chemical, and the plant ultimately had to

be converted in part to making other less corrosive chemicals. That was the only plant we ever built that didn't work as designed, and virtually all of them are still producing. It took Stauffer some time to forgive us, since the contractor always gets blamed in such a situation!

The Financial Results

Many companies that are honored by The Newcomen Society are able to point to growth in sales revenues, profits, employees, etc., as a measure of their success. We are not going to do so directly, since we are still a private company, and don't have to! Indeed, we have plowed back virtually all our earnings into research and development, and later into investments in our manufacturing ventures. The stockholders have been patient indeed. But the bias of the tax laws against savings and risk-taking investments is so great, and the distractions of the regulatory bodies so enervating of real entrepreneurial activity, that we have deemed privacy as the only way we could grow without serious injury to our mobility and imaginativeness. This may well change, but not now.

A recent listing of the 100 largest privately held companies,[3] headed by Cargill at $10 billion in sales, and the smallest of which was H. B. Zachry with $200 million in sales is shown in table 7.1 We fit right into the approximate middle of these 100 companies, and consider that we have joined a very distinguished fraternity. But even more interesting is the fact that there appears to be no other of these companies engaged in the chemicals manufacturing and marketing business, nor in high-technology

Table 7.1

No.	Company	Estimated Sales (Millions)
1	Cargill	$10,800
3	Bechtel Group	2,080
7	Hughes Aircraft	1,600
8	United Parcel Service	1,600
14	Deering Milliken	1,000
17	Reader's Digest Association	750
22	S. C. Johnson & Son	600
29	Hallmark Cards	500
43	E. & J. Gallo Winery	400
49	Estee Lauder	375
62	Allen-Bradley Co.	300
68	Triangle Publications	270
85	Encyclopaedia Britannica	225
100	H. B. Zachry	200

research in this field. The capital-intensive nature of our industry is a sufficient explanation for our uniqueness, but it is because of the patience of our
stockholders, and the foresight of our partners, that we are able to stay
private, and thereby enhance our entrepreneurial and research skills. Governments are constantly seeking to reduce the rewards for risk-taking, and
it is the entrepreneur task to seek ways to mitigate these trends. As I once
wrote in paraphrase of Wordsworth: "Government is too much with us;
late and soon, getting and spending, it lays waste our powers...."

People Make a Company—Especially an Entrepreneurial Company

Still another way of looking at our history is to study the nature of the
people who have built it. We were always special in that we appealed to a
variety of individuals, many of whom would simply not have been productive in a large bureaucratic organization. And we were flexible in what and
how we paid them. We had no limits of any kind, and so attracted quite a
mix of all kinds of people, whose interaction produced enormous vitality.
Our situation in a great metropolitan area also contributed, because creative people cannot and should not be kept in an ivory tower. We did not
insist always on promotion from within, as many larger companies do, but
felt that bringing in people from other companies and countries contributed
to cross-fertilization and new ideas. Indeed, the entrepreneur and the entrepreneurial company must always be receptive to the new; they must listen
carefully to the world outside, and be submerged in the widest possible
stream of reality. One can never tell where the next opportunity or the
next idea will come from. I remember in 1963 when we reorganized our
company as Halcon, in order to start the search for a partner for our
propylene oxide technology, we drew up a short list of possible and logical
candidates; naturally, ARCO was not on that list! How could we have
known then of their own still secret work in this field, or their proposed
plans to organize an ARCO Chemical Company? But we circulated around,
talked to lots of people, and, one day, the blocks fell into place! And
ARCO can justly be proud of its great progress in chemicals since 1966. As
they said at their shareholders meeting in May, 1978, "But we are still
happy with the potential of a business that turns a $13 barrel of crude oil
into a range of products worth many times as much. We'll stay in that line
of business and do well."

We were fortunate that from the very beginning we were invited to
meet the top leaders of our industry, both foreign and domestic. Presumably, this hospitality was due to the circumstances prevailing in the post-

war world, but it must also have been due to the recognition that we were experts in our field, and even a casual visit might bring useful ideas or information to both parties. Thus we have come to know the leaders of the great (and not so large!) chemical, oil, and associated industries, and many of their colleagues. This has been a rare privilege indeed from a personal point of view, but it has also permitted us to gain invaluable perspectives and insights. One must know one's industry thoroughly if one wishes to innovate in it—its history, its technology, its markets, and its people. It is one of the reasons among many that I have concluded it is not enough to be a good general manager in order to manage any kind of company: to be truly creative and progressive, one must be steeped in one's industry, and always learn from it.

Throughout our evolution, then, we were very pleased with the selection of the people who joined us or worked with us. For many years we have had a flow of the brightest young people into all aspects of our work, and we are very strong in the younger generation of management. Many young people prefer an entrepreneurial organization in a way which is most heartwarming to us. Indeed, our ratio of Ph.D. chemical engineers and chemists to technical personnel is greater than that of DuPont or Exxon. We maintain fellowships at selected universities to improve our contacts there, and have recently created the Halcon Professorship of Technological Entrepreneurship at the University of Pennsylvania, which will permit young people to obtain, in four years of undergraduate study, the equivalent of the basics of engineering and management. The first incumbent, Dr. William Hamilton, is with us tonight.

We are working on other creative arrangements with the academic world, to bridge disciplines, and encourage a new breed of sophisticated would-be entrepreneur to emerge. And entrepreneurship, as I have found in my teaching assignments, is very much alive among the young people in the United States! It gives me great pleasure to tell this distinguished audience that our partners at ARCO are likewise very innovative in these areas, bridging the gaps between the industrial world and the other worlds that exist outside. Bob Anderson, of course, is very well known for his tremendous contributions as Chairman of the Aspen Institute, but recently another example appeared in the form of a $1 million award by the Atlantic Richfield Foundation to the University of Pennsylvania to establish the Robert D. Bent Professorship in Chemical Engineering. As many of you know, Bob Bent was the first president of ARCO Chemical Company and the co-founder of our Oxirane enterprises, and I am happy that he is in our audience tonight, as is Professor John Quinn, who is the first occupant of the Bent Professorship.

But, obtaining bright people from any source is not enough: they must be organized—loosely, but effectively. I am convinced organization has a great deal to do with the way any company can succeed in technological innovation. The top management should be actively and personally involved in the business, *and* the technological leadership and planning. England's Professor Bradbury (who has had industrial and academic careers) put it very well in his paper, "Constraints to Innovation": "Effective leadership today demands not the good practical man, but the well-trained and broadly trained professional."

From the very beginning, Halcon was managed primarily by technically trained people, chemists and chemical engineers. Our CEO is the man in charge of strategic planning, but we have chemical engineers right in the laboratory, working with our chemists at every stage of process development. Again, to cite Bradbury, "without an explicit strategy, well understood at the laboratory bench as well as in the board room, the failure rate in innovation may be unacceptably high and ruinously expensive." We have followed this concept from our inception. When you are underfinanced, you really have no choice. Even now it is part of our fundamental thinking, and we are organized so that our entire top management constitutes our entrepreneurial core, mostly freed from daily operating responsibilities. This structure differs from many larger companies in that we control the R&D directly, for the company as a whole, together with the more conventional control over our cash flow. This permits us to deploy all our strengths rapidly, in accordance with the market, existing and potential, with the most effective feedback possible. The Oxirane group is similarly organized, and, as mentioned, Halcon Chemical is still another entrepreneurial center. All this is based on our experience that even the larger companies, if they are to be successful in new venture strategy, must imitate the strengths of small company technical entrepreneurship....

... Mr. Robert Malpas, an executive director of Imperial Chemical Industries, who is joining us this fall as our new president, also said it very well in applying this same thinking to even big companies: "... organizations must cater both for the optimization of existing assets and fundamental change. They probably need two different cultures existing within the same organization, staffed by different types of people. There must not be a conflict between the full utilization and improvement of existing technology and the creation of the new. The first must finance the second, and the second is needed to remain profitable in the long run."

Mr. Soltanoff, in the article mentioned earlier, shows how difficult this can be:

You may think it presumptuous to believe that you can help a major, multinational company achieve its new product goals. Of course you can.
The strength of such companies is not in their innovative ability but rather in their capability to produce and distribute products competitively. They do this by being capital intensive, structured, disciplined and specialized. These are the very qualities that inhibit the entrepreneurial, nonstructured, risk-taking and creative spirit required for invention.
Some progressive companies understand this dilemma and try to solve it by creating an environment for a special group that has a freer hand. However, this environment lacks the special incentives that motivate the individual inventor. (Compensation for success or failure must be buffered from the real world lest it fatally stress the relationship between this elite group and the rest of the company.) So one powerful incentive that is typical of our way of life is missing entirely from theirs. That is, if we don't succeed we don't eat. In their environment, the paychecks are issued weekly, regardless.
Further, you must keep in mind that there is an inverse relationship between size and creativity in the art of invention, just as there is in other art forms. You would regard it as preposterous for a large corporation to claim that it can write a better play or novel than an individual by virtue of numerical superiority.

Dr. Alan Fusfeld, in the same issue of *Technology Review* cited above, puts this thought another way: "Most U. S. corporations are organized around the production process. They are not organized to recognize or to reward the uncertainties, risks, and time constraints of the technological innovation process. Not surprising, then, that most significant technological change originates outside of the firm—or even of the industry—that eventually uses it."

Peter Drucker has also spoken to this theme in his book, *The Age of Discontinuity*:

Now we are entering again into an era in which emphasis will be on entrepreneurship.... It will not be ... the ability of a single man to organize a business he himself could run, control, embrace.... It will rather be the ability to create and direct an organization for the *new*. We need men who can build a new structure of entrepreneurship on the managerial foundations laid these last ... years ... and who ask: Where are the opportunities for a new industry, or at least for a new major process or product? ... In an age of rapid change, a technological *strategy* is essential for the success and indeed for the survival of a business and perhaps even of an industrial nation. The market is the most potent source of ideas for innovation....

Thus, Professor Drucker says what I am convinced is deeply true: *Innovation geared to market demands is vital to the solution of man's many problems of the future.*

Continuing Innovation Is Vital to the United States Economy

Innovation, however, is threatened by many things, including the actions of government, as a recent article in *The New York Times* says, which includes some remarks of mine. I have recently written a long paper on this subject for the National Academy of Engineering symposium entitled "Innovators and Entrepreneurs—An Endangered Species?" I have also testified on these matters before the House Ways and Means Committee in April, and have delivered lectures at the University of Pennsylvania and Stanford University on an allied theme entitled "Technology, Economics, and Public Policy." This is not the time to dwell on these matters, but our declining national productivity increase, our large deficit in the balance of payments, our increasing inflation, and the mounting shrillness of our national dialogues are warnings that society and our economy can not stop growing without evil consequences, and that innovation is required everywhere to reverse the unfavorable trends of the last decades. Our international competition is increasing, and the momentum of the new technologies and industries created after the Second World War has begun to run down. We will soon be following Britain's path to a bleak future. A very graphic picture of that path is portrayed in the Hansard transcript of the debate in the House of Lords on 19 June, dealing with the subject of industrial growth. Therein reference is even made to Mr. Malpas's decision to leave ICI after a distinguished career of thirty years in order to join us. Particular stress is laid in this review on Britain's confiscatory tax rates, especially on individuals.

Unlike Britain, however, we can still create and innovate the major new high technologies of the future, and the organizational patterns to exploit them. Nevertheless, we too are engaged in an intense debate about the requirements for greater technological innovation. Special attention is being given to America's unique contribution to high taxation—our recently greatly increased capital gains tax (the highest in the free world). While it is hard to quantify the deadening effect on innovation and capital formation which the capital gains tax increase in the last decade has had, I am convinced it is the basic reason for the decline in risk-taking capital investment, which alone fuels the innovative process. Institutional investors, as a result of ERISA [Employee Retirement Income Security Act] and other fiduciary restraints, are very conservative. Furthermore, a study recently completed on the profile of the American individual stockholder made by two Wharton School professors shows clearly that all but 3 percent of individual investors are "overwhelmingly averse to taking risks" (these being mostly in the highest income or stock-holding groups). They point out, therefore, that the "benefits of many types of proposed tax reductions related to common stocks would, at least initially, benefit primarily a limited number of families." But as the above-cited British debate brought out, if this be so, then let us make the most of it! What is inequitable about letting the biggest risk takers get and keep more money, so long as it ultimately benefits society as a whole? Government cannot substitute itself for such individuals in judging when to take risks with their money, and it would not be successful if it could. That indeed is how our American capitalist system has become the strongest in the world, and the freest!

Thus, in order to encourage risk-taking capital investment, there has to be a recognition at the highest levels in the United States that a trade-off is necessary between encouraging new risk-taking wealth among corporations and individuals—wealth that will translate into investment—and the desire for equity and redistribution of income. Considering the great need for breakthroughs, this trade-off will have to be settled largely in the direction of wealth creation and new entrepreneurial incentives by tax reduction and regulatory reasonableness. *Nothing else will realistically work.* This wealth formation would not be encouraged for its own sake, but because it is the only way the country's economic and social welfare can be improved—for all the people—in a free society. It is certainly true that some of the new wealth that would thus be created might turn out to be employed in less useful investments than would be optimal, but this is an inevitable consequence of the alteration in economic climate. Such wealth formation incentives may be viewed as quite analogous to the limited monopoly our patent laws permit—another form of wealth creation which aids society in the long run. Both are needed for the processes of innovation and productivity improvement to flourish, and these are essential for our national health, as a recent report of the National Research Council Workshop (in which I participated) makes clear.

Old wealth tends to be conservative and non-risk-taking; new wealth tends to support new ventures, growth stocks of the riskier types, and new technology investment. A healthier stock market would be a reflection of such underlying changes. A good example of this distinction may be found in a recent history of the richest family in America, the Mellons. In their heyday, as investment bankers, the Mellons supported many new entrepreneurial companies, and their income today mostly comes from these earlier investments in Gulf, Alcoa, Mellon National Bank, Koppers, Carborundum, First Boston, General Reinsurance, Hewlett-Packard, etc. But today they are much less active in this type of funding. As one review of the book said:

"... today the Mellons are no longer accumulators, they're only spenders." Undoubtedly an exaggeration, but the book does make my point clear.

If there is any lesson to be learned from Halcon's history, it is this: if the prospect of money-making does not inspire people to innovate, then our society in the end will become coercive, and unfree, so as to spread the poverty around. True, we had other ideals as well, as I mentioned earlier. Our burning passion was always to be the best there is; but without the expectation of making money, none of this would have mattered. It is time government recreates the climate for more innovation! The cost of research and development is perhaps as little as 10 percent of the total cost of bringing new technology to commercial fruition; it is this 90 percent phase which is so sensitive to the regulatory, tax, inflation, and uncertainty barriers continuously erected and changed by government.

Where Do We Go from Here?

Obviously, we haven't come this far to rest on our laurels. There are many challenges for us yet—to help build Oxirane further, to establish other ventures for Halcon, to seek acquisitions, to continue to innovate in new technology, and to wrestle with the constantly changing problems posed by governments and tax laws. The entrepreneur is never satisfied, and that is our best reason for hope for the future.

8   Corporate Partnering
Can Spur Innovation

Not only are new technologies of great importance, but so are new institutional arrangements—social innovations, as it were—which will permit greater flexibility in the formulation of advanced and highly competitive technology. Corporate "partnering" is one such social innovation. Experiences at my former company belong to this category, although we never heard of the word at the time we employed the concept.

In my view, corporate "partnering" fundamentally applies to "cohabitation" of large and small organizations. If two big companies are organizing some form of collaborative organization, it would have been more commonly referred to in my day, and perhaps still today, as a joint venture; and since both partners are perfectly capable, in most instances, of looking after themselves very well in such an organization, there is nothing really new to say about joint ventures. But in the combination of a small and a large company, it is much too easy for the large to smother the small; hence this is my worm's-eye view of how the small company not only avoided smothering but came out with honor and rewards for all!

I emphasize that I am not dealing with "intrapreneurship" This term signifies an effort on the part of a large company to create in some parts of itself a culture which is more like that of the entrepreneurial world, and to keep out the suffocating culture of the large bureaucratic organization as long as possible. Some companies have managed to maintain "skunk works" for lengthy periods with quite good success. But there are many problems inherent in this organizational pattern. From my perspective, the culture of the true entrepreneurial company is very difficult to sustain inside a large organization, however good the intentions are on all sides.

One of the fundamental prerequisites for an entrepreneurial environment is the chance for high financial rewards; this creates great jealousy in a

Published in *Research Management* 30, no. 3 (May–June 1987): 21–26. Reprinted with permission from *Research-Management Technology*.

structured organization. At the same time, entrepreneurs recognize that they are taking a risk with their money and their futures; it is difficult for large company personnel, even those assigned to a "skunk works," to feel that the price of failure may be permanent loss of their jobs. Decision-making in the entrepreneurial company is often done instantaneously and the committee culture is seldom or never found. Work habits may be informal and the type of people employed may, in fact, be quite different from those in the typical large company.

Once in a philosophical discussion with a representative of ARCO (the large corporate partner which I will be discussing here), we examined why our relatively small research organization seemed so consistently to produce extraordinary results whereas many other such organizations in large companies did not do so, despite the obvious advantages they offered. The conclusion was that we had a unique advantage in that we had people living close to the large metropolitan center of New York who were intimately involved with global problems through the participation of the entire organization in world affairs. This gave them an extremely cosmopolitan perspective.

In private life, these people enjoyed many of the features that only a large city can offer. In fact, the kind of person who is attracted to New York is very often the kind who would not even fit into the culture of a large company. For New York one can substitute a few other major cities in the United States; nevertheless, research organizations are often located on predominantly semi-rural or rural campuses where it is supposed that people can think more effectively. I have felt that this is not always so and that the research environment for an industrial organization requires a feeling of intense energy—even pressure—and the knowledge that there are important problems that must be solved every day.

Finally, it seemed to us that the person who would be employed by a relatively free-wheeling smaller company would be much more likely to be individualistic and hard to fit into a conventional organization. Many of our employees, in fact, had left large companies precisely because they wanted the relative freedom and excitement which they hoped to find with us; and we had a very good record of keeping most of our able people. These factors may have aided us in assembling a unique team of brilliant technologists, in a concentration seldom if ever found in larger companies. Many smaller companies today also have superb teams of specialists, and it is their concentration in the smaller company which can make fruitful partnering so rewarding for both sizes.

The Small Company Culture

A small company has a number of cultural features which it would be to the advantage of the large company to preserve. It is well known that small companies are responsible for a large share of the major technology innovations in the United States. I am convinced that this is largely due to the nature of this culture and of the desire of the individuals for visible success, participation and reward. Gordon Moore, chairman and CEO of Intel Corporation and himself a successful entrepreneur at least twice over, had this to say: "Start-up companies are frequently the exploiter of innovation, if not the innovators themselves, because they have 'focus' and because small companies are often a more efficient instrument to get things done"[1]

A fundamental characteristic of the small entrepreneurial company is its adaptability to risk-taking. While a few fortunate companies have been able to grow so rapidly that they can offer essentially lifetime employment (perhaps a firm like Digital Equipment), this is generally not possible. There must, therefore, be the combination of excitement, wide experience, freedom from bureaucratic interference, and high compensation to offset the risks involved. A particular type of person fits these characteristics, and he or she is not easily found in large companies.

It is no secret that our society has become increasingly risk-averse. At all levels, in government as well as in the private sector, individuals no longer wish to accept the consequences of their actions, but seek to blame some other person or organization with deeper pockets and seek recourse thereby. This has inevitably been accompanied by an increasing emphasis on short-term horizons in management circles. But let us not blame our managements too hastily. The macro- and micro-economic climate in this country since the early 1970s has hardly been conducive to the formation of longer-term strategies, which in the end pay off better than constant devotion to the short-term. The extraordinary fluctuations in the price of energy since 1973 and the accompanying inflation-deflation cycles have further added to the difficulty of setting forth on a steady long-term course for an individual company, even a very big one. When interest rates exceed 20 percent as they did as recently as 1979, it is difficult to imagine thinking about much more than the next three months. If discounted cash flow methods are used to evaluate projects, as is often the case, such interest rates, plus the inevitable risk premiums associated with projects, would make it virtually impossible to justify any capital expenditures that do not pay out in a year; and it is well known how hard it is to find such projects, especially those based on new technology. Yet Japan and some other countries seem to be doing better at this economic management than the United States.

I have written about this subject more fully in two recent books[2], and raise it here only to underscore that the entrepreneurial company is much more likely to be able and willing to take a longer-term view under today's conditions than the large organization; i.e., a roller-coaster existence. If a capital investment is to be made, even if it is called R&D within the context of a "skunk works," management will be held accountable by its stockholders and its board while the entrepreneurial company will treat the subject of its cost of capital and its expected return quite differently.

Although our experience in corporate "partnering" began in the middle 1960s and the search for it had commenced earlier, nevertheless we lived through a great many of the rapidly changing conditions I have described and have seen the way they influence large company decision-making. To be sure, we always remained a private company, and that is less common today when venture capital is so abundant and the initial public offerings market so attractive. But entrepreneurs and venture capitalists really have a different financial environment and are, therefore, well-suited to taking the early risk in new concepts.[3]

Other characteristics of a smaller entrepreneurial company are that it is independent and can, therefore, bring other ideas to the partnership. Also, it is a flatter organization, which makes it much easier to produce decisions than in a typical joint venture between two large companies. Lastly, it is recognized that the entrepreneurial small company, which is more highly regarded in the U.S. than in any other country, is the great creator of jobs. Consequently, it is much admired in Washington, and political circles generally, as a source for good—R. L.

Although a successful partnership with a small entrepreneurial company brings a large company many advantages (see editorial box), one may ask why a small company would want to be associated with a large company. Is it not afraid of being taken over, its best ideas siphoned out and its best people enticed away? Of course, there are these risks, but agreements can be written to minimize such dangers; the large company offers capital, markets, greater resources and manpower, wider varieties of technological skills, and many other assets which would be virtually impossible for the small company to duplicate. The new technology that a smaller entrepreneurial company develops must be put to work as rapidly as possible in order to prevent obsolescence, maintain a lead over the inevitable competition, and pay for further R&D.

In the earlier years, young, small companies like ours are usually compelled to license to bigger companies in order to accomplish these ends. Recent examples are found in some of the biotechnology companies. If this cannot be accomplished, some companies start to sell pieces or all of themselves to larger companies (some foreign) to achieve positive cash flow. However, this can truly become a Faustian bargain, both for the company and the country. In most cases, I have discovered that because technology is capital it ought to be invested for the optimum return on the R&D which brought it into being. This means having a "piece of the action." It was this conviction, formed as we saw our licensees increasingly willing to pay only for our successes and not our failures, that led to our searching for ways to enter into the manufacture of the chemical products our novel processes would make it attractive to invest in. As in all cohabiting arrangements, if each partner has something the other needs, they can live together indefinitely if not necessarily until death do them part.

Partnership with ARCO

Scientific Design Co., Inc. was co-founded by [Harry Rehnberg and] me in 1946 and ultimately transformed into Halcon International, Inc. and the Halcon-SD Group, Inc. Even in the early 1950s, when initial plant sizes were so much smaller than they are today and capital requirements were so much less, we had no means of doing it on our own. A partnership with the right large company seemed the best avenue to pursue.

Our first opportunity arrived in 1955 when we invented the Mid-Century process for the bromine-assisted oxidation of paraxylene to terephthalic acid, the main ingredient of polyester fiber. After numerous discussions, we entered into serious negotiations with Standard Oil Company of Indiana (now AMOCO). When I proposed a corporate partnership, their vice president for research looked at me and said, "Ralph, that would be like the mating of an elephant and a mouse." Clearly, cohabitation was not as prevalent in the 1950s as it subsequently became. At any rate, we wound up selling the technology to AMOCO, and I don't think they regret it, although we mourned our first lost opportunity.

From another attempt at cohabitation, which involved our buying into an existing joint venture of two other companies, we learned a great deal about the problems of organizing a corporate partnership. In particular, it seemed to us that no provisions had been made for the future expansion of the venture, or its dissolution, so that new negotiations would be required each time any kind of capital investment was called for, or the partners' interests no longer coincided sufficiently. Although the plant in question was located at the site of one of the partners' other plants, many of the products were sold exclusively by one partner who, therefore, controlled the market; and pricing of the intermediates could not be done at arm's length because of varying market conditions.

There were many other problems. At any rate the experiences were helpful in preparing us for the moment when we did succeed with our third attempt at corporate partnership, this time with Atlantic Richfield Company. One learns from one's failures as well as from the successes. I might add that this was not an immediately obvious choice; we had canvassed many possibilities to determine where the mutual needs and opportunities coincided.

The technology involved our discovery of a process for the production of propylene oxide, the principal ingredient of urethane foams, and other polyurethane polymers. Why was ARCO interested? They had an entrepreneurial management in both the chairman of the board, Robert O. Anderson, and in the head of their newly formed chemical company, Robert D. Bent. They had ambitions to enlarge the chemical company rapidly but did not yet have all of the necessary people or technical resources. Although they were researching in an area somewhat similar to our own, we were able to convince them that we were likely to dominate the patent position, and this proved to be the case. Perhaps it was simply that we knew each other from previous contacts and that the reputation of both companies, I am proud to say, was one of integrity and skill; these are fundamental prerequisites for making a corporate partnership work. Furthermore, it was a unique moment when the oil industry had a keen appetite for expansion in petrochemicals and a good raw material position to support it.

Our motivations were obvious. ARCO had all of the advantages large companies enjoy, and yet their new chemical division was sufficiently small and unstructured that decisions were reached much more rapidly than would be customary in a major oil company. It took us only six months to negotiate the agreement which was signed on June 30, 1966, and which governed most of our relationships for quite a long time thereafter even though the top management of their chemicals group changed several times. Their CEO, fortunately, remained the same throughout our association, although we seldom dealt with him directly. I shall describe a few of the basic principles:

1.   Management

We set up a separate 50:50 corporation called the Oxirane Corporation, headquartered midway between the Philadelphia and New York offices of the parents in Princeton, New Jersey, to manage the business and technology of the parents in the defined fields. This corporation, with an equal number of directors from each partner, was a non-manufacturing entity primarily concerned with R&D, engineering design, and general manage-

ment (including the provision of general advice to the manufacturing partnerships and overall marketing strategy). There was a chairman selected by
each of the partners, and rotated between them annually. The president and
executive vice president were permanent employees.... A separate manufacturing partnership was set up at Bayport, Texas, to build the first plant.
I use the word "partnership" in its legal sense; the first and succeeding
plants were indeed structured as partnerships directly by the two parent
corporations through intermediate holding corporations who were the actual partners on a 50:50 ownership basis. In this way each parent was able
to deal with the finances of the venture according to its own methods of
accounting and avoid the double taxation that usually takes place if a
corporation form is used. Joint decisions had to be taken regarding depreciation, investment tax credit, and so forth, but each partner handled its
respective share of tax by itself. Each partnership had a general manager
and a chief technical officer.

2.   Personnel

It was agreed in the contracts that the CEO of every organization involved
in this corporate partnership would be nominated by ARCO and approved
by us; the chief operating-technical officer, the Number Two man, would
be nominated by us and approved by ARCO. Personnel on loan in this
manner would remain on their respective company's payrolls but would be
granted a leave of absence so that the benefits flowing to them from length
of service, etc., would continue as if they were still employed by the
parents. In other words, since ARCO's pensions, for example, were more
generous than ours and the new partnership could not afford those pensions
for everyone, the arrangement preserved the benefits of having been an
ARCO employee. On the other hand, a number of our key people thus
transferred were participants in our stock and executive compensation
plans which seemed so potentially attractive if Oxirane succeeded that
even ARCO personnel wistfully asked to join in—obviously impossible.
Other personnel from each company were assigned to various positions in
the organizations where they were best suited.

There was also a hands-off agreement that neither party would raid the
personnel of the other. The result was free movement of people from both
companies into the new corporate partnership, which thus profited from
widely different cultures mixing intimately; we contributed a substantial
percentage of all of the technical people in the various organizations, for
the reasons mentioned above. Certainly, some "culture shocks" might

appear in some such transfers but every effort was made to establish a reasonable balance. Most understood that there were pros and cons to be considered. Other employees were obtained from outside, and a benefits plan was adopted to apply uniform standards as widely as feasible.

3.   Financial

Obviously, the most important of all the arrangements was on the financial side. From the beginning ARCO recognized that we could not possibly carry an equal load in the financing of the enterprise, but they insisted that we should always own a 50 percent interest. In their view this was particularly important because an equal arrangement of this kind would give us a real voice in the affairs of the business and a strong incentive to exert maximum efforts on behalf of Oxirane; that is what they wanted in addition to the technology rights that were contributed to the partnership— not a dutiful subordinate but an active complementary equal. Consequently, it was they who proposed the basis of the financial arrangements that were incorporated in the original agreement. The basic features of this arrangement were as follows:

• The objective was to permit Halcon to obtain a half-interest in Oxirane, while allowing ARCO rapid recovery of its investment and a satisfactory rate of return.

• ARCO provided 90 percent of the project's initial capital requirements, while Halcon provided 10 percent.

• ARCO's contribution was divided into two parts; 50 percent for its share of the venture and 40 percent as a non-recourse loan to Halcon to be used solely to fund its interest in Oxirane.

• ARCO had done enough work to satisfy itself that the technical risk was acceptable. Had the venture failed, ARCO would have borne most of the loss. Despite the 90:10 ratio, however, any loss would have had a much greater effect on Halcon, by far the smaller company. The initial 10 percent funding was *very* earnest money for us, and that was what ARCO wanted us to express as a measure of *our* confidence in the technology and the project.

• The 40 percent of the total project cost (grass roots capital cost or "GRCC") lent to Halcon was divided into eight notes. These notes could not be retired until three years after the venture started and, even then, only one note could be prepaid every six months. The number of notes outstanding governed the distribution of cash flow between the partners.

• Project cash flow was distributed quarterly. The financing agreement was structured to maximize distribution. Fifty percent of the cash went to each partner but, if eight notes were outstanding, 40 out of Halcon's 50 percent was dedicated to servicing the notes. If seven, the dedicated cash flow dropped to 35 percent and so on at five percent per note.

• The notes had a nine-year amortization and a 10 percent rate of interest. If the five percent dedicated cash flow per note exceeded the sum of scheduled principal and interest, a portion of the excess was allocated to additional retirement of principal. Consequently, with very successful ventures, as the Oxirane plants proved to be, the principal was paid back substantially ahead of schedule and prepayments reduced in amount.

• ARCO's rate of return was less than the project return but not by much. For a project having a pre-tax return of, say, 25 percent, ARCO's return significantly exceeded 20 percent. This was due to the fixed 90 : 10 distribution in the first three years; as is known in discounted cash flow analysis it is the early years that are the most important. As a private company, we cared less about "up front" payout, but were very interested in building long-term cash flows.

Some of the secondary issues should be mentioned. If additional cash was required for plant modifications or working capital while any notes were outstanding, Halcon could borrow an additional amount from ARCO basically by increasing the notes. If no notes were outstanding, Halcon had to provide all of its share; if all notes were outstanding, it could borrow 80 percent of its share.

As new units were added, it became necessary to layer the financings and to create methods for allowing Oxirane's operating management to make the correct decisions without worrying about the mechanics of the funding. For example, the second plant was much larger and more efficient than the first. It started up while most of the notes on the first were still outstanding. This was handled by creating a full-capacity financial model for the first plant and allocating cash flow as if the first plant ran at full capacity regardless of actual operations.

How the Partnership Fared

That the whole complex scheme was developed so successfully is due in large measure to ARCO's financial officers. They clearly understood their management's objectives and found creative ways to support them. So often large companies suffer from the "not invented here" syndrome, and fail to grasp opportunities available from external sources. This applies to technology, of course, but also to "social innovations."

The key, in all cases, was that each partner valued the other's contribution and set out to build agreements designed for the long-term strength of the partnership, rather than as a temporary device which should be collapsed as soon as feasible.

How did the partnership fare? I believe on the whole very well from the point of view of both parents. Our first plant started up on January 1, 1969; before it began, we were already building a larger second unit at Bayport and a substantially equivalent unit at Rotterdam in the Netherlands (this was financed in part by off-shore bank financing combined with the inter-partner financing as a result of American currency restrictions, now long forgotten). Simultaneously, we began negotiations in Spain for a plant to produce propylene oxide by a variant of our technology, with the Spanish Government as our third partner. In this case we produced a *menage a trois* which succeeded quite well because of the care with which the agreements were written.

After the second Bayport plant and the Rotterdam plant had started up, a third Bayport plant was commissioned and an agreement was entered into with two prominent Japanese companies. This agreement differed from the others in that the Japanese agreed to arrange for all the financing and give ARCO and ourselves 50 percent of the equity in return for the rights to the technology. This was a landmark decision by the Japanese Government, and it has become, somewhat modified, the largest petrochemical joint venture in Japan. A substantial degree of the initiative in forming overseas ventures came from Halcon, which had had twenty years of diversified international experience, while ARCO was then mainly a domestic oil company.

Neither partner had ever made propylene oxide before, which was a market served by at least twelve companies in the United States, as well as numerous companies abroad. Dow Chemical Co. was the leading producer. All of the existing producers employed the chlorohydrin process which had been invented around the time of the First World War. The possession of very modern technology made it possible for us to pick up a substantial amount of the market growth in the products we made, and because there was excellent growth in the derivatives we were fortunately never really involved in any major price wars to gain market share. There was no conflict of interest among the partners since neither one made the principal products; although one product was used by ARCO, which developed a wholly new market for it, it was easy enough to establish a market price.

Engineering design was performed by us with approval by ARCO, and in this way our long experience in plant design and scale-up of new technology would be best realized. Furthermore, a number of our R&D and design people proved to be immensely valuable in plant operations as well as general management. We found that plants incorporating new technology need to be saturated with such highly technical people, who understand the technology and the plant design. In this way start-ups were mostly rapid, and the learning curves descended quickly. This not only improves productivity, product quality and profitability; it also reduces the chances of other competitors entering the field in the earlier years. In fact, our experience in this area contributed to accurate and rapid estimates for the cost of capital involved in new projects.

By 1980, we knew we had a tiger by the tail. The volume of business generated by our corporate partnerships on a worldwide basis had now reached the billion-dollar-a-year level. This is exceptional for a new company that made its first pound eleven years earlier, and was based entirely on original technology. The time had come for us to give serious thought to whether we could stay the course indefinitely. For one thing inflation and high interest rates had arrived. Although the financing arrangements of our initial agreement had worked very well for the three Bayport plants and the Rotterdam plant, and as mentioned above had presented no problem in Japan or for that matter in Spain, our newest plant which had started up around 1978 at Channelview, Texas, had cost many hundreds of millions of dollars. This plant was not financed under the original arrangements for a variety of reasons, including the fact that ARCO was by now deeply involved in the north slope of Alaska, and the relative abundance of capital of the early years was gone. We had to resort to large off-balance sheet financing, which meant a floating rate of interest.

When the prime rate reached 21 percent, we were all working for the banks and not for ourselves. Obviously, we at Halcon had been counting on the cash flow from our previous ventures to sustain our investment in future ventures, but even that cash flow was being absorbed in interest payments, or so it seemed. This experience of the 1978–1980 era and the arrival of Paul Volcker at the Federal Reserve are now history, but they demonstrate how even the very best technology and management can fall victim to bad macroeconomic policy, which inflation certainly represented. Of course, some of the problems were ours. One of the plants at Channelview entailed a new process for ethylene glycol, which, while it eventually proved operable had been designed for an era of low energy costs, and those days were gone!

We came to the conclusion, therefore, that it would be prudent to sell our interests, and we did so in May 1980 when ARCO bought us out. It is worth noting that some of the Halcon people elected to stay with Oxirane (ARCO) and of course were free to do so; most returned to Halcon, because they preferred a less structured environment. Some of those who went with ARCO rose to high positions.

Needless to say, we got a fair amount of cash for the labors of so many years, and a large number of our people benefited personally. I think I can also say that the return on our research was spectacular! However, ARCO got a chemical business which is still a major part of the ARCO Chemical Company; and while I have had no private access to the records since then, I know that they have been expanding and further improving the status of this technology. In 1986, they announced a new plant in the South of France and enlargements at Rotterdam. They have increased the output at Channelview. They are now the world's Number One producer of these products, and most of the other producers have discontinued their operations. New technology does pay off if one is patient and entrepreneurial.

Would this business exist if ARCO and Halcon had not combined? I doubt it. Would it be as healthy as it is if they had not combined? I doubt it. Would ARCO have been able to accomplish the same result on its own? I am sure not. Did ARCO treat us too generously in order to acquire our technology, our best people, and our entrepreneurial skills? Although some of their staff may have thought so in private, the great and continuing success of this business and the absence of any other analogous success stories elsewhere argue for a firm No—only by this kind of arrangement could ARCO have gained the soul of a wonderful group of people, while we not only did not lose our own souls, but found fulfillment.

I do not mean to imply in this account that ours is the only—or even the best—way to accomplish successful corporate partnering. Many such efforts have been undertaken recently, in a variety of forms, but it is still too early too tell how they will mature. Let us invent even better ways for more such applications, as IBM, General Motors and other companies are doing.

Our experience is one illustration of how this feat can be managed, but it takes a bold and enterprising large company management to pull it off. ARCO was such a company, and I have previously praised their foresight and imagination; I happily take this opportunity to repeat my great respect, admiration and affection for that singular company. It is obvious to me from my long observation of the working of many companies, that there is no substitute for great and inspired management. Successful companies usually have that in abundance; many companies do not, unfortunately. They will have an increasingly difficult time in this competitive era.

References

1. Gordon E. Moore, "Entrepreneurship and Innovation: The Electronics Industry," in Ralph Landau and Nathan Rosenberg, *The Positive Sum Strategy: Harnessing Technology for Economic Growth*, National Academy Press, Washington, 1986.

2. Ralph Landau and Nathan Rosenberg, Ibid; this book is the outgrowth of a conference at Stanford University cosponsored by the National Academy of Engineering which is actively probing into this area. Ralph Landau and Dale Jorgenson, *Technology and Economic Policy*, Ballinger, Cambridge, 1986 (based on a conference sponsored by the Harvard Kennedy School of Government).

3. See Ralph Landau and George Hatsopoulos, "Capital Formation in the U.S. and Japan," in Ralph Landau and Nathan Rosenberg, Ibid.

Professional Issues

Ralph Landau is known not only for the number of innovative processes that his company developed, but also for developing one of the first companies to combine chemical process research, design, and construction in a single package that could be tailored to each individual customer. When Landau and Rehnberg began Scientific Design in 1946, few people even in the chemical industry fully understood the role chemical engineers would come to play in the development of the industry. At that point most doctorates in chemical engineering joined the research departments of chemical companies. Firms of scientists and chemical engineers that developed chemical processes and designed and built the plants for other companies were so rare that Landau had to spend a great deal of his time in the early years explaining exactly what it was his company could do for potential clients.

The benefits of special engineering firms (SEFs) that combined research, process design, and construction soon became quite clear. Scientific Design could provide not only the engineering, but also many of the processes needed to turn basic petroleum-derived feedstocks into the major intermediates required for manufacturing plastics, polyesters, and an entire range of petrochemical products. Other SEFs could do the same for the large number of crackers required to generate these feedstocks. It was much simpler and cheaper for a company to procure all or most of its needed technology from a single company that could coordinate the project from basic design to start-up and pass along know-how and training in the process. By the 1960s, according to Landau and Nathan Rosenberg, nearly three-quarters of all the major new chemical plants in the world had been built by SEFs.

"Whereas Warren K. Lewis [of MIT] created a discipline, I helped utilize and expand it within the chemical industry." Landau has said. Much of what Landau learned in these early years was embodied in the book *The Chemical Plant: From Process Development to Plant Operation*, published in 1966 and still the only book written by industrial designers on how products and plants are really designed and put into operation. More recently Landau has urged that the distinctive systems approach of chemical engineering be applied more widely by other branches of engineering. And he has chronicled the role of the systems approach in the rise of the American chemical industry to its present highly competitive status.

Landau's abiding interest in the chemical engineering profession can be seen in his support of the chemical engineering schools at MIT, the University of Pennsylvania, Stanford, and the California Institute of Technology. It is also reflected in several papers addressing the appropriate education for chemical engineering students and the role of the chemical engineer in industry and society.

Chemical Engineering in West Germany

The Federal Republic of Germany (West Germany), of all the major industrial powers, is alone in not holding chemical engineering a special branch of engineering. In spite of this negative attitude, the flourishing condition of the West German chemical industry is too well known to permit any doubt that the West Germans have found adequate means to handle the development of their chemical process industries.

It is the purpose of this paper to examine briefly current West German practices, some of the reasons for the differences which exist, and to express a few constructive comments gained primarily from West German representatives themselves as to the virtues and defects of their present system. . . .

Present Conditions in West German Chemical Industry

Nature of Chemical Industry

Before World War II, the I. G. Farbenindustrie A.G. constituted approximately 80 percent of German chemical production. Today, the four largest companies, Farbenfabriken Bayer, Badische Anilin und Soda Fabrik, Farbwerke Hoechst, and Chemische Werke Huls, represent rather less than half of this proportion of West German production, each ranking with the larger United States companies.

West German Education Pattern

Some 95 percent of graduate industrial chemists hold a Ph.D. Their education includes thirteen years schooling through the secondary curriculum,

Published in *Chemical Engineering Progress* 54, no. 7 (July 1958): 64–68, 115. Reproduced with permission of the American Institute of Chemical Engineers. © 1958 AICHE. All rights reserved.

and eight of college-level work; the average age at graduation is about twenty-seven years. Universities and technological institutions (hochschulen) both teach chemistry. Engineers are not generally graduated from universities but only from technische hochschulen. They usually require four years of training after the secondary schools, and are therefore about twenty-three year old when they receive the degree of Diplom-Ingenieur, which is perhaps more like the M.S. in the United States. The Dr.-Ing. degree is rare in West Germany.

The principal engineer encountered in the West German chemical industry is the mechanical engineer. More recently, the Verfahrens Ingenieur (Process Engineer), a mechanical engineer with some chemical engineering training, has appeared.

There are also engineering trade schools which give less training than the technische hochschulen, supplying technical assistants, designers, and some draftsmen.

Team Approach

Evolution of Process Engineer

The accelerated requirement for process engineers has been brought about by the greatly changed character of the postwar chemical industry. Since, however, most of this demand is unsatisfied as yet, the West German industrial technique still involves the traditional team approach, in particular the combination of the chemist and the mechanical engineer, who learn their respective roles in industry. Neither in industry nor in the schools is there found the individual trained both as a chemist and an engineer.

The demand for process engineers is recent. The first technische hochschule to originate such a curriculum was Karlsruhe (1928). The other five technische hochschulen curricula for process engineers, at Berlin, Aachen, Braunschweig, Hannover, and Munich have been in existence only since 1952. The technische hochschule at Darmstadt teaches chemical technology rather than process engineering; Stuttgart's technische hochschule teaches neither.

Education for Chemical Process Industries

Table 9.1 presents a typical picture of some comparative curricula.

With regard to the process engineer's curriculum, in West Germany the process engineer is considered to be largely an equipment engineer. His

Table 9.1

Course	Percent of total time spent in higher education (est.)		
	U.S. chem. engr. (B.S.)	West German process engineer	West German chemist
Chemistry	20−27	8−9	81
Chemical engineering	24	12−15	5
Other engineering	8−18	25−35	—
Mathematics	13	12	3
Physics	8	14°	7
Mechanics	4	11	—
Cultural	15−21	10	4

° With fluid dynamics and thermodynamics.

chemical engineering training is primarily in unit operations, based on methods quite similar to those used in the United States. The curriculum does not pay much attention as yet to process design, instrumentation, material and energy balances, applied chemical kinetics, and applied chemical thermodynamics. Cultural subjects, as well as mathematics and basic sciences, are partially covered in the secondary school, so that these percentages should normally be lower than those for United States chemical engineering undergraduates. Instead, there is heavy mechanical engineering training, and more physics. Process engineering is a branch of the mechanical engineering faculty....

The distribution of courses for the increasing number of master's and doctor's men in United States chemical engineering would be different from those shown with higher percentages in chemical engineering.

The chemical technology course at Darmstadt involves special industrial chemistry courses, less pure chemistry and research, and recently some engineering and design subjects.

Other information on curricula may be found in various publications.

Some Statistics

The West German technische hochschulen graduate roughly 100 process engineers per year, who constitute about 1 percent of West German engineering graduates. At Karlsruhe there is one process engineering graduate to two mechanical engineering graduates; in the other five the ratio is more nearly one to six. Altogether in West Germany there are about 1,000 graduate, process engineers. There are several thousand more who are process engineers by practical experience and interest. There are only about twenty chemical technologists graduated annually from Darmstadt among 1,000 total chemical graduates, 70 percent of whom are university men.

Since the graduates in process engineering supply less than about 10 percent of the demand for their services, the other more than 90 percent must be obtained from the mechanical engineering graduates.

By comparison, the United States graduates some three thousand to four thousand chemical engineers every year, who constitute about 10 percent of all engineering graduates. Perhaps 20 percent of these chemical engineering graduates obtain advanced degrees. The number of graduating doctor's men in chemical engineering in the United States is probably of the same order of magnitude as the number of process engineering graduates in West Germany.

Philosophy of Educational Program

The West German educational system is designed to train chemists in research and research-mindedness, as scientists of profound understanding in their field. By and large, the Ph.D. chemist has little or no knowledge at graduation of industrial equipment or the many problems associated therewith.

For process engineering the goal of the educational system is to adapt the traditional mechanical engineering curriculum so as to permit the process engineer to understand the language of the chemist.

The West Germans insist that a process engineer must not be a specialist, not even for the chemical industry, but must be trained to fit into a wide type of industry such as foods, minerals, etc.; hence, their preference for "process" instead of "chemical."

Chemical Engineering Practice in West Germany

Comparison

Table 9.2 presents in summary form some of the similarities and differences between United States and West German industrial practices.

Table 9.3 shows how the various professionals are distributed in the United States and in West Germany.

The American chemical engineer is distributed in a somewhat wider functional spectrum than is any one of his counterparts in West Germany.

Chemical Engineering Research

In West Germany, fundamental research is usually done by the faculties of the universities and associated institutes (such as Hamburg, Göttingen, Berlin), and at the technische hochschulen. Little is as yet done by industry, unlike the United States. Process engineers are beginning to move into the field, and mechanical engineers have also been active, for example, in fluid flow and heat transfer, much as in the United States.

Some West German Achievements

It is generally recognized that unit operations, and more recent concepts in kinetics, applied thermodynamics, etc., are primarily attributable to the United States chemical engineer. He has also figured prominently in the evolution of new techniques such as the turbo-grid tray, centrifugal extractors, cyclonic scrubbers, sorption systems, gaseous diffusion methods for isotope separation, etc. In general, fewer such innovating concepts and methods have appeared in Germany, although names such as Eucken and Jakob are world famous, and West German teams have produced such new equipment and techniques as the Winkler generator, thin film evaporators, and other novel designs.

There have been, nevertheless, important contributions by German mechanical engineers to this area, as in fluid flow and boundary layer work, heat transfer and fluidization. Moreover, German contributions to chemical process work have been outstanding and have been made primarily by chemists, assisted by mechanical engineers and more recently process engineers. Many of these process developments involved continuous processing, and in fact the Haber process goes back to World War I; it was one of the first really continuous chemical process techniques in the world. Frequently cited by the West Germans in this category are ammonia synthesis, methanol synthesis, Fischer-Tropsch and Oxo processes, Bergius coal hydrogenation, Linde low-temperature liquefaction, Buna-S rubber, Reppe acetylene chemistry, acrylonitrile and acrylonitrile fibers from acetylene and HCN, diisocyanates, polycarbonates, and Ziegler low-pressure polyethylene.

Differences between U.S. and West German Practices

An examination of the industrial practices as described above suggests that both the United States and West Germany really employ a team approach

Table 9.2
Chemical engineering practice in U.S. and West Germany

Function	Example of functions	Who performs in U.S.	Who performs in West Germany	Where performed in West Germany
1. Provision and correlation basic data	Correlations such as Benedict eq. of state	Chem. engr. and chemist	Chemists (occasionally process engrs. and physicists)	Research lab; also occasionally in process eng. lab
2. Dev. design information	Pilot plant dev. of processes or equip.	Chem. engrs., aided by chemists and mech. engrs. and technicians	Chemists (90%); process engrs. and mech. engrs. (10%); aided by technicians	Res. center (pilot plant, mostly in glass); plant lab (semicommercial units)
3. Process dev.	Economic comparison of processes; translations of data and designs to probable commercial form through process flowsheets, equip. sizing and selection; direction of res. programs	Chem. engrs.	Chemists, aided by process engrs., physicists, and mech. engrs.	Pilot plant or eng. dept. large chem. cos.
4. Equip. dev.	New processing techniques such as fluidization; new equip. dev.	Chemical engrs. and mech. engrs.	Chemists and mech. or process engrs.	Large chemical co. eng. departs., and equip. mfrs.
5. Economic evaluation	Definitive capital cost & project profitability studies; dev. of costing procedures; decisions to build to expand	Chem engrs., aided by mech. engrs.	Chemists with extensive industrial experience; mech. engrs. aided by process engrs.	Large company eng. or administrative dept.; also, executives (vorstand members) often decide on selection of processes and programs

			Large company eng. dept.
6. Detailed plant design	Piping, civil, electrical, pressure vessel, instrumentation, design	Mech. engrs., and others; chem. engrs. often act as project mgrs. or coordinators	Mech. or process engrs., aided by others such as technicians and draftsmen	
7. Plant operation and improvement	Removing bottlenecks; maintaining production; reducing costs	Chem. engrs., also chemists	Chemists, aided by process or mech. engrs. and physicists	Plant
8. Management	Direction of enterprises at highest or intermed. levels	Chem. engrs. and chemists (among others, often nontechnical)	Chemists, also lawyers, commercial specialists (process or mech. engrs. in certain tech. depts. such as eng.)	Chemist dominant in direction of res., mfg., and in gen. management (vorstand)

Table 9.3
Estimated percent distribution of employment

Function	U.S. chemical engineer	West German process engineer	West German mechanical engineer	West German chemist
Chemical and engineering research and development	31	20	5	20
Consulting	4	5	5	1
Management	10	1	2	5
Teaching	3	2	—	2
Technical writing	1	—	—	1
Design	13	40	35	5
Analysis and Testing	5	5	—	6
Production	28	25	50	55
Technical sales and services	3	1	—	3
Other	2	1	3	2

but that the leadership in the United States is more often in the hands of the chemical engineer, and in West Germany in those of the chemist. Aiding the chemist in his team are the mechanical engineer, and in smaller but increasing numbers, the process engineer.

Industrial practice in the United States most often involves a larger team consisting of a chemical engineer (frequently of graduate caliber) with a chemist and a mechanical engineer. In some cases, a United States chemical engineer thinks much like a chemist, in other cases more like a mechanical engineer; but he is usually a distinctive type of engineer, and in this respect is a specialist *in addition* to those working together in West Germany rather than *in place of* any one West German specialist.

Eight Reasons for Differences between U.S. and West German Practice

1. *Chemical engineering arose earlier in the United States than in Germany.* As a result of a forty-year head start, there are many more schools of chemical engineering in the United States than there are schools teaching process engineering in West Germany, and far greater numbers of chemical engineers.

2. *West Germans credit the rise of the petroleum industry for the rapid growth of the American chemical engineering profession.* Refining necessarily had to be

on a continuous scale and because adequate fundamental data applicable to the complex mixtures handled were rarely available, the applied physico-chemical approach, the pragmatic attitude so suited to the genius of the American people, and the unit operations concepts found just the right reception from the petroleum refining industry. The West Germans also point out, quite justly, that the chemical aspects of petroleum refining were comparatively simple compared with those of the dye-stuff industry, so that the heavy emphasis on the engineering function in the American chemical engineer's training was proper.

3. *The size of refining and petrochemical units forced the American chemical engineers to design carefully and conservatively, with semi-empirical methods and minimum experimentation.* In Germany, however, before the war, the scale of operation was generally smaller and the variety of products was much greater; there was also less competition than in the United States and more time to work problems out in the plant, including training of "chemical engineers" in fact. The great postwar expansion in both the United States and West Germany has resulted in many more large continuous plants, so that the older West German practical learning methods have become less economically permissible.

4. *Industrial training of technicians has been more extensively practiced in Germany.* I. G. Farbenindustrie before the war had less than 1 percent turnover per year, and dominated the industry. On-job training was there-fore an excellent and secure investment. However, the lack of the system-atizations introduced by the American chemical engineering discipline cost the German industry much difficulty, money, and time; such practices prob-ably were not excessively burdensome to a large entity like I. G. Farben-industrie, which had the advantage of evolving people trained especially to suit its requirements. Dr. Carl Bosch's account of his struggles in de-veloping the continuous ammonia process gives an excellent perspective on this period in German chemical history.

5. *Geography has had an important effect.* United States plants are widely scattered, and even today, except in some cases, make only limited num-bers of products in one plant. One does not often see in the United States such huge complexes as exist at Hoechst, Leverkusen, Ludwigshafen, etc., in which much of the West German chemical industry is still concentrated. Therefore, in the American plants, chemists are not overwhelmingly more important than engineers, and one person can combine the function of both, according to the West Germans.

6. *While chemical production facilities in West Germany are no longer very dissimilar to those in the United States, the West German goals are not identical*

with those of the United States. Only lack of time and educational facilities have retarded development of West Germany's chemical plant techniques. But the West German executives stress that in the future their chemical industry can not compete with the United States mass-produced chemicals on a purely economic basis. To succeed, they will need new, complex, and original chemical reactions, e.g., new polymers. This work requires the type of training exemplified by the Ph.D. West German chemist. Hence, the West Germans still stress the chemist's role in their industry, but they freely recognize that the process engineer (or mechanical engineer), and also the chemical technologist, are his increasingly important collaborators, and the differences between the United States and West German approach are thus diminishing. However, the West Germans do not yet fully understand the important advance represented by the M.S. and Ph.D. U. S. chemical engineering training, in dealing with the more complex chemical and engineering problems of today's industry.

7. *Chemical engineering has been the glamour field in the United States as against chemistry in Germany.* The glamour of chemical engineering in the United States comes partially from the high social standing of engineering in a country which had a continent to develop, and comes partially also from monetary considerations. In Germany, on the other hand, chemistry has been an honored profession for a hundred years.

8. *The large engineering and contracting firm has not yet developed as widely in West Germany as in the United States.* Most of the West German engineering design work is done by the large chemical companies themselves (who occasionally do a job for others, particularly if they are licensing a process), and this permits not only on-job training but an acceptance of a certain amount of experimentation in the plant. The United States engineering company's development accelerated the demand for the chemical engineer since a properly trained chemical engineer was economically more justified than a team might be.

Some West German Self-Criticisms

Opinion in West Germany is not complacent about the situation today, and healthy differences of viewpoint exist. Industry is bringing great pressure to bear on the technische hochschulen and universities to modify the curricula, add teachers, and increase [the] number of students. The long traditions of the schools change too slowly to satisfy many. The absence of important industrial consulting activity by university professors, the relatively low salaries but the high standing of scholarship and scholars generally in West Germany, and the universal shortage of funds tend to keep the faculties from responding immediately to the industrial viewpoint.

The influence of a pure chemist if misapplied has sometimes tended in the eyes of experienced West German management to result in processes being commercialized before they are ready economically or technologically. Industrial orientation courses are helping to reduce this risk.

Some West German executives feel that the wide gap in viewpoint and training between the members of the two-man team tends to make more difficult invention in the broad territory that lies between them. One outstanding individual is still the principal source of fundamental inventive creation. Where it is the chemist who is inventive, his contributions tend to the pure chemical side; where it is the mechanical engineer, his inventions go to fluid flow, heat transfer, design of special high-pressure equipment. But what is missing, these executives say, is the invention in the middle: either of techniques or equipment design (largely developed as mentioned above by chemical engineers in the United States), or in those areas of process development which involve both engineering and chemical insight. Many German executives expressed the view that still too few people in the West German chemical industry possess a really rounded view of the process as a whole. This is particularly important in the continuous heavy organic or inorganic plant. It is here that the United States chemical engineer's training, particularly of advanced degree caliber, has provided some outstanding example. Two are cited here:

a. The silver catalyst for direct oxidation of ethylene to ethylene oxide was found by a French chemist in 1930, and basically the chemistry and the catalyst have not changed since. But yields have been raised at least twenty points and the capital greatly lowered by the application of U. S. chemical engineering concepts. The improved process has now been reintroduced to Europe and Asia from the United States.

b. Suspension polymerization of polyvinylchloride has been until recently operated only in large plants both in West Germany and in the United States. A chemical engineering analysis (aided by chemists) resulted in purely engineering design changes which in no way affected product quality but reduced the capital investment to half of what had previously been deemed possible, so that small plants for captive users became feasible. No laboratory work at all was necessary in making these designs, but only a profound understanding of both the polymerization itself and the heat transfer and diffusion characteristics of the system.

These few examples suggest that it would be shortsighted to ignore the special contribution of the chemical engineer, particularly in view of his leading role in the great accomplishments of the American chemical industry, not only in economy, but in innovations.

A criticism voiced in West Germany has been that there is insufficient mathematical skill in the West German training of both process engineers and chemists, and insufficient use of computers. As a result the viewpoint tends to be somewhat more qualitative and intuitive. Where the individual is able, this can result in remarkable discoveries. But for the average, a quantitative technique is surer, if less spectacular. In the United States, mathematical aspects of design are more prominent in modern chemical engineering training, contributing to the aforementioned over-all process perspective. Mathematicians are appearing increasingly as members of the team. In this same area the West German approach to applied chemical kinetics and thermodynamics still lies behind the United States level of quantitative chemical engineering treatment. There is substantial but not unanimous sentiment in West Germany for slightly greater chemical training in the process engineering curriculum, with more thermodynamics and kinetics and less machine design.

One difficulty shared by both nations' chemical industries is the necessity for secrecy. Where on-job training still is important, this secrecy may hinder the attainment of a rounded viewpoint.

Conclusions

1. West German and American chemical industry conditions are sufficiently dissimilar to have evolved along divergent paths, but within ten to fifteen years there will be fewer differences, as the world chemical industry becomes less national and more universal in character.

2. The West German emphasis on compatibility of teams working together, surprising perhaps in a European country where people are generally more individualistic, is basically very much like that of the United States.

3. The West German approach of training a number of technological assistants without giving them college degrees is apparently sound.

4. The West German stress on science and fundamentals in educating chemists and engineers is valid. The high level of training of their chemists should be carefully noted; in fact, it is just possible that proportionally too few young men are studying graduate level chemistry in the United States today, and that perhaps too often semiroutine work is their industrial

destiny. However, beyond the research stage lies a very broad area of application. To help fill it, perhaps both countries will evolve a new type of engineering science specialist with doctoral training who can cope with the increasingly complex physicochemical, nuclear-mechanical problems of the future.

In the United States this could well emerge from the present doctorate in chemical engineering by gradual evolution along the following lines: More science and humanities would be taught in the primary and secondary schools; the four-year undergraduate chemical engineering curriculum, now well defined, would largely continue, with further reductions in such courses as shop practice, analytical chemistry, and increasing stress on mathematics and humanities; in the graduate curriculum there would be more mathematics, statistics, physics, chemistry, and basic engineering sciences as well as chemical and nuclear engineering theory, probably at the expense of some of the thesis work which is increasingly unlike actual research practice in industry. American chemical engineering curricula of the future should include more mechanical engineering training and discipline, and in this way will tend to assume some of the aspects of the process engineer's training in West Germany.

5. American chemical engineering can help other countries in a more rapid increase in their standard of living (as it has so signally done in the United States), and America can benefit from the viewpoints of other countries if such could be expressed in interchanges and meetings of American, European, Asiatic and other technologists. Such meetings have been held on a limited scale before, but without a sufficiently broad participation to permit a really rounded presentation.

Acknowledgment

The help of R. S. Davis and A. W. Gessner, of the Scientific Design Company, Inc., is gratefully acknowledged, as is also the invaluable cooperation of many German industrial figures who must remain anonymous.

10   The Chemical Engineer—
Today and Tomorrow

There are 60,000–70,000 chemical engineers in the United States today; *36,000* are members of our American Institute of Chemical Engineers [AIChE]. The great majority (approximately 75 percent) are employed in private industry, the balance (25 percent) primarily in the universities, government, etc. It has been a profession primarily related to industry, and not dependent on government sponsored programs. As a result, it has had a great growth, and great stability. Chemical engineering, as we know it today, has been primarily a post-World War I development. In October, 1970, I was privileged to serve as Chairman of MIT's 50th Anniversary Convocation of Chemical Engineers—an occasion marking the establishment in 1920 of the first independent university department of chemical engineering. At that time (1920), the AIChE had 344 members. In 1941, when I received my doctorate, AIChE membership was 2,574. This exponential growth is equivalent to a compound rate of over 9.3 percent per year.

It was the petroleum refining industry that fueled the initial demand for chemical engineers, followed shortly by the chemical industry, and later by other process industries such as paper, rubber, glass and others. These great growth industries in turn created even more demand for chemical engineers.

Recently, however, we have been feeling some recessionary effects, both in industry generally and in employment of chemical engineers in particular.[1] Statistics on such unemployment are somewhat contradictory, but suggest that there has indeed been a rise in joblessness among chemical engineers, from perhaps 1 percent to under 3 percent. These figures should not be confused with statistics for *all* college graduates; the future, in my opinion, is much more serious in other areas and public discussions of this matter obscure the fact that certain disciplines will continue to be in demand. Unemployment is a distressing phenomenon for all of us, employed or unemployed. However, matters are already starting to improve, as a recent Institute survey shows. The *New York Times* stated, "The worst decline in job openings for college graduates since the Depression of the nineteen-thirties appears to have ended. . . . Graduates in technical fields— such as engineering, business and accounting—are expected to have the best job prospects. Majors in nontechnical disciplines—liberal arts—will be worse off than last year, the survey found."[2] Thus, considered in the perspective of the great rise that has occurred in the past half century, current difficulties are only ripples in the tidal wave of the progress in our industry and profession. Nevertheless, industry must and will do a better job of forecasting its demands for chemical engineers, and must not allow itself to be panicked into sudden moves of excessive hiring or insufficient hiring of chemical engineers and chemists, who are the professional backbone of the chemical process industries.

One of the consequences of the rise of chemical engineering has been the rise of chemical engineers themselves into the topmost levels of management. Many chairmen and presidents of our leading corporations are now card-carrying chemical engineers. I have put together Table 10.1 which gives a listing of such officials, without any claim to completeness.

It is also well known to most of you that chemical engineers are widespread in marketing, in process design, and project engineering, as well as in their obvious roles in manufacturing and research and development. In fact, it has been my conviction and experience since the days of World War II that a properly trained chemical engineer is the best qualified *executive* for research and development in the process industries because of his unique combination of technical and economic skills.

This brief recital of an altogether satisfying picture of a dynamic profession has excluded certain areas, which are less well penetrated by chemical engineers. One is administration of our universities and colleges. Another is the almost total absence of chemical engineers in the fields of government and politics, or in consumer protection (there are no known chemical engineers among Nader's Raiders, which is understandable considering the widely held opinion that the group is biased and ideological, but consumer protection is an important field, and good chemical engineers could make quite a contribution to it). The Soviet Union's top woman political figure,

Table 10.1
Top chemical engineering executives in major U.S. corporations

Company	Chairman	President
Du Pont	Charles B. McCoy	Charles B. McCoy
Du Pont of Canada		R. J. Richardson
Union Carbide	F. Perry Wilson	
Dow Chemical	Carl A. Gerstacker	C. B. Branch
Borden	Augustine R. Marusi	
PPG Industries		Joseph A. Neubauer
American Cyanamid		Clifford D. Siverd
International Minerals & Chemicals	Nelson C. White	
Universal Oil Products	Maynard P. Venema	
BASF Wyandotte Corp	Robert B. Semple	
Texaco	M. F. Granville	J. K. McKinley
Gulf Oil		B. R. Dorsey
Gulf Oil Canada		Jerry McAfee
S. O. California	Otto N. Miller	
S. O. Indiana	John E. Swearingen	Robert C. Gunness
Sun Oil		Robert H. Sharbaugh
Union Oil of California		Fred L. Hartley
Uniroyal	George R. Vila	George R. Vila
B. F. Goodrich		Harry B. Warner
American Biltrite Rubber	David W. Bernstein	
Kimberly Clark		Guy M. Minard
Alcoa		W. H. Krome George
American Can Co.	William F. May	William F. May

Minister of Cultural Affairs Mme. Furtseva, is a chemical engineer by training.[3]

In my opinion, these failures should be viewed seriously, and methods found to encourage a change in the future, particularly in government and politics. I know that this view is not shared by all of my fellow chemical engineers, and that the current standards and training in politics is very different from the standards of engineering. Nevertheless, based on my own experience recently, I do not believe that technical men acting solely as advisers in a governmental or political area can have the influence that I believe society needs in order to solve some of its most pressing problems of the future. Perhaps a good deal of my conviction in this regard stems from the fact that I believe politics and government are about to undergo a very substantial change in their standards, and our younger generation is going to be much more demanding of truth in politics. This is a particularly advantageous climate for chemical engineers and technically trained men generally to consider a career in politics at some point in their lifetime. Recent events show that government will occupy a prominent role in our lives for the foreseeable future, and to paraphrase a well-known cliché, "Government and politics are too serious to be left solely to the politicians."

The Chemical Engineer in the Future

Study of the figures on graduates in chemical engineering over the last thirty-five to forty years, together with every indication that current trends in college graduates will continue about as they are for the immediate years ahead, indicate clearly that by the end of this decade the chemical engineering profession will have reached *zero growth rate*. By 1980, therefore, as many people will be leaving the profession as are entering it, and the growth rate in the rest of this decade is going to be very small.

Since there is no doubt that industry will be producing more and a greater variety of products in more installations during this decade, the inevitable conclusion from the above facts is that industry will have to use chemical engineers not only much more efficiently than in the past but will have to adjust itself much more rapidly to the future than it has ever had to do before. The number of chemical engineers per unit of sales volume has been steadily decreasing over the years but this decrease will be greatly accelerated during the rest of this decade.[4]

This being the case, we shall soon see that the present temporary small scale unemployment will give way to a steady rise in demand. By the end of this decade the real gap between demand and supply will be substantially higher than can now be visualized.

Such a shortfall in the later 1970s will be accentuated as the chemical engineer moves further into the fields which are properly made to order for him and which are generally recognized to be high-priority demands of our society. It is my opinion that the shortfall of chemical engineers by the end of this decade may approach 10,000, and we have very little time to get the message into the high schools where the initial decision is made regarding careers.

Energy Requirements of the Future

Energy is the "first limit on growth" of our society, correctly editorializes the *New York Times*,[5] but then it goes awry in proposing solutions. This section of the paper is an attempt to present the real nature of the problems and solutions.

Most of us do not yet realize the great changes coming in this area, which is the basic underpinning of an industrial society. We know natural gas supplies are dwindling and that even some quite old European technology is suddenly being imported to make synthetic natural gas at $1.00 or more per thousand cubic feet. But the far-reaching demands of society and population pressure will produce much more strain on all our industry and government to cope with the needs for cleaner energy.[6]

Low sulfur oil is only a simple example of this imperative. But with power plants increasingly faced with delays and uncertainties, we are going to be experiencing serious power shortages in the near future. At the same time, nuclear energy as a fuel for the 1980s and thereafter to replace dwindling fossil fuels is slow in developing, and faced with many local and environmental questions. This whole area, in its *technological* aspects, is the domain of the chemical engineer.[7]

It is clear, however, that the ways and priorities in which the energy supply-demand relationships will be worked out in the future are also going to be *politically* influenced to an even greater extent (this is true of other aspects of our technology and industry as well). Certain of our leading university critics of the ecological "crisis"[8] or of the general economic growth trends involving growing population, depletion of natural resources, etc.[9] have gone so far as to either hint, or state unequivocally, their convictions that only a "socialist revolution,"[10] and the strongest *coercion* imaginable on a world scale, can cope with these future problems. In this they speak not as experts from their chosen specialties of biology, computer science, or whatever, but as amateurs (laymen) in the fields of politics, sociology, history, and economics, with little or no experience in industry or the problems of government. In so doing, they invite all of us to study more objectively, and with less emotion or apocalyptic visions the true nature of the societies which have actually attempted to become "socialist," particularly as set forth by prominent participants who have managed to provide their witness for all the world:*

A. The *coercive society* incarnate, the Stalinist regime in the U.S.S.R., is well characterized by his daughter[11] who was in a position to know, and succeeded in escaping from it. Reading this book should be required of all college students.

---

*Having said this. I do not want to imply that these critics do not raise many important issues such as the desirability of limiting population growth and reducing pollution; careful study and actions will be required to solve them.

B. The East European Communist regimes, even as independent a one as Yugoslavia, are brilliantly described by Milovan Djilas, who likewise was a top participant, but, unable to escape, nevertheless dared to expose the real facts, as in these sharply written passages from one of the most important books of our time: "All the demons that Communism believed it had banished from the forthcoming as well as the real world have crept into the souls of Communism and become part of its being. Communism, once a popular movement that in the name of science inspired the toiling and oppressed people of the world with the hope of creating the Kingdom of Heaven on earth, that launched, and continues to launch, millions to their deaths, in pursuit of this unextinguishable primeval dream, has become transformed into national political bureaucracies and states squabbling among themselves for prestige and influence, for the sources of wealth and for markets—for all those things over which politicians and governments have always quarrelled, and always will.... The Communists became so completely absorbed and engulfed in greed and the lust for power than their power became absolute, totalitarian; and in their struggle for power they showed themselves to be ordinary mortals, as fallible as other men, rather than initiates of a 'a special mould,' as Stalin called them.... The concepts Communism, capitalism, even socialism ... all belong to earlier ages.... And the reason ... is to be found in the fact that ideas are like vampires; ideas are capable of living after the death of the generations and social conditions in and by which they were inspired."[12]

C. In Chile, the press frequently reports the growing need for coercion to overcome the ills that a democratic socialist state cannot cure. The *New York Times*, e.g., reports that the "nationalized copper mines, cement plants ... taken over by State administrators have shown large increases in costs, declines in productivity, and either reduced profits or losses ... covered by ... currency issues, contributing to inflation." The article goes on to cite the need for "revolutionary forces to go beyond the legal limitations on the Government."[13]

D. In Cuba, only massive coercion and $750 million per year from the U.S.S.R. have kept the economy from bankruptcy.

And in the few cases of "democratic socialism" the results are equally disappointing. The veteran radical Silone says "We are in a tragic epoch ... reform and revolution have both failed. You cannot consider even Sweden the realization of man's hope. We are passing through a kind of middle ages marked by bureaucratic centralization."[14] (See also[15] re Sweden.) And in an extensive and very stimulating study of British Socialism and its lessons for the United States, Worsthorne says.

The first thing to note about a collectivist society is that it increases the range of decisions taken by officials; requires, that is, an enlarged bureaucracy. Decisions which in a predominantly capitalist economy are taken as a result of the dictates of the market are determined instead by central planners.... It means that these men and women have to give orders, the authority behind which depends not on the impersonal forces of the market, but on their individual judgments of what is right and wrong.[16]

Worsthorne's book deals with the fundamental question of whether an attempt to attain more social justice or a different set of national priorities can be accomplished without coercion, and without a massive increase in bureaucracy and government controls. Therein, he dismisses, in a carefully reasoned book, the hope of some university economists and others that somehow one can visualize an egalitarian society without a large bureaucracy and without coercion[17], but one that still functions efficiently.

Coercion, in one form or another, is what certain of these critics of our American society ultimately offer us, in spite of the record cited very briefly above, and in spite of the fact, quoted by Worsthorne from Henry Fairlie:

Removed from his own discipline, no one is more vain than the intellectual. Precisely because his mind is able to handle ideas with ease and excitement, it is all to easily turned when he is invited to discourse outside his own field. Inside his own field, the intellectual would never lay claim to omniscience, and seldom to authority. Outside it his claim to both is breathtaking. A man who, having devoted his life to the study of some exact historical event, would hesitate to suggest the multiple reasons why it occurred, has no hesitation in analyzing the situation in Vietnam and predicting, say, the Vietcong reaction to a hypothetical situation.

The fundamental choice facing the world in the rest of the century is between sliding into universal totalitarian rule, which will be required to force *sharing of the poverty* if the "zero economic growth" and ecological fanatics are allowed to have their way, or developing a much higher level of technology so as to permit a reasonable economic growth while ameliorating ecological problems, but in a voluntary and democratic manner. An excellent short analysis of this stark choice is contained in a review of the books mentioned [footnote 9]. This latter points out one of the basic fallacies of all the "doomsayers" who use extrapolation to arrive at future disaster, that is, they ignore the real impact of future technology. "If the telephone company were restricted to turn-of-the-century technology twenty million operators would be needed to handle today's volume of calls. Or, ... an extrapolation of the trends of the 1880s would show today's cities buried under horse manure."[18]

The chemical engineer thus must see how important is the interplay of technology and politics in the future, and why I believe he is well suited to becoming active in both of these areas, regardless of his own personal political convictions. The chemical engineer is taught to anticipate the outcomes of the solutions he proposes, to weigh and compare alternatives, to take into account the economics of any situation, and to understand that there are no ideal solutions, only practical ones. Few scientists, or for that matter lawyers, and certain other politically active professionals, are able to think and perform as well in this way. An example of such an approach, without ideological overtones or "revolutionary" talk is given in the proposals by the presidents of the five borough chapters of the New York State Society of Professional Engineers in New York City to ameliorate power consumption in that city so as to reduce its electrical demands by one million kilowatts by 1980, but without imposing arbitrary reductions in living standards, or freezing the status quo for the more fortunate residents against the less so.[19]

I have dwelt at some length on these matters because they are the basic issues. We must as engineers dig below the superficial and the misleading, so often emanating from the "intellectuals"* of Fairlie's description, particularly those of limited experience outside of the academic environment.

Amelioration of the Environment

As mentioned above, the word "pollution" is on everyone's lips. But it is the chemical engineer who is uniquely qualified to deal with the problems which require solution in this area, ranging from design of lead-free gasolines through purification of air and water to alteration of chemical processing sequences to permit abatement of their polluting effects. These are all engineering problems with economic parameters.

Recently, Dow Chemical has emphasized not only its ability to clean up pollution, but to do it profitably[20] So have other companies.[21,22] That, indeed, is the challenge to the chemical engineer!

And, from abroad, Holland's Prince Bernhard, international president of the World Wildlife Fund, had this to say: "The United States, with its unparalleled industrial technology, has brought on tremendous pollution problems, but Americans also 'set the world's pace' in solving thee problems."

The Prince said that the solutions developed by the United States "can and should be exported and adopted by other countries." The affluence of America, he said, allows huge expenditures on ecology control, which in poorer countries are given low priority. "In some cases," he added, "it is only if the United States does the spadework and takes the lead that other countries in one way or another will come around to follow suit."[23] This is particularly appropriate when one considers there is no evidence to indi-

---

*We engineers consider ourselves intellectuals as well, so we had better be careful to heed Fairlie's warning ourselves!

cate that pollution is any less prevalent in the U.S.S.R.; quite the contrary. A recent article underlines that America is much more sensitive and questioning in these areas, because it is a free society.[24]

Dr. Jerome B. Wiesner at his presidential inauguration at MIT spoke on this subject eloquently, and pointed out how many such problems of society have already been solved even in the last decade, such as the nuclear test ban, elimination of DDT spraying, and many others.[25]

The Medical-Engineering Interface

It is now becoming clear that the chemical engineer will have a unique role in the increasing emphasis by medicine on new chemical and mechanical tools, organs, diagnostic methods, and the basic study of the body as a dynamic physicochemical system, involving highly complex dynamics and kinetics. Words like "biomedical engineering," "biochemical engineering," "enzyme engineering," etc. have already sprung into use, but I feel strongly that our profession should resist such glamorizing attempts at specialized branches. Realistically, of course, universities do have to provide a certain amount of glamor to attract the best students, but the important point is that the programs have broad engineering concepts rather than limited specialization. All of these fields are legitimate chemical engineering work. Our professional training is and should be broad enough to encompass all these ranges of activity. Chemical engineering and *breadth* are virtually synonyms, in my view—it is the broadest of the engineering professions. This same breadth applies in the coordination of research, development, design, and operation of pollution control systems, medical systems, nuclear reactor systems, rocket systems, factory-made housing systems—you name it—so long as changes in the composition of matter are taking place or are required. That covers a lot of our civilization! Let's keep chemical engineering broad, and aim at controlling such systems (although the medical field is not likely to allow this for the foreseeable future).

New Challenges in the Traditional Fields

As stated above, there is no reason to doubt that new technological demands will be made of the chemical engineer in his widely recognized fields of activity. Plastics will have to be better able to be disposed of; detergents must be changed to meet pollution requirements; new housing materials must be devised to reduce the now almost prohibitive cost of housing for everyone but the rich; new materials for automobile bodies and even for all construction are going to be required; synthetic foodstuffs and improvement of present day food supplies will be required; better synthetic fabrics will be needed to simplify an increasingly servantless life (including the effects of women's liberation!); new fuels will be required for transportation of the future; better methods will be required to manufacture many industrial chemicals and their derivatives, so as to conserve the world's natural resources and to adapt to rapidly changing economics. Examples of the latter are not difficult to cite:

(a) The manufacture of ethylene and related olefins will shift rapidly away from ethane and propane (except possibly from certain quantities of imports) because of the rise in price and increasing scarcity of gas. The heavy end of the barrel will become the feedstock of the future, but better technology is needed to permit this to be done most economically.

(b) The manufacture of ammonia will soon feel the effects of methane shortages and high price. What will be the appropriate feedstock of the future, and how can existing plants be converted?

(c) Electricity is going to become much more expensive, for reasons likewise related to the scarcity of traditional energy supplies. Processes now involving electrochemistry will have to be replaced. Chlorine manufacture has already undergone a serious change in that mercury cells are rapidly being phased out in favor of diaphragm cells because of the pollution question, but even more serious problems loom—such as imbalance between caustic (in short supply) and chlorine. We need a good caustic process without chlorine (shades of Ernest Solvay!). The development of safe chlorine-consuming compounds would have real economic benefits.

(d) The growing scarcity of high-grade metallurgical ores will call for new techniques effective on lower grade ores, as well as plastic materials capable of replacing more and more of the commonly used metals.

(e) The ecological balance will surely call for development of synthetic papers; economic factors will also demand preparation of superior materials cheaper than lumbering and paper production can permit. Recycling of many such materials will become necessary, and superior waste disposal techniques will be required.

(f) Improvements in the economics of the chemical industries: We as chemical engineers can get very interested in the solutions of some of the problems mentioned above but in all of this we can never afford to lose sight of the fundamental underlying economic realities which have permitted our industries to grow and prosper over the years. It is certainly well known to most of you that in recent years the rate of growth has hardly been an awe-inspiring one and many serious ills have appeared which are going to need some intensive effort to cure in the 1970s.

Examples of some of these economic problems are the following:

Profitability
There is an overriding urgency to increase the profitability of the chemical process industries. The 1960s have had a very debilitating effect on them. In 1969 and 1970, net profits after taxes for basic chemicals represented 7 percent and 5.6 percent, respectively, of total capital employed, less than *all* manufactures of 8.3 and 6.7 percent. It is easy enough to see from various published figures that during the decade costs went up but selling prices declined below what they were at the beginning of the decade, and the industry was caught in a severe cost-selling price squeeze. While other industries passed increased costs on to their customers in increased selling prices, the chemical industry did not. There are many, many reasons why this took place, and I certainly do not feel that this is the occasion to ventilate my views on this important subject. Nevertheless, I would like to say that, based on my experience in chemical manufacturing, as well as process licensing, I am convinced that a great deal of the blame falls on management—in particular, in two areas: deficiencies in chemical marketing, particularly in pricing policy[26,27] and inadequate realization that new technology when translated into very large plants does not necessarily guarantee greater profitability despite lower costs. However, there are other villains: entrance of too many companies into chemicals manufacture; ready availability of technology at low prices; inadequate understanding of the differences between costs and adequate selling prices to permit a reasonable return on capital invested; excessive concentration on "share of the market" instead of profitability; the need for early buildup to full capacity of large plants with many coproducts, without attention to the effect on price of many other such projects existing simultaneously, but looking only at costs at full capacity; and many others.

Balance of Payments
The United States, as is well known, has had some considerable balance of payments problems—a subject little discussed when most of us were at school. Looking solely at the trade balances, the United States in 1971 experienced a deficiency in its trade balance slightly over $2 billion, for the first time in this century showing a loss. However, in the chemical

industries we enjoyed a surplus of payments of slightly over $2 billion.[28] There is considerable doubt in my mind whether this favorable contribution of the chemical industries to the American balance of payments can continue very long under present circumstances, and a great deal of attention is going to have to be paid to this problem by the chemical industries in the 1970s. We need much innovation in products and processes.[29]

Improved Functioning of Our Economic System
The chemical engineer can help the economist understand and guide our economic system better than is now the case, because of his more objective and frequently less academic turn of mind. He can also help in the improvement of world standards of living. The magnitude of this latter question can best be realized when looking at the three-quarters of the world's population which together shares less than a third of the total world gross national product. This should be challenge enough even for the most idealistic of our youth, and it won't be done on the barricades but by hard and imaginative work.

Having taken this peek into my crystal ball, it should be apparent from the foregoing remarks why I am optimistic about the future of the *well-trained* chemical engineer. If we can continue to attract the top students and educate them correctly (a subject I will touch on below), I am confident that not only will these problems be solved, but the chemical engineer will be very satisfied with his work, his compensation, and his contribution to society. And, I continue to believe that the managements of the future that deal with the systems I have described above must also come from the chemical engineering profession to a large extent, because only technically trained management in an increasingly complex technological era can deal most effectively with the multifold problems.

Future Education of the Chemical Engineer

I have alluded several times above to the question of proper education of the chemical engineer of the future. Obviously, we have been doing something right when the success of the chemical engineer to date is recognized. How should it change to meet the new challenges of the 1970s and 1980s?

In considering these questions further, it must first be clear to all that private industry will continue to be the employer of the greater part of the chemical engineering profession (as it has in the past). This is not only historically true, it is also very good for the profession, and for the society which it serves. For, basically, our system of mixed private enterprise operating in a democratic framework has two overwhelming advantages when properly organized—(1) it permits decentralization of decision-making, and provides criteria for judging the performance of managers and employees at various levels within general ground rules laid down by the government and other bodies (e.g., taxation, anti-trust, accounting principles, etc.); such a process greatly contributes to the efficiency with which society gets things done; and (2) it releases men from total bureaucratic or state control over their lives by allowing self-development, liberty for advancement, and shifting of employment and occupation. Freedom for the individual is much more assured. In the totalitarian state there is no place for the individual to go without the approval of the bureaucracy, and no other employer to escape to. I have emphasized other aspects of this same basic issue earlier in this article.

Efficiency and freedom—these very simple words mean an enormous amount when they are absent. Any one of you who has experience with large organizations, including government, can testify, as I can, to the dead weight which bureaucracy assumes, the freer it is of checks and balances against its power. In the totalitarian states, the direction of all social activity is from the top and goes down very far, and in very great detail. Our educators must understand these facts, and must make their students understand them too, or there will be a very grim future indeed, not only for chemical engineers but for all of us. It is a heartening fact indeed that a very significant percentage of chemical engineering graduates at MIT, for example (about 25 percent of the doctor's men), are hoping to become entrepreneurs, and found science-based companies. This is a very recent trend.

In order, then, to provide proper education to the future chemical engineer, the teacher must understand industry, the user of the majority of his graduates, and the way our mixed economy really functions in comparison with others, permitting Americans to enjoy the highest standard of living among all major industrialized countries, but with substantial freedom. (This is no accident.)

Here we come to the first point of challenge to our educational system. Many of our younger teachers have never had this experience. The enormous impact of the government funding programs of the 1950s and 1960s on educational institutions has resulted in a vast expansion of faculties recruited directly from the recent graduates of the educational system itself. This recycling has been going on for too long a time, and I fear the consequences if allowed to continue. The schools *must* recruit faculty from people who have had industrial experience, not alone from recent graduates. Consulting work with industry, while valuable, is not a substitute for a real interchange between industry and the university. With the earlier retirements now foreseen for many in industry, a whole new category for possible recruitment to teaching becomes available (as an example). It also permits the possibility that engineers who take early retirement could become much more active in politics, where the pay is often not very good! In this connection, I feel that a significant improvement is going to be needed in the pension programs in this country including the introduction of fully portable pensions, and more generous provisions for early retirement which, for some of the reasons cited above as well as for others, may well turn out to be beneficial for society as a whole as it faces even greater demands for improvements of every kind in the human condition.

A second, and related point, is the need to understand economics, business management, political science, accounting, and the like, on the part of both teachers and students. Classical economics courses alone are ill suited to the needs of tomorrow's chemical engineer, who needs to know a great deal about the processes of capital formation, investment criteria, the operation of our financial institutions (domestic and international), the tax system, the actual working of the so-called "socialist" economies, and many subjects not understood by most engineering graduates today. Cooperation between faculties of engineering and economics will be required to develop optional subjects and "minor" programs suited to the chemical engineer, who can thus combine technology with a strong business-economics oriented education. Industry should take an active interest in this area, so as to improve the understanding of economic reality on the part of university faculties. Engineers trained in this way can have a profound influence on our developments in the rest of this century.

A third point is the absolute necessity to maintain the breadth of the chemical engineering curriculum, which I have already discussed earlier in this address. Fundamentals only should be taught, and preferably in the manner of problem solving.

Fourthly, in order to prepare properly trained chemical engineers of the future, it would appear that a well designed Master's curriculum will represent an optimum for a long time to come (with plenty of need for the B.S. training alone). There have been too many Ph.D.s graduating from our universities in the 1960s, and they have been taking an inordinately long time to complete their theses. This has resulted from the distortions brought about by the government-sponsored research programs mentioned above, and also by the effects of the Viet Nam war, the draft, etc. The great growth in faculties during this period used up the new Ph.D.s (as mentioned above) but this trend will no longer continue in the 1970s, or, most probably, thereafter. Perhaps a new style Doctor of Engineering degree (with no experimental thesis), already introduced by some institutions, will continue to develop, for the preparation of especially well-trained men and women for careers in process design, for example, or general management (with strong economics and business training), rather than the wasting of years in an experimental thesis little resembling the kind of research work actually practiced in industry. I believe industry-university cooperation in developing process design studies is very important for the future, as the process engineer is one of the most essential individuals to the future of chemical engineering practice.

Despite these strictures, I do not want to overlook the possibility that the Ph.D., if broadly trained, can still find many areas of value to himself and society.

Methods and emphases in education can certainly be improved, taking into account the interests of today's freshmen. Thus, chemical engineering principles can be taught just as well by considering the problems of scrubbing sulfur dioxide from gas effluents as by study of the manufacture of sulfuric acid, but the flavor of an anti-pollution step is used to demonstrate basic principles.

Fifthly, the curriculum of the chemical engineer should not be cluttered up with a number of "humanities" courses, which are fashionable today. (An exception to this generality should be psychology, which over the years has proven to be an extremely important part of the engineer's requirements; but, very few engineering curricula provide for this.) School is for learning the tools of one's lifetime occupation; culture is something one acquires on one's own over a lifetime. Interests in history, music, art, and the like are best developed outside of formal educational circles, and preferably by travel, reading, outside studies and practice, rather than formal courses. Social science courses as taught today in most universities are mainly confusing and negative, and it is better for the student to develop his interests in these areas over a lifetime of study, and with the objectivity resulting from a sound engineering training.

Sixthly, there is a related problem for the future—the proper evaluation of the role of mathematics. It is surprising, if you look back on your own career, how little mathematics you really need to practice the profession. Of course, the development of new techniques requires great mathematical sophistication, but only a few specialists are really needed in this area. The computer is now recognized as a tool, but not an end in itself, and this is good. There has been too much mathematical orientation in chemical engineering education lately. Indeed, this trend is observed abroad, and in other fields. The French have recently launched a counterattack on the increasing abstractions of mathematics which turn young people away from physics and engineering.[30]

We should begin emphasizing the *chemical* part of our title more widely, because it is the backbone of our profession. I don't believe chemical engineers are getting enough chemistry, and I believe our chemistry departments have also fallen victim to the postwar mathematical craze, to the point where they have often succeeded in making chemistry dull, a feat I would never have imagined could be accomplished!

And, finally, minority groups should be informed early (in high school, at least) that the opportunities for rapid advancement are substantial in the field of chemical engineering; not the least of these "minorities" is woman, whose participation thus far in our profession is negligible, but who clearly is beginning to enter it very successfully.

Some Other Needs

The chemical engineering profession needs an even stronger Institute, to help in expressing the voice of the profession to the public and to government. In this activity, it should not be the spokesman for any industry, company, or university, but for the profession. Further effort is also needed to explain to high school, grade school, and college freshmen what the profession is really like, how it is being practiced in all its diversity, and the opportunities that lie within it. We must explain to laymen and youth why our modern "witches" and anti-technology cranks are just that—unreal voices in a society that is already too technological ever to go back to the compost pile for food production, or to return to slavery so that more cotton can be grown instead of replacing it with polyester fiber production!

No profession has any future which does not secure the next generation by attracting the finest minds, and educating them superbly. Since, clearly, I believe, as I think you do too, that chemical engineering is alive and well and ought to continue, we—the industries, the universities, and our Institute—must cooperate together to secure this future for us all. If the past is any guide, we shall succeed in this effort.

Literature Cited

1. *Chem. Eng.*, 79, No. 6 (Mar. 20, 1972), p. 62; *Chem. Eng. Progr.*, 68, No. 4 (Apr., 1972), p. 134.

2. "College Graduates' Hopes for Jobs Turning Brighter," *N.Y. Times*, Jan. 19, 1972.

3. "In the Soviet Union, She's the Highest Ranking Woman," *N.Y. Times*, Jan. 19, 1972.

4. *Chem. Eng. Curr. Rev.*, June, 1970. Dept. of Chem. Eng., MIT.

5. *N.Y. Times* Apr. 10, 1972.

6. Gunness, R. C., "The Energy Crisis: Real or Imaginary?" *Chem, Eng. Progr.*, 68, No. 4 (Apr. 1972), pp. 26–32.

7. Hottel, H. C., and J. B. Howard, *New Energy Technology—Some Facts and Assessments*, MIT Press, Cambridge, Mass (1971).

8. Commoner, Barry, *The Closing Circle*, Knopf, N.Y. (1971).

9. Forrester, J. W., *World Dynamics*, MIT Press, Cambridge, Mass. (1971) and Meadows, Donella, et al., *The Limits to Growth*, Universe Books, N.Y. (1972).

10. "Space Ship Earth," a discussion organized by *The Observer* (London), Gerald Leach, moderator, as quoted in the *Jamaica Daily Gleaner*, Mar. 19, 1972.

11. Alliluyeva, Svetlana, *Only One Year*, Harper & Row, N.Y. (1969).

12. Djilas, Milovan, *The Unperfect Society*, Methuen & Co., Ltd., London (1969).

13. *N.Y. Times*, Mar. 19, 1972.

14. *Ibid.*, Mar. 22, 1972.

15. Huntford, Roland, *The New Totalitarians*, Stein & Day, Inc., N.Y. (1971).

16. Worsthorne, Peregrine, *The Socialist Myth*, Weybright & Talley, N.Y. (1971).

17. *Bus. Week*, Mar. 18, 1972, pp. 72–74.

18. *N.Y. Times Book Review*, Apr. 2, 1972, p. 1.

19. Report of the N. Y. State Soc. of Prof. Eng., headed by Joseph D. Lewin, Sept., 1971.

20. "Dow Cleans Up Pollution at No Net Cost," *Bus. Week*, Jan. 1, 1972, p. 32.

21. "Union Carbide Claims Nonpolluting Process to Treat Solid Waste, *Wall St. J.*, Jan. 12, 1972.

22. Quinn, James Brian, "Next Big Industry: Environmental Improvement," *Harvard Bus. Rev.*, Sept.–Oct., 1971, pp. 120–131.

23. "Prince Lauds U.S. on Cleanup Work." *N.Y. Times*, Oct. 18, 1971.

24. "Soviet Sees No Peril in Greater Output," *N.Y. Times*, Mar. 30, 1972.

25. Wiesner, Jerome, "Opportunity for Affirmation," *Tech Talk*, Oct. 13, 1971.

26. "Dow, Seeking Earnings Boost, Looks at Pricing, Capital Outlays, Cost Controls, Olefins Picture," *Oil, Paint & Drug Rep.*, Dec. 20, 1971.

27. Gibbons, Donald R., "What's Ahead for Profitability," *Chem. Eng. Progr.*, 67, No. 12 (Dec., 1971), pp. 13–19.

28. *Chem. & Eng. News*, 50, No. 12 (Mar. 20, 1972), p. 19.

29. Harr, Karl G., Jr., "Technology, Trade and Government," *Wall St. J.*, Jan. 13, 1972.

30. "Down With the New Maths," *New Scientist*, Dec. 30, 1971.

11 From Chemical Engineering to Moral Philosophy

What does one say on an unconventional occasion like this? So, as I stand here, like a drowning man searching for words to express my emotions, bits and pieces of my life and thought speed before me. Perhaps, as these memories bob to the surface, some may be worth rescuing. Anyway, let me try:

1. I came to this Institute in 1937 with a Tau Beta Pi fellowship that paid me $65 a month for ten months, plus my tuition. That's all I had to live on. And I was lucky to have it. But, even in those depression days, MIT reached out the hand of aid to its needy students, and in the following years a teaching assistantship and then a research assistantship were offered me until I finally graduated with my Sc.D. degree in 1941. There were many outstanding students at MIT in those days who were in equally modest circumstances, and I can remember no case in which the necessary form of help was not found. Of course, this tradition goes on today—it is the essence of the requirements for a great university, and it is one of MIT's many virtues that it concentrates so much attention on this vital matter. It believes in equality of opportunity.

2. In my time here, the era of the great master teachers and creators of chemical engineering was at its zenith. There parade before us the names of Sherwood, McAdams, Walker, Hottel, Weber, Hauser, Whitman, Meissner, Reed, and numerous others. But, leading even these, in my estimation, were Warren K. Lewis and Edwin R. Gilliland. They were not only men of genius —they were the most inspiring teachers and examples to us all. Their relation with the *practice* of chemical engineering was profound: it was not just a science for intellectual enjoyment, but primarily a technology for the widest possible application in industry, and for the benefit of mankind. It

Address on the occasion of the dedication of the Landau Chemical Engineering Building, Massachusetts Institute of Technology, March 5, 1976.

was this attitude, and the presence of these leaders, which distinguished MIT's chemical engineering department from all others, and ranked it as the first in the world. A stream of some of industry's most important executives has come from this department (many are happily with us today): Butch Granville, Jerry McAfee, Brel McCoy, Bob Gunness, John Haas, Carlos Paya, and others; in addition there are prominent entrepreneurs like Paul Cook, Bob Purvin, and the Koch Brothers; also the new editor-in-chief of Reader's Digest, Edward Thompson; engineering executives like Bob Siegfried and Dave Brown; and many technical and business practitioners throughout the world. The fruit of these eminent teachers still grows on the tree of chemical engineering, and, by one of the typical recycle processes for which chemical engineering is famous, some of us have been fortunate enough to be able to return to the soil of the Institute and this department its first new facility ever built specifically for chemical engineering.

3. Bricks and mortar are a necessary but not a sufficient condition for the continuing health of our beloved chemical engineering department. Most of the great names I have cited are gone or retired. In their place we have many bright and able younger men. New directions for chemical engineering applications have been perceived by them, such as in the biomedical sciences, enzyme technology, materials science, and the like. But there must be eternal vigilance and attention by the department and the Institute to strengthening and deepening the ties between the department and industry, which employs three quarters of its graduates and provided the capital for our magnificent new building. There is much that needs to be done in this connection, including bolstering of our unique Practice School. Industry and the department's graduates have funded not only this new building, but also a relatively high proportion of MIT's total named professorships, including, most recently, those established in honor of Warren K. Lewis and Edwin R. Gilliland. It would be consistent with the department's history and the accomplishments and ideals of these men if both professorships were regularly filled by prominent engineers of strong industrial bent and experience, who can help maintain and enlarge MIT's long leadership in the *practice* of chemical engineering.

4. Proceeding from the particular to the more general, I should like to say a few words about the role of a private university like MIT. It seems obvious that government-owned or -controlled institutions cannot normally be very innovative or experimental. A dean of engineering in a famous Midwestern state university told me recently that, once one leaves the Northeast, and especially MIT, educational innovation falls off all the way

across the country until the West Coast is reached. In between, he said, the legislators and citizens who pay for their state or local universities expect a generally uniform and standard undergraduate curriculum, much as if they were expanded high schools. Of course, in graduate schools there is more room for individuality, and some excellent chemical engineering departments have been developed, which offer much competition to MIT's. But I am convinced that, with this new building as a start, we shall once again be on the road to unchallenged worldwide leadership in chemical engineering education. *Only a private university, funded by money which is intelligently unselfish, can lead the intellectual world of the future.* President Wiesner has written a very eloquent summary of his vision of MIT in the book, *The MIT Leadership Campaign* ("The Case book"), which I hope everyone will read carefully. We are very fortunate to have such thoughtful and outstanding leaders as Howard Johnson and Jerry Wiesner, and, indeed, I should hasten to add, MIT is exceptionally well managed among institutions generally and universities in particular. Additional names from the past and present, like Jim Killian, Jay Stratton, Paul Gray, Walter Rosenblith, and others, shine among their contemporaries, and give assurance that the MIT of the next generation will play an even more important role in our free society than ever before. It is why our new fund-raising "Leadership Campaign" is so important.

5. Lastly, flowing from the foregoing, I want to comment on an even broader subject, that of moral philosophy, and how this unique private university of MIT might achieve a still more exceptional role in the life of our country during the rest of this century. The eminent constitutional scholar, Alexander Bickel of Yale University, who died so early in his brilliant career, wrote in his last testament, *The Morality of Consent*, a remarkable chapter, "Moral Authority and the Intellectual." In it he has these words to say about the university: "... scholars often bring a valuable detachment to affairs. All too little information and opinion enter the universe of political discourse with the credit that attaches to disinterestedness. Much of what there is comes from academic and professional persons, whose credentials are certified by universities ... and are known to be certified in accordance with neutral standards, not political objectives. Persons so certified then speak with a certain moral authority; they inject ... dispassionate, informed, disinterested judgment, which looks beyond the interests and objectives immediately engaged in the debate." I certainly believe this is an accurate description of how MIT sees itself, and is seen by others.

Yet, there is another step to be taken in this dispassionate search for truth, and that is special to MIT's talents—namely, its integration into an overall perspective, a moral philosophy of the political, the ethical, the scientific, the technological, the economic, the rational elements of our free society. Drawing upon the best philosophical concepts of the free world, it should be MIT's task to anchor such a correctly synthesized moral philosophy firmly to the *realities*, bringing it out of the clouds in which it has rested up to now. No other university in America, in my opinion, could perform such a role in a way comparable to MIT, which is so strong in so many of these areas, and in the interdisciplinary search for deeper and more complex knowledge.

Raymond Aron, Professor of Sociology at the Sorbonne, has dealt with a number of these considerations in his book, *The Industrial Society*, published ten years ago, well before some of these ideas became commonly discussed. I quote a few of these:

Is the rationality of modern societies more than a means? Does it imply—must it logically imply—the application of moral principles to societies, a trend toward respect for humanitarian values? Modern science is the product of an attitude of mind that is rational in its ends, and not only in its means—regard for facts, sound reasoning, trust in other scientists, a critical attitude toward oneself and toward evidence. The scientist as a scientist lives according to the dictates of reason. Does he as a man also live so? ... To carry over the scientific virtues—prudence, humility, and deference to fact—into the field of action is praiseworthy. But it is dictated purely by philosophical considerations, which most scientists do not consider as valid or as binding as the scientific establishment of facts and laws. Personally, I agree that there is no logical or scientific connection between science and a scientific attitude in other fields. One can only move from the one to the other by a realization of the human ideal implied in scientific research, and that realization is philosophical.... In interpreting sociology and forecasting history, can we safely say that government and social customs will become more moral as a result of scientific and technical rationality? In the present state of our experience, moral and humanitarian progress, whether in political institutions or in the individual way of life, does not seem to be a necessary result of rationality.... At present, we are apt to think that in the scientific age every system will be based on democratic watchwords.... In has been proved, however, that these watchwords do not exclude the possibility of even the worst features of tyranny. The alternative stated by Tocqueville [in comparing America and Russia of the early nineteenth century]—that ... society must be either despotic or liberal—seems to be more in turn with our experience than any theory according to which the economic-social infrastructure results inevitably in one particular system and only one [i.e. Marxism].... In the past, class inequality was essential in order that a minority might enjoy the comfort and leisure without which culture was impossible. Now, an even larger proportion of mankind is gaining access to culture—ultimately, all mankind. But our object in giving the masses of the future the luxury enjoyed in the past by the elite is to place culture within reach of all. Only if this goal were achieved could scientific and technical rationality be confidently affirmed to be an advance in human progress.... There is no certainty, however, that this will be so. The quality of existence is not determined by the amount of goods available to each person.

For any reflective observer, history from now to the end of the century will be dominated by two facts: the hydrogen bomb and the population explosion.... There is no longer any common measure between the consequences of a thermo-nuclear war or the possible tripling of the world population and the scope of political party quarrels.... *There is one way of instilling fresh life into Western ideas ...: this is to try and discover the meaning of the historical phase we are now living in....* [Emphasis mine] The confrontation between Communism and the West ... shows ... that the same volume of resources can be shared out in entirely different ways.... Social organization can aim either at the absorption of the individual into an entirely state-controlled society, or ... at the widening of the individual's margin of initiative.... The collectivism-individualism dilemma retains its significance, because industrialization can be oriented toward either. Similarly, on a political level, human liberties will never be guaranteed by prosperity; the single-party system and the indoctrination of the masses are and will remain threats or temptations.

Many other aspects of these fundamental philosophical questions are covered in such recent books as *The Socialist Idea—A Reappraisal,* which analyzes the many failures and moral and philosophical dilemmas of Marxism as seen from the perspective of 100 years, mostly by Marxist scholars, and the book just published by the eminent physicist and Nobel Peace Prize winner, Andrei Sakharov, *My Country and the World.* In the latter appears the following interesting quotation, "In my opinion, contemporary Soviet society can be concisely characterized as a society based on state capitalism; that is, a system differing from contemporary capitalism of the Western type by virtue of complete nationalization, a Party-State monopoly of economic affairs—and therefore in culture, ideology, and the other basic aspects of life." Thus, the synthesis I am describing is not just about capitalism, or what type of capitalism, but the far wider one of *freedom versus unfreedom,* in all its many ramifications.

In this context, note should also be taken of MIT's unusual relation with industry and the private sector generally. This not only gives the Institute a good opportunity to engage in constructive dialogue with many entrepreneurs, and business and financial leaders; it also leads to a symbiotic relation by which these same leaders help MIT sustain its vigorous growth and yet independence. In a smaller but still essential sense, this same relation carries over to the more mundane necessities of life for MIT. The men who helped Ken Jamieson raise millions of dollars for our new building could only do so because their companies (mostly from the much maligned oil industry) were able to generate some profits, and indeed I would not be here if entrepreneurship were dead! Chemical engineering has no important role to play in the communist states, makes little impact on their society, and where used is copied or purchased from the innovations of the West, particularly those of the United States. Today, moreover, the American private universities and the private economic sector are also sharing in many of the same dangers. Professor Robert Nisbet, in his most thought-provoking new book, *Twilight of Authority*, speaks of the efforts of many men to bring as much of the economy and society within the purview of law and litigation as possible. "Those of revolutionary disposition have abandoned the barricade for the courtroom, ... seeing the manifold accomplishments of the latter in the whole realm of the New Equalitarianism and the New Despotism that goes with it.... The university alone is a superb case history.... Within the past quarter of a century we have seen a formerly free and largely autonomous social body reduced in a score of ways to becoming the handmaiden of legislature, law office, regulatory agency, and the courtroom." Welcome to the pariahs' club, although here too I am confident some pariahs are more equal than others, and this gives you still some hope for the future!

As an illustration of the necessity for the synthesis I advocate, I would like to point out that scholars from other institutions of learning, often those not closely based on technology but active principally in the political and economic spheres, have generated some very dangerous nonsense (up there in the clouds!) that in my judgment is the exact antithesis of the preceding statement of our fundamental philosophical problem. Again to quote Bickel, "The moral authority of liberalism is lost when the fundamental principles and attitudes of liberalism [i.e. freedom] are compromised or abandoned, for these principles are the essence of the American political tradition. They touch Lincoln's mystic chords of memory." One such scholar, for example, has become a major advocate of "tax reform," which basically stems from his strange concept that the government owns all our income, and graciously allows us to keep some of it for ourselves. While this is an interpretation of his philosophy and he may not himself put it into such crude terms, I am satisfied that this is the real meaning of his teachings. Clearly, from this, flow all kinds of concepts for compulsory redistribution of wealth, including the latest attempt once again to reduce charitable contributions to universities which so alarmed us all just a few months ago. We will hear more of this again, as such philosophy is attractive to many politicians seeking votes.

Another prominent economist has recently come out four square for socialism and in an embodiment of that dogma has been preaching reinstatement of wage and price controls, this time under someone (like himself, no doubt) who really believes in it! What he basically advocates, of course, leads directly to an authoritarian if not totalitarian state, as our Canadian and British friends have been discovering. Certainly, no entrepreneurial company could long survive price and wage controls, as my own experiences amply testify, nor could any other part of our complex economy. Thus, we see once again that symbiotic relation by which MIT, the spawner of so many entrepreneurs, has ample justification to study the ways in which they can be encouraged. Entrepreneurship in totalitarian states is illegal!

Still another scholar has become the modern theoretical spokesman for the founders of the French Revolution, in restoring the doctrine of "egalitarianism." He means much more than that, however, and basically is attempting to change our American concept of "pursuit of happiness" to a guarantee of equal results for all. This can only lead to a totalitarian state. Again, I quote from Alexander Bickel: "[Such] ideology represents 'intellectual and emotional imperialism.'" He then quotes from Burke, "... all men have equal rights, but not to equal things ..." and explains this by saying, "since a leveling egalitarianism which does not reward merit and ability is harmful to all and is unjust as well." That eminent educator, Professor Clark Kerr, in his lecture here last fall, also touched on some of these same themes, and, in particular reference to MIT, said, "In a struggle between those who favor expansion and continuation of equality of opportunity, as against those who favor equality of results ... it is easier for a great research university to prosper in a century concentrated on *growth* than it may be to prosper in a century where one of the fundamental themes is *egalitarianism.*"

I refer to that same Edmund Burke, eminent British statesman and writer, who was the friend of the American Revolution, and the critic of the totalitarian tendencies of the French Revolution, having correctly predicted the rise of the Napoleonic dictatorship, the first but not the last of the European revolutions to drown the world in blood. As Bickel points out, "true believers ... theorists, and ideologues made the French Revolution, and for Burke a politics of theory and ideology, of abstract, absolute ideas was an abomination, whether the idea was the right of the British Parliament to tax the American colonies or the rights of man. Such a politics cannot work as politics. It begins and ends by sacrificing peace, and it must proceed from one bloodbath to another and from one tyranny to another.

Ideas are the inventions of men and are as arbitrary as their will. The business of politics is not with theory and ideology but with accommodation." The contrast between the American concepts of freedom and two centuries of European revolutionary developments, culminating in the present Russian totalitarianism, could not be more eloquently stated. Here at MIT we have indeed always believed in excellence, in merit, in rewards for it, and for incentives to create it. We believe the same in industry. It's what makes our great economy flourish so much better than any other.

Professor Nisbet, who touches on many of the same issues as Professors Bickel and Aron, sums it all up by saying, "At the present time the ascendant moral philosophy in the West is that which, as I have noted, takes what is in effect leveling as the desired norm of justice. How welcome would be Burke's words today: 'Believe me, Sir, those who attempt to level never equalize.'"

The recent policy reversal in Britain, after two decades of leveling egalitarianism, and the contrast in postwar development between East and West Germany are sufficient examples to show what our tasks should be! This recent British swing away from the European socialist-communist tide is well described in an editorial of the *New York Times* of February 27, 1976:

The four-year austerity program introduced by Britain's Labor Government is based on the American axiom, "There is no such thing as a free lunch." Three decades of a cradle-to-grave welfare state have exhausted the tax-paying capability of wealthy Britons and have imposed such tax burdens on lower income groups that it is sometimes more advantageous to stay home and collect unemployment insurance than to work and pay taxes.

This "poverty trap" for the individual is forcing Britain's governing socialists to come to grips with another poverty trap affecting the nation as a whole It has become increasingly clear that redistribution of the nation's wealth can no longer serve to lift living standards for lower income groups and that a more rapid rate of growth in national output to provide a larger pie is essential.

Chancellor of the Exchequer Denis Healey has pointed out that further taxes for Britain's wealthy, investing class—already the world's highest imposts, with rates up to 83 percent on earned income and 97 percent on unearned income—would only bring in $800 million, even if all income over $10,000 a year is taxed away. Meanwhile, the British worker receiving the average weekly wage of $125 now pays a quarter of it to the Government, as compared with a tenth in 1960, and will be paying half of it in three years if government spending continues to increase at the present rate.

Let us hope this keen perception by an arch-spokesman of similar trends in this country will support comparable policies by our own politicians. What they say about Britain applies to us also.

My own view of the importance of all these subjects, and what led to the title and theme of today's remarks, was embodied in a paper I wrote on the future of chemical engineering in 1972: "The fundamental choice facing the world in the rest of the century is between sliding into universal totalitarian rule, which will be required to force *sharing of the poverty* if the 'zero economic growth' and ecological fanatics [I should now add 'egalitarian philosophers' and 'collectivists'] are allowed to have their way, or developing a much higher level of technology so as to permit a reasonable economic growth while ameliorating ecological problems, but in a voluntary and democratic manner." Technology and leveling egalitarianism are fundamentally antagonistic to each other! And anyone who doubts this should read a recent publication by an ecologist who claims to have found his way to Marx via the second law of thermodynamics and, in my view, basically advocates the Maoist solution for America, so that we can undo altogether the effects of the industrial revolution. His is probably the most violent totalitarianism of all, if it were ever realizable!

Such a challenge is worthy of MIT's some day esablishing an Institute of Freedom, a world center for the synthesis of philosophy and technology of which I have spoken. This Institute would be devoted to the examination of freedom from every viewpoint, and to the development of policies for the preservation and strengthening of freedom, rooted in the hard practical approach for which MIT is so famous. It should be funded solely by private means, and be absolutely free itself to pursue the truth in the manner Professor Aron has described. What a contribution to our society this would be!

But, until such a center exists, I hope our many distinguished faculty members will work on more and more of these problems. And, finally, I am confident that the whole MIT community will engage in the relatively simpler but still vital task of lending a hand to help in our "Leadership Campaign." We are all united in our faith in MIT's role in the future.

In this Bicentennial Year of 1976, it is particularly pertinent to look back at the awesome achievement of our founding fathers in having created the first free society in the world; as Professor Kerr said, however, the shape of the next century is in our hands. The great majority of nations is unfree; our own freedom is imperfect; our task is great.

12   The Chemical
Engineering Trilemma

Undergraduate chemical engineering education has changed a great deal since I was a student. In the pre–World War II era, the basic training ended with a bachelor's degree. The curriculum was heavy with required shop and laboratory courses from the major engineering disciplines, as well as with numerous chemistry lectures and labs. In addition, there were courses in industrial chemistry and stoichiometry, unit operations, electrochemistry, etc. Despite this load, students also had to take two years of English (including composition), a foreign language, and mathematics and physics for two years. Needless to say, it was more than a forty hr. week! Graduate work was relatively rare, and few doctorate degrees were awarded in chemical engineering. These usually required about three years after the baccalaureate for completion.

The purpose of the bachelor's degree in those days was to prepare students for industrial work; the doctorate, for research and teaching. There were a few universities that had a good M.S. program, such as MIT, which featured then, as now, its Practice School, and also prepared students for industrial careers. The cost of research and teaching was borne by the university from tuition and general funds; the professors earned extra income by consulting for industry. In the 1930s, at least, industry contributed little to academic research.

Only a Partial Resemblance Left

Today's undergraduate curriculum bears only a partial resemblance to that of the 1930s. Gone are virtually all the required courses in other engineering branches. Gone is the four year chemistry concentration. Gone

Paper presented to a seminar on the future of chemical engineering at the Massachusetts Institute of Technology on April 4, 1976. Published in *Chemical Engineering Progress* 72, no. 8 (August 1976): 13–16. Reproduced with permission of the American Institute of Chemical Engineers © 1976 AIChE. All rights reserved.

from many departments is the unit operations laboratory, where a large number of practicing chemical engineers first got the "feel" of the engineering side of their profession. In their place one finds a far wider choice of electives including the humanities, computer science, and additional chemical engineering subjects such as transport processes, kinetics, thermodynamics, polymers, surface and colloid chemistry, and the like, most of which were graduate courses in the old days. It is clear that such a curriculum is both more substantive in the content of the courses taken, and more limited in the lack of broad engineering and laboratory studies than the earlier curricula. As a result, there is increasing doubt that today's four year curriculum is sufficient. Much debate has centered on whether a fifth year leading to the master's degree should be considered a necessary prerequisite for the first professional degree. Several programs of this kind, which prepare chemical engineers for a variety of careers in industry (where more than 80 percent of all Ch.E. graduates are employed) have already been established. Research is still not the major emphasis in such a master's curriculum, although it is an important part. There are, at some universities, cooperative courses for chemical engineering study that provide an opportunity to work in industry. There are also a few industry-university programs such as those in the area of process design.

Industry probably does a great deal more on-the-job training than heretofore, because even the five year M.S. program is lacking in certain essential respects. I have the strong impression that training by industry takes longer all the time, due partly to the deficiencies in academic programs, and partly to the greater sophistication required in industry. Of course, industry is a great deal more technically advanced than it was forty years ago, with a much wider sphere of activities, so that the education of its new recruits must of necessity adhere more to certain fundamentals.

Many chemical engineering faculties have claimed to notice, over the years, a decline in the average quality of the student body. To whatever extent this was a real trend, it can be traced to competition for the brightest students among many more disciplines than were ever imagined in the 1930s, for example, aerospace, computers, electronics, oceanography, biological and medical sciences, etc. There is probably a relatively small fixed percent of the student population that stands at the top of the distribution curve for ability in mathematics and science, and these have simply been partitioned among many more fields, some of them much more glamorous than chemical engineering. Certain of the curricula alterations can thus be attributed to changing enrollment trends and student desires.

Now there is evidence of a return to chemical engineering, both in numbers and quality. The reasons for this development are no doubt related to students' perceptions of job opportunities in the new glamor fields. After all, by contrast, chemical engineers have had a remarkable record for stability of employment. But another reason surely is the growing interest in the areas of energy and environmental problems. I find this a healthy trend. We can teach the broad principles of chemical engineering with many different types of problems, and still retain the students' interest. The important thing is to maintain the breadth of teaching the fundamentals so that we graduate *chemical engineers* suitable for employment in all kinds of jobs, and not a scattering of narrow specialists like biomedical engineers, enzyme engineers, polymer engineers, etc., who will find themselves with limited job opportunities.

Another Force Pulling on the Faculties

Today we can discern another force that is tending to pull faculties of chemical engineering into just such specialized areas, at least as far as their research interests are concerned. I refer to the major change that has taken place due to the great emphasis placed by many universities on the doctoral program, and its consequences. Of those schools that train the largest number of graduate chemical engineers, such as California, Minnesota, Wisconsin, Delaware, Stanford, etc., only MIT is unique in that it graduates a high percentage of M.S. degrees compared to doctorates (of the order of four to one). The fundamental reason for the tremendous growth in doctoral enrollment was the funding of academic research by government that started in the 1950s and expanded steadily until the late 1960s. This not only included research grants directly to the professor of faculty member; it also resulted in large numbers of fellowships, student grants-in-aid, etc. Most of the students who obtained doctor's degrees during this time stayed on at the university with the confident expectation that their careers would be a continuation of these developments, in an ever-expanding universe of education and research. The time to receive the doctor's degree lengthened greatly (to about five years now), but many of the later postwar students were married, and life in university research was thus very agreeable. The ties between faculty and industry, which were basic in the pre-war era, began to loosen, and students were increasingly taught by faculty who had themselves only limited industrial experience, and whose research interests spread into many specialized areas in order to attract government funding.

As we all know, the bubble burst a few years ago, but the basic landscape of the university seems to have been permanently changed, in that government-funded research is still the principal source of support for faculty and doctoral research programs which, in turn, now dominate the attention of most faculties because of the growth I mentioned previously. Meanwhile, all universities, particularly the private ones, are feeling the pinch of adversity in their general budgets, so that there is little extra money available for the teaching as distinguished from research activities. Most universities, public and private, are out trying to raise massive sums of capital.[1] Yet, it is the teaching activity that was the original purpose of a university and that prepares the great majority of graduates who find their careers in industry. In essence, many universities are now running two separate businesses, one, that of traditional education, the other, that of sponsored research. It is true that the research approach is an excellent way to prepare students for the creative solution of original problems in contrast to cook book education. Our own company has a high proportion of Ph.D. chemical engineers relative to most companies, and after a period of training they have worked out very well. But this may not be valid for every type of company.

Universities Should Hold No Illusions

Unfortunately, advanced education by research is very expensive and time consuming, and has, as noted above, been funded almost entirely by the government. Tuition alone pays less than half the costs of educating a student in this fashion, and as fees inexorably rise, many segments of our society find themselves priced out of doctoral programs.

Larger student and research grants are thus needed. There is no real prospect, in my opinion, that this squeeze will ever end. In fact, it is possible that it may get worse. People of diverse political viewpoints are now asking what specific value is obtained from tax dollars invested in academic research. The British House of Common's Select Committee on Science and Technology has just filed a report on this subject, in which it states, "We are deeply disturbed about the effectiveness of the universities' present contribution to the national scientific effort." While we in the U.S. do not feel so strongly, particularly about certain branches of learning, the question may well be asked of a department such as chemical engineering. As *The Economist* magazine said in commenting on the House of Commons report, "Universities should hold no illusions. For the most part, industry gets along without their reasearch."[2] I think this may be largely true also

in the U.S. It is a most unfortunate fact, because if there were closer association between industry and academia, who knows what major advances
would be possible that are otherwise lost forever, or delayed for a long
time? At any rate, what will happen if politicians, struggling to allocate
priorities among conflicting groups in our society, decide to reduce academic research as being irrelevant to the common weal?

Thus, one of the major consequences of government domination of
university research has been the pull it exerts on the faculties' interests.
Whereas industry seeks students who are well and broadly trained in fundamentals, faculties are compelled to develop a variety of specializations
that will be attractive to those who hold the government's purse strings.
There results a basic conflict between the needs of the university and those
of the faculty, and the demands of industry on engineering graduates. Of
course, much work in traditional and basic chemical engineering research
continues, and I am speaking only of shifts in pattern, not absolutes. Indeed, the appearance of the Energy Research and Development Administration, and its ambitious plans to fund many new programs at universities,
may not only reverse government spending patterns, but bring back much
needed attention to "traditional" chemical engineering.

Ratings Depend on Research Work

Still another consequence of these developments has been that the standing
of various faculties of chemical engineering … depends almost entirely on
the perceived quality of the Ph.D. research work performed by that faculty,
and not at all on the excellence of the teaching or the suitability of the
graduates for industry. Thus, a school such as Manhattan College may
specialize in training process engineers for the large industrial requirement
in the New York area and contribute a very useful service to society, but
its rating doesn't compare with that, say, of Minnesota. And, unfortunately, these ratings, which increasingly seem to outside eyes to be self-
serving, are important—for fund raising, for attracting able faculty, and for
attracting superior graduate students. We can see, therefore, the origins of
the typical recycle process so familiar to chemical engineers, whereby research has come to dominate many aspects of chemical engineering education. And again, let me echo *The Economist*: industry, by and large, can get
by quite adequately without much of such university research, although
this doesn't necessarily represent an optimization of society's goals and
accomplishments. It is pertinent to note, however, that some companies are
more sophisticated than others with regard to their in-house capabilities, so

that this observation needs to be a qualified one. But, basically, industry needs the good, well-trained students, and it will seek them out regardless of the college from which they come.

This is the fundamental trilemma I see for the future of chemical engineering; the change in relationship between industry, government, and academia. How it is handled and evolves will surely have a major impact on our profession during the rest of this century. Industry and private money must provide funds by the millions for bricks, mortar, and equipment, endowed professorships, etc., because government will not do so. In return, industry expects an increasing attention to its requirements in the future education of chemical engineers. But, on the other hand, the increase in the budget required to take advantage of such facilities will come (it is hoped) almost entirely from government-sponsored research! And still industry will take at least the same overwhelming proportion of the graduates as before! This three-legged stool may, contrary to simple geometry, be a prescription for instability, especially if one leg is cut off!

The Situation Bears Watching

It should be stated clearly that I do not foresee an imminent crisis—short of another economic catastrophe in this country. But the situation bears watching, and careful consideration of alternatives. I have previously made specific recommendations regarding changes that would be desirable in the university so that chemical engineering education could better relate to its primary customer, the private industrial sector.[3] I especially expressed concern about the often over-theoretical nature of modern chemical engineering training, the great difference between research practiced in industry and that required for the Ph.D., and the lack of real teaching in the economic aspects of chemical engineering practice, such as process design and cost evaluation. Here, I want rather to give some broad philosophical observations, based on my thirty-five years of industrial experience both as a chemical engineer and employer of chemical engineers, as well as my membership on the MIT Corp. where, as a trustee, I am privileged to see the broad university scene. And as a Councillor and Executive Committee member of the National Academy of Engineering, I have access to the atmosphere of government. From these vantage points I urge continuous rethinking both of the curriculum and the faculty in the departments of chemical engineering. It would be ideal if there were less dependence on government, but industry is not likely to take up all of the slack. All three legs of the stool are needed, but in my opinion industry can help more than it is doing so far.

For example, the Practice School is not really doing as well as it should because of the absence of modest grants from industry both to the stations and the students. I think such additional participation by industry can and should be found. My organization believes that collaborative research programs with some universities, based on a careful division of labor and patent rights, can be quite promising for the development of advanced industrial technologies. We consider that one year "academics in industry" fellowships, under appropriate secrecy agreements, are an important tool to bring the industrial viewpoint back to the campus, and vice versa. We are interested in pursuing this avenue in the future.

Many departments of chemical engineering favor summer work in industry for faculty members as a technique for the improvement of university-industrial relations, but the realities have shown that this type of work will not really accomplish the purpose: the time involved is too short, and the resulting tasks too untypical of the true industrial practices of today. We believe in visiting professors and lecturers from industry to the university, and we have long sustained fellowships in several departments. Many companies do likewise, but there is need for more.

New Industry/Academia Arrangements

There must also be a heightened receptivity by the university to new arrangements with industry, and faculties must orient themselves more toward actual industrial chemical engineering practice. Some of these new arrangements can be for novel types of curricula such as those being instituted by the Univ. of Pennsylvania, where it will soon be possible for an undergraduate to obtain two bachelor's degrees, one in applied science and the other in economics, after a four year program at the Engineering School and the Wharton School. Another variant is a five and one-half year program leading to the B.S. in engineering and the M.B.A. Industry very much requires this type of combined training in engineering and business, and the future for such graduates is bright; unfortunately, there isn't much government money associated with this type of curriculum. At MIT the visiting committee to the Dept. of Chemical Engineering has recommended, and the School of Engineering has agreed, that there be established a Dr. Eng. (or perhaps Dr. Engineering and Business) degree (without a thesis) that would permit a student to obtain the equivalent of the M.B.A. degree from the Sloan School of Business as well as that of an advanced engineering program, such as in process design. Some other universities like California and Dartmouth are also trying such an approach. But this concept still basically remains to be implemented in the future, because, again, of financial problems caused by lack of general funds, and industry needs to work out ways of assisting in the interest of obtaining graduates truly suited to the changing and more intense demands of chemical engineering practice.

There are other types of combined programs that are possible and currently offered, but what I am emphasizing is the need for universities to study their markets more carefully. The solution does not lie, broadly speaking, in turning out more researchers, or more teachers. The trends against these opportunities for employment are unmistakable, particularly in view of the declining college enrollments foreseen in the 1980s.

I have mentioned MIT's visiting committee system. There are some other universities which have long had similar committees, but most either do not, or have only just recently commenced. AIChE [American Institute of Chemical Engineers] recently received a study indicating, among other steps, the advisability for all chemical engineering departments to set up some such outside review board, so as to strengthen the link between industry and academia.

The future of chemical engineering is in the hands of industry and the university. Government plays a supportive but in some ways disruptive role—possibly more so in the future. Let us try to manage our situation in the most constructive manner possible, without closing our eyes to the true nature of our trilemma.

Literature Cited

1. *The Wall Street J.*, p. 16 (December 29, 1975).

2. *The Economist*, p. 15 (January 31, 1976).

3. Landau, R., *Chem. Eng. Progr.*, 68, p. 9 (June, 1972).

13

The Chemical Engineer and the CPI: Reading the Future from the Past

In an address at a symposium to celebrate the one-hundredth anniversary of the first curriculum in chemical engineering at the Massachusetts Institute of Technology, I traced the rise of modern chemical engineering and its intimate association between the university and industry at various critical periods of U.S. history, in particular, the rise of the petroleum refining industry that facilitated its evolution.

A major theme in this backward look was that the chemical engineering discipline always focused much of its effort on solving real-world problems. This has led the profession to emphasize the design of continuous automated processes for the production of a wide variety of products. Chemical engineers, unlike professionals in most other engineering disciplines, are trained to consider entire production systems and, thus, are encouraged to discover cheaper and better production methods. An institutional feature of this development was the flourishing of a number of process engineering design firms, which became powerful sources that supplied many firms with the latest techniques for applying basic principles to everything from small-scale experimentation to large-scale plant design and construction. Thus, the predominant American chemical engineering discipline was in place when World War II ended, and it helped to propel the American chemical process industries to a leading position. This article seeks to peer into the future by reviewing the past.

[T]he chemical process industries ... flourished, especially during the first twenty years after the war. There was a lack of pervasive intrusion by government, which fostered a stable economic climate and aided overseas

Paper presented at the Centennial Celebration of the Chemical Engineering Department, Massachusetts Institute of Technology, October 8, 1988. Adaptation published in *Chemical Engineering Progress* (September 1989): 25–39. Reproduced with permission of the American Institute of Chemical Engineers. © 1989 AIChE. All rights reserved.

countries struggling to recover from the war's devastation. Regulatory policies were mostly economic survivors of the prewar era [e.g., the Securities and Exchange Commission (SEC)]. The tort law system was also far from the level of litigation experienced today, and product liability and toxic waste questions were low key. The chemical trade balance remained (and remains) positive; a result of, as we shall see, a combination of innovation, plant scale, the best chemical engineering, favorable raw materials, some tariff protection, international presence, and sheer competitive need.

Although profits of U.S. chemical producers grew rapidly into the mid-1950s, so did those of other basic industries. By 1955, chemical equities sold at a 70 percent premium to the U.S. market, based on cash flow and research productivity concepts. I owe my information on the financial performance of the chemical industry largely to Edward M. Giles of Peter S. Cannel & Co., in my opinion the most astute observer of the industry. By the early 1960s, however, the exuberant expansion of the industry, supported by all of the favorable factors previously described, led to overbuilding and some overcapacity.

Nevertheless, the earnings of the industry grew about as fast as all manufacturing up until 1966, but balance sheets were deteriorating. There was no premium for chemical stocks by 1966. The signs of growing competitive pressure, both domestic and international, were unmistakable. Also, the entrepreneurially minded employees who came out of the extraordinary talent pool of the war years with rich experience and contacts entered into various existing companies and stimulated their creativity. But as the scale of operations became bigger and the financial stakes grew, entrepreneurial risk taking began to lose its allure. Greater bureaucracy also entered into the picture to change the "can-do" atmosphere of the two decades following the war. Inevitably, there was a greater temptation to imitate others.

Unlike electronics and computers, where many small companies did a great deal of the innovating, their chemical counterparts did little (except in end-use firms, such as plastic fabricators). Entry costs were becoming too high, especially as the petroleum company surge into chemicals focused attention on large-scale, more commodity-type chemicals and resources. This moved the industry away from markets and higher value-added products.

Large companies must make special efforts to become skilled at differentiated products. Nevertheless, the chemical industry did maintain itself in the face of the challenges that will be described. In many ways, entrepreneurship flourished in the process-design companies. In two recent articles, I described how the firm I cofounded developed and responded to the challenges of the times, and told of the lessons we learned.[1,2]

It was with this benign postwar climate in America that many new companies, product lines, and processes appeared. The modern petrochemical industry would be inconceivable without the many developments that were fundamentally American. They spread rapidly around the world to make petroleum and other hydrocarbon feedstocks the irreversible prime raw material source for the chemical industry. The dominance of American chemical engineering was never more proudly displayed than in this triumph. This opened the door, however, to many new and vigorous foreign competitors. Coupled with numerous changes in the world economic climate that were signaled by the arrival of the Vietnam War, the Great Society, and the baby boom, the road was clear for a major shift in the environment for the United States and, of course, the chemical process industries.

The Turbulent Period, 1966–1981

Although difficult to detect in the beginning, the decline in the improvement of America's annual productivity began around 1966; by 1973 it had collapsed to virtually nothing. This was a very important change because productivity improvement is the measure of the increase in the standard of living per person in an economy. During the 100 years after the Civil War, the average real productivity increase per capita was slightly below 2 percent, which enabled standards of living to nearly double every generation. Such is the power of compounding. The merchandise trade balance also started to deteriorate, so that by 1972 the balance became negative in real (inflation-adjusted) terms, although the nominal trade balance, because of rapidly rising prices, did not sink into the red until 1981.

Only three of the research-intensive industries shown in figures 13.1 and 13.2 have had consistent positive trade balances: aerospace, chemicals, and the considerably smaller scientific apparatus. Others were affected early, especially petroleum after the 1973 oil shock.

American competitiveness in world markets had begun a long-term erosion. What began to appear in macroeconomic policy might well be called "Vietnamics," and it had powerful, lasting effects on the world economy.

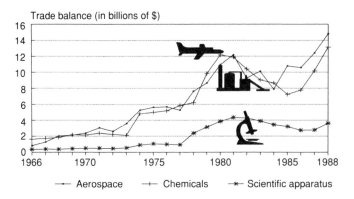

Figure 13.1
U.S. industries with heavy R&D and positive trade balances. Source: U.S. Census Bureau.

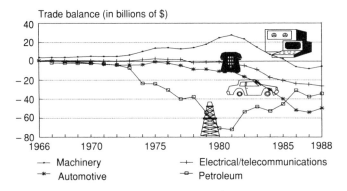

Figure 13.2
U.S. industries with heavy R&D and negative trade balances. Source: U.S. Census Bureau.

• There was great demand overstimulation featuring loose fiscal and monetary policies; inflation and interest rates consequently rose, escalating globally throughout this period. Lyndon Johnson preferred to finance the Vietnam War in part by creating debt rather than by tightening civilian consumption. A structural budget deficit resulted.

• The value of the dollar declined sharply in the early 1970s, and the United States abandoned the Bretton Woods regime of fixed monetary exchange rates.

• Net savings declined, but, aided by tax incentives, gross investment rose slightly. A significant proportion of the savings pool, however, went into residential and commercial construction as investors fled from financial to real assets. These types of investments contributed little to productivity or international competitiveness. The cost of capital rose.

• Capital investment per worker declined as the baby boom peaked. No doubt this was a key factor in the decline of productivity gains, which have averaged not even 1 percent per year since 1973 (in the 1980s, there has been some improvement, led by manufacturing). Japan and other countries had two to three times as much annual capital investment per employed person, with resulting high productivity gains. The United States, however, unlike Europe, created a large number of jobs mostly in small companies and the service sector between 1955 and 1987: United States, 50.2 million new jobs; European Economic Community (EEC), 6.6 million new jobs; Japan, 17.2 million new jobs.

• Unemployment, therefore, became high in the EEC, where the baby boom peaked later. The United States absorbed a large number of women, minorities, and so on into the labor force. Developing new jobs became an important part of U.S. economic policy during the later 1960s and the 1970s.

• Two massive oil price increases in 1973 and 1979 approximately quintupled the cost per barrel of crude oil and siphoned enormous wealth out of the industrial world.

• American firms encountered increasing and strong competition from abroad—our strategy for rebuilding a prosperous and stable postwar democratic world had succeeded!

• Increasing environmental regulation and litigation made it necessary for businesses to invest large sums to clean up the excesses of the past, which were now perceived in a different light.

• In contrast to the first two postwar decades (partly because of government policy), economic conditions became very volatile. As a result, the planning horizons for business became almost myopic. This was to have long-range effects on American competitiveness.

• The ravaging effects of the inflation of the 1970s could no longer be tolerated, and by late 1979 Paul Volcker was brought in as chairman of the Federal Reserve Board to subdue it, and he did this by forcing interest rates up and limiting the supply of money. It broke with the sharp recession of 1981–82.

The chemical industry was, of course, strongly affected by these immense climatic changes.

Inflation and the Vietnam War provided a large demand that was misread by many companies (which had been weaned on the postwar stability) as indicating a larger potential market than actually existed. This led to much overbuilding, especially of large "world-scale" plants that each company thought would give the advantages of scale. This trend also forced operation at capacity above demand; because companies could not fully pass on their cost increases, they sought to cover fixed costs by selling full output at distress prices. Profits were subordinated. In addition, they were dismayed by other companies, including newcomers, that rushed in, also with large facilities.

The obsession with the experience curve concept promoted by the Boston Consulting Group, which was correct as far as its assumptions permitted, failed to take into account the enticement of slightly better economics on would-be entrants. Most of the usual incremental process improvements gained from experience were given away to customers in a desperate attempt to retain or gain market shares.

It was almost always impossible to shut down a competitor's plant, except when a truly major development (such as Union Carbide's UNIPOL or Halcon's propylene oxide process) appeared. Continual technical change made full use of the learning experiences impossible, and, in many instances, the expected benefits were postponed indefinitely.

There also was a perception that, during a period of rising inflation, the first company to build a plant would have a capital advantage over latecomers. In addition, the notion of "optimum" scale expanded. This trend was aided by the skills of the engineers involved, who learned how to design and build ever-larger single train plants to extreme design limits. The engineers have been accused of "overselling" this concept because, too often, both the engineers and their managements were willing to go along as it built their own domains. This was, however, only a minor factor in the overbuilding. Much more responsible was the absence of tight linkage with the marketplace and the financial world, a phenomenon understandable in an era of rapid growth.

Changing Conditions

It took years before many companies realized that the ball game had changed. In hindsight, the successful survivors (such as Dow) became the lowest-cost producers in the world and, therefore, world-class competitors. It was not until long after, when market conditions and slow economic growth prevented operations at capacity, that it became evident that somewhat smaller plants operating at full capacity could be more profitable because they could have a higher average load factor over their economic life. Moreover, smaller plants can better adjust to the vicissitudes of economic cycles. In fact, George Hatsopoulos and colleagues have pointed out that U.S. management has invested more than financial considerations alone would have justified in the last fifteen-twenty years or so.[3] Competitive zeal in industries such as chemicals accounted for much of this.

In general, profitability for the chemical industry dropped significantly as shown in figures 13.3 and 13.4. Nevertheless, at least in recent years where data are available, the chemical industry had a higher profit margin than all

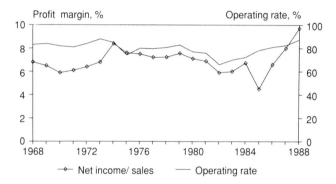

Figure 13.3
Total chemical industry profit margin and operating rate. Source: Chemical Manufacturers Association.

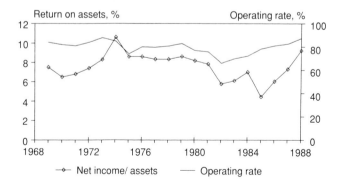

Figure 13.4
Total chemical industry return on assets and operation rate. Source: Chemical Manufacturers Association.

manufacturing companies, despite large, nonrecurring charges during the 1980s, especially in 1985. (The most difficult year for basic chemical producers came in 1982.) A good deal of this is due to the high profit margins in pharmaceuticals (where, however, R&D costs are very high and not all products are easily successful), but it is even true for industrial chemicals.

The oil shocks created panic and resulted in the misallocation of resources. For example, much of the equipment for plants in progress was rendered obsolete even before commercial operation started because energy-efficient designs had not been perceived as necessary. This can also be seen in the increased uncoupling of the gross national product (GNP) growth rate from the growth rate of energy consumption. Between 1950 and 1973, this difference in average compound growth rates for the United States was only -0.72, but from 1973 to 1984 it was -2.24. The chemical industry experienced a similar but even greater adjustment.

Management found financial conditions in an era of rising inflation to be critical to survival. While technologists still were prevalent in the industry (even at the highest levels), MBAs and financial officers also became indispensable. Management also had to deal with increased foreign competition that was facilitated by extensive licensing of technology, which became a significant factor in all markets. Because the U.S. chemical industry enjoyed many of the advantages we have noted previously, the trade balance continued to be positive, as it has to this day.

Entry costs became much greater; now only large companies could play. The oil companies, however, seeking downstream outlets to compensate for the loss of control over crude, realized they had possession of the key raw materials for petrochemicals and moved forcefully into an already crowded and overbuilt arena. Chemical companies integrated backwards, and other resource-based companies (such as paper and steel), lured by higher apparent returns on investment, also moved in. Smaller, entrepreneurial companies, except for specific end-product applications, found entry barriers prohibitive in this capital-intensive industry.

The same pattern occurred in pharmaceuticals. Until Genentech entered with genetically engineered products in the later 1980s, no new pharmaceutical company had been founded since Syntex in 1957. Significant foreign competition was developing, however, and the regulatory process became more active. The American development in pharmaceuticals featured companies specializing in these products, whereas in Europe this was a growing segment of the chemical industry proper.

The early phase of chemical innovation (both product and process, but the dividing line is often difficult to distinguish) occurred during the prewar era when such petroleum-based chemical products as styrene and polystyrene, vinyl chloride and polyvinyl chloride, low-density polyethylene (high pressure), ethylene oxide and glycol (by direct oxidation), alkylamines, and methacrylates were pioneered on a small scale. It was only after the war that immense new markets and large-scale demand produced the great surge in petrochemical development and the need for the design skills of the chemical engineer.

Postwar Technologies

Not only were many new technologies developed during the postwar period, their diffusion throughout the world followed as numerous competitive firms entered the industry. The real impact on growth comes, of course, from the extent of the diffusion, Nevertheless, for individual innovating firms that seek maximum appropriability to justify the risks of innovation, diffusion has a dark side. Some scholars have contended that the industry's innovative urge declined decade by decade. Not only is this factually incorrect, but it fails to recognize the time required for diffusion to take place. The truth is that innovation in chemicals changed in character over time.

Table 13.1 is an updated summary of significant chemical industry innovations from the 1950s onward that I first presented about ten years ago.[4] (Pharmaceuticals have been excluded because they represent a separate success story that requires a discussion of the potential threats of generic drugs and increased regulation.) Table 13.2 lists the important agricultural chemical innovations. In this field, the effect of environmental considerations has been exceptionally strong. Important chlorinated pesticides such as DDT have been phased out, and some of the "newer ones" are likely to be replaced by more environmentally friendly products produced by biotechnological research.

Until the mid-1960s or so, major commercialization was accomplished for important new plastics (polyurethane, high-density polyethylene, polypropylene) and new fibers (polyesters, nylons, acrylics). Each required the building of large, new olefin and aromatic plants so that raw materials could be made at attractive prices. Also, a large segment of the innovations commercialized during this period included significant process improvements for precursors of plastics developed earlier—maleic anhydride, terephthalic aid, cyclohexanol-cyclohexanone mixtures for nylon, vinyl chloride, acrylonitrile, and hexamethylene diamine (HMDA) for nylon. After 1966, the tonnage plastics already in place were extended in properties and compositions, and become more and more differentiated. More sophisticated fibers and plastics such as Kevlar, engineered plastics, and composites

Table 13.1
Major postwar commercial chemical developments

Approximate date	Product	Development	Company
Postwar	Low-pressure polyethylene	Ziegler chemistry	Karl Ziegler
Postwar	Phenol acetone, cumene	Air oxidation	Distellers Co., British Petroleum UK, Hercules
1953	Dimethyl terephthalate	Four-step air oxidation	Imhausen, Hercules
1953 +	Ammonia	High-pressure synthesis gas (large single train)	Pullman/Kellogg
1955	Maleic anhydride	High-yield benzene oxidation	Halcon
1957	Irradiated polyethylene	Memory plastics	Raychem
Through 1957	Isocyanates-urethanes	Urethanes and foams (polyether polyols, one-shot foam, etc.)	Bayer, Houdry, Wyandotte
1958	High-density polyethylene; polypropylene	New catalysts	Montecatini-Natta, Phillips, Avisun, Amoco
1958	α-olefins and linear alcohols	New catalysts	Gulf, Ethyl, Conoco
1958 +	Terephthalic acid	Air oxidation of p-xylene pure product	Halcon, Amoco
1959	Acetaldehyde	Vapor-phase ethylene oxidation	Hoechst/Wacker
1960–70	Oxo alcohols	Improved catalysts	Exxon, ICI, Shell, Union Carbide
1960–70	Acetic acid, etc.	Oxidation of paraffins	Celanese
1960–70	Polycarbonates	Engineered plastics	GE, Bayer
1964	KA (cyclohexanol-cyclohexanone) Oil (for nylon)	Cyclohexane oxidation, boric system	Halcon
1965	Acrylonitrile	Propylene ammoxidation	Sohio
1965	Hexamethylene diamine (HMDA) (for nylon)	Acrylonitrile electrohydrodimerization	Monsanto
1965 +	Vinyl chloride	Oxychlorination of ethylene	Goodrich, Monsanto, PPG, Stauffer
1967 +	Vinyl acetate	Ethylene + acetic + O_2, vapor phase	Bayer, Celanese, Hoechst, USI
1968	Acetic acid	High-pressure methanol + CO	BASF, Du Pont
1969	Phthalic anhydride	High-yield o-xylene oxidation	BASF

Table 13.1 (continued)

Approximate date	Product	Development	Company
1969	Acrylates	Propylene oxidation	BP, Celanese, Rohm & Haas, Sohio, Union Carbide
1969	Polyethylene terephthalate	Plastic bottles	Du Pont
1969	Qiana (now abandoned) fiber	From cyclododecane KA Oil	Du Pont, Halcon
1969 +	Propylene oxide, glycol, TBA	Epoxidation with hydroperoxide	Arco/Halcon
1970	p-Xylene	Recovery by adsorption	UOP
1970	Methanol	Low-pressure $CO + H_2$	ICI
1970	Aniline	Phenol + NH_3	Halcon, Mitsui
~1970	Ethylene oxide	Catalyst improvements	Halcon, Shell, Union Carbide
~1970	Polyphenylene oxide and noryl polymers	Engineered plastics	GE
1972	Hexamethylene diamine (HMDA) (for nylon)	Butadiene + HCN	Du Pont
1972	Styrene and propylene oxide	Epoxidation with hydroperoxide	Arco/Halcon
1973	Acetic acid	Low-pressure methanol + CO	Monsanto
1974	Kevlar	High-tensile fiber	Du Pont, Akzo
1974	Polypropylene	Vapor phase	BASF
1974 +	Maleic anhydride	From butane	Amoco, Halcon, Monsanto, Denka
1977	Linear low-density polyethylene	Lower pressure	Union Carbide, others later
1978	Ethylene glycol (and vinyl acetate) now abandoned)	Via acetoxylation	Halcon/Arco
1980	Acetic anhydride	Coal-based CO + methanol	Halcon, Tennessee Eastman
1981 +	Methacrylates	Isobutane or isobutylene based	Mitsubishi, other Japanese companies, Halcon/Arco (Development)
1985	Polypropylene	Improved catalysts and processing techniques (e.g., catalloy)	Montedison/Himont, Shell, others

Table 13.2
Major postwar commercial chemical developments: pesticides, fungicides, and herbicides

Class	Product example	Introduction	Company
Pesticides			
Phosphorodithioates	Thimet, Malathion	1953	American Cyanamid
Carbamates	Sevin	1956	Union Carbide
Synthetic pyrethroids	Resmethrin	1967	NRDC,* Oxford
Fungicides			
Sulfenimides	Captan	1953	Chevron
Chlorthalonil	Bravo	1965	Diamond Shamrock
Systemic fungicides	Benomyl	1967	Du Pont
Herbicides			
Ureas	Monuron, Diuron	1950	Du Pont
Triazines	Simazine, Atrazine	1955	Ciba-Geigy
Pyridinium salts	Paraquat	1956	ICI
Nitroanilines	Treflan	1960	Eli Lilly
Thiocarbamates	Sutan	1962	Stauffer
Acetanilides	Lasso, Dual	1969	Monsanto, Ciba-Geigy
Glyphosate	Round-up	1974	Monsanto
Sulfonyl ureas	Glean	1983	Du Pont
Imidazolinones	Scepter	1985	American Cyanamid

Source: S. Allen Heininger, Monsanto Co.
*National Research & Development Council, United Kingdom.

began to appear. Additional process developments for precursors of previously commercialized polymers such as ethylene oxide, glycol, and p-xylene also were introduced.

Several of the new processes involved switches in raw materials because the energy price shocks were seen to be permanent. Development such as vinyl acetate from ethylene, acetic acid from carbon monoxide and methanol, acrylates from propylene, HMDA from butadiene, and maleic anhydride from butane are examples. More recently, innovative developments have continued to focus on further product differentiation and adaptation of lower-cost processes for precursors. Some commentators have worried that the last major plastic to be introduced (polypropylene) is now thirty years old. But there are enough basic polymers available; the game today is to develop an infinite variety of finished products by manipulating the process and the product to produce what sophisticated markets demand.

Table 13.1 also shows that the oil companies and process engineering firms did much of the innovating. Their entrance into the chemical industry was not just "me too"; it also involved general participation in the innovative core of the industry. Foreign companies were increasingly active as well, particularly in Europe. All of this points to the vigor of the international technological competition among chemical and oil companies and how companies can develop the ability to commercialize inventions made elsewhere. Virtually all of the products mentioned were very large-tonnage items. This provided an economic basis for innovation and a need for the talents of chemical engineers who were grounded in design and economics. But there was also much new chemistry and close cooperation between chemists and engineers. This approach was found in all of the companies involved in the industry to some degree.

By the end of the 1960s, the poor results accompanying these processes of change (absolutely and relatively) and the depressed earnings of the industry were reflected in the discount to market of chemical equities. During the early 1970s there were signs that the returns on capital had dropped to a level where differentiated producers could support new investment while others (except for oil companies) could not. This suggests growth in market shares, primarily by the industry leaders.

Aside from a short-term boost after the first oil shock of 1973, optimism dropped after 1976 when many companies finally realized that growth in the industry (which had been at least twice that of the GNP) had slowed. Gross margins in the commodities had disappeared, and increases in hydrocarbon prices had a major negative effect on future earnings. Before this perception crystallized, significant new capital unfortunately had been committed to the commodity sectors (partially because of the large-plant syndrome and partially because of the ease of adoption). Many of the judgments about future markets turned out to be in error.

The 1979 oil price increase, while less dramatic, resulted in a significant inventory liquidation in the industry that culminated in a recession. By 1982, many major product sectors earned very little in the United States. In the absence of large new capital investment possibilities, chemical companies turned to increased R&D efforts, a traditional tool in this research-intensive industry. This trend, shown in figure 5, clearly indicates that the funds used for R&D exceeded 50 percent of those spent on capital expenditures for the first time in 1982. Figure 6 reinforces this concept and also illustrates the importance of capital investment in the chemical industry.

The chemical industry has proved to be particularly vulnerable because the public suspected that it generated environmental and toxic hazards. At times, some companies were spending up to 25 percent of their capital on investments to abate these long-standing problems. Inevitably, some innovative activity had to be diverted to these urgent needs and to energy conservation. Young people began to find the industry unattractive, and chemical engineering enrollments began to waver.

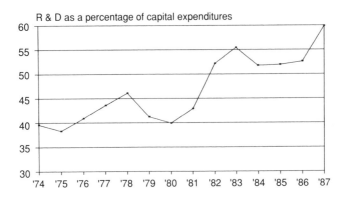

Figure 13.5
Chemical industry R&D vs. capital expenditures.

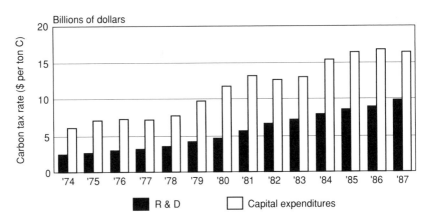

Figure 13.6
Chemical industry R&D vs. capital expenditures. Sources: For R&D, National Science Foundation; for capital expenditures, S. H. Brooks Co., Inc.

One Company's Experience

Obviously, what was happening in the nation and the industry had profound effects on individual companies. In my company (Halcon International), for example, it was apparent by 1963 that opportunities for our
traditional lines of business (licensing) would begin to shrink. With the
discovery of our propylene oxide process, we started a major search for a
partner with whom we could exploit it through self-manufacture. It was
clear that the right partner would be an oil company that lacked good
original technology but had ample technical and financial resources and
was eager to enter the industry. Such a company was found in Arco. We
set up the Oxirane venture in June of 1966 with a commitment to build a
$26 million plant in Houston, TX, largely financed in a creative, novel
way by Arco.[5] Arco also contributed substantial research and market
development.

The U.S. Chemical Industry to 1941

The U.S. chemical industry was founded shortly after the American Revolution by E. I. duPont, who built an explosives plant in Delaware. During the
latter part of the nineteenth century and the early part of the twentieth
century, other companies arose. A largely inorganic chemical industry developed that had a larger dollar volume than the German chemical industry
(more heavily based on dyestuffs and coal tar chemicals).

The First World War showed that the U.S. must become more self-
sufficient in all important chemicals. Major growth took place between the
wars in the number of both companies and products.

As the Depression took hold, a world cartel arose in the major chemicals;
American antitrust laws inhibited American participation. Because there was
no access to the markets, entry costs for new companies were prohibitive.
Innovation tended to be inhibited, but overcapacity was avoided.

The industry was largely based on batch operations; the chemical engineer was not yet perceived as a critical resource. A few companies, particularly Union Carbide, Shell, Dow, and Exxon, ventured into what were the
initial stages of what became the petrochemical industry. How this came
about is well detailed by Peter Spitz.... Here, the need for chemical engineering skills rose sharply as the scale of operations made resorting to
continuous processes necessary, as had occurred previously in the petroleum
refining industry. The techniques and skills developed in the refining industry now would apply to the petrochemical industry. Chemical raw materials
began the epochal shift from coal to petroleum.

But this was to be more than a single plant. By establishing a corporate partnership with a long-range agreement on all kinds of matters, we moved rapidly overseas (to Rotterdam in 1972, to Japan and Spain by the middle of the decade) and built three more U.S. plants by the end of the decade. From a zero market share, we rose to not far from half. New products were also developed, such as Oxinol motor fuel and tertiary butyl peroxide.

This is a graphic illustration that one can establish a dominant position not by copying what others are doing but by striking out boldly with new, patented (although risky) technology. Instead of going to a whole flock of imitators, benefits flow from future exploitation, which stimulates more research and investment by the innovators.

One of the reasons for our success was that we combined the best features of small and large companies. Another was that our technology was so efficient that there were far fewer environmental problems than exist in older plants. Efficient new process technology is often much more benign environmentally.

By 1980, however, the traumatic events in the general economy could not be overcome by our advantages. The prime interest rate in the winter of 1979–80 rose to 21 percent. At that point, our share of the venture's cash flow was going solely to the banks. The time horizon of the management was very short indeed! No one, least of all we, could foresee whether it would get worse.

We therefore decided to sell our share to Arco; we were back to where we were in the early 1960s. The recession of 1981–82, however, imperiled even that, and I sold our company for good in 1982; our interest in Brazil was sold shortly after (as economic conditions deteriorated there as well). Then I turned to academic economics in search of an explanation for the buffetings, which had affected not only my own company but American industry in general.[6,7] Many other companies have also gone through similar major restructurings and transformations.

I do not imply that our efforts were not well rewarded. The return on our R&D efforts for this technology was spectacular, far better than licensing would ever have been. Jeffrey I. Bernstein and M. Ishaq Nadiri have studied the pretax rates of return on R&D and physical capital for five R&D-intensive industries.[8] In four of the five, the gross private rate of return on R&D capital was, on average, 1.5 to 2 times greater than the rate on physical capital (which is an essential follow-up on R&D). Four of the industries had rates of return on R&D of 15–20 percent. In transportation equipment, the two types of returns were essentially equal.

These same authors calculated a social rate of return of R&D that measures the total returns to society as a whole (including items such as spillover effects, which can be significant). These are substantially larger than those attained by any single company and are especially noteworthy in the nonelectrical machinery category, which includes computers, and in scientific instruments. Chemicals come out high—essentially tied with electrical products for third place. Of course, it must be remembered that this industry sells its products mostly to itself and other industries (only 25 percent goes to consumers), so problems in other industries tend to feed back negatively. Nevertheless, research pays! The chemical industry is clearly one of the major players in American innovation and competitiveness.

The handicaps of a broad licensing strategy are a lesson other chemical companies have also been learning. Somewhat surprisingly, Union Carbide's breakthrough in linear low-density polyethylene (the Unipol process) during the late 1970s was widely licensed, and many companies then competed vigorously with Carbide's own production. On the other hand, Arco has taken the Oxirane technology further, doubling its revenues, expanding to France in 1988 (and to Korea by 1990), and holding the dominant position in the marketplace. Similarly, Amoco has also succeeded in dominating the world terephthalic acid market by steady product and process improvements ever since they purchased the basic development from us in 1956. Their improvements include the use of pure terephthalic acid as a direct feedstock to polyester fiber manufacture. These two cases, as well as perhaps Sohio's acrylonitrile process, are good examples of strategic management of technology supported by management involvement at the highest level. Technology is capital of the most expensive kind—equity, and should be invested, not devested. If only RCA had seen this potential when they invented color television rather than relinquishing it cheaply to Japan!

The Present Era: 1981–1989

"Vietnamics" was, more or less inevitably, succeeded by "Reaganomics" in 1981 (although Jimmy Carter had begun the corrective process in 1979). Deflation, not inflation, became the prevailing climate. We are all familiar with this history: the sharp recession of 1981–1982, followed by seven years of uninterrupted growth, some revival of gains in productivity (up to 3.5 percent per year in manufacturing), marginal tax cuts, and growing budget deficits. High real interest rates combined with the need to finance the growing budget deficits, however, created a strong international demand for dollars. The dollar appreciated against the yen and the deutsche mark to a point where many American exports became uncompetitive

Table 13.3
U.S. savings and investments, 1982–87

Percentage of GNP

Year	Gross savings	Net savings	Net foreign investment	Net private domestic investment
1982	17.1	1.6	0.2	1.8
1983	17.3	1.6	1.0	2.9
1984	18.4	4.0	2.6	6.4
1985	17.5	3.1	2.8	5.1
1986	16.2	1.9	3.4	5.1
1987	15.0	1.9	3.5	5.3
1988	13.3	2.9	2.8	5.7

while imports became cheap. The current account deficit grew rapidly after 1981 (and is now at about 3 percent of the GNP), mirroring the inflow of dollars for investment in the United States.

As shown in table 13.3, an even more serious trend arose. American savings and investments both declined—the former for a variety of reasons, such as demographic changes and changing pension plans, the latter because industry was suffering from the overcapacity of the 1970s. The overall trade imbalance and rapid technological change introduced heavy competition for American companies, not only in international markets but also domestically.

Furthermore, U.S. net investment rates were very low compared to those of Japan, Germany, Britain, and France. A majority of domestic investment capital came from abroad—about $140 billion in 1988. By accounting definitions, the current account imbalance is equal to the net investment minus domestic savings. Because net investment is clearly already too low, domestic savings must be raised in order to eliminate the deficits. Productivity has been increased by management practice improvements, but unemployment rose sharply during the early part of the decade, diminishing as the recovery and growth continued. The cost of capital, however, was and is still high.

In summary, the investment and production structure of the U.S. economy has been adjusting to the growing scarcity of savings. As a result, the service sectors, which have lower productivity, are expanding (because they are not sensitive to high interest or exchange rates) while the capital-intensive manufacturing sector is retarded. This trend, if not reversed, is a recipe for a relative decline in living standards.

The era has seen additional growth in litigation, especially in product liability, even though the pace of regulations has slowed and some deregulation has occurred. Public perception of the industry as dangerous and possibly toxic continues to force much research effort and capital into prevention rather than expansion. If not arrested, this trend may seriously affect the future of the industry. Nevertheless, it is only this industry and the profession of chemical engineering that can solve the problems; no one else has the technical expertise. It must remain economically healthy while addressing these issues.

The huge debt created by the government and the private sector moved first into the financial markets, not into the real world of goods and services. This and the tax code that permits interest to be deducted from debt but not dividends on equities are key elements in the rise of junk bonds, corporate takeovers, leveraged buyouts, and other creative financial manipulations that substituted debt for equity. The tax code has also favored increasing the indebtedness by households.

The high cost of capital contributes to short-term horizons everywhere. Although some bad managements *were* driven out, the general atmosphere of fear has also reduced the propensity for taking risks. The new world of international competition and rapid technological change added to the uncertainties for management.

As the dollar weakened by the mid-1980s, exports from the United States improved. Foreign companies, however, were encouraged to buy U.S. assets and companies. The need to limit this and to finance the deficit has led, at least in part, to a government macroeconomic policy that continues to maintain relatively high real interest rates.

Beginning as early as 1976–77 in some cases, chemical companies began to respond to these external pressures. In an age of high energy costs, plant shutdown economics needed to balance supply and demand were no longer related primarily to new process developments but to differential feedstock advantages. The successful survivors needed rapid improvements in their processes and products. High yields were essential for expensive raw materials; and high energy costs necessitated efficient heat conservation. (The new Arco propylene oxide plant in France, for example, operates without an external energy source.)

Because many lacked these advantages, by late 1982 several major chemical company stocks sold at the same absolute level as in 1959! Investors saw these companies as mature commodity manufacturers threatened by new sources of low-cost production (such as Canada and the Middle East). Although understandable, this view underestimated the degree of

---

The War Years: 1941–1946

The United States entered into a crash program to build many new facilities for synthetic rubber, petroleum refining, chemicals, munitions, pharmaceuticals, light metals, and many other products. The massive effort required many companies that normally were competitors to collaborate. Universities were overwhelmed with fast-track trainees, while the pool of undergraduates dried up.

Under U.S. government auspices, much of the know-how and processes were shared. Many new companies undertook chemical manufacturing, and personnel were widely interchanged. Engineering design firms were swamped with orders, participated actively in crash development programs, and became an enormous reservoir of widely experienced chemical design engineers.

Unbeknownst to most, the country engaged in a massive effort to build the atomic bomb. While this had many tremendous impacts, it was also important in demonstrating the versatility of American engineering and development. Most significant to me, as a participant, was that it showed that bringing together the very best talent from many different sources was a powerful process development tool. One of the features of the postwar engineering firms was the extensive movement of personnel into and out of companies. While sometimes disconcerting, it more often brought fresh blood and new insights.

The government sold the newly built plants to many newcomers and competitors of the traditional chemical industry. The GI Bill brought a flood of new students to the universities. At the same time, the European chemical industry lay in ruins, their schools were severely injured, and the prewar cartel had ceased to exist. The chemical industry landscape had permanently changed.

---

change that had already taken place as well as potential future developments. Even in the trough year of 1982, while many major product areas were unprofitable, the differentiated (specialty) businesses of some companies contributed a large share of the profits. These businesses, however, accounted for only a small fraction of their sales and assets.

Productivity, Demand, and Cash Flow

As shown in Figure 13.7, productivity in the chemical industry was also improving.[9] The multifactor productivity index in figure 13.7 measures the productivity of both labor and capital. From 1960 to 1967, this productiv-

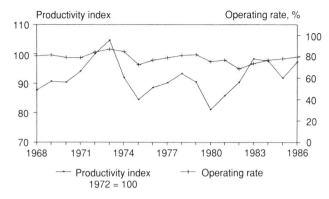

Figure 13.7
Total chemical industry productivity index and operating rate. Source: S. H. Brooks Co., Inc.

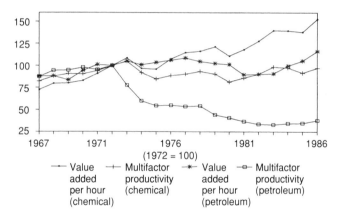

Figure 13.8
Productivity index comparisons, chemical and petroleum industries. Source: S. H. Brooks Co., Inc.

ity increased at an annual rate of 3.4 percent; it then increased to 4.4 percent until 1973, after which it generally declined until the 1980s. Industry's restructuring resulted in emphasizing its lack of labor intensiveness, a reflection of the largely automated plants in the chemical industry. Its total employment (which had reached almost 900,000 by 1970) remained at slightly over 1 million for ten years. During that time, total sales nearly doubled.

In real terms, labor productivity, as shown in figure 13.8 (represented by value added per hour), was essentially flat from 1973 to 1981 but has been

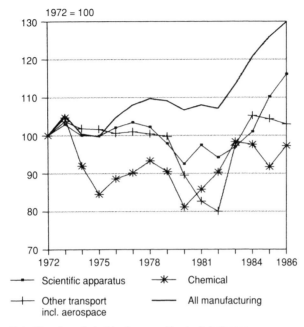

Note: The above industries have positive trade balances.

Figure 13.9
Productivity indexes of U.S. industries with heavy R&D. Source: S. H. Brooks Co., Inc.

improving rapidly. The chemical and petrochemical industries are relatively immune to the inadequately educated workforce problems experienced by more labor-intensive industries. Because the multifactor productivity in real terms has been essentially flat, however, it is clear that the chemical industry's capital productivity is not satisfactory. This shows how essential capacity utilization is for the chemical industry; it is even more crucial for the petroleum industry.

Furthermore, other industries, as shown in figures 13.9 and 13.10, have shown greater productivity improvements. This is especially true for machinery (computer), electrical, and scientific instruments. These are rapidly growing industries that were based on new technology. Chemicals had gone through such a phase earlier. As a result, all manufacturing also showed significant improvements in productivity.

When a better demand environment appeared in 1983, the net result of this series of constructive changes was a rapid buildup of cash flow. In

1972 = 100

Machinery
Electrical
& telecommunications
Automotive
Petroleum
All manufacturing

Note: The above industries have negative trade balances.

Figure 13.10
Productivity indexes of other U.S. industries with heavy R&D. Source: S. H. Brooks Co., Inc.

1984–85, while American manufacturing was still struggling against powerful overseas competitors and the strong dollar, the chemical industry's growth slowed as its customers suffered. But from 1986 on, there has been a buildup in cash flow. The chemical industry is benefiting from lower oil prices, a weaker dollar, and growth in the world economy.

Cash flow has been used in various ways: to buy back stock in order to raise stock prices; to expand into new areas that promise future growth; for increased related R&D expenditures; for capital investment in modernization and rationalization of major commodity manufacturers; and, finally, for some new capacity in certain sectors such as plastics. Commodity plants have not become obsolete even though companies seem to seek out specialties. In fact, the chemical industry today combines a large commodity-based, capital-intensive substructure with a proprietary product-based overlay.

While pharmaceuticals are almost all proprietary products (except for generics), the chemical industry as a whole is also made up of manufacturers of olefins, aromatics, methanol, various intermediates, and inorganics. These businesses require skills that are different from those needed for proprietary products, but it is the *combination* of skills that the best-managed companies have attained. This close association is found in parts of the polymers and fibers industries, some major organics, and inorganics. It is these skills that define the competitive companies of the future. In many ways, we are now truly in a "financial golden age" of American chemical manufacture.

But there may be bumps ahead. Has the restructuring process of the late 1970s and the 1980s, necessary though it was, gone too far and compromised many companies as they enter the global competition of the 1990s? Perhaps the pendulum has swung too far. Perhaps the R&D commitments of today are still not enough to compete with the giant European companies (which are 30–50 percent larger than even our largest). They are increasing their R&D more than we, in part because of the longer time horizon permitted by their macroeconomic environment. The stock market still hesitates to give the chemical industry the price/earnings multiples of more pedestrian companies. Perhaps this is because of the concerns given previously; perhaps it also due to the industry's complexity and difficult-to-understand technologies. In addition, there is concern over various potential legal and regulatory liabilities discussed previously. These (and our unique accounting practices) impose special penalties on innovative American companies.

Few industries are as thoroughly pervaded by strategic and tactical issues involving product, geographic and customer diversification, forward and backward integration, technology, advances, economic and noneconomic competitors, international financial structure, environment and safety questions, capital, marketing, and research intensity as the chemical industry. As a high-tech industry, chemicals support what is probably the world's largest privately financed research and development budget. The current R&D expenditures for a number of industries and the extent of private funding are shown in table 13.4. Obviously, R&D alone is not enough to account for a positive trade balance. Industries that are successful in international trade must have several favorable factors going for them.

The relative importance of each industry with respect to the overall manufacturing sector is shown in figure 13.11. Chemicals, machinery, and

Table 13.4
Major R&D investment industries (more than $1 billion), 1989 estimates*

Industry	R&D Expenditures (billions of dollars)	How financed
Aerospace	19.16	82% government
Electrical machinery and communications	18.55	57% industry
Machinery	12.13	86% industry
Chemicals	11.52	97% industry
Automobiles, trucks, transportation equipment	11.41	83% industry
Professional and scientific instruments	6.52	85% industry
Petroleum products	2.09	99% industry
Rubber products	1.24	75% industry
Food and beverages	1.17	100% industry
Total	83.79	

*Total U.S. R&D is estimated at $129.2 billion, of which all industrial R&D is $92.7 billion (67% comes from companies and the rest from government); the industries given here, therefore, represent the bulk of the investors in R&D. Source: Battelle Memorial Institute.

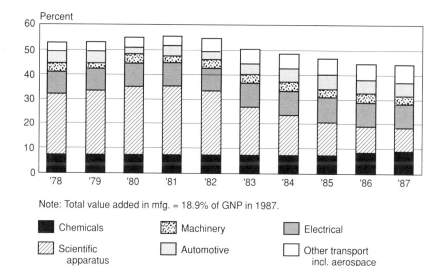

Note: Total value added in mfg. = 18.9% of GNP in 1987.

■ Chemicals   ▨ Machinery   ▨ Electrical
▨ Scientific apparatus   □ Automotive   □ Other transport incl. aerospace

Figure 13.11
U.S. industries with heavy R&D, percentage of total value added in manufacturing. Source: S. H. Brooks Co., Inc.

Table 13.5
Value added per employee (thousands of 1982 dollars)

Year	Chemical	Machinery	Electrical, telecommunications	Automotive	Scientific apparatus	Other transport including aerospace	Petroleum
1967	29.6	27.9	17.6	36.2	22.7	33.4	117.3
1968	32.7	28.1	18.3	41.4	23.8	33.8	118.0
1969	33.0	28.4	19.1	39.6	25.7	32.3	111.3
1970	34.1	29.1	18.7	33.2	23.5	33.4	127.3
1971	37.3	29.8	20.2	42.7	25.4	34.8	135.5
1972	41.3	32.4	21.8	44.1	27.2	35.4	133.9
1973	45.0	33.4	22.6	46.8	27.5	35.5	139.7
1974	39.7	32.0	21.0	40.7	28.0	37.2	132.8
1975	38.9	31.6	22.4	43.4	29.9	37.4	134.2
1976	44.0	33.3	23.7	51.8	30.1	35.6	139.9
1977	47.3	34.1	26.7	55.5	31.3	35.0	146.0
1978	48.1	34.3	28.4	54.6	31.8	36.0	143.3
1979	50.1	34.0	28.7	48.2	33.2	34.8	141.0
1980	45.5	34.5	30.2	42.4	31.4	34.9	132.2
1981	48.6	35.9	30.9	42.7	33.2	30.3	121.4
1982	51.7	36.2	31.1	42.0	32.1	31.5	124.5
1983	57.5	43.5	33.2	51.4	33.9	39.4	125.7
1984	57.9	53.0	35.5	56.6	36.3	41.0	136.6
1985	57.3	62.5	36.8	58.4	34.9	40.0	143.1
1986	63.5	73.0	38.3	52.0	36.5	41.5	160.4
1987	68.3	81.1	40.1	47.6	37.1	42.5	166.3

electrical are the "big three" with, respectively, 9, 9.5, and 10 percent of total value added (the manufacturing sector constitutes about 18.9 percent of the value added of the total output of the United States). How the relative size of value added for chemicals has increased since 1978 is also noteworthy.

The value added per employee for the industries shown in figure 13.11 is given in table 13.5. Despite continual real cost reductions and the passing on of many of the benefits to consumers, the per capita contribution to the economy of chemicals ranks above all others except petroleum and machinery. The value for petroleum reflects oil price increases and large volumes of relatively few products, but these factors produce low profit ratios. That for machinery reflects the rise of the computer industry. Every industry is different and generalizations must be made cautiously.

The rapidly changing quality of many of the chemical industry's products (such as fibers and plastics) is not reflected in the conventional expressions of productivity. Certainly, many fibers and plastic consumer products today are much better than they were, and now include recyclable and biodegradable products but, in the final analysis, it is profitability and international competitive positions that really reflect the health of the industry. The chemical business is adaptive and, if it adjusts successfully to the many new technologies and markets it faces, could become the world's leading industry in the 1990s. Indeed, if crude oil remains below $20/bbl., chemical growth rates may be at least one-and-a-half times that of the GNP.

At present, certainly, the U.S. chemical industry is relatively strong and can succeed even at somewhat higher values for the dollar relative to other currencies. The trade balance indicates this because production is close to 100 percent of realistic capacity levels. Nevertheless, the rapid pace of global technology requires the replacement of obsolete facilities. For example, apparently half of the world's polypropylene capacity is technically obsolete. This polymer was virtually a commodity for thirty years, but it has now entered the stage of high value-added differentiated products and requires new plant facilities. This is an illustration of the change from the "assembly-line" mode of production (typical of commodity chemicals and much of American industry) to a tailor-made product.

Foreign Investment

Although the industry is quite international in its positions, it missed an opportunity while the dollar was even stronger in the early 1980s to buy

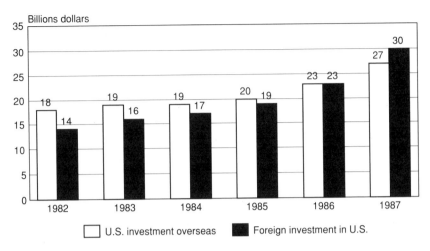

Figure 13.12
U.S. chemical industry, international direct investment. Source: Chemical Manufacturers Association.

or build more assets in foreign markets. Within the past decade, in fact, there has been a substantial divestiture of overseas businesses that were established years earlier as companies realized that they had insufficient resources to maintain a leading position in all their markets. Now the flow is the other way, and foreign companies are buying American chemical companies. In the past three years, approximately one-third of foreign investment in manufacturing in the United States has gone into the chemical industry. Recent trends in overseas investments in the chemical industry are shown in figure 13.12. It is estimated that perhaps 25 percent of the industry is in foreign hands—more than most others, and, in an ironic sense, a tribute to the very success of this industry. This is a warning of the potential structural vulnerabilities we have discussed.

Foreign large buyers may indeed raise their ownership of America's industry to a much higher level. It may well be that some mergers will occur in the chemical industry as a result of fending off such takeovers. Some of our chemical companies are too small to stay in the race. One should take the fact that the U.S. dyestuffs industry is now nearly 100 percent foreign owned as a cautionary note. American companies did not back this area with a sufficient amount of R&D. In an era of limited resources, companies have rationalized their businesses to optimize growth potential.

Overseas earnings for U.S. chemical companies are, nevertheless, still very significant. The 1987 remission of payments from abroad ($2 billion) represented about 13 percent of U.S. chemical company profits. In the chemical industry we see the same pattern as for other U.S. industries. American companies really prefer to grow abroad by reinvesting earnings rather than by acquisitions. In an era of volatile external conditions, the real protection for a company lies in diversification, especially into higher val-ue-added differentiated products and globalization. This is particularly true now that American companies no longer enjoy feedstock advantages. And as the economies abroad recovered during the mid-1980s, so did American foreign reinvestment. In fact, American investment abroad continues to rise at a rate greater than foreign investment in the United States. Chemicals show a slight trend in the other direction, but it is not great. U.S. multina-tional companies account for 75 percent of our merchandise exports and for about 45 percent of our imports. Hence, the recent rise in domestic investment suggests a significant multiplier effect on domestic output and trade.

Despite its technical and business accomplishments (which are immense), the chemical industry over the past thirty years has not been able to establish *sustained* high profitability. Because much of the industry cannot integrate backwards economically to control the cost and supply of the raw materials, it clearly must integrate forward by using advanced technology. This may be the price for remaining such a competitive industry.

And what of the process design firms? Obviously, the problems of the industry were bad news for most of them. The chemical companies are doing their own modernizations. My company Halcon (now Scientific De-sign Co.), for example, shrank rapidly but still exists with limited horizons as a subsidiary of the German Linde Co. There may be a real shortage of experienced design and construction supplies in the future as a result of the heavy attrition of the past.[10]

The entrepreneurial new company has virtually ceased to exist in the chemical industry. Gordon Cain and Jon Huntsman have shown how to use economic conditions to salvage many of the commodity chemical plants that no longer appealed to their owners during restructuring. At the right time, a leveraged buyout worked wonders in improving efficiency.

Others, like Alexander Giacco of Himont, restructured and refocused their growth areas in a relatively unbureaucratic organization controlled by a patient foreign stockholder. They are concentrating on a stream of new technology developments as they move to valuable differentiated poly-mers. The chemical industry will face few new strong entrants in the future, such as Paul Cook's Raychem, which has built a high value-added business since the 1950s. There is always an opportunity for entrepreneurial

The Stable Decades—Innovation and Entrepreneurship: 1946–1966

There was a large, pent-up domestic demand that came from the restrictions of the war years; this led to a requirement for large plants and a need for reconstruction abroad. The United States, the only major center of undamaged and new industrial facilities, was the financial powerhouse of the world. It faced relatively little competition from abroad, either in products or in finance. Many companies established operations overseas and became international in strategy.

The experiences of the Depression and the war years led the U.S. government to maintain, on average (except for the immediate postwar years), a low-inflation, low-interest economy with a low cost of capital. Annual output gains were higher than ever, averaging 3.5 percent per year of the real gross domestic product. Marginal tax rates were high, but, because of various "loopholes," corporate profits after taxes were acceptable in an era of high demand. Capital gains tax rates were low, which helped some entrepreneurs find financing. The venture capital industry as we know it today as well as the new issues market was inconsequential, so individuals could not easily form small, technologically based companies.

Technology moved rapidly around the world, through investments and process licensing and design (frequently by American engineering companies, but also by manufacturing firms that earned additional returns on their investment and by equipment manufacturing firms.) Processes for olefins and aromatics production were pioneered by engineering firms, as were many organic chemical processes utilized for plastics, fibers, and synthetic rubber. European inventions (such as polyethylene, polypropylene, and polyester fibers) were adopted not only in the United States but elsewhere.

Pharmaceuticals experienced a major expansion, but engineering design was not at first a key ingredient of commercial success because the scale of production was relatively small and process economics were subordinated to marketing, research, and regulatory costs.

companies, which have enough funding but are not too large, to avoid becoming bureaucratic and become truly innovative. John Welch, for example, seized the opportunity to build a large chemical business based on the concept of engineered plastics, mostly in isolation inside of the much larger GE.

Because of his success, he became the chief executive officer of GE. In today's takeover mania, however, can we expect to find many such situations in independent companies, without their soon succumbing to larger predators or the large corporate structure?

The Future

The history reviewed here provides little confidence when it comes to predicting the future. Nearly everyone thinks a domestic recession will occur sooner or later, that our deficits may diminish, that there may be a world recession, that oil prices are uncertain (low at the moment) but domestic oil production is clearly shrinking. There is also talk of new tax bills, yet the new administration took office with few commitments. No one seems to know how to increase the savings and investment rate of American society. Many companies need to catch up with the many more modern installations abroad.

When "hurdle" rates for new investments are 15–20 percent in the United States and perhaps only 8 percent (or even less) in Japan, it can be seen how big our problem really is. At a 15 percent discount rate, for example, a $1 investment in the United States must produce at least $2.60 in seven years in order to break even. Few projects will qualify. Here is a major reason for the short-term perspective of the financial markets that, because of the increasing role of pension funds (themselves seeking maximum quarterly earnings increases) in corporate equity ownership, influence management's myopic planning. Interestingly, although the Japanese are formidable competitors for several of the major industries we have surveyed, they are not in the case of chemicals.

Particularly in a time of capital shortage (and high cost), proper allocation among projects and products becomes so critical.[11] For many of the reasons we have discussed, the profitability of the chemical industry has suffered from misallocation to overlarge commodity-type plants for quite a while. I do feel, however, that, given a reasonable macroeconomic and regulatory climate, the American chemical industry will survive, grow, and remain competitive. It will certainly participate in the newer fields of materials, electronics manufacture, biotechnology, and complete systems (including fabricated equipment and instruments) as well as in extending and deepening its traditional products.

Chemicals are developing as a mixed industry, part chemical, part electrical, electronic, mechanical, and biotechnological. There will be few pure chemical companies in twenty years, but chemical engineers will still be employed in larger numbers in traditional chemicals manufacturing, whose products are indispensable, as well as in the newer specialty products, which will require continuous processing and astute scale-up design for flexibility and quality control.

An appropriate question at this point is this: What of the future of chemical engineering? There are some disturbing signs. College enrollments are down, and many other fields also attract the best students as well, so that they are spread more thinly. While the total numbers may well be larger, chemical and oil company expansions have not been as great as in the past; chemical companies may feel that they need talents different from those of the typical undergraduate-trained chemical engineer. The public sees chemicals as toxic, polluting, and unsafe.

There is an increasing lack of a strong industrial orientation in many chemical engineering departments, a trend that began in the late 1950s as government funding of university research became the dominant financing mode. Engineering science moved the discipline closer to a more academic orientation. Are we training theorists rather than practitioners? Is this because faculty, as they become more profound, tend to lose touch with practice?

There is a real doubt in my mind whether such a complete shift is desirable. Perhaps a partial return to the prewar days, which had a significant proportion of industrial funding, would be a better balance for the future.

The need for an integrated chemical engineering education—with a total systems approach and an emphasis on design—is greater than ever. This is for both old and new fields of application. Thus, not only is the scale-up skill important, so is the ability to lead a diverse team of specialists while retaining an overall economic marketing and technical perspective. If we cannot convey this to prospective new chemical engineers, we risk the loss of our identification and the employment contest to chemists, biochemists, biologists, and material scientists.

In rethinking the future of the chemical process industries and the role of the chemical engineer in shaping that future, certain key elements of our past success should still serve as a guide. Process design, tightly linked to market demands and research and development, fueled our rise. This model should serve not only as a paradigm for our future, but also for other engineering disciplines that have not had this tradition. We have seen the Japanese (knowingly or not) adopt such a model for the manufacture of automobiles, machine tools, semiconductors, microprocessors, computers, and consumer elecronics.

At the same time, we must become more aware of the larger environment that shapes our practices and our industries. We are entering a new world of intense international competition, global markets, and rapid diffusion of technology. Obsolete national domestic policies will be increasingly disciplined by the world financial markets. We do not want to conduct research that will be unprofitable because of an infatuation with technology. We cannot overlook the fact that financial considerations will play a large role in the next decade because we are in an era of high-cost capital.

There is no automatic assurance that past successes can be indefinitely sustained. If chemical engineering as a discipline is to survive for another 100 years, it must continually adapt to changing conditions. But, at the same time, the United States and the chemical industry must also adapt and change. Relative to other competing nations, the U.S. growth rate is too low. The world market will not forgive relaxation or a lack of zeal. Most of all, we must create a more favorable saving and investment climate so that we can once again plan for the long-run future well-being of our people.

Literature Cited

1. Landau, Ralph, *Chem. Eng. Prog.*, pp. 31–42 (July 1988).

2. Landau, Ralph, *The Newcomen Society in North America*, Publication 1088 (June 21, 1978).

3. Hatsopoulos, George N., P. R. Krugman, and L. H. Summers, *Science*, 241, pp. 299–307 (1988).

4. Landau, Ralph, "Chemical Industry Research and Innovation," in "Innovation and U.S. Research, ACS Symp. Ser. 129," W. N. Smith and C. F. Larson, eds., American Chemical Society, Washington, DC (1980).

5. Landau, Ralph, *Res. Manag.*, 30 (1987).

6. Landau, Ralph, *Sci. Am.*, 258, pp. 44–52 (1988).

7. Landau, R., and Nathan Rosenberg, "Strategies for U.S. Economic Growth," in "Globalization of Technology, Proc. Sixth Convocation of the Council of Academies of Eng. and Technol. Sciences," Janet H. Muroyama and H. Guyford Stever, eds., National Academy Press, Washington, DC (1988).

8. Bernstein, Jeffrey I., and M. Ishaq Nadiri, *Am. Econ. Rev.*, pp. 429–434 (May 1988).

9. Jorgenson, Dale, Frank Gollop, and Barbara Fraumeni, "Productivity and U.S. Economic Growth," Harvard Univ. Press, Cambridge, MA (1987).

10. Jacobs, Joseph J., *Chem. Eng. Prog.*, pp. 26–29 (June 1989).

11. Landau, Ralph, and George N. Hatsopoulos, "Capital Formation in the United States and Japan," in "The Positive Sum Strategy," R. Landau and N. Rosenberg, eds., National Academy Press, Washington, DC pp. 583–606 (1986).

Technology and Trade in
the Global Market

The postwar decades were a golden age for chemical technology. The worldwide demand for new products and the new technologies developed to meet that demand allowed the large-scale growth of a world chemical industry. A primary tool of that growth was the specialized engineering firms (SEFs) like Scientific Design that licensed proprietary technology to companies worldwide. Because process engineering was such a new concept, particularly in developing countries that were just beginning to manufacture chemicals, the SEFs had to market themselves as well as their technologies.

The result of this technology transfer by SD and the other SEFs was healthy international competition and widespread wealth creation. Robert Malpas, an executive with the British-based ICI (Imperial Chemical Industries) before joining Halcon as president in 1978, has written that Landau's small company had an "extraordinary impact … on Britain's postwar development and in building ICI to become a world leader in petrochemicals." The four large petrochemical plants that ICI licensed from and built with Scientific Design in the 1960s "were major elements of ICI's petrochemical strategy and the nation's ability to meet the growing demand for plastics, fibers, solvents, resins, antifreeze, and many other products."

Licensing technology was not without problems. In 1964 Landau learned that one of his licensees, a subsidiary of the Italian state oil company ENI, had built ethylene oxide plants in Czechoslovakia and Poland using a technology very similar to one it had licensed from Halcon. Halcon sued the Italian company for violating its license and also asked the U.S. Commerce Department to take action under the Export Control Act. Despite concrete evidence of an infraction confirmed by an independent expert, the Johnson administration refused to give Landau any support. That position was reversed in 1969, when the newly installed Republican secretary of commerce promised to take action. In 1970 the government won a cease and desist order against the Italian firm, and Halcon won a multimillion dollar settlement.

The incident reconfirmed for Landau that protecting intellectual property, in this case embodied in technology, is essential to maintaining one's competitive advantage. The incident also taught him that the federal government would not always back the interests of its businesses and could in fact adopt positions and policies that were detrimental to those interests. In this attitude, Landau realized, the U.S. government differed significantly from the governments of its principal industrial competitors. (The incident also made Landau an active Republican.)

14 Role of American Engineering Design Companies in the Chemical Process Industry

History of American Engineering Design Companies

The forerunner of the chemical engineering company as we know it today began in the petroleum industry in the U.S. about the time of the first World War. The first engineering companies were formed as research-minded, process development firms, to assist in furthering the wide technological exchanges then beginning in the petroleum industry. The engineering company even then grew of necessity—many of the oil companies spent all their efforts searching for crude oil and establishing retail marketing facilities. The engineering organization led in the development of processes and manufacturing techniques that were needed in the refining industry.

By developing and licensing processes, these engineering companies spread the know-how they created and helped in the building of the giant world-wide petroleum industry. Prominent among early companies were M. W. Kellogg Company and Universal Oil Products Company, each of whom first because well known by offering important thermal cracking processes for license.

The chemical field developed more slowly in this regard and there was little interchange of information between manufacturing companies in the chemical process industry or between a manufacturing company and an engineering contractor. A chemical producing company would expand by doing its own process design and contractors would be called in to handle construction, piping and mechanical work, electrical work, and other separated facets of the project.

Paper presented to the 32d International Congress of Chemical Industry, Barcelona, Spain, October 25, 1960. Published in *Chemical Age of India* 13, no. 1 (January–February 1962): 9–15. Reprinted with permission.

The petroleum refining industry installations of that period were much larger in scale, and more continuous in operation, than had theretofore been required by the chemical industry: Unusual demands were placed upon the designers—it was no longer possible to scale up equipment by the prevalent semi-empirical methods. The profession of chemical engineering suddenly received a tremendous boost. However, the supply of chemical engineers was limited and the many refining companies could not obtain or justify the teams of specialists required to design the occasional refining units that were needed.

This trend encouraged the growth of contracting firms capable of handling the more sophisticated engineering and construction requirements of such refineries. These firms grew out of pure construction contractors, or from equipment fabricators, and evolved into integrated contractors from a direction opposite to that of the process firms mentioned above. They were equipped with experienced skilled personnel, and specific knowledge of how to coordinate and produce a plant for a process company (particularly refining) that would meet the producer's specifications. The formation of this type of company was an important step forward. With all responsibility placed in one organization, complete coordination of a project was possible with savings in time and money resulting. Generally these activities were *not* part of the chemical manufacturer's or oil company's organization....

As the chemical and refinery processing industries forged ahead, other types of engineering firms found that an important job was still not being done adequately—that of providing *interchanges of know-how among companies in the chemical industries and of the development of processes universally available for licensing* (somewhat like the activities of the first engineering companies in the refinery field). Companies with strong chemical engineering background emerged—some limiting themselves solely to research and development—others doing research, development, licensing, engineering, and construction.... It should of course be realized that from time to time some of the general contracting companies ... also offer proprietary processes or act as licensing agents for other companies' processes, but these do not normally provide a major portion of their business.

Incidentally, there have arisen a number of manufacturing companies which do licensing in certain fields, but do not act as contractors, e.g. Texaco, Esso Research & Engineering, California Research, Phillips, Shell Development, and a few others. There are relatively fewer general contractors or chemical engineering organizations ... in Europe. A few examples are Lurgi, Power Gas Corporation, Air Liquide, British Oxygen, and Linde.

There are many reasons for the growth and importance of process research and licensing firms specializing in the design and construction of chemical plants. To begin with, not all chemical producing companies are large enough or diversified enough to support their own research programs. Also in the course of their work, engineering companies have made widespread contacts with chemical producers all over the world, and have gained knowledge in all phases of engineering and in many different processes. In some cases the engineering firm may have contributed to or collaborated on a new process, in other cases the firm may have adapted a new process for a company, or even may have provided the process itself.

The engineering company, as a natural organization, looks upon all producers as potential clients. It is thus able to negotiate or work with all companies without being in competition with any producing company.

One of the most important roles played by the engineering company has been in acquiring, trading, and disseminating know-how. Immediately after the end of World War II, the flow of chemical and petrochemical technology was from the U.S. to Europe and the Far East. Today, there is a considerable and ever increasing flow of technology in both directions.

The engineering company, with international experience, is in a unique position to aid and contribute to know-how interchange. This type of company has an intimate knowledge of engineering standards and process equipment, and can translate a foreign chemical operation into a successful American plant incorporating the latest American technology and design methods, just as it has in the past translated American processes into successfully operating European and Far Eastern plants, utilizing the best available equipment, with local procurement whenever possible.

By aiding in the know-how importing and exporting business, the engineering firm helps companies in many ways:

1. to save money, since the purchase price is almost always less than the original cost of research, development and operating trials upon which it was based.

2. to gain advantage in time, and to establish a sound commercial position in the field before potential profits are watered down by widespread competition.

One of the failings in the chemical process industries is the strong determination of many companies to favor internal development against technology which can be bought outside. Although arising from wholly creditable motives, such policies are obsolete today, and stand in the way of the forward march of progress in the face of fierce competition. The Russians have no hesitancy in adopting useful western patents and technical papers, sometimes even giving credit to the original. This has permitted them to concentrate their limited high-quality scientists on problems of unusual importance to the state. Admittedly it takes courage for a technical administrator not to research "surefire" areas already plowed over by others, or to resist putting a high gloss on already satisfactory techniques previously developed, but it is not in the interest of his company or country.

The engineering company makes it possible to obtain comprehensive know-how, which goes considerably further than the purchase of licenses to practice inventions under patents. A patent disclosure is carefully worded to substantiate the broadest possible claims for the inventor, while at the same time divulging somewhat less about how to practice the invention. Thus, the patent license is little more than a hunting license to acquire practical operating knowledge for an invention's commercial practice. The most recent world-wide example of this difference has been the very divergent evolution by many licensees of the famous Dr. Karl Ziegler's initial patent grant [for producing polyethylene under low pressure] (without know-how).

The know-how provided by an engineering company often embraces operating data, based on actual experience in the practice of a chemical process. Obviously know-how will vary widely in its comprehensiveness. It can include only the data accumulated in small bench experimentation, or it may derive from more extensive operating experience gained from a pilot plant or semi-works unit. It is most valuable, and most expensive to acquire, when it comprises not only the fundamental chemistry of the process, but engineering design and operating data based on a successfully operating commercial plant.

In its performance, the contractor company must have assembled a highly skilled staff under one roof, that is capable of engineering all phases of design and construction. Complete coordination and control of all basic services—structural, electrical, instrumental, etc. is thus vested in a single organization, permitting an efficient project, economic cost, and considerable time savings.

The key to the successful operation of the company and the plant actually goes back to the process itself, and process selection and design are paramount in importance. Here, research and development companies have made many contributions, and one of the most important roles has been played by the research-and development-minded engineering design and construction firm.

In view of the high cost of research today and the scarcity of good research scientists, it appears increasingly probable that more and more chemical companies will concentrate their research activity in the future on new product development which they alone can do, and leave the development of new processes for intermediate manufacture to research-minded engineering companies, or to purchase from other manufacturing companies when available. To be sure, some companies have such a strong position in certain fields that they will continue to do research in these, but, in general, such areas represent a relatively small part of a modern chemical company's diversified activities.

Importance of Engineering Design Companies to the Chemical Industry

The important role played by the engineering company become readily apparent when one considers the list of postwar chemical process developments in the chemical industry—all of which were licensed by or through engineering companies [see table 14.1]. It is safe to remark that many of these processes would have been considerably delayed in their introduction by many of the companies involved if it were not for the engineering companies who made time and manpower savings possible with the introduction of the needed know-how.

Standardized Plants—Pre-Engineering

One of the good ways for an engineering company to introduce the required know-how of chemical production is through the integrated plant concept—that is, where the engineering, design and construction of a chemical processing plant are provided simultaneously and in total. The proof that this is a practical method can be seen in the numerous "standardized" petrochemical plants producing polyvinyl chloride, ethylene, polyethylene, maleic anhydride, ethylene oxide, phthalic anhydride, etc., in the United States. Europe, and Japan.

For the small to medium-sized chemical processing company that is not equipped or financially able to research, develop, design, engineer and build a new plant and equipment, this "package" provided by the engineering

Table 14.1
Partial list of important processes licensed by or through engineering companies

A.   Heavy inorganic chemicals

Ammonia—Chemical Construction: Girdler; Blaw-Knox; Lummus; Kellogg; Fluor; Foster Wheeler; and others.

Nitric acid—Fluor; Chemical and Industrial Corp.; Chemical Construction

Sulfuric acid—Chemical Construction; Titlestad; Leonard Construction

Urea—Foster Wheeler (Pechiney); Vulcan (Inventa); Kellogg (Montecatini); Braun (Staats-mijnen); Chemical Construction.

Phosphates—Fluor; Chemical and Industrial; Dorr-Oliver.

Chlorine—Braun (Solvay); Krebs; Hoechst-Uhde

Iron ore reduction—Hydrocarbon Research; Chemical Construction; Kellogg.

B.   Heavy organic chemicals

Ethylene—Stone and Webster; Kellogg; Lummus

Benzene, toluene, xylene—Universal Oil; Houdry Process Co.

Naphthalene—Univeral Oil

Butadiene—Houdry Process Company

Acetylene (from natural gas)—Chemical Construction Co. (BASF); Kellogg (Soc. Belge. Azcte); Braun (Montecatini)

C.   Organic Intermediates

Ethyl chloride—Scientific Design

Styrene—Scientific Design; Universal Oil.

Phenol—Kellogg (Hercules-Distillers); Scientific Design

Ethylene oxide—Scientific Design; Lummus (Shell)

Phthalic Anhydride—Scientific Design; Badger (Sherwin Williams); Foster Wheeler

Perchloroethylene and chloromethanes—Scientific Design

Terephthalic acid—Scientific Design (Mid-Century Corp.)

Maleic anhydride and fumaric acid—Scientific Design

Isoprene—Scientific Design-Goodyear; Houdry Process

Xylene isomerization and purification—Scientific Design

D.   Finished chemicals

Fibers—Von Kohorn.

Polyvinyl chloride—Scientific Design

Polystyrene—Scientific Design

Polyethylene—Scientific Design

E.   Refining

Cracking processes—Stone and Webster; Kellogg; Lummus; Universal Oil; Foster Wheeler

Catalytic reforming—Universal Oil; Kellogg; and others.

Synthesis gas—Hydrocarbon Research—Texaco; Kellogg; Chemical Construction and others.

company offers the only practical solution. Even very large companies have found that such a plant can save time and money.

Before going further, it is necessary that the term "standardized plant" be well-defined—many misconceptions exist as to what is meant or implied whenever the term is used. A "standardized plant" is a chemical processing plant based on a given process, whose unit design is adaptable to a wide range of small to medium-large capacities through standardization of certain design features, involving substantial investment by the vendor of such a plant in the form of pre-engineering. The plant components included, in combination may often be adaptable to a variety of requirements and circumstances. A modern "standardized plant" is a low cost, fully adequate, and up-to-date facility—not a series of cheap units—but one specifically aimed at doing a complete job.

Process license, engineering and construction, training of operating and supervisory personnel, often guaranteed price and guaranteed performance, are all frequently part of the "package." Purchasing, equipment, legal fees, other forms of insurance, technical supervision, and the like may be among the many details included. Size alone does not distinguish the "standardized plant"—it may be very small or very large. But its distinctive feature is standardization and unit responsibility in a single "pair of hands." ...

The processes that already have reached a marked degree of commercial success are most easily adaptable to standardization. Here, the engineering company, that has broad chemical process and design experience, has acquired the necessary process know-how (on a commercial scale) and can translate this know-how on a predictable cost-performance basis. The advances in process techniques inaugurated and observed through long and continued experience lead to fewer variations in product specifications, and permit simplification of operating procedures....

Of course, in practice, not all custom work is eliminated. In any new area there are differences in local conditions—in physical building sites, in utilities, etc. and each new company or country can pose new and exotic problems. Thus, "standardized plant" designs are continually modified to meet the existing conditions....

An extremely important concept that must be developed through experience is that of economical size of a plant. In the United States the mass market is huge, and it is assumed that plants must be large to operate efficiently and economically.

In many instances, however, in the United States as well as the other countries, small plants can be practical, and in many instances may be the only possible solution. Thinking behind these problems requires knowledge of engineering "down" chemical processes, and in successfully translating from continuous to batch processes. One of the questions most often asked of SD's chemical engineers is "What is the smallest-sized economical plant you can build for me?" The answer of course, lies in a full analysis of all local factors, and the application of acquired technical skills. Another important factor here is labor optimization—in areas where labor is relatively inexpensive, scaled-down plants and lack of mechanization can still produce profitable operation.

It would be simple to say at this point that the solution of a problem lies in leaving a sizable safety factor for each item considered. Competition, however, rules this out. Not too many years ago foreign countries needed American know-how and processes, and price was not the main object. Today there is competition between American companies, between American and foreign companies, and between foreign companies. Close figuring is a necessity to remain in this competitive race....

Special Problems of International Engineering By Chemical Engineering Companies

The American engineering design companies, because of their relatively greater number, have become very active abroad, and have ... contributed very substantially to the growth of the world chemical industry. This has not been accomplished without travail. A few examples are described below.

A. Language

The differences in languages between countries are an obvious barrier to mutual understanding. Americans by tradition are monolingual, and a real obstacle thus exists to achieving a mutual understanding in the delicate business of negotiation—whether for process, plant, or just technical details. Sound planning and a full meeting of the minds of all parties are difficult enough under any circumstances, but they become increasingly involved when all discussion must take place in two or more languages.

It is not enough merely to acquire enough understanding of another language to make known one's wants and necessities. There must be, for engineers, a full technical understanding of the meanings and shades of meanings involved in all design, engineering, and calculation work, as well as in construction. An engineering company that has successfully performed internationally has acquired this additional know-how—the know-how of interpretation. This type of company knows well enough how to avoid the numerous pitfalls that are possible—and makes sure that only terms that are mutually understood are used, that little or nothing is taken for granted, and that even universally accepted symbols and terms are re-defined for positive clarification. . . .

There are of course legal as well as technical misinterpretations that can be made if extreme care is not exercised. Conversational facility with a language is not sufficient—business translators must be technically qualified, and legal counsel must be thoroughly aware of international law and the nuances of language.

B. Standards

Perhaps the biggest single obstacle in international design and construction is the lack of common engineering standards from country to country, and sometimes even within a country. Regional differences alone can have a considerable effect on electrical design, mechanical design, acceptable types of construction. So simple a matter as cooling water temperature must be known from previous experience or determined—it cannot be assumed even for preliminary calculations that the cooling water temperature will be the same as that used for the last design prepared for another company.

As countries reach industrial maturity, various groups increase the acceptance of design standards and building, trade, and technical codes. Some codes that have been in effect for some time are antiquated, and a hindrance—to change the code, however, is as difficult as trying to establish a new and needed code. In any country, and the United States is certainly not an exception, building codes vary and conflict with each other in different cities and sections. With little uniformity within a country, it is a great deal to hope that there will be uniformity between countries.

The problem, although great, is certainly not insurmountable. It is only necessary to start by understanding that the problem does exist, and then determining the scope and magnitude of the essential differences. A thorough technical knowledge of the subject, care and full attention to detail, and continuous checking will produce a wholly satisfactory result.

Here again, the international engineering company is set up and geared to this type of problem. By background and experience it can define the problems and successfully interpret and translate engineering and construction from one client company to another or one country to another. By having full control and command of the process as well as engineering and construction, all work and problems can be coordinated with maximum efficiency to insure that all parts will fit together to produce a smoothly operating whole.

C. Legal

The legal problems concerned with patents and licenses, as well as those concerned with contracts, would fill many volumes and still not cover the subject. A brief suggestion of the types of problems that exist follows.

One of the first aspects of foreign licensing that needs to be considered on the part of the American licensor is his relationship with the Federal Government. This can be classed as: (1) Atomic energy legislation, which places considerable restrictions on any prospective licensor and is, in essence, a governmental function. (2) Export control of technical data, which is a function of the Bureau of Foreign Commerce of the U. S. Department of Commerce. (3) The Patent Codification Act, which permits issuance of secrecy orders by the [patent] commissioner in instances in which the publication or disclosure might be detrimental to the national security. Further, a license must be obtained for filing in foreign countries if it is to be filed prior to six months after the filing of the application in the U.S. . . .

The foreign company which has launched the commercialization of a new product or process that is of considerable financial value will often find itself beset, not alone by active competition in the United States by the American companies, but will be frustrated by being thrown into interference with one, or even a plurality, of applications filed by American inventors on inventions arising out of the basic idea. The foreign company also discovers that while it cannot claim an earlier invention date than that of their date of filing in their country, an American inventor can cite his actual date of conception (if adequately supported by records) to bolster his claim of priority.

The problem of settling an interference is somewhat complicated, and can be very expensive and time consuming. Further, no patent can issue until the termination of the interference proceeding which decides which of the contending parties is, in fact, the first and original inventor. No royalties must be paid by anyone until a patent finally issues. The foreign discoverer is not able to skim off the cream as he expected and this peculiarity of the American patent system ties up such inventions during the time when there is still cream on the top of the bottle.

One needs to consider the various aspects of legal relations of licensor and licensee with foreign governments. A primary consideration is the need for complying with the currency regulations. This has, in the past, been a problem of considerable concern to the prospective American licensor. Also, the question of whether or not a prospective licensor is doing business in a particular country can have a very serious consequence, particularly with respect to taxes. If there are performances, such as servicing of a license, in the proposed license deal, one must consider whether or not employees may be required to visit the particular country and thus comply with particular rules and regulations.

Among the many legal problems are: (1) The negotiations and the provisions of the license itself—who the parties of the license are, and what the language of the license will be when the licensor is other than an English-speaking country. (2) The definition of the field in which the license is granted—this has consequences with respect to patents and know-how and requires very careful attention. Care should be exercised that the breadth of definition given to the field in contemplation of an expected exchange of license rights or information should not be such as to be a catchall which would be embarrassing at a future date and include inventions and discoveries not contemplated by the parties, yet within the actual and literal definition of the field. (3) Method of execution of a document. This may vary from country to country. (4) Tax laws.

D. Economic

One of the difficulties in the adaptation of a foreign manufacturing technique to United States conditions and vice versa is caused by the great difference between the national economies of the United States and the other countries of the free world. Almost without exception, a plant in this country will be considerably larger than its foreign prototype, and economic considerations will dictate continuous operation with a high degree of automation, which cannot be said to be typical of all foreign chemical plants. These design factors may require radical changes in technology, with resultant delay and cost for further process development work. The foreign operating company technical staff is often very unfamiliar with American practice, and the burden of adaptation ultimately falls very heavily on the purchaser. In consequence, if engineering design on an operating plant is included in the know-how package, its claimed value must frequently be discounted because of the fact that foreign engineering standards and design bases are not directly applicable to American conditions. Considerable engineering skill and experience in translation and adaptation of plants and processes from abroad to this country are necessary in order to avoid costly delays in execution of the project and excessively high costs in bringing the plant successfully onstream.

Conclusion

The engineering-construction contractor is a valuable tool for management in the establishment of new enterprises or manufacturing units. It is especially valuable when it is experienced in international activities. Many chemical process companies as yet do not have enough experience with such contractors and are still trying to do many of the new projects alone. If they will learn to work with these contractors they will gain a new insight into the possibilities of saving time and money.

15 Technology and Obsolescence in the Petrochemical Industries for Developing Countries

There is no longer very much argument as to whether the developing nations should build a petrochemical industry. Almost every country, starting on the road toward industrialization, is giving serious attention to building up the manufacture of heavy chemicals and particularly petrochemicals, so that the question really becomes when and how to get started. From the inception of the petrochemical industry in the U.S.A. through its adaptation and creative contributions thereto, particularly by the Federal Republic of Germany and the United Kingdom,[1] this industry has become, in the industrialized countries, one of the major growth industries, perhaps the most important of all. Hence, its applicability to less-developed countries, is surely of prime importance. . . .

It is important to consider that the petrochemical industry generates further industrialization through the consumer products introduced—fertilizers, plastics, detergents, synthetic rubber and synthetic fibers. International manufacture of these products will not only meet present consumption, but provide for and make possible the anticipated increases in standard of living. A petrochemical industry, therefore, represents one of the early goals in the desired consumer-oriented economic planning. It is evident that, except in the most unusual circumstances, it is impossible to import for any length of time, a substantial portion of these consumer products, since there is rarely enough foreign exchange available for such large-scale purchases. These reasons for the early establishment of such an industry are compelling enough to sweep aside a number of initially unfavorable economic aspects.

Excerpt from a paper presented to the United Nations Inter-Regional Conference on the Development of Petrochemical Industries in Developing Countries, Teheran, Iran, November 16–30, 1964. Published in *Chemical Age of India* 16, no. 3 (March 1965): 213–225. Reprinted with permission.

The establishment of a new petrochemical industry in a developing country must cope with many important problems. A partial list of these frequently includes most or all of the following: (1) lack of raw materials; (2) small domestic markets and low consumer purchasing power; (3) difficulties in breaking through on the foreign market; (4) low priced competition from the industrially developed countries; (5) inadequate technical manpower and lack of skilled construction and operating labor; (6) little or no heavy industry to supply the sophisticated equipment and instrumentation required, and (7) lack of capital and, particularly, the foreign exchange component necessary to acquire the technology and the special equipment. These serious handicaps, among others, obviously present such formidable road-blocks to the establishment of a petrochemical industry, that a tremendous challenge is created. Fortunately, there are several mitigating aspects so that, with good planning and a comprehensive knowledge of the economics and future technological trends, it is possible in many cases to proceed on a program that can overcome or abate at least some of these problems. It is the objective of this article to discuss some rational approaches that may help the efforts of countries starting along this treacherous road. In presenting these viewpoints, it is recognized that the problems vary from country to country so that it is almost impossible to make broad generalizations. Partly for this reason, examples will be offered, whenever possible, in striving to present a logical approach to petrochemical planning—based on present and future technology. It is further recognized that such viewpoints may not be universally accepted. Thus, each country must obviously judge for itself what aspects of this presentation, if any, apply in its case.

Let us now turn to certain advantageous factors, present in many cases, that tend to mitigate the adverse conditions listed above, and consider these factors in some detail:

Simpler Consumer Market and Demands

The manufacturer in the industrialized country caters to a very demanding consumer. In the case of plastics, this leads to a multitude of formulations and a great spectrum of products. These conditions burden the manufacturer with higher investment, more storage facilities and working capital, and higher operating costs, due to meeting the extreme specifications demanded—sometimes with little justification—by the fabricator and thus the ultimate consumer. It is easy to see that a new manufacturer in a developing nation will—at least initially—have an easier market to satisfy. For instance, a manufacturer of plastic dishes and cups may be able to restrict himself to a few colors of one grade of plastic material, such as polystyrene, and thus install a low-cost molding plant that may soon build up enough capacity for a small, simplified polymerization plant. This method of starting with the manufacture of basic consumer products, and then integrating backwards into more capital-intensive production industries, was used successfully in Europe, and is ideally suited to many developing nations.

Similarly, a polyethylene industry could be based primarily on supplying a general purpose resin for injection molding of various containers and for making a heavy duty film for various types of bags. The demand for these two items alone—neither of which would have to satisfy the critical properties of transparency of most resins offered for sale in the U.S. and Western Europe—could bring about the construction of a single polyethylene train. Special refining facilities for making the various other resins would be added later.

Special Raw Material Situations

Some countries are favored with indigenous raw materials suitable for the production of petrochemicals. It seems obvious—but does not always follow—that these countries should stress the manufacture of petrochemicals derived from such materials. It is interesting to note ... that natural gas is still being flared in some developing countries. This valuable resource is an ideal raw material for several important petrochemical processes. Thus, an abundance of natural gas should lead to immediate consideration of ammonia and other nitrogenous fertilizers. Other possibilities might involve consideration of methanol, acetylene, and trichlorethylene. While acetylene generally is losing out to ethylene as the raw material for the vinyls (the largest consumers of acetylene), it is not necessarily economic to import naphtha and crack it to make ethylene, when acetylene can be produced from available natural gas. On the other hand, liquid ethane and propane may be present in sufficient amounts to permit economic extraction from natural gas; a cracker for production of ethylene and propylene can be built near the source of such liquid hydrocarbons, or near the point of consumption. If this is feasible, vinyl manufacture from ethylene obtained from cracking of such feedstocks may become more attractive than the acetylene route, and may swing the balance away from making acetylene at all, even from zero value methanes.

Low cost electricity is an important product of very cheap natural gas, and it can also lead in the direction of chlorine, since salt is almost always available from sea water, if not otherwise. Likewise, the availability of fermentation alcohols in large quantities at low cost can be the basis for numerous products. It is interesting to note that up to two years ago, Imperial Chemical Industries of Australia and New Zealand, Ltd., based its polyethylene manufacture exclusively on alcohol-based ethylene. Yet Australia is much further along the road toward becoming a full-fledged industrial nation than the countries now considered in the ranks of developing nations. Brazil is also operating an ethylene-from-alcohol plant and another is under construction in Pakistan.

Another typical situation is an excess of chlorine due to the relatively high requirements for caustic and soda ash. In one South American country, a project has just been authorized to use an entirely new process to make ethylene dichloride (for vinyl chloride) from byproduct HCl, since no other use could be found for the HCl.

High Shipping Costs for Low-Priced Commodities

Although many misconceptions exist regarding the economics of shipping raw materials and intermediates, it is a fact that many high volume, low-cost products frequently cannot be landed in the developing nations at a price low enough to present serious competition to a proposed indigenous industry. We are witnessing, today, a tremendous, world-wide buildup in fertilizer capacity, largely because of this economic reality. The awakening interest in advanced agricultural methods, based on synthetic fertilizers, has provided the impetus for an almost explosive increase in demand, which may serve as a useful background for certain countries' ... modest petrochemical industry. In particular, the hydrogen and carbon monoxide (synthesis gas) available in every ammonia plant, should be looked at most carefully as valuable feedstocks for other petrochemicals (for example, oxo alcohols, toluene diisocyanate, etc.). On the other hand, where the raw materials for ammonia synthesis are not available at low cost, it may be reasonable to import the ammonia in tankers and go on from there. Recently a trend has begun for certain less-developed countries, (for example, Kuwait and Trinidad and Tobago) to build large ammonia plants from low-cost raw materials, which would permit shipment thereof over very long distances and yet land it at cost below what could be produced economically in the respective importing countries on a smaller scale.

National Policy May Be Decisive

While the many existing problems could be used to slow down the establishment of a petrochemical industry, this does not usually happen. There is the recognition that it is inevitable that some petrochemicals manufacture will eventually commence and that it may be desirable to create the industry first and let the demand catch up. This method also permits the orderly and careful planning of an industry, and allows time for the proper groundwork to be laid and direction to be established. The move must be bolstered by a series of supporting steps, including adequate tariff policy, allocation of foreign reserves to purchase the needed raw materials, and similar measures. Although these measures can impose a strain on other parts of the economy, it is expected that, given time, the industries formed, will generate income through exports and conserve funds usually applied to imports. But the justification for such action is not necessarily only the creation of markets but also the establishment and training of a cadre of technologists and administrators who can then act as a nucleus for further growth. Thus, such pragmatic reasons may also bulk large in the overall consideration of when and how to proceed. Under these conditions, usual economic considerations, such as payout and return-on-investment calculations, so necessary to the industrialized nations, may be quite out of place, except by the application of an entirely different set of ground rules, which go far beyond those governing investment decisions in the industrial nations and include such items as "increase in national income produced per unit of investment" and "social rate of return." The base question becomes the needs of the society.

"Skipping" an Industry to Favor Domestic Advantages

Although the promise of plastics has long been known, the strides now being made in the application of the various plastic materials in replacing more traditional materials such as wood, paper, glass, aluminum, and steel are truly astounding. We may now be at the point where countries will start to consider a plastics industry as one of the basic foundations to build on, and may thus defer the installation of some of the other industries, until a later time. Since hardwood is not always available and the capital investment for a glass, steel, paper, or aluminum industry is one or two orders of magnitude greater than for plastics, it is not surprising that developing nations are giving most serious attention to the latter. Trends in the use of polypropylene and PVC for pipe, PVC and polystyrene and glass-reinforced polyesters for building materials, and polyethylene for bottles, other containers and heavy duty bags, are being followed extremely closely.

This is a good example of the use of new technology in a "leap-frogging" role. Japan has partly followed this path, and has created an extraordinary plastics and fiber industry, fully competitive with the world industries in these fields and in some respects more advanced.

Labor-Intensive Products

Although the preponderance of petrochemical manufacturing processes are capital-dependent, there are some products that are more labor-oriented than others. Most certainly, this includes plastics end-uses and, to a somewhat lesser extent, synthetic fibers. By their nature, the petrochemical process industries do not require much labor but what labor is required tends to concentrate toward the consumer product side rather than the preparation of raw and intermediate materials. Hong Kong may be cited as an area where the availability of low-cost labor has resulted in a highly active plastics industry. For the raw material and intermediate industries, however, the labor requirements are so small, as never to justify site or size selection solely for employment reasons.

Regional Groupings and Trade Associations

The small size of markets and the problem of competing with the heavily industrialized countries, has led to the formation of trade associations and this trend may become even more pronounced. By pooling several countries' markets and apportioning the manufacture of the individual countries' particular advantages in terms of raw materials, energy sources, or trade patterns, it may be possible to realize a sufficient plant capacity to make a project viable. Thus, it is less necessary for each country to be self-sufficient, and thus often compelled to build uneconomically small-sized units. . . .

Oil-rich countries like the Middle Eastern nations could specialize in large crackers and ship ethylene and propylene to other developing countries less endowed in raw materials, even those not in regional trade groups. A similar approach to ammonia manufacture has already been mentioned. However, unless the countries seeking to export such chemicals, have a sufficient market to purchase their customers' products in return, such schemes are obviously bound to result in creating as well as solving problems.

Imposition of Protective Tariffs

The need to protect a fledgling industry with adequate tariff is *sine qua non* but this policy must be regarded as a two-edged sword, for it frequently results in two major dilemmas. First, it may raise the price level of the commodity in question and thus hurt not only the consumer but also the potential exporter of a product fabricated from the imported petrochemical. Again, in Australia, the Tariff Board allegedly encountered serious objections from plastic molders, when it recently raised the tariffs on polyethylene and polyethyrene. By attempting to maintain resin prices at levels 50 percent or more above U.S. prices, the cost of the fabricated products was raised to such levels that competition with the imported fabricated products became extremely difficult. This illustrates that, in a free market economy, various elements tend to influence such decisions, which are never easy. The second problem with high tariffs is, of course, their effect on the country's ability to trade with other nations and thus maintain a reasonable balance of payments. From these considerations, it may just not be feasible and would be foolhardy, ever to set a tariff high enough to protect a very small, uneconomical plant. However, some tariff protection is obviously essential, as long as it is applied in the country's best overall interest....

Technological Factors

The preceding section has illustrated the interplay of economic factors which make up the background for the planning decisions. Such decisions may be strictly in the hands of government bodies or, in other cases, private industry. Frequently, as in India, government and private industry engage in joint planning studies, with the government in primary control particularly with regard to setting price levels. In Japan, which actually developed its petrochemical industry mainly within the last ten years, government planning, such as the approval of new projects by the Ministry of International Trade and Industry (MITI) has been carried out within a framework that is more closely based on commercial economic criteria and private financing. Japan's impressive progress in petrochemicals manufacture has been described recently.[2] However, regardless of the mechanism used for project approval, the key question remains: Is this a viable project, and how can the economics be improved?

The following list presents some of the most important criteria that should be considered in analyzing the path a country is charting for its petrochemical development:

(1) What are the most important products to start with?

(2) Can the intermediates be imported? If not, should the raw materials be imported? This leads to a serious consideration of whether a cracker (naphtha or liquid hydrocarbons) is desirable for the initial installation.

(3) Have all possible indigenous raw materials and other potential special advantages been considered?

(4) What is the minimum economic size for (a) a vertically integrated plant and (b) an end product plant only?

(5) Is the shipping cost for certain raw materials or intermediates less than the difference in manufacturing costs between the proposed high cost, small capacity plant and and the giant installation in another country? Freight costs will rarely be more than two or three cents per pound, whereas the penalty for small plant scale may be far greater than that....

(6) Can a packaged plant using standardized or otherwise modified design concepts result in better economics for a small installation?

(7) Will products that instinctively appear a "must" on any list of proposed petrochemicals, fit the country's present and future needs?

(8) What processes and/or products are doomed to partial or complete obsolescence in the years ahead? Can a "leap-frogging" operation be carried out on the basis of new technology?

(9) Has the list of proposed products and processes been reviewed by the most competent authorities in the field, or is it influenced by financial considerations which dictate the use of certain processes and/or equipment?

(10) Has a given amount of money, presumably available for the construction of petrochemical facilities, been utilized to get the highest capacity of end products and the greatest increase in national income per unit of investment?

Consider the following example: A country desires to start a petrochemical industry based on polystyrene and polyvinyl chloride. Available are surplus chlorine—a situation fairly common in developing countries as mentioned before—and a small molding industry that supplies a modest market of several thousand tons per year of PVC and somewhat less polystyrene. This, then, is to serve as the backbone for a petrochemical complex. The plan is to erect a naphtha cracker to make the ethylene raw material for the two plastics. It is recognized that the cracker cannot be built with a capacity of only 3,000–4,000 tons per year of ethylene, as required to supply the two monomer plants. Thus, a polyethylene plant is added to the complex to put the cracker into a more reasonable size range. Naphtha is to be obtained from a local refinery at reasonable cost and effectively without the use of foreign exchange. A realization of the fact that the large quantities of naphtha required to make the ethylene gives rise to numerous potentially valuable additional petrochemical raw materials, leads to further additions to the complex. Butadiene is to be extracted and used for the manufacture of SBR rubber, thus increasing the capacity of the styrene plant to a more economic level. Propylene—which is inevitably coproduced at the rate of about 0.5 pounds or more per pound of ethylene—is to be used for the manufacture of tetramer and dodecyl benzene destined for detergents. The aromatic by-products, particularly benzene, are also separated. The cost of the complex is estimated at close to $50 million. It will parallel similar installations set up in the 1950s in a number of the industrial countries and thus appears to be a well-conceived venture.

Now, what is wrong with this scheme? Perhaps a great deal. An initially modest plan to start a plastics intermediates industry, has mushroomed into a giant complex that may be impossible to finance, and that will make, at least, one product probably doomed to obsolescence and another of dubious importance. It may also exhibit prohibitive economics. In an attempt to justify a naphtha cracker, the planners have loaded the project with products that were never contemplated in the original plans and may help to scuttle the entire project. The naphtha cracker, sized for very limited ethylene requirements, cannot hope to produce raw materials at anywhere near world market prices. Including any reasonable return-on-investment, ethylene will be priced at eight to ten cents per pound, as compared to present world market prices of four and half to six cents per pound.... In a vain attempt to justify an economical cracker, two future problems have also been created. Dodecylbenzene sulfonate-based detergents and SBR rubber may not at all be desirable for a new petrochemical industry. The former is not biologically degradable and is rapidly being phased out in the United States, Europe and elsewhere, by linear alkyl sulfonates and various nonionic detergents based on primary and secondary alcohols. Styrene-butadiene rubber production is flattening out since the advent of stereo-specific rubbers such as polyisoprene and polybutadiene. Now it may be quite reasonable to produce the more old-fashioned, non-biodegradable detergents and SBR to satisfy the local market. However, forward-looking planners would read the current technological trends to say that where there is still a choice, the newer products should be made. In this way, the developing country may actually gain an advantage over the industrialized countries by avoiding investment in anything but the latest technology. There is now also a growing realization that soaps may still be the most imporant detergents in many developing nations and that syndets should be deferred at present.

Let us, therefore, go back to the initial objectives of this imaginary project, which were polyvinyl chloride and polystyrene. A careful and objective analysis of the economics may well show that the best course would be to delay the use of chlorine and to import vinyl chloride monomer and either styrene monomer or ethylbenzene. Without prohibitive tariffs, both commodities could be landed (including shipping and insurance costs) at well under twelve cents per pound—perhaps ten cents for styrene and vinyl chloride, and less for ethylbenzene. These prices are easily 30–40 percent under those calculated for the small cracker-based complex described above. These intermediates would supply new polymerization plants which can be erected with modest capital. Such plants should be reasonably large and should supply an expanded fabricating industry that is geared to the export trade, as well as to the supply of domestic demand. Having established a growing market, attention could then be paid toward promoting a market for other end-products upon which the ultimate cracker could eventually be based. Naturally, as consumer demand and, hopefully exports increase, it becomes more desirable to reduce the expenditure of foreign reserves for raw materials. The next step might then be to manufacture the monomers from imported liquefied ethylene. While this is not yet readily available as a market item, the advances in shipping liquid methane make refrigerated ethylene a sure thing of the future. This commodity may be available in ocean-going tankers at a cost not very different from world market prices. This is because incremental ethylene made in locations where hydrocarbons are at fuel value or flared can be priced at three to four cents per pound and shipping and handling charges should add no more than one and a-half to two cents per pound. Since in the case of both styrene (ethylbenzene) and vinyl chloride, the ethylene contributes well under 50 percent of the molecular weight, the quantities of ethylene required for reasonable volumes of polystyrene and PVC are not enormous. This is just the reason why it is difficult to get naphtha crackers up to an economic size level. By purchasing liquid ethylene, and reacting it with indigenous chlorine and benzene (from a steel or petroleum source), the second step is taken on the road toward building a viable complex, still without a naphtha cracker. Meanwhile, it may be decided to start importing isoprene monomer and building a polyisoprene plant with a view towards achieving an ultimately favorable balance of ethylene and propylene. New technological trends toward more flexible ratios of ethylene to propylene may also assist in achieving an overall olefins consumption on a sufficiently large scale. Polyisoprene is the only true "all purpose" synthetic rubber. When polyethylene demand builds up to the point where a plant can be built, the naphtha cracker then becomes an economic reality.

In another approach to circumvent the time factor necessarily involved in the foregoing example, the government itself might consider the construction of a large naphtha cracker and aromatics plant as a stimulus to industry, even though it may operate at a loss for some years. The plants could be financed on a long-term basis, and fully justified over the time period. Raw materials would then be available to several small producers, allowing them to maintain a competitive position, that they could never have achieved with their own raw material plants.

Thus, it may be seen that the developing nations must always be vigilant to avoid the twin pitfalls of uneconomical plant scale and obsolescent products and technology. Obsolescence, as employed in this paper therefore, applies in the broad sense to obsolescence of scale factor as well as that of product and process. Each year the minimum plant size, on the world scale, becomes larger; the rate may even be increasing. The scale factor involves the most careful study of each project in terms of the country's own situation. Obviously, in the more heavily industrialized nations, it is easier to arrive at minimum economic plant sizes. Japan has now recognized the fact that its early petrochemical efforts were on too small a plant scale. Projects now being authorized by M.I.T.I. are on a much larger scale, in some cases involving several companies at the same location.... This situation is made even worse if the country proposes to construct a number of widely dispersed petrochemical complexes, each of minimum size, as has been recommended in certain cases (although poor and therefore expensive internal transportation may, in rare situations, justify such planning as the lesser of two evils).

To appreciate the effect of plant capacity on production cost and required selling price, it is necessary to analyze the individual elements that are included in these calculations. These elements, in their broadest form, include (1) raw materials costs, including catalysts (if any), (2) utilities and other services, (3) operating and maintenance labor supplies, (4) taxes, insurance, administrative charges, and other overheads, [and] (5) depreciation and interest. Items (1) and (2) are frequently termed "Variable Charges" and Items (3), (4) and (5) are called "Fixed Charges." Assuming raw materials and utilities are always available at a given price—which is not necessarily true as discussed below—labor and maintenance cost will generally remain relatively constant over a fairly wide range of capacity while the other fixed costs will bear a direct relation to plant investment. This investment is related to plant capacity by an exponent that may vary from the 0.45 to 0.8 power,[3] depending on the process.[4]

These economic considerations lead to the following realities that must be faced when planning a petrochemical installation:

1. A small plant will be very heavily burdened by capital charges, since the investment in terms of dollars per annual pound will be high. For most of the petrochemicals under consideration, the investment expressed in these terms is of the order of five to fifteen cents per annual pound, for the large plants being built in the industrial nations. The lower part of this range would be representative of styrene or ethylene oxide; the upper part for polyethylene or TDI. Since depreciation is frequently taken at 10 percent per annum and taxes, insurance, overheads, etc. can, in general, be assumed as a function of capital investment, it turns out that capital-related cost-of-production items (excluding interest or capital-return) can usually be approximated at 20–25 percent of the investment, that is, one to three cents per annual pound, at full design capacity.

High tax burdens and capital return charges can be offset by various actions taken by governments to foster and support industrialization. Most common methods, now in use even in some of the more industrialized European nations, are high investment allowances, rapid tax write-offs on new investments, and highly favorable government loans with low interest rates.

However, the important effect of "fixed charges" on production cost at low capacities cannot be over-stressed.... For styrene and vinyl monomers and polymers, a penalty of eight to ten cents per pound relative to plants of world market scale ... can easily result for undersized plants. While the absolute value of the cost data employed in these figures will vary, depending on the exact situation, the shape of the curves is quite general.

2. If a plant is operated at lower-than-design capacity, the fixed charges are spread over a smaller number of annual pounds. This has a particularly damaging effect on economics....

3. Up to now, only cost-of-production or "mill cost" as it is often called, has been considered. Since a return on investment or loan repayment and interest charges on borrowed capital are usually required, a further penalty is imposed on a small plant operating at low capacity. By this time, capital

charges may become unbearably high. This is the reason why production costs in small plants frequently exceed those in large plants by far more than half the shipping charges of the product that is to be manufactured.

4. Going back now to the assumption of constant raw materials prices, it is evident that if the raw material to Small Plant No. 2 is the product of preceding Small Plant No. 1, all the adverse factors discussed in paragraphs 1 to 3 above come into play in raising the raw material "transfer" price to Plant No. 2. This is really the crux of the problem in building an undersized petrochemical complex.

... In general, it becomes evident that small plant economics can become very unfavorable if care is not taken in selecting the economic size level. Although one would think that processes intrinsically exhibiting low capital investment will be more adaptable to small economic plants, this may not necessarily be the case at all. This is because such processes also enable the industrial countries to put up huge plants, for modest investments, which drops world market prices to the point where the much smaller plants in the developing countries find it just as hard to compete. Examples of this may be found in vinyl chloride, ethylene glycol, and cyclohexane.

Various approaches have been considered to arrive at smaller economically viable plants. These include:

(a) The use of standard or packaged plants where the engineering component is greatly reduced and the complexity of the plant is sharply restricted.

(b) Examination of each section and piece of equipment to see whether it is economically justified in view of the abundance of labor and other factors in the developing nation. Certainly, such a plant should not be overinstrumented to save the cost of one or two operators. Batch vs. continuous operation could also be carefully scrutinized.

(c) Eliminiation of "gold-plated" construction standards that tend to be used in highly industrialized countries, especially in the United States. These have generally emanated from the petroleum industry, where continuous operation is paramount and plant cost is rarely a deciding factor. Such factors are frequently not applicable in quite the same way to petrochemicals manufacture. All standards adopted should reflect the latest developments in materials and equipment with prime consideration still being given to safety....

When considering the processes to be used in the new undertaking, the need to maintain vigilance for obsolete technology and for processes that may lose their importance cannot be overstressed. We have already mentioned dodecylbenzene sulfonate detergents, although obsolescence in this case may not be an important factor in some developing areas. . . .

The utilization of new technology to gain special advantages may be illustrated with several other examples. A new oxo alcohol process recently developed makes butanol and 2-ethyl hexanol directly from propylene and synthesis gas (hydrogen and carbon monoxide). The latter can be made automatically available when an ammonia plant is installed—and at very attractive price levels when calculated on an incremental basis. The new oxo technology can, therefore, point the way toward a simplified entry into the field of plasticizers, solvents, acids, etc., which in turn may lead to a favorable local export situation. A development scheme of this sort would "leapfrog" over a fermentation alcohol-based derivatives industry, such as may be found in many sugar-rich countries of the world. A second example is afforded by the possibility of building a small, economically viable caprolactam plant. It is now anticipated that new routes under development will greatly reduce the size of economical plants and, for the first time, put one of the "miracle fibers" within the reach of most countries with a petrochemical industry. It is, therefore, deemed desirable to wait until the technology catches up with the need and makes the construction of a small, modern plant a reality. A third example is the case of building a cyclohexane derivatives complex to manufacture a number of important derivatives as satellite operations to a large oxidation plant. Thus phenol, aniline, cyclohexanol (for plasticizers), cyclohexanone (for caprolactam) and cyclohexylamine (for sweeteners and rubber additives) can be simultaneously produced in an integrated plant, not by a number of unrelated processes, each of which individually would be more expensive than in this new way of following the cyclohexane path. . . .

Notes

1. This topic has been touched on in another paper by the author, "Growth of Chemical Processing in Western Europe and the U.S.A.," *World Petroleum*, August 1962.

2. R. Landau, T. P. Brown and G. S. Schaffel in the July 1st, 1963 issue of *Chemical and Engineering News*.

3. This relationship is frequently plotted on log-log paper.

4. It should be noted that on a graph showing production cost as a function of plant size, fixed charges per pound must increase as production capacity decreases. Variable charges are constant, being related to production capacity.

16

The Chemical Process Industries in International Investment and Trade

A Case of Copying

... A few years ago, it came to our attention that one of our own licensees (a government-owned company in a friendly country) for an important original process of ours had sold what appeared to be a close analog of this process to a country in the communist bloc. After our own extensive investigation, we succeeded in obtaining evidence of what appeared to be outright copying of our process. We initiated litigation to recover damages, and succeeded only after intensive effort in persuading the Commerce Department to invoke the provisions of the Export Control Act. The result of these combined actions was a settlement by the foreign government entity involved: with us, for monetary compensation, with our government, for cessation of such activities. To my knowledge, this was the only time a foreign government organization was so penalized under the Act with respect to improper technological exports from the U.S. Unfortunately, one of the terms of the settlement was a reduction in the period of secrecy obligation by our licensee and that group is now offering a process somewhat like ours in various countries of the communist bloc, at least. Of course, we are counting on our own R&D to help maintain our leadership in this area, but our new competitor gained at least a twenty-year head start by having access to so much of the latest American technology in this area.

My account of the foregoing experience is intended to underline what I feel ... are the legitimate areas of government intervention in our field: namely, to help protect American patent and trade secrets from abuse or

Reprinted with permission from *U.S. Technology and International Trade: Proceedings of the Technical Session at the Eleventh Annual Meeting on U.S. Technology and International Trade, April 23–24, 1975.* Courtesy of the National Academy of Sciences, Washington, D.C.

piracy and to recognize the vital role of government in helping private industry ... in its efforts to earn foreign exchange and profits by trade and investment abroad. The know-how of our industry owes nothing to government inspiration or funding (with surprisingly little defense budget fallout except in a few instances, such as government research in high technology metals like titanium, used in many chemical processes), and it should, therefore, be up to each owner of such know-how to decide how best to exploit it to maximize his earnings. Usually, if not always, the owner is in the best position to assess the competitive merits of his technology as against that available from others.

Priorities in Exploiting New Technology

It is my observation that, increasingly, owners of such know-how follow a system of priorities whenever they have new or improved technology to exploit:

1. First preference clearly is to mount a manufacturing plant in the U.S. at the earliest possible time, to prove out the technology and to secure a favorable position in the marketplace. Included in this strategy would be a major effort to export the products to foreign markets, thereby permitting faster loading of the domestic plant, and development of market penetration abroad. In our industry, however, the cost of shipping the great majority of its products abroad is quite high relative to the selling price, and most countries have erected substantial tariff barriers (as indeed have we) so that there are limits to the amounts of products that we can export in the face of foreign competition.

2. ... Second preference would go to investing in a plant abroad, as early as market considerations permit, to exploit the same technology, with, if possible, the same ownership as in the U.S. If the foreign market has been prepared by exports from the American plant, it is ripe for a "world size" plant to be built. The risks here are inherently greater, but if the investment is timely and well chosen it can gain for the American company a possibly commanding lead in the foreign markets and ensure its ability to compete successfully without freight or tariff barriers. Furthermore, such foreign manufacturing usually leads to further needs for imports from U.S. plants (such as raw materials and intermediates), and the net result is definitely greater exports from the U.S. than if no foreign manufacture were undertaken. Finally, if such action is not taken, sooner or later, other foreign companies will figure out how to move into this market, and

despite patent and trade secret protection (which are highly variable and weak depending on the country involved), the American company will see the loss of its former technological lead. In some countries, also, the laws or practices make sharing the investment with domestic entities mandatory, and this can lead to complications for the American investor.

3. In the absence of opportunities to invest, third preference would be given to judicious licensing of the technology in friendly countries abroad. The high cost of R&D today makes licensing of an important discovery generally very unattractive because the royalties allowed by trade practices are too low to permit an adequate return compared with manufacturing the product. Just when the new technology is really well established and production is rising, the royalty payments cease, and secrecy obligations usually expire. Furthermore, the high R&D cost is due in large measure to the percent of failures found in all company research efforts. A licensor wants to pay only for the successes, and does not contribute to the cost of the failures. . . .

4. The last preference would be given to sale of the technology to countries whose foreign policy is often unfriendly to us, particularly in the communist bloc. Here, the concept of a joint venture as we understand it is particularly difficult, if not impossible, to implement, and enforcement of secrecy agreements and protection of patent rights held by the western firm is uncertain. . . . Moreover, competition in the international marketplace from products made in such licensed facilities often comes back to bite the licensor hard, for many of these countries do not price their exports in a rational way, but in any fashion to earn foreign exchange, or to accomplish their government's foreign policy goals. However, no evidence is available to me to suggest that communist countries are not scrupulously honoring their contractual obligations; still these run out eventually, and the country is free to use the technology in any way it sees fit.

Our experiences with Japan, a friendly power and one whose economic health is important to us, show what can be done by application of the imported technology and its effect on the trade of the countries providing the technology. In any case, unless the cash return or equivalent in valuable raw materials or products is high enough, this path may well turn out to be a poor one in the long run for any really advanced technology.

5. The above sequences, while representative of present thinking, do not cover all the real possibilities in our complex industry. Thus, an American invention may first be commercialized abroad, then introduced into the U.S.A.; the reverse is also possible. . . .

How Technology Is Traded

... Consider the pattern of trade in technology:

1. The great bulk of the technology exported from the U.S. goes to Western Europe and Japan.

2. The great bulk of the technology exported from the West to the East bloc (and now possibly to the Middle East) comes from Europe and Japan.

3. The east bloc (and third world countries generally) prefer to buy complete packages wherever possible, including financing, supply of equipment, engineering design, know-how, license rights for same, and consulting services during start-up. This practice has given Western European and Japanese companies great advantages over the U.S. firms for a number of reasons. To mention just a few:

a. Financing of the type favored by the customers is not feasible in America. Loan terms considerably in excess of five years are now common, and government insurance and other schemes are much further advanced in Europe than in the U.S.

b. Europe and Japan have had lower costs of equipment and personnel than we do.

c. European and Japanese technologists are much more willing to live in Eastern Europe and communist China for long periods during construction and start-up, despite such episodes as the sentencing of one Vickers-Zimmer engineer for espionage in Red China a few years ago, and cancellation of the contract.

d. European and Japanese entities are much more willing to engage in barter arrangements, even including output of the proposed plants, so as to permit the communist bloc countries to finance the projects largely from the West.

e. As mentioned before, many European organizations, particularly those in which governments are involved, are willing for national prestige purposes or balance-of-payments reasons to sell technology very cheaply compared with what would be considered an adequate return by comparable American entities.

f. American companies have generally felt that once a sale of process know-how or other form of know-how takes place behind the Iron Curtain, it is difficult to police copying of this know-how elsewhere; therefore the compensation should be reasonable, not bargain-basement pricing. However, the extensive European and Japanese competition described herein has made this philosophy very difficult to achieve in most instances.

g. It is known that the Italian Communist Party and very possibly the French counterpart are very active in promoting sale of technology from companies inside their countries to the communist bloc countries. Luigi Barzini stated in *The New York Times* several years ago that the Italian Communist Party received a commission on all sales to the Iron Curtain countries.

4. Although, as mentioned above, there exist technology export controls in the United States, and the COCOM countries to a lesser extent, their effectiveness is diminishing. Of course, it has been difficult to persuade [members of] COCOM and OECD [the Organization for Economic Cooperation and Development] to cooperate very effectively in this area. But the greater problem is due to the fact that technology is increasingly leaking from Western Europe and Japan (even though originally of U.S. nationality), by a variety of means (instances of each kind are known to us, and to others in the industry), namely:

a. Outright misappropriation. It is the widely held belief by American industry that many such cases of misappropriation of American technology have occurred, but it is exceptionally difficult to prove this for any specific case.

b. Disclosure by American personnel employed by foreign entities, emanating from their knowledge of American secret know-how. Often these instances involve contravention of personal secrecy agreements with former employers.

c. Disclosure by European personnel who have worked on projects involving American know-how, to other European companies which are not yet bound by any formal secrecy obligations, and who then retransmit the data behind the Iron Curtain. A ring of this type was recently uncovered in Italy, but the same practice has been known to occur in France and elsewhere.

d. Espionage by employees of one company with relation to employees of another company which has American technology and which the first company then retransmits to the Iron Curtain. It is believed that at least one such case is known to have occurred in Japan.

e. Espionage by East bloc government and technical personnel in Western Europe and less often in the United States.

This question of Soviet espionage is at last receiving more public scrutiny. Recently, Mr. Tom Normanton, a member of the British Parliament, made the following remarks at the European Parliament in Strasbourg: "We need not remind ourselves that the greatest leap forward in aeronautical technology, namely, the Concorde aircraft, has been copied in almost every detail by the Russians. That stems from the fact which I am sure nobody can deny that copies of blueprints, copies of designs—the product of research of the [European] community—have been handed over in totality to the U.S.S.R."

Other examples are contained in recent articles ... published by the *London Economist*. One such issue deals with the KGB (Soviet Secret Police) activities relating to multinationals. "The KGB delegates who sit in on the Soviet Council of Sciences regularly point out—when the discussions turn to the purchase of technology from the West—where techniques can be stolen more cheaply than bought. (KGB spies in West Germany succeeded in 'borrowing' the most sophiscated railway computer technology on offer.)"

f. The required publication of patent applications in Western patent offices often signals to observant Iron Curtain technologists important directions being taken by the West.

g. The talk of a "Technology Gap" has encouraged and justified to some inaction regarding prevention of the leakages of technology as described herein by propagating the idea that Robin Hood should get technology from the richer nations and give it to the poor!

Plugging the Leaks

This being the case, how can the leaks be plugged more effectively than they are at present? Here are some recommendations:

1. The American government should encourage the writing of contracts by private companies for license or sale of American technology to foreign entities that include a clause prohibiting the sub-licensing or further transfer by the licensee or purchaser of technology in the same field as the subject licensed. There are too many cases known to exist today where the foreign licensee, through an affiliated or associated company, alleges to have developed an independent source of technology similar, if not identical, to the acquired American technology, which it proceeds to sell behind the Iron Curtain and elsewhere. Actually, our government should prepare detailed recommendations and warnings to private companies regarding all the security problems mentioned herein.

2. Efforts should be exerted, by treaty and otherwise, to strengthen trade secret rules and judicial precedents and practices; talks should be undertaken with foreign governments to suggest improvements from our own experiences in the loose legal protection provided to trade secrets and patents by much of foreign law. Even in the United Kingdom, for instance, there is very little restraint on an individual who works for a company which may itself be obligated to secrecy. Perhaps international courts with expertise might be established to deal with technology matters. It is not illogical that "know-how," which originated as an American concept, should also be followed by an international legal doctrine which adopts some of our experiences for the benefits of the more orderly international flow of technology.

3. Government bureaus abroad should be better staffed so they can feed to American industry and the various governmental agencies at home commercial intelligence concerning technology flow and trade opportunities.

4. As a corollary to the above, the government could give a great deal more general help to private business in all of its international affairs, without getting involved in the business itself. The current philosophy of some government agencies—and too many government personnel, including some Congressmen and their staffs—is that any government help to private industry under any circumstances is per se bad. This all-too-prevalent attitude presents a marked contrast to that obtaining in the foreign ministries of most of our allies and certainly of our opponents. These ministries are regarded as essentially organs of business and government in promoting international trade to the maximum possible extent. *One of the biggest changes that can be brought about under any administration is to help develop a clearer understanding of the vital role of private business in creating and maintaining our technological lead.* And, it would help if younger engineers, businessmen, and the like would vie for election or placement with the (mostly) lawyers who are active in the political process.

5. A "Robin Hood" type of problem has arisen among some friendly countries of the third and fourth worlds, whose leaders are insisting that the price they pay for modern technology is too high (the President of Mexico, for example). But no one questions that they should pay prevailing interest rates for monies. Why this discrimination? Our friends in these countries should be helped to understand that because of the limits of skilled U.S. manpower, and the initially small scale of their requirements, the time and cost required to transfer the technology are often inordinately high, and the compensation must be equally so. The risks of leakage to third parties must also be evaluated.

6. A more flexible policy could be adopted by U.S. sellers of technology regarding the kind of information which might be exported as part of a know-how sale in selected cases. For instance, detailed equipment drawings might be excluded from being supplied with the equipment bought (catalyst manufacturing information is already prohibited from being exported to certain countries, but exports of the catalyst itself are allowed).

7. Particular attention should be called to enterprises that are established and owned by some of our allies and friendly countries. These organizations sometimes evidence a cavalier disregard for the origin or protection of know-how when they determine to use such know-how for political or commercial reasons. An example of this type of opportunism is found in the recent agreement between some American companies and the French aviation industry with regard to data on swing-wing design. The British were more than slightly disturbed because they cooperated with the French in the development of the swing-wing designs and they felt that much of their know-how was incorporated in the material which the French proposed to sell to the U.S. This example demonstrates that other countries have sensitivities which could be utilized in developing much more carefully thought-out trade secret and export policies than now exist. Our government can be more effective here than most private companies.

8. It might be possible to develop patent doctrine in treaties with friendly countries which would prevent the export of technology (and sometimes products) to the Iron Curtain as well as countries not covered by an adequate system (as mentioned before), where the technology is protected by patents in the allied country. Many American companies do not obtain patents in the Iron Curtain countries because there is considerable doubt that these have any value, or in other countries because of the lack of an organized patent system. Consequently, companies in allied countries, utilizing disclosures in patent applications filed by American companies, proceed to develop technology for export to these other countries. Such technology would not be saleable in the exporter's own country because of the American's patent protection. Perhaps this anomalous situation might be changed by appropriate treaty.

9. Additional efforts might be made to permit action against American individuals who transmit valuable know-how (even though they have personal secrecy agreements) while working for foreign entities.

10. A new problem has recently surfaced: the strong possibility of control being acquired in American companies with a strong technological base by foreign countries which have gained great wealth, beyond their own needs. This is a most complex question that is beyond the scope of

my remarks here, but, again, one must not oversimplify. If government is to oppose such take-overs, it must also provide alternate financial mechanisms to compensate the shareholders involved—a most difficult task.

I have devoted a perhaps inordinate amount of space to the issue of protecting American technological know-how because it really underlies all decisions which private companies and our government must make each day in the many areas of activity touched on at this seminar. It is important to understand the nature of this problem, and my long experience in it may be of value to the further studies this Academy may undertake.

In conclusion, I want to reiterate my feeling that the role of government must not be that of a top centralized administration overseeing our technological posture. Let us avoid the mistake the Soviet Union has made, and which keeps it in the position of seeking our know-how. However, in a true complementary relationship between private industry and government may be found the American way to maintain a proper and long-lasting preservation of the dynamics and statics of our technological leadership....

Technology, Innovation,
and the Economy

Ralph Landau believes that the principles embodied in the systems approach typically used by chemical engineers can be employed to great benefit in many other areas, including manufacturing and the resolution of problems of economic policy.

Although Landau recognizes that a consensus is emerging among policymakers, economists, and business people on the central economic issues facing the United States as it enters a new era of global competition, he worries that most participants in the debate continue to approach these issues from their own particular, comparatively narrow perspectives. Too often, Landau notes, politicians and policymakers fashion macroeconomic policy without fully understanding the effects that policy is likely to have on individual industries and firms or the consequences, good and bad, that actions by industries and firms are likely to have on the broader economy.

In essence, Landau wants policymakers and scholars to view both macro- and microeconomic actions as a chemical engineer would—as parts of a full-cycle process in which there are always feedbacks or recycle loops between the different layers of economic activity. Instead of achieving an optimum balance for a particular chemical system, however, this process would be aimed at improving the standards of living of the population.

Landau's colleague at Stanford and frequent collaborator, economics professor Nathan Rosenberg, has summed up Landau's approach well:

One of the things that Ralph has taught me is that I have no business being surprised that a splendid chemical engineer would also be a splendid economist. A good chemical engineer must always think in terms of tradeoffs and opportunity costs within the system he is designing. He is continually being confronted with situations involving maximization of some magnitude subject to certain unalterable constraints. And, obviously, these kinds of situations are precisely what microeconomics are all about.... By any reasonable criterion, Ralph Landau is a distinguished economist. Moreover, the profession is badly in need of people with his vision, wisdom, and deep sense of commitment. It needs people who understand, as Ralph does, the fundamental role of risk-taking in the innovation process, the pervasive importance of financial incentives throughout the economy, and the absolute necessity in economic affairs of distinguishing as clearly as possible between short-run effects and long-run effects.

The following papers illustrate the variety of venues and forms in which Landau has carried his message to policymakers, economists, and his business colleagues.

17 Financial and Capacity Needs

A. Capital Requirements and Availability

The major constraint faced by entrepreneurs and innovators in the chemical industry (and in others) today is the drying up of capital of all kinds. Money is the entrepreneur's major problem—both in getting started and in expanding. He does not usually have the resources available to large corporations. In this inflationary era, it costs more to get started, the size of the first production unit must be bigger in order to be competitive with existing plants, and the risks are greater than ever. Let us examine the state of the available sources of capital:

1. From Sales of Stock

The equity markets have died insofar as the new company is concerned. For instance, if a small entrepreneurial company decided to raise capital by selling some of its shares to the public today, the result of such a sale would probably realize only 25 percent of the amount that could have been expected in 1968, and this only if one could find buyers at all, which is very unlikely under today's conditions. Currently, only a handful of new issues is selling at or above their earlier issued price; most are far below. Virtually no new issues are announced these days. Not even large and prominent corporations are offering equities issues, for similar reasons, although some of them might find buyers. Whereas a decade ago the debt-equity ratios for industrial companies were commonly about one to three, today the ratio is often three to one. And, over this same period, the nature of the investor in securities has changed similarly; in 1961 the value of all trading on the

Testimony before the U.S. Congress, Joint Economic Committee. *Financial and Capacity Needs*. 93d Cong., 2d sess., October 1, 1974.

Big Board originated with individuals, institutions accounting for only 39 percent. By 1971, these proportions had almost exactly reversed, and institutions accounted for 68 percent of the value of all trading.

The virtual destruction of confidence of the average investor in stock issues of any kind, coupled with the high interest rates now prevailing, has caused what may soon be irreparable damage to this vital source of capital for the venturer into a new business or product.

2. From Banks and Other Financial Institutions

Because of the huge demand for loans accelerated by the collapse of the equity markets, and the chronic borrowing by governments, interest rates have shot up, and the demand for such money far exceeds the supply of capital. Where on the totem pole does the would-be entrepreneur come when confronted by competing demands of America's largest corporations, federal and local governments, etc.? Credit allocation is a very tricky weapon to use in such cases, and involves a possibly dangerous interference with the forces of the marketplace. It is never safe to start a new business on much borrowed capital, as the high risks and difficulties in the early years make repayment uncertain, and the burden of carrying fixed interest oppressive.

3. From Private Wealthy Investors

These have often been a principal source of venture capital for new enterprises, but with the Wall Street market in such poor shape, and the higher capital gains taxes now in effect, fewer and fewer such risks are worth taking even by very wealthy families, individuals or venture capital firms. Without a healthy equities market, the private investor faces the prospect of his capital being locked into the new enterprise for the foreseeable future without receiving a reward for his patience and risk-taking by selling some or all of his ownership to others when the enterprise is successful. But, if he should be so fortunate as to find such buyers, the current capital gains tax, irrespective of how long he has been willing to wait for any return on his money, is about 40 percent effectively. Since the return he gets is in depreciated dollars to boot, the longer he waits, the less he gets back in this sense also. Yet, the entrepreneur needs handholding for quite a few years before his success can be demonstrated. With the incentives and risks going in opposite directions, it is not at all surprising that this important source of capital is disappearing. And, if a capitalist craves equity investment as part of his portfolio, he finds some of America's soundest corporation stocks selling today at three to five times earnings, and with good security why take a risk on an untried venture?

4. From Larger Corporations

In recent years, some corporations have been adopting a policy of assisting entrepreneurs by investing in their enterprises. Now, with even the largest corporations strapped for cash to meet expansion, pollution, safety, and other requirements, such activities are bound to suffer. Large corporations are vital to the entrepreneur—he needs also their raw materials for his plant, he needs them as customers, and as further developers of his products. Their health is vital to his success, as our own history has proved repeatedly. But large companies are not great risk-takers in the entrepreneurial sense—they have too many constraints on them, and they are bureaucratic in outlook for this reason. If we want innovation and new ideas, we must encourage the individual and the small company to take risks which larger organizations do not take. Large corporations are faced with the increasing need for capital to provide buildings, materials, and equipment for their own expansion and replacement. As a result of the premium charges on borrowed capital funds, they tend to limit added expenditures to those areas directly related to their present production.

In thinking about the role of large corporations one should never forget that the United States Government takes half of the profits made by large and small corporations, but puts up none of the capital. Hence, the modest tax incentives for entrepreneurial businesses which are government's only investment are repaid many times over to everybody's silent partner. There has been much talk of tax "reform" and tax "loopholes," but, again, the real facts are quite different. Virtually all "loopholes" (or "tax shelters") are tax incentives or deterrents to accomplish some social or economic objective, and "reform" means changing these from time to time. But today our media use it as a code word for "soak the rich," or "the corporations." I have tried to show in these remarks that capital formation has received insufficient incentive, and consumption too much incentive, and what I am suggesting herein is not such "reform" but changing the ground rules toward a more efficient society. Government not only gains generally from this; it also gets back more tax revenue from the businessman's and industry's success, and labor gets more jobs and a higher standard of living.

B. Other Constraints

While money is the single most important problem for the entrepreneur, there are other constraints which increasingly militate against his success.... His biggest problem is government, and most particularly in the rapidly changing ground rules with which the businessman and entrepreneur are constantly being confronted. Any fledging businessman needs an army of lawyers and accountants just to help him fill out all the forms he is required to prepare; the cost and time for their preparation are a heavy burden on the entrepreneur. Economists must evolve their discipline in the direction of less governmental intervention, fewer stop-start programs, more long-range climate creation. Fine tuning of the economy has been proven to be less than perfect, and we should go on a steadier pace over longer periods of time.

In searching out what other constraints there are, I asked myself the question, "Could we do this over again if we were starting today?" I came to the conclusion that this would be most unlikely, and I would like to quote here a passage from my speech of one year ago ["Industrial Innovation: Yesterday and Today"] before "double-digit" inflation became a household word. "The reasons for my caution are based on the different climate existing today, as compared with 1946. It is unbelievable how many obstacles to the international technological entrepreneurial enterprise (and to industry generally) now exist because of the heightened role of national governments.

"Except for the excess profits tax, all the obstacles (some reasonable, many not) we encountered are still here, and *being added to year by year*: greater restrictions on currency transfers; foreign investment controls; higher taxation in many years; price, wage, and profit controls; increased reporting and bureaucratic procedures; increasing ecological restraints; anti-trust and consumerist legislation; political restrictions on imports and exports; and others. It takes many more lawyers and accountants to stay out of trouble, and litigation consciousness is much greater than ever. Inflation has arisen at unprecedented rates. Resources and energy limitations are becoming very restrictive of economic growth. Non-governmental organizations of all sizes, all over the world, are more and more subject to governmental regulations, frequently changing, and politically unpredictable. Incentives are increasingly chipped away, including raising capital gains taxes, reducing the attractiveness of stock options, reducing depletion allowances in many areas—in short, the formation of capital is constantly undergoing erosion while government's spending increases steadily. As a result of these and other forces, the profitability of industry has declined materially since World War II, and the willingness and ability to take risks has been reduced accordingly. Why take risks if the rewards are less than the penalties? With this has come the unwillingness of the securities markets to take similar risks."

It should be clear that my whole experience suggests the conclusion that the only decent hope for mankind is for more and better innovation— technological, educational, economic, and social—but in the direction of less government, less oppression, more freedom, more decentralization of decision and judgment making, and especially of risk-taking. We all accept that each society has the basic political right to set the ground rules and establish the priorities under which its citizens can work, but it must be based on a greater historical and practical understanding of the limits within which successful results can be obtained. Above all, governments should stop changing so rapidly the ground rules under which business operates. Innovation takes years to accomplish; businessmen and entrepreneurs cannot take risks if the rules change frequently in mid-stream. A quotation from Herr Schmidt, the West German Chancellor, is particularly apt: "Despite our abstention from controlling prices and wages, we have the smallest price increases. The whole of our economy is more adjusted to respond to market forces than to regulations.... This is said by a Social Democrat.... The deeper you get into regulations the deeper you get into red tape and the more you hamper the dynamic development of your economy." ... The contrary British experience is an object lesson of another kind to us.

It is in my opinion more important to recognize the deadening hand of bureaucratic restraints and rapid shifting of ground rules than it is to ask for any particularly new incentives or legislation. However, from my experiences in the business world (where economists, politicians, and financial people seldom immerse themselves, and therefore cannot really grasp how the objects of their laws and practices actually are affected by their actions, and what their reactions will be), I would like to make some suggestions which certainly could improve the capital availability situation for the entrepreneur, and for business in general, since the health of each is very much interwoven.

1. The restoration of a healthy equities market on Wall Street ranks as a vital priority for our country, which for the first time in its history faces a shortage of capital to cope with all the needs and desires of its people. Much attention should be given to improving the rules and behavior of large financial institutions vis-à-vis the purchase and sale of securities, but

this is not a subject on which I can pretend to have any expert knowledge. In addition, it is obvious that a reduction or elimination of governmental deficits (which can be achieved by various methods) will shrink the competition for capital between government and private industry, and lead to a lowering of interest rates. This in turn will make equities look like better investments, and we must never forget that equities and risk go together. But one very worthwhile legislative change would be to make dividends up to some reasonable limit tax free.

The burden of the double tax on corporate profits would thus be lifted for the smaller investor to whom dividends are essential, even more than capital appreciation. Professor Peter Drucker, in his *Age of Discontinuity*, discussed this matter in much greater depth, and while I do not share all his ideas, he is a very innovative man on the economic-business scene, and is worth listening to.

2. The large private investor will in no way be tempted back to risk-taking unless something substantial is done to reduce the capital gains tax. As I pointed our earlier, such investors have to be patient, and take great risks. The longer they hold on, the less their capital gain tax should be. This is so obvious that it is difficult to understand why so little has been done in this direction. It is a mistake to equate lower capital gains taxes with income taxes in any way.

They serve different purposes, and I am entirely willing to see the income tax on individuals adjusted in accordance with society's ideas as to equity—such as lowering individual taxes for the poor, and somewhat raising them for the rich. (But for this latter category, the difference between earned and unearned income should be eliminated, and a maximum of about 60 percent imposed. We cannot go higher or an important source of risk capital will begin to disappear, and the manager of a company will lose incentive to improve his position if he pays so much incremental tax. . . .

In all of these suggestions I have tried to keep in mind that a better balance between consumption and investment is needed in our country in order to reduce the long-range impact of inflation and to provide us with the resumption of economic growth. In this regard, the fundamental fallacy of equating increases in wages or salaries with increased profits should be clear to any person who studies the workings of our economic system. A very small part of the recently somewhat improved corporate earnings has gone into dividend payments to individuals, and because of the double taxation very little winds up in the hands of the stockholders.

The bulk of corporate cash flow is used for reinvestment or reduction of debt, and to that extent does not directly contribute to increasing consumption of consumer goods. Increases in wages that go beyond the national ability to increase productivity simply mean a forced redistribution of income to those individuals able to exert clout from those individuals less able to defend themselves. In fact, wage earners themselves must be made to understand that this process has not truly helped their real standard of living grow very much, because of the concomitant inflation it causes. A corporation is not an individual, and its entire economic role is completely different. As *The Wall Street Journal* points out ..., government deficits also have contributed to the increase in consumption patterns and to the rise in inflation.

But the capital gains tax reduction is a vital necessity for capital formation and risk-taking by entrepreneurs. I am not talking about helping Wall Street trading here, but of making risk-taking investments attractive enough. Otherwise, the entrepreneur may be tempted to sell his whole company out prematurely to a larger listed company, and so another entrepreneur's business disappears.

It is interesting to note that West Germany does not have long-term capital gains taxes, nor Holland. The "socialistic" Scandinavian governments waive taxes on gains after assets have been held for five years. Only Britain, which, as *The Wall Street Journal* says, "remains intent on bankrupting itself," follows the U.S. example of steep taxes on capital. Again, the experiences of others can teach us to avoid their mistakes. Are we more likely to follow the German or the British pattern? Another aspect of this problem is the treatment of capital losses, a possibility very frequently encountered by venture capitalists. The taxation of these should be liberalized to help induce more such capital to be risked in new enterprises, or in expansions of such companies.

3. As I mentioned above, corporations are going to be strained to provide the cash needs of the private sector. One tool that can be made available to them to assist in risk-taking and new investment and which will in the long run increase the government's income by participation in company profits is to permit total flexibility as to the time period over which the investor may take depreciation of his new investment. This is a system used in other countries, and it certainly would assist the assumption of larger risks in individual cases, such as in entrepreneurial organizations. It permits each manager or investor to draw up his own rules of the game, and as such it is a tool which would be valuable in shifting more capital

immediately into the private sector where it is badly needed and from which most of the increase in productivity in this country is to be expected in the forthcoming years.

4. Stock options for corporate managers should be made attractive once more, and the negative effects of the Revenue Act of 1969 eliminated. This is particularly applicable to the small entrepreneur who has to use the stock option to attract skilled help from larger companies who generally can afford to give greater security and higher wages to such people. The combination of the reduced ceiling on earned income contained in the Revenue Act of 1969 and the elimination of stock options has led to the predictable result (although it is by no means a straight cause and effect), namely that corporate salaries in the higher executive brackets have risen sharply while at the same time the value of the stock of their company has been declining more sharply. The stock option represents a real way for entrepreneurs and business managers to have a stake in their company without having a large amount of capital at their disposal, and it seems to me that this is a vital aid in improving the performance of industrial enterprises as well as assuring a greater interest by the public in the equities market.

5. Much has been said in the press and in recent discussions about the high cost of pollution and the quality of life. As an engineer and businessman, I can certainly confirm that the sharp change in society's demands that has taken place in the last few years in this regard has confronted business both large and small with an unusually heavy burden coming on top of the needs for more production capacity in many industries. My own interests in conservation and preservation of the quality of life are as great as anybody's, and I certainly approve of the national goals in this direction. The problem, however, is that the pendulum swung too far the other way in legislation which was passed at the height of the emotional feelings on the subject and essentially confronted industry and municipalities with too idealistic a set of standards. It is clear that the costs and the benefits of each particular potential or actual pollution have to be studied and a reasonable balance struck. For example, the country accepts as a necessary price for its standard of living an annual death toll on our highways of scores of thousands. In the long run we should be perfectly able to cope with the pollution problems and to provide for them routinely in new investment in the future, but it is a major undertaking to try to correct what has already been built in a short period of time, especially when jobs and rising income may be adversely affected in the near term. But if some of my suggestions just

below regarding energy were to be adopted, we could gain a very substantial improvement in the quality of life at no cost at all!

6. One of the major causes of our double-digit inflation, as has been so clearly brought out in recent days by the President and the Secretary of State, is the unconscionable rise in the price of oil that took place last year. The effect of this rise has been to extract approximately $100 billion per year from the industrial world and effectively to put it into cold storage, which means removing it from the standard of living of the industrialized world.

Much is being made of recycling this money back to the industrial and the less developed world, but in my opinion this will be a vain hope insofar as any meaningful effect is concerned, at least over the next five years or so. I fully agree with our government's efforts in this regard, but I feel also that a major and sustained effort has got to be maintained to reduce immediately the energy consumption of this country by conservation measures of all kinds. As an example, we should adopt the European system of placing heavy taxes on any automobile of larger than a minimum size, and make them progressive so that the gas gulpers which are still so popular in America will once and for all disappear. Other excise taxes on luxuries might also be reimposed, especially those that are high in energy consumption.

In particular, higher taxes on gasoline, even if only a few cents a gallon, will not only discourage excessive use of an expensive material that costs us a lot of foreign exchange, but will contribute enough additional revenues to the Treasury to make up for some or all of the reductions suggested herein (even, perhaps, supporting a public job program if unemployment rises too much). European nations have long had much higher gasoline taxes than we do, and France has just shown determination to reduce its imports of oil. We too should consider anew the idea of gasoline rationing, whereby essential uses for lower income people are covered while incremental consumption requires much higher cost "free" coupons. Energy is at the root of our inflation problem.

The recent study, ... "U.S. Energy Prospects—An Engineering Viewpoint" issued by the National Academy of Engineering, deals with many other aspects of this vital question, and it is my hope that some considered policies will emerge based on the results of that study.

7. In effect, the federal government has subsidized borrowing by state and local governments by virtue of making tax-free issues possible. This has of course attracted large investors and institutions who furnish the

necessary capital. If it is deemed vital in the national interest to do the same, let us say, for the housing industry (below a certain value for houses or apartments), then it should be equally justifiable to make, say, $1,000 a year of interest from savings and loan institutions tax-free. This would be a much better basis than tinkering with the interest rates as has been the practice in recent years where the small saver has been compelled to accept a much lower rate of interest than the large saver.

8. It should be clear from what I have said before that I am totally opposed to the re-imposition of price and wage controls. They represent the worst kind of governmental intervention in the private sector, and we are still paying the price for the distortions that were caused by our last bout of such controls. They are particularly bad for the rapidly growing entrepreneurial company because historical criteria for fixing of prices and profit margins have no real validity in such cases and prevent the entrepreneur from generating sufficient internal cash flow to maintain his forward progress.

9. There is a real misunderstanding outside the business world about the recent rise in prices instituted by large companies in such fields as metals, chemicals, autos, etc. Somehow, it is fancied that competition doesn't really work in these fields, that prices are "administered," and the fact that prices go up despite falling demand proves this theory. Well, I have worked with (but not for) large organizations all my professional career, and I do not believe any of the foregoing.

The rise in prices reflects not only the effect of higher energy, labor, and other, costs; it also reflects attempts to recover from the debilitating effects of price controls, and to restore profit margins (only partially) to former levels so that new capital can be generated for expansion of productivity. A new capital investment costs far more today per unit of capacity than did a similar plant just a few years ago. If the price of the product remained too low, the new investment on such a higher capital base would show an unacceptably low return which no management responsible to its stockholders could justify.

This is particularly true in the capital-intensive basic industries. But as such prices needed for new investment go up, the consumer can delay purchase of a new car, for example. This is the risk a management takes when it raises prices, or puts in new capital for more capacity. Alternate products may even take a market away altogether. Imported goods may be priced lower than a company's own products, and threaten this market or his return. There are many such consumer choices. That's how the price system allocates the production and consumption patterns of a country.

Rather, we should pay attention to removing the large number of governmental rules and restrictions which force high costs upon the public, restrict imports and exports, and generally prevent the maximum competition in the marketplace, which we believe will aid in holding down inflation.

In conclusion, may I say that I am privileged to be invited to appear before this distinguished committee, and thank you for allowing me to submit my views. As I said before, what I have tried to express is the result of thirty-three years of industrial and technical experience on the front lines, that is, the entrepreneur's world; not a macroeconomic view but a microeconomic analysis. You might also call it the worm's eye view—how the fellow in the trenches feels when he gets contradictory and frequently changing orders from his commanding officers, and what he tends to do about it. In short, I have tried to express what the reality of our economic functioning is from the participant's point of view and not from any vested interest's point of view. I am lobbying for nothing at all!

18

Innovation for Fun and Profit

Broadly speaking, what we are setting out to explore is INNOVATION, particularly technological innovation, in its various ramifications. Economists define an innovation as the first commercial application of a new or improved process or product.[1] Nowadays we would extend this definition to include a system—the supermarket, time-shared computer, satellite communication, etc.

The innovative process consists of two distinct stages:

- Conception or invention

- Subsequent commercialization

Thus the economist would point out that the invention by itself is not an economic good; it is only by commercialization that it becomes one.

Whereas the former task is that of the inventor, the latter role falls to the entrepreneur. Fundamentally, entrepreneurship is the process whereby people, money, markets, production facilities, and knowledge are brought together to create a commercial enterprise which did not exist before. Doing so need not embody an invention: it can simply be the founding of a new drycleaning establishment on a block which did not have one but where a need existed, or a new plant by a corporation using existing technology. If invention is involved, the importance of the entrepreneurial activity is even greater, because inventive novelty implies new risk and completes an innovation.[2]

Usually, the inventor and the entrepreneur are not the same person, though in rare cases they are. Thomas Edison fell into this rare classification, as did Henry Ford (a systems inventor!), Edwin Land, and Messrs. Hewlett and Packard.

Published in *Chemtech* 9, no. 1 (January 1979): 22–24.

There are also sub-classes of innovators: we may have an individual inventor, not supported by corporate facilities and staff, who makes inventions of fundamental importance and drives them forward. John Kilby, inventor of the monolithic integrated circuit ... is an example (for at least part of his career). There is also the corporate inventor, who has functioned within a corporate structure where he has had to champion his idea, probably in the face of much opposition at various times—for example, ... Sir Alastair Pilkington, inventor of the float-glass process. The inventor-entrepreneur is, as mentioned, a rare bird; ... Alejandro Zaffaroni, a principal at Syntex and inventor of controlled drug delivery at Alza, would fall into such a category. There is also the purely technological entrepreneur who stimulates and participates to some degree in the research and development, but basically guides the creative invention of his colleagues and leads the group in the commercialization of the new technology, thus completing the innovation. As a congressional report put it, "The technical leader is the individual who matches the world of science to the world of society, with a foot in management and a foot in science."[3] I have had the honor of doing just that at Halcon for the thirty-two years of its existence....

The Real Problem

It is seldom appreciated that the invention, the R & D, usually costs far less than the process of first commercializing it. Where large capital-intensive projects are concerned, the R & D portion may be as little as 10 percent of the total cost; the remainder needed to convert the invention to an innovation may consume 90 percent of the total cost. Professor Edwin Mansfield and his colleagues at the University of Pennsylvania have been studying this kind of relationship and, as might be expected, found in seventeen chemical innovations that R & D costs ranged from 7 percent to 71 percent of total project cost.[4] Though for new products the percentage is higher than for new processes, the important conclusion is that the invention itself (the R & D expenditure) usually costs less than half of the amount spent on the innovation. This relationship has been slow in coming to the majority of economists, who pay little attention to the economics of technology, and it has been even more tardily perceived by politicians who listen to the economists, although their advice has been mixed. Although R & D expenditures, as a percent of GNP, have been falling, it is only recently, as we in the United States start to probe into the reasons for our apparent decline in innovation, that it is being discovered that it is the risk-taking entrepreneurial side of the innovation process, costing the greater part of the innovation, which has been faltering.[5]

It is not surprising that this should be the case: most politicians take for granted that the present (presumably satisfactory) state of the nation will continue forever unchanged. In our country, the great successes and dominance of our technology since the Second World War have blinded us to the changes which are taking and have taken place both internally and externally. Alexis de Tocqueville, writing over 120 years ago, put his finger on one of the reasons for this apparent blindness, "In America there are no nobles or literary men, and the people are apt to mistrust the wealthy; lawyers consequently form the highest political class.... They have therefore nothing to gain by innovation, which adds a conservative interest to their natural taste for public order.... These (legal counselors) secretly oppose their aristocratic propensities to the nation's democratic instincts, their superstitious attachment to what is old to its love of novelty, their narrow views to its immense designs, and their habitual procrastination to its ardent impatience." Doesn't that have a contemporary ring to it?

Of course, a democracy must be founded on a legal system; we cannot do without lawyers. Allied with them are the accounting, financial, and other professions which control the pace of social and political change. Opposed to this social conservatism, which our legally trained politicians prefer, stands the technologist, the architect of *change*.

One of the few economists of technology, a recent specialization, is Professor Nathan Rosenberg of Stanford. He points out that the machine-based technology that emerged in the nineteenth century owed little to scientific knowledge.[6] Although mechanization has continued into the twentieth century, a succession of new sources of technology has developed—chemical, electrical, electronic, biological, and nuclear—each of which requires a scientific base for technological achievement, rather than cut-and-try empiricism. Nevertheless, it is important to realize that often technological development led to important scientific discoveries; indeed, often the invention never does gain a complete scientific explanation.

The Impact of Innovation

To illustrate how technology has grown, look again to Rosenberg. He points out that the electric motor "represents an extraordinarily versatile technological innovation by which it is possible to 'package' and deliver power in ways which have had very far-reaching consequences for the growth in manufacturing productivity.... Electric motors accounted for less than 5 percent of total installed horsepower in American manufacturing in

1899; ... by 1909 their share ... was 25 percent. Ten years later the share rose to 55 percent, and by 1919 ... over 80 percent.... The sharp rise in productivity in the American economy, in the years after World War I, doubtless owed a great deal ... to the [rapid spread of the] electrification of manufacturing."

This thought brings us to the question. How much of today's growth in the American GNP has been due to technology? Here we find difficulties in economic estimates,[8] but one can safely say that a third to a half of the growth rate in GNP is based on innovation. Dr. R. Atkinson, head of the National Science Foundation, has spoken of 45 percent.[9] These numbers usually understate the facts, because the *quality* of new products and of new capital investment cannot readily be measured. But clearly, technology has been a major contributor to the advances in the American standard of living since the middle of the last century. Dr. William Nordhaus, a member of the Council of Economic Advisors, says "... the effect of technological change substantially outweighs that of increase in capital stock." The full import of this finding has not yet been digested by many; it is laden with policy implications.

Slow Down

Why are we faltering? What evidence is there that we are? Let us consider signs that might give clues to the second question:

• For the first time in its history, the United States has run a deficit in its balance of payments, now reaching unprecedented heights.

• The international competitiveness of our exports is diminishing and we are experiencing intensified competition from Japan, Germany, and other countries.

• "Stagflation" has appeared with its concurrent high unemployment and high inflation rates.

• Capital investment is lagging in an unaccustomed manner.

• Growth rates have slowed down, with increased social stress.

• Taxes take an increasing share of GNP, and the governmental sector of the economy, where efficiency and productivity are difficult to maintain, has increased substantially.

• Industrial R & D turns steadily toward shorter-range, surer projects and away from risk-taking ventures; away from new products, and toward improvements in existing technology.

- Five industries alone perform over 80 percent of all R & D in the United States. They are aircraft and missiles, electric equipment and communication, chemicals, motor vehicles, and machinery.
- The others are not advancing very much technologically, relative to our international competition.
- The United States government is running unprecedented annual budget deficits, even in prosperous times.

The reason which underlies these changes, in the opinion of many, myself included, lies in the failure of our political masters to understand the *positive* role of technology. The negative side has been overemphasized in recent years (there is a negative side), and this has resulted in too many often contradictory regulations. Simultaneously, taxation on entrepreneurial individuals and on companies has increased. *Most of the technological progress made in this country was accomplished in an era of few taxes and minimal regulation.*

Partially, the current trend toward egalitarianism, to the redistribution of wealth, has contributed to the present situation. People are either innovators or imitators; wealth creators or spenders. The prevailing moral philosophy of the Western world favors the imitators, the less productive, the "disadvantaged," the spenders. Innovators, the wealth creators, are a small minority, and in a democracy cannot politically defend themselves readily against such an onslaught. Yet we have never been in greater need of innovation, particularly because the problems cited above are not susceptible to the accountant/lawyer standard "quick fixes"—fiscal and monetary manipulation, wage and price controls, restrictions on the movement of goods, services and capital across international boundaries, etc.

As I've wrestled with such concerns I came to the following conclusion: In my opinion, it is unassailable that technology is at the heart of our national dilemma, and that money in the private sector (capital and incentives for its formation) is the key to unleashing it: There has to be a recognition at the highest levels in the United States that a trade-off is necessary between encouraging new risk-taking wealth among corporations and individuals—wealth that will translate into investment—and the desire for equity and redistribution of income. This trade-off will have to be settled largely in the direction of wealth creation and new entrepreneurial incentives by tax reduction and regulatory reasonableness. *Nothing else will realistically work....* [10]

References

1. Mansfield, et al., *The Production and Application of New Industrial Technology*, W. W. Norton & Co., Inc., N. Y., 1977, p 12.

2. Applied Science and Technological Progress, a report to the Committee on Science and Astronautics, U.S. House of Representatives, by the National Academy of Sciences, June 1967, Introduction, p 1, and Applied Research Definitions, Concepts. Themes, p 21.

3. *Ibid.*

4. Mansfield, et al., *ibid.*, p 72.

5. Blumenthal, W. M., Address Before the Annual Conference of the Financial Analysts Federation, Bal Harbour, Fla., May 8, 1978. This address also gives many statistics and confirmations of the items listed [in] this paper.

6. Rosenberg, N., *Technology and American Economic Growth*, M. E. Sharpe, Inc., White Plains, N.Y., 1972, pp. 118 et seq.

7. Rosenberg, N., *Ibid.*, pp. 160 et seq.

8. Nordhaus, W. D., at A.A.A.S. Second Annual Colloquium on R & D in the Federal Budget, June 15, 1977; Edwin Mansfield, Congress of the International Economic Association, Tokyo, 1977.

9. Atkinson, R. Basic Research, The MacNeill/Lehrer Report, televised N.Y., Nov. 30 1977.

10. Landau, R., "Entrepreneurship in the Chemical Industry and in the United States," National Academy of Engineering, Washington D.C., April 1978.

19 Taxes—Their Impact on Innovation Decision-Making

... Innovation cannot flourish in today's climate. The steadily mounting inflation rates have totally distorted the investment and savings processes in this country:

• What average individual has been putting his money into a savings account at 5 1/2 percent, the income of which is still taxed, when the inflation rate is 18 percent (that is, the real return on such savings is strongly negative)? Only government rules, just now changed by Congress and the President, kept this unfair discrimination against small savers for so long, thereby forcing them to subsidize home mortgage buyers. The inevitable recognition of this rip-off is leading to a quick decline in home mortgages, which now reflect the real underlying inflation rate with rates of interest of 15–17 percent.

• What upper-income investor will be interested in any dividend-paying stock or corporate bond when he is taxed by the federal government (and more by some states) at 70 percent because dividends are deemed "unearned income"?

• What large corporation can build new risk-taking plants when the interest (at perhaps 20 percent) it would have to pay is itself approaching or in excess of what was once considered a suitable return on the investment? Usury was once deemed a crime; now it has become an instrument of government policy, which itself contributes to the increasing rate of inflation.

• Who wants to invest in the stock market when interest rates are so high, and only a few stocks really show long-term growth potential?

Excerpt of a speech delivered before the Science and Technology Committee of the National Association of Manufacturers, Washington, D.C., March 21, 1980.

• Consumers pay lower interest rates than business. Why should we wonder as consumption has been roaring and investment dropping, particularly eroding small business' ability to generate funds for survival, let alone capital formation and growth generally?

• Recent indictments of a major company subsidiary officers for counterfeiting only underline what *Business Week* has recently said: "In the diversified corporation run by financial people who have no feel for the fiber and texture of a business, the bottom line is all that matters. They manage the bottom line to produce a desired ... profit, and they order division executives to produce ... or else.... In some divisions, the project goal is met by postponing the introduction of new machinery ... or new projects to make the company more competitive." In brief, the long run is now being largely sacrificed to the short run. That is one of the major hidden costs of inflation.

You all know the answers. Only the politicians and the economists act as if had just discovered this strange new phenomenon: that people act in accordance with their perceived economic interests and incentives, and that markets reflect the collective judgments of many individuals. Now we recognize that this leads to misallocations which affect the current concern with "supply-side" economics, in addition to the more traditional "demand-side" economics. Yet the bulk of our economists and politicians continue to be surprised by the consequences of people acting exactly as we might expect—they don't save.

Whatever the underlying economic theories, the facts are indisputable. The personal savings rate in this country has virtually disappeared; instead, people buy anything tangible they can afford: gold, precious stones, real estate, homes. Corporations invest only in the sure and short-term things —projects usually associated with debottlenecking, squeezing more out of our aging industrial plant, reducing energy consumption, or expanding only where absolutely safe and with little or no new technology. For most of these, the returns are still high enough. Also, they are compelled by law to invest for pollution control, with often little or no economic benefit to the firm. While such investment may benefit society in other ways, it most certainly reduces the capital available for risk-taking innovation.

The national result of these trends is the declining productivity, the reduction in the proportion of gross national product which goes to manufacturing, and the decline in the growth rate of investment in absolute dollars. We are becoming a nation that takes in one another's laundry, but because we do not live in an isolated economy, this is no longer an economically competitive society except in a limited number of sectors. Meanwhile, in Japan, Korea, Taiwan, and Singapore, where savings and investment have resulted in new and modern productive plants, the standard of living is increasing as productivity increases.

One symptom of our growing uncompetitiveness was our recently unfavorable balance of payments, which, contrary to popular opinion and encouraged by our administration, was *not* the consequence of OPEC [Organization of Petroleum Exporting Countries], as the very different experience of Japan and West Germany (who import virtually all their oil) clearly demonstrates. No. Our industrial plant is aging and increasingly unproductive; America is becoming de-industrialized (only one third of its employed force is engaged in manufacturing) as it continues to wound itself by continuously inflicting the lashes of controls, regulations, and income redistribution from the productive to the unproductive elements of the population, achieved by ever higher taxation. Look at some of the warning signs:

• One of the major American corporations, and its second largest automobile manufacturer, lost $1 billion on its North American business in 1979, while the third largest automobile company was temporarily rescued from bankruptcy by the federal government.

• All but one of the big tire companies is floundering, and even the leader is so constrained that it has little room for any new innovations.

• The basic steel industry barely survives by virtue of a "trigger-price" mechanism instituted by the federal government.

• Automobile imports now account for over 25 percent of domestic sales, in an industry once considered highly technologically advanced relative to that of other countries. The leader of the automobile union goes to Japan to threaten their more efficient industry if they don't reduce their exports! Obviously what the American consumer wants is not being made available to him by these failures.

• Japanese cameras and electrical appliances dominate the domestic market.

• Even the oil companies, whose profits will be needed to find alternate sources of energy, face the certainty of highly confiscatory taxation by the federal government (the "windfall profits tax").

Of course there are still bright areas: in aluminum, in aerospace, in chemicals, in semiconductors, in computers, in agriculture. But there are already warning signals flashing here also:

• Aluminum capacity is not being expanded greatly in the U.S., but is moving abroad, to Australia and Brazil, for example, where energy supplies are more certain, and can be expected to be more economical (by contrast, look at the shambles in the Pacific Northwest Power situation).

• Although Boeing has done very well, the Airbus Industrie consortium now has 15 percent of the world passenger plane business in the class it manufactures, a significant upward climb.

• The domestic dyestuffs industry is passing into foreign ownership.

• Even in agriculture, we face increasing competition from countries like Brazil.

• A recent conference showed major Japanese advances in semiconductor manufacturing technology.

• Our most efficient worldwide competitor in computers is under attack from our own government, seeking a breakup....

The Causes

Such deep-seated ills as I have described did not develop overnight. They are basically the fault of the Johnson, Nixon, and Carter administrations (obviously not a partisan matter), and the associated Congresses, all of whom have put politics above economics, above growth, above the nation itself. Harsh words, but true. Under them, taxes have gone up, or, ironically, failed to go up when really needed (during the Vietnam war), and investment has gone down, despite needs created by the OPEC oil shock. Even President Ford, who vetoed many bills which would have led to excess government spending, nevertheless signed into law the highest capital gains taxation bill in history, which saw the virtual extinction of the venture capital and indeed most of the new equities markets. Budget deficits have been swollen. R&D as a percent of GNP [gross national product] has declined. The regulatory burden on society has been immeasurably enlarged.

The net result of these ill-conceived policies is the steadily increasing level of inflation, to the point where it (and its inevitable concomitant recession) is as great a threat to America in 1980 as the Depression was in 1930. As Hugh Thomas says in his *World History*, "Bad politics cause poverty more often than bad business."

The bulk of our politicians and most economists have refused to see that the causes all came from the same basic error: the growing lack of incentive to save, to take risks, to produce, to innovate. Inflation is used as an excuse to avoid cutting taxes, but in fact secretly, insidiously, and inexorably raises them, since taxpayers are pushed into ever higher tax brackets with inflation. Thus, from 1965 to 1975, the proportion of taxpayers who fall into the 20 percent or higher tax bracket skyrocketed from 19 to 53 percent. The number of people paying a quarter of their income in taxes jumped from 7 to 29 percent. This change accelerated between 1975 and 1980. The present administration then says that in order to reduce the budgetary imbalance while raising expenditures even more, no real tax cuts are possible, but rather adds new, often concealed taxes, and the incentives for ... capital formation and risk-taking shrink further. ...

What Is to Be Done?

The solution to the problem of inflation is not within the scope of my remarks herein, although the press is littered these days with proposals ..., most of them based on imposition of controls of all kinds, and more taxes. I think it is clear to all of us who are actually involved in the production and innovation process that these remedies will not work in the long run, and that models exist in West Germany and the Far East which show how we can encourage growth with low inflation. In fact, we can look back at our own development from 1945 to about the early 1960s to find a similar model, basically characterized by low inflation, low government spending, high private investment, strong productivity increases, and low controls. ... But even the West Germans are finding it difficult to learn from their own experience. Although their inflation rate has been kept low and money supply tightly controlled, the German government spending is increasing, and crowding out the private sector, so that economic growth is slowing down. This accounts for the expansion of the great German companies outside of Germany, and soon this will be followed by an increase in the German inflation rate.

Thus, although it is my conviction that generally lower taxes (particularly those affecting savings and investment), and lower government spending, are the keys to revitalization of American productivity and innovation, nevertheless I now believe that the likelihood of this happening soon enough and on a big enough scale is not great, and that it is urgent for our country to target some specific tax actions which are *not* tied to a general tax reduction, and which can encourage capital formation, productivity, new investment, and technological innovation, even in an era of high inflation. Just as we recognize, all too slowly, that the energy crisis demands unusual and specifically targeted national policies, so also must the situation regarding lagging capital investment and declining productivity be considered a grave national crisis.

The argument now fashionable that a balanced budget must precede a tax cut is fallacious. *Balancing the budget* per se is not necessarily anti-inflationary, nor is an unbalanced budget per se inflationary. Germany, Switzerland, and Austria, for example, run a deficit but have low inflation. The *level* of government expenditure and the amount of monetary expansionism do matter. Savings and incentives for them do matter a great deal, so that the general level of taxation is indeed critical.

Tax Changes to Encourage Investment

Therefore, I would like to delineate the kinds of tax actions that would be immediately effective. I can speak from a many-sided experience as an active participant: a technological entrepreneur, a small businessman, a C.E.O. responsible for investment decisions running into the hundreds of millions, a board member of a Dow-Jones company where large sums are invested every year; a head of R&D; an investor of personal funds, and, last but not least, a taxpayer of substantial amounts!

An Increased Refundable Investment Tax Credit
This kind of incentive can be most directly targeted at new industrial investment, and produces the most immediate results. The 10 percent present level is too small; it should be raised to at least 15 percent, and perhaps more for certain types of energy-related and new technology investment (along with certain continuing tax credits to help the operation of early versions of pioneering technology-containing plants such as synfuel plants), and also for mandated investments. The refundable feature is particularly important to encourage growing firms with high R&D costs and no offsetting profits to invest in new plants incorporating their technology.

A Change in Corporate Depreciation Policy
At the present time, the use of long-term depreciation schedules on historical investment greatly understates the replacement costs for the plants and equipment involved. As a result, American industry is decapitalizing itself, and paying a disproportionately high corporate tax rate. This year one will see many more companies reporting their earnings on an inflation-accounting basis of some type, and these will clearly reveal that the *real* cash flow is reduced. There is urgent need for a correction of this fundamental error, so that corporate cash flow can be increased to levels which will encourage more investment and risk-taking.... By more rapid recovery of the initial investment, industry would calculate a higher return on invest-

ment, to compensate for the negative factors in today's climate. This approach may be tailored even more precisely by allowing more generous depreciation on *new* investments made from now on, such as unlimited depreciation on new plants, entirely within the choice of the investor.

An Investment Tax Credit for New R&D
It is well established that the social value of R&D far exceeds its value to the individual firm. In order to induce more R&D which may become a precursor for later innovation, it seems perfectly reasonable for the general public to subsidize additional R&D done by firms, above some base line, measured in appropriate terms. An investment tax credit for such new R&D would help accomplish this purpose. As mentioned above, our R&D has been declining in real terms, particularly if one considers the high proportion of it which goes toward military and defense purposes, which do not encumber our foreign competitors. While R&D by itself is a *cost*, it is certainly a fact that, coupled with appropriate capital investment, under the spur of foreign and domestic competition, R&D becomes technological innovation, which has been for many years the principal driving force of the growth in the American economy—an economic *benefit*. It should always be remembered that the cost of an innovation is largely in the capital required to commercialize it, and to a much lesser extent, in the cost of the preceding R&D expense. In short, today's R&D portfolio is tomorrow's capital budget. An increase in the formation of both R&D *and* capital is therefore greatly in the national interest.

But this investment tax credit for new R&D does not necessarily, except where competition is vigorous and cash flow adequate, result in its commercialization. It is for this reason that a large investment credit for new plants incorporating new technology offering an economic advantage, must be a companion measure. Only then will improved productivity and better product quality be worth risking, and the newer plants with the latest technology will ultimately force older plants to modernize as well, thus improving the competitive situation, internally in the U.S., and on the export market. No government planning can possibly perform this service in our complex economy and the Japanese model is simply inapplicable.

Recent studies for the Joint Economic Committee of the Congress demonstrate econometrically the power of even modest cuts of the kinds described above. Furthermore, all three of these proposals, which are primarily aimed at the corporate world, are characterized also by the interesting fact that they would really cost the federal government very little in taxes, while going far to create new wealth and new technology, higher productivity, and ultimately more taxes! The changed depreciation rules, for example, in the longer run, would cost no more at all in taxes, and the initial, short-term cost would be offset by a five-cents-per-gallon. tax on gasoline, which is below what the President now proposes. But, unlike the President, I am saying that any increased tax such as this (which is by itself inflationary) must be passed back to the economy in the form of tax benefits for capital investment and risk-taking (which are not inflationary), instead of allowing more governmental expenditures to take place (which is the President's real policy and which are inflationary). The investment tax credits would be specifically associated with productive new investment.

Tax Changes to Spur Innovation

In addition to these measures, there are others that must be targeted at individual investors, new business formation, venture capital, and the technological entrepreneur where historically many of our new innovations and new industries have originated.

The Capital Gains Tax

This tax is an interesting example of how so many economists and politicians have grossly misjudged the real world of the individual risk-taker. Ever since 1969, this tax has been steadily increasing, until, in 1976, it rose to 49.1 percent as a maximum. Although inflation at that point was much lower than today, [the tax] successfully stifled venture capital and the new equities issues market. Despite all the conventional wisdom (in fact, I can remember only one prominent academic economist who spoke out in favor of a cut, and that was Dr. Martin Feldstein of Harvard), the Congress and the American people proved smarter, and forced on a very reluctant administration the reduction to 28 percent in the Revenue Act of 1978, the only real capital-formation benefit to come out of Washington in years. Already, we have seen a partial revival of the new issues market, and more venture capital can be found. But the high interest rates of today occasioned by our increased inflation make risk-taking ever so much more unrewarding, and the only remedy would be to reduce the capital gains tax even more, since it still taxes gains that are largely due to inflation alone (especially if the securities have been held for any period of time). Consequently, the capital gains tax should be reduced with the length of time the investment has been held, so that say, after ten years, it is no more than 10 percent. One additional advantage of such tax treatment would be that the entrepreneur would be less tempted to sell out to a larger company on a tax-free merger, but would find it more advantageous to seek a public market for his shares.

I recognize that the full deductibility of capital losses against ordinary income is a highly controversial issue (although it applies to certain types of agricultural activities within limits), but it would really improve risk-taking by individuals if there were such deductibility permitted.

The "Unearned Income" Tax

The present tax rate of 70 percent on investment income is confiscatory, and totally designed to discourage investment in growing enterprises. This should be reduced to 50 percent, or perhaps even less.

More Favorable Stock Option Treatment

New ventures need to attract very able technologists who are willing to accept less job security provided they can look forward to substantial rewards if the new venture is successful. Salary is an insufficient lure compared to the big company benefits. We need some kind of more favorable stock option, such as lengthening the time between grant and exercise to ten years, and making the tax due only when the stock is actually sold rather than when the option is granted.

Again, these measures do not really involve very much short-term tax loss to the Treasury, but would have great importance in encouraging new risk-taking investments by individuals. And, the dynamic effects they would produce in the economy would soon in fact add additional revenues.

Recognizing the Real World

One of the fallacies which governments of recent years have used to discourage tax reduction for capital formation is to consider that companies are like individuals, and that if companies get one-third of the tax cuts and individuals two-thirds, then it may be politically palatable. But companies and businesses are *not* individuals—they are delegated agencies of our society to generate capital and provide jobs. The money they make doesn't go to consumer goods—it goes to either new investment or to pay the bills of the workers and suppliers; the investors, who put up the capital, historically have gotten only a small proportion of the proceeds. But, by equating individuals and companies, the amount of tax reductions available at any one time is nowadays considered too large, because the budget would become too unbalanced, and so no tax cuts at all are recommended by government. Indeed, taxes keep on going up.

We must finally separate the two types of taxation. It is the responsibility of government to encourage the capital formation process regardless of what else is done to or for the economy generally, or whether there is a general tax cut at all. There is no justification for price controls when the economy needs more capital formation, and when the returns on investment as measured by the real cash flow of the private sector are already too low.... Controls are particularly unfair and stifling to younger and growing enterprises, so that, paradoxically, a real price-wage control system would in the end perpetuate an oligopolistic control of America by industries which, however, would steadily decline in competitiveness compared to their overseas rivals (British Steel and British Leyland are good examples).

In a paper delivered at the December meeting of the American Economic Association, Professor Martin Feldstein of Harvard once again showed a refreshing recognition of the real world and its problems. He stressed that the effect of taxes on economic decisions by individuals and firms has not been appreciated by classical economists and politicians, so that even the high interest rates of the recent past were perceived as being, in real net terms, below the rent value of money. This encouraged a spending and consumer binge, and a great decline in savings, investment, and innovation. In this way, inflation crept up on the American people while no one in charge noticed! He thus proposes tight federal monetary policies, with reduced government spending, so as to permit major tax cuts to favor investment and capital formation, while discouraging excessive consumption. He too considers budget balancing not necessarily good, especially when it is done at high levels of government spending and taxation. My proposals herein are suggested in this vein, based on actual experience in the decision-making processes to which he refers. But as inflation moderates with the resumption of technological growth and productivity, and with tight control over government spending, interest rates will also moderate. However, attention should really be given in the present interim climate to some kind of system which would make low interest loans available for new technological investments; credit controls on consumption may help correct some of the current imbalances, but the present high interest rates for small businesses or entrepreneurs are impossible. It is better by far to subsidize such growing and technologically progressive businesses by reduced interest than to bail out a Chrysler.

Professor Burton Klein of the California Institute of Technology, in his book, *Dynamic Economics*, is also one of the few academic economists who understands the real world of incentives, of innovation, of human imagination, of technology, of dynamic equilibrium and unstable conditions. While my proposals and recommendations herein are not by any means the same as his, because I arrive at them from a much harder experience base, nevertheless he is definitely on the right track, and it is hoped that the economics profession will increasingly recognize the importance of his attempts to modernize it to describe the world as it actually is. One of the great mysteries to me has been the only very recent discovery by a handful of economists of the decisive importance of technological progress to economic growth, and the failure of much of classical economics even to inquire why the growth of the American economy has so significantly exceeded the usual inputs of land, labor, and capital.

A few other economists such as Dale Jorgenson at Harvard, Nathan Rosenberg and Michael Boskin at Stanford, and Edwin Mansfield at Penn have also done important fresh thinking in these areas, as have Edward Denison, formerly at Brookings, and John Kendrick at George Washington University in productivity studies.

Thus, we are finally beginning to realize that there is no other way than the aforementioned for our economy to survive the rigors of world competition. A greater level of fixed capital investment, coupled with increased R&D will more rapidly embody the new technology in plants which can become world leaders. The relatively old American industrial plant is technologically obsolescent when compared with the newer plants of its foreign competitors, particularly because so many of our plants were designed to use cheap forms of energy.

America has abundant energy resources, a high-technology base, an educated work force, a huge home market, many entrepreneurs, a marvelous Constitution—all the inherent power to resume its position as *the* dominant economic power of the world, which desperately needs our leadership. All we have to do is get our act together! But I must issue the most solemn warning: a continuation of the malign neglect of innovation of the past fifteen years will ruin this country within twenty-five years. Innovation cannot be turned on and off like a water tap. New technology takes years to discover and even longer to commercialize. The start-stop economic policies of these recent years, the zig-zags of government, which will soon lead to an enormous squeeze on the private sector with attendant liquidity problems and even greater reluctance for risk-taking capital investment, have been disastrous, and must be completely changed to a long-range, steady, imaginative, predictable program that is determined to allow the creative genius of the American people to renew itself. We must take the control of industry out of the hands of the financial people, or we will all go the way of the railroads. But this can only be accomplished when inflation is beaten into the ground. No one can guarantee under those circumstances that company managements will be any smarter than were those of the railroads, but, unlike these, most industries must face fierce competition from abroad. If we provide the right macro climate with much less government interference, managements and workers must sink or swim. That is the path to reinvigorate our economy.

20

Technology, Economics, and Public Policy

... [The United States is now] confronted with a plethora of new tax proposals—making it possible that there will be a major tax bill in 1985 or 1986 as there was in 1981, 1982, and 1984. The dangers that face the country if inappropriate tax policy is adopted can best be illustrated ... by some comments on proposals made November 1984 by the Treasury, which would form the most radical change in the tax laws since the income tax was introduced in 1913. Although the president's proposals of May 1985 are different in some respects, and the final bill, if any, that emerges from the political process will certainly be different still, it is instructive to review certain aspects of these proposals ... :

1. The most fundamental philosophical question is whether the United States wishes to abandon its principal postwar policy of favoring in its tax policy certain economic and social activities, hoping that everything will just work out in a "neutral" environment, while its competitors abroad (most especially the Japanese) follow the *opposite* strategy. It may be added that the United States does not follow a neutral policy in its budgetary approach, or in trade matters. In fact, even this [tax] proposal is not neutral. All "profits" are not the same across industries and companies, and there is no realistic way they could be. Housing is still a favored investment because interest on primary home mortgages would be deductible in full; to maintain adequate investment in productive facilities, favorable tax incentives for business must also be contained in the code, especially in industries that face severe international competition. Tax-exempt institutions still compete with private individuals for investment opportunities, often to

In Ralph Landau and Dale Jorgenson, eds. *Technology and Economic Policy.* Proceedings of the Conference on Technology and Economic Policy, Harvard University, Washington, D.C., February 4–5, 1985 (Cambridge, Mass.: Ballinger, 1986): 44–55. Reprinted with permission of the program on Technology and Economic Policy at Harvard University.

the latter's disadvantage, as they must act on after-tax considerations. Enterprise zones have been praised by the president as a special incentive for high risk-taking but there are many other high-risk enterprises. The capital gains tax experience of 1978, and the impact of other features of the Reagan tax programs, argue strongly for continuation of proven effective policies. In short, nowhere has neutrality of tax policy as advocated by certain tax policy purists ever been applied, let alone shown to be worthwhile; hence, proponents of such a philosophy have the heavy burden of proof. There is little evidence that these proponents have seriously studied the realities of the business and technological worlds in reaching their conclusions, or that they understand the implications of modern economic theory and research. At the same time, there are important social goals embedded in the present code which should not lightly be abandoned or damaged: low-income rental housing; charitable contributions (where the United States has achieved a truly enviable mix of social benefits); state and local tax deductibility, which provides for favorable education and aid to the disadvantaged of much of the United States; tax-free accumulation of various insurance and other benefits by employers for the account of their workers, and others, all drastically altered in the Treasury ... proposals.

2. Another illustration is afforded by the experiences of many companies which took advantage of the accelerated depreciation (ACRS) and investment tax credits (ITC) in the 1981 and 1982 tax bills, designed to encourage new capital investment and increase American technological competitiveness. It is not well understood that perhaps only twenty companies export over $1 billion of goods annually, among them General Motors, General Electric, Boeing, Ford, DuPont, IBM, Kodak, and United Technologies. Many of these used such tax credits to advantage in their work, and funded investment without recourse to external debt. Particularly in an economy of high interest rates, which favors housing and where hurdle rates for investors are high compared with the Japanese, such tax features are essential to encourage new investment. Indeed, in preserving American companies' competitiveness, a higher proportion of equity capital is being employed so as to combat Japan's lower interest rates and more accommodating financial system in the face of economic uncertainty. This is done despite the higher cost of equity versus debt and underlines the need for compensating incentives for new investment. The recovery from the 1981–82 recession has featured an extraordinary investment boom. Spending on plant and equipment rose more during the first seven quarters of the current recovery than during corresponding periods of any of the last five economic expansions, being more than double. The tax policies of

the 1981 and 1982 acts were certainly conducive to these results, although it is too short a time period to provide good correlations. The real question is whether such an investment surge would have been as great without these tax incentives, and this seems most improbable. Furthermore, much of this investment is in modernization and cost reduction, thus restraining inflation and promoting competitiveness by improving productivity and product quality. Half is in high-tech investment, and half of that is in computers alone! However, as noted, if the hard dollar persists, Stephen Roach ... of Morgan Stanley points out that U.S. capital goods producers may be increasingly squeezed out of participating in the most dramatic transformation in the U.S. economy since the Industrial Revolution. The mostly young high-technology companies have boomed and have created jobs at the cutting edge of economic growth. Yet, too many American companies are still illiquid. Here, also, the health of the total equities markets matters profoundly. This is no time to destroy the successful tax policies of the Reagan first term. The more capital intensive the firm or industry, the more significant does the tax policy affecting it become; but it is more and more clear, *all technology is capital intensive.*

One example pointed to in the recent press is the case of General Electric, which paid no income tax in the period 1981–1983 while earning $6.5 billion domestic pre-tax profits. But, in addition to various local and payroll taxes they did pay, GE invested $18 billion since 1981 in new plant and equipment, which may well have sustained at least 250,000 jobs per year in the United States. Does anyone seriously contend that the government could have spent the deferred (its effective rate is about 32 percent) or reduced taxes more wisely than did GE—an outstandingly well-managed company prominent in its R&D and strategic planning approach and headed by a Ph.D. engineer? In fact, if lowering the corporate tax rate requires abolition of such favorable tax treatment for investment, then there is a high probability that many companies would elect to *reduce* innovation and increase their dividends pay-out, especially considering the partial deductibility of dividends that the proposals contain. The better solution is to amend the ACRS and ITC regulations to correct known and unproductive abuses, which cause much inequality and envy between firms. These incentives to invest serve as at least a partial offset to the triple taxation of capital in the present income tax system as it pertains to shareholders. John Shoven and Toshiaki Tachibanaki in a comprehensive paper ... have calculated that the overall effective marginal cost of capital to Japan, taking all levels of taxation into account, was − 1.5 percent at the actual inflation average of several indices, while the U.S. figure was 37.2

percent for the year 1980. Thus, in Japan, the marginal investor is *slightly subsidized*. Further calculations in their paper indicated that at the corporate level, the effective marginal tax rates at different measures of actual inflation are in the range of 7 to 17 percent, so that they have an approximation of an expenditure tax. Japan since World War II has adopted a firm strategy of favoring savings and investment over consumption by a variety of incentive policies described in their paper, and these have proved highly effective; before the war, Japanese savings and investments were much lower. This provides another example of how careful incentives do indeed work in this direction; prior to the events of 1978–1981, the United States had few such incentives. This highly uncompetitive situation needs far more tax reductions for firms and individuals that invest in new technology and equipment than even the 1981 bill has provided; the Treasury ... proposals move in exactly the opposite direction, almost suicidally so!

3. Neither the Treasury nor anyone else seems to have made reliable economic forecasts for the overall impact of this bill on the economy and its component parts, especially for the longer range. The few that have emerged since November 27, 1984, are somewhat negative about the proposals in the short run, with quantitiative effects probably overshadowing any favorable qualitative effects, but what the effects would be over the five to seven years necessary for the economy to absorb them are very difficult to predict by any model, because of the great complexity of the interrelated effects. Yet it is the overall long-term result that is critical. New classical economists would say that any change in policy can alter the entire structure of an economic model, not just measure the specific effect of the policy change. How can the U.S. government seriously make the entire economy of the United States a guinea pig in this way? There was no political demand for such drastic experimentation, only a vote not to raise taxes; the performance of the Reagan first term does not require surgery, just a corrective. Engineers would be severely criticized if they built a large-scale plant without going through the pilot plant and other preliminary phases.

4. The overall impact of the proposed bill is not only anti-investment (it will raise the cost of investing in equipment by perhaps 15 percent at a time when Japanese capital costs only half of that in the United States, and reduce incentives to save)—it is *anti-risk-taking*, the precise opposite of what is needed to remain competitive and to encourage growth and job formation. The partial dividend exclusion will favor established low-growth companies; the capital gains tax provisions will militate against new companies and risk-taking; the provision for partial indexing of inter-

est will cause a great influx of buyers into government and other fixed income securities at the expense of the equities market; indexing of depreciation for inflation will attack new investment after 1988, but not existing investment; the elimination of the progressive corporate tax on small companies will make it harder for them to finance their growth; and the nondeductibility of state and local taxes will cause a rearrangement of business and individuals who will then be too busy to gaze at distant horizons in time. These are only a few examples, but they illustrate what appears to be a strong bias in favor of safe and secure government obligations.

Consider the case of a New York investor purchasing Treasury bills (at whatever interest rate eventually occurs) with inflation at 4 percent. [One Treasury proposal would] exclude 40 percent of the interest from taxation, so that the new maximum effective tax rate would be $0.60 \times .35 = 0.21$ (21 percent). On the other hand, an entrepreneur starting a company with stock at a nominal price, which appreciates quite substantially in five to seven years would pay nearly 35 percent plus the applicable but nondeductible state tax (nearly 14 percent in New York) as a capital gain. This tax rate of nearly 49 percent is more than *twice* the tax rate on investments in federal securities, not counting a possible New York City tax as well. What incentive is there for risk-taking, or entrepreneurship? The return on venture capital would have to average more than twice the return on bonds just to break even; but since the losses due to failure are not deductible, there must be a substantial risk premium as well. Hence, the expected return would have to be three or four times as much from the venture as from the bond. This is obviously very unlikely even in the most ideal circumstances, and risk would be avoided completely. The proposed increase in capital gains taxation not only flies in the face of hard recent experience—it is a signal to the entire country to beware of risk-taking. And the data show conclusively that raising this tax will reduce revenue, certainly not increase it. In any event, the amounts are too small to matter in the deficit; yet this very tiny segment of a huge total capital market is the lubricant of entrepreneurship and technological progress. The capital gains differential and stock options are at the very most only offsets to the deductibility of home mortgage interest. Why take this grave risk for some theoretical reasons of "neutrality"? Neutrality will almost certainly translate into safety and risk aversion; there must be non-neutrality if there is to be risk-taking! *Most important, these proposals are not neutral as between investment and consumption—they clearly favor the latter.*

To be sure, nontaxable institutions also invest in venture capital and new issues, but the data show the decisive importance of the tax to individuals

—the entrepreneurs, the investors who lead institutional commitments, and those who buy stocks (42 million now). Stanley Pratt, publisher of the authoritative *Venture Capital Journal*, has recently pointed out that "the organized venture capital industry has currently committed to it about $16 billion, of which at least 62 percent is from taxable sources and only 38 percent from tax-exempt investors. If one considers informal venture investments from taxable individuals, which some analysts estimate to be greater than the organized activity, tax-exempt investors are even less significant.... Even though many like to credit them with a leadership role, the fiduciary responsibilities of pension, endowment and foundation investors mandate a follower's role in new investment trends, after others have served as pioneers." He explains that the $16 billion comes from independent private venture capital firms ($11.4 billion), small business investment companies ($1.6 billion) and corporate subsidiaries ($3.0 billion), both of the latter being almost exclusively taxable entities. He also points out that the entrepreneurs and their employees *do* perceive the importance of the capital gains differential, which is the most potent device in the code to stimulate the creation of *new* wealth, whereas the Treasury proposals for decreasing the tax rate for dividends and interest favor those already wealthy, and discourages them from further risk-taking....

Recently, the Joint Economic Committee of the U.S. Congress ... released a study which shows that institutional nontaxed venture capital flows more to the better known, less-risky, and larger investments and venture funds, while the taxable funds go more to the seed capital and startup companies, where the smaller venture capital companies are essential—that is, those that are the greatest risks. Thus, ... the growth of venture capital coincides with the rise in real interest rates. Therefore, growing companies could not have been financed by borrowing but by plowing back capital gains realizations. As the capital gains tax was reduced, the stock market revived and the initial public offerings (IPO) increased. It is also known that institutional capital has been less abundant in the recent months, because it sees lower returns ahead as the venture capital industry, in the face of a poor IPO market, is compelled to increase its secondary and tertiary financings. It is necessary to understand the dynamics, and not be fooled by any simple average calculations.

The entire equities markets, if adequately liquid, provide the outlet for risk-takers to "cash in," for investors to move from one asset to another, and for companies to raise capital in the face of high real interest rates. It is impossible to single out one narrow part of the equities market (such as venture capital alone) for favorable tax treatment, for all these reasons, and many more. The markets are all interrelated. Institutions are not heroic—people are! It was from considerations such as these that the people most knowledgeable about how the system really works urged the government to retain the capital gains tax differential. In February 1985, the American Business Conference, the American Electronics Association, the U.S. Chamber of Commerce, the National Association of Manufacturers, the National Association of Small Business Investment Companies, and the Securities Industry Association, among others—including high technology and basic industries, small and large businesses, mature and emerging companies, agriculture and manufacturing, and Wall Street and the venture capital community, all joined in a strongly worded statement that said, "In our view, the Treasury Department's capital gains tax proposal, if enacted into law, would reverse two of the most successful tax changes in history, the lowering of capital gains taxes in 1978 and again in 1981." They attributed this particularly to the fact that by these changes the government had restored the reward for risk-taking and investment. They also pointed out that maintaining incentives for venture capital alone does not address the fact that elimination of the capital gains differential for all other equities will raise the cost of capital to American firms at a time when Japan already enjoys at least a 2:1 advantage in this regard. All equities investors (42 million) are influenced by after-tax considerations. . . . Instead of dealing with . . . static models of the economy and theoretical considerations of neutrality, the Treasury should pay attention to the way individuals and firms *actually behave*, and how they adjust their actions if unfavorable tax or other policies are promoted based on such theoretical models, which the Treasury admits it still uses. Business firms use dynamic models regularly; why is the government so retrograde?

It is curious that the Treasury proposals support R&D credit for firms but deny them the tax credits needed to implement the results of R&D! The lack of neutrality of the proposals is again shown by this example favoring only one part of the innovation process. It would be more appropriate to show concern for the substantial number of excellent research organizations that have disappeared or are endangered, by the vicious takeover practices now permitted by law, and to propose appropriate corrective legislation, and correct economic policy.

Does this bias imply that the federal government under President Reagan foresees indefinitely large deficits which must be financed with such federal obligations? And if so much attention is paid to indexing against inflation at a time when inflation rates are low, are the American people to expect that this administration really considers that inflation will come roaring back again and is preparing for it? If so, it is a naked admission of failure, and the history that will be written will be very harsh. Yet it is unjustified: the Reagan administration has some real economic accomplishments to its credit and a chance to create a long-lasting favorable climate for growth.

5. Any new efforts in the direction of tax simplification are to be applauded, but great care must be exercised before major steps (or even lesser ones, if untried) are undertaken. Many economists have shown that the most fundamentally positive approach to encouraging growth and prosperity would be to move toward an overall consumption tax system. Several studies comparing the efficiency loss to the economy form distorting the consumption/investment choice relative to the decision about the types of investment to be made suggest that such intertemporal distortions are several times more important than the distortions in the allocation of investment. Thus, a consumption tax system could be truly neutral among investments and classes of investors (such as tax-exempt or taxable, residential or productive) leaving investment decisions to the marketplace, and could eliminate tax shelters, mergers, or buy-outs of an unsound or highly leveraged character, increase savings, etc. Jorgenson ... has shown, using an econometric model incorporating rational expectations concepts, that a pure consumption tax generating the same total revenue as under today's codes, would permit growth in the wealth of this country almost three times more (in percentage) than a pure flat tax .... Because no econometric model can be "correct" in real terms, Jorgenson's model should be looked at particularly to distinguish the relative advantages of alternate policies. One could approach such a system incrementally, for example, by broadening substantially the scope of Individual Retirement Accounts (IRAs) and similar tax-free savings, which do impose taxes when money is withdrawn (consumed), and by adding a value-added tax on certain types of goods, while lowering marginal tax rates, or by phasing in over several years full expensing of capital investment in the year it is made. Or, perhaps as The Economist ... recently suggested, by a large increase in the tax on gasoline, or a tax on imported crude oil, to compensate. What is relevant is John Shoven's ... observation that the tax code today is already midway between an income and consumption tax at the personal level. Why not move closer to an all-consumption tax system?

The recent book by Charls Walker and Mark Bloomfield ... New Directions in Federal Tax Policy for the 1980's, and the Brookings volume edited by Alice Rivlin ... discuss consumption or similar taxes in great detail. They are admittedly radical departures from precedent. Any transition from an income tax to a consumption tax would be very difficult to engineer, particularly as a way must be found to reward risk-taking—the key to innovation and growth. But, if the pain of a wholesale restructuring of the tax code is ever justified, it should be only for a very large probable benefit which a consumption tax represents, and not for an extremely uncertain outcome such as the Treasury income tax proposals, which do not even have the virtue of greater simplicity than the present code (the indexation features and the transition rules which will endure for at least ten years, guarantee that this will be the case).

6. The proposed increase in corporate taxes would add over 30 percent to the corporate sector taxes while reducing those of individuals by 8.5 percent. Corporations would pay $45 billion more in fiscal 1990. (However, those corporations that require heavy capital investment would pay much more and those that do not might pay less. As stated above, the United States cannot afford to abandon its manufacturing sector by such methods!) This is absolutely the wrong way to go in an era of increasing need for technological innovation in a competitive world economy. In Ralph Landau and N. B. Hannay ... an extensive analysis of the relation between taxation, technology, and economics was undertaken by a number of experts who had real world experience. It is worthwhile to quote the major policy conclusions for policymakers drawn from their papers by the editors: "You are justified in making—indeed obliged to make in view of the national urgency—extensive business-oriented and pro-investment personal tax cuts. It is better to include a very broad mix, all at once, rather than piecemeal, as a real business stimulus to investors." There was no real consensus on the desirability or extent of general personal income tax rate cuts, and no such consensus exists today. There is little doubt that lower marginal tax rates would be beneficial in the long run, but these can only be truly feasible when government deficits and hence the required taxes can be reduced.

Under conditions where greater economic growth and investment are essential, as today, it is desirable to target incentives for *new* capital investment. If the incentive is too wide, extending also to existing capital, it is less efficient in its "bang for the buck," that is, stimulus of new investment per dollar of lost revenue. Thus, an investment tax credit, which applies only to new investment, is more efficient from a revenue point of view than lower corporate taxes, because these also benefit old capital investments. Another example is the first year expensing of new asset investments, giving a zero effective tax rate on the new investments but not applying to returns from old capital. Alan Auerbach ... has dealt extensively with this subject in a chapter of a book devoted to improving economic growth (Wachter and Wachter). There is still an unsolved problem of how to provide investment incentives for companies with tax losses that cannot take direct advantage of such incentives. Often, such companies require high equity/debt ratios because of their risky nature; low capital gains taxes tend therefore to offset the risks and attract investors and new capital. The R&D tax credit is similarly of little use to such companies, unless there is an actual rebate from the Treasury (a most unlikely occurrence), but R&D partnerships have tended to provide at least a partial offset. Thus, neutrality, as between old and new capital or between risky and safe investments, is clearly undesirable, another fault of the Treasury I proposal.

In fact, the first Reagan tax bill (ERTA, the Economic Recovery Tax Act of 1981), even though modified somewhat later, had many of the desirable characteristics and has been quite successful to date. It targeted its incentives very well, even though some companies and activities might not have been as socially desirable as others, and some features of accelerated depreciation were of little value to rapidly growing high-technology companies which are less capital intensive than the smokestack industries. Since the cost of capital to the former companies is often based primarily on equity investment, however, the capital gains provisions have been important to them; the situation would have been even more favorable if interest rates were lower, contributing to more robust equities markets generally. It is not necessary to demolish its basic accomplishments in 1985, although improvements in specific instances may be justifiable.

More generally, the high cost of capital to American companies mandates that the budget deficits first be reduced by cutting expenditures so that interest rates fall, and equities rise. Until that happy day American entrepreneurs and industrialists need all the tax advantages that ACRS, ITC, capital gains, and the like provide them as a partial offset to the low Japanese capital cost, as well as the abundance thereof.

It must be clear from everything said before that uncertainty leads to very short-range viewpoints, and lack of long-range planning which is essential for technological progress and growth. Any sweeping change will inevitably lead to just such uncertainty, and economic regression. The very announcement of this Treasury ... proposal, and of the debate in Washington, has already introduced significant delays in investment planning by individuals and companies. Yet, any fundamental overhauling of a tax code which has been in existence for many years (although with numerous modifications) *must* require extensive national deliberation and examination; the very uncertainty of its effects requires an exhaustive investigation of every feature. Hasty action for political ends will be judged very harshly indeed as future unfavorable trends unfold. *Markets hate uncertainty!*

The greatest danger facing the country is a gridlocked political process which would result in small budget cuts and a tax increase incorporating the worst features of the various tax proposals. In such a case, all semblance of tax neutrality and logic would drown in a sea of hasty political compromise! That would be a recipe for economic failure!

21

Introduction to
The Positive Sum Strategy

Why this volume? We start from the premise that engineers and economists share a common interest in technology and technological change. They do, however, approach the subject from different vantage points, and the very differences in these vantage points have been intensified by the inevitable increase in specialization that has characterized industrial societies.

Specialization has been not only the source of well-known benefits in economic activity but also the source of spectacular advances in the production of knowledge. However, increased specialization of disciplines has fostered compartmentalization and fragmentation of knowledge about particular subjects that can, in some instances, prove to be dysfunctional and therefore costly. This occurs when one group of specialists no longer has even minimal comprehension of bodies of information that are highly relevant to the successful performance of some of its responsibilities.

We have prepared this book because we believe that we are now at such a juncture in our understanding of the determinants of successful technological innovation. We believe that engineers and economists can benefit from a dialogue in which each group of specialists acquires a deeper understanding of the concerns, priorities, insights, and methods of the other.

Thus, this volume presents chapters by engineers who are knowledgeable about technologies and by economists who are knowledgeable about the functioning of markets. A fruitful exchange of views between these groups of specialists should lead to a better understanding of the conditions under which technological innovation can be made to function more effectively in the generation of economic growth.

With Nathan Rosenberg, coeditor of *The Positive Sum Strategy*. Reprinted with permission from *The Positive Sum Strategy: Harnessing Technology for Economic Growth*. Copyright 1986 by the National Academy of Sciences. Courtesy of the National Academy Press, Washington, D.C.

Why Dialogue Is Needed

Technology has been *the* critical factor in the long-term economic growth of modern industrial societies. But it functions successfully only within a larger social environment that provides an effective combination of incentives and complementary inputs into the innovation process. Technology may be thought of as an extroverted activity: it involves a search for workable solutions to problems (the practice of technological innovation). When it finds solutions that are workable and effective, it does not pursue the "Why?" question very hard. Moreover, the output of technological activities is a product or a service that must eventually stand the test of the marketplace.

Science, by contrast, is an introverted activity. It studies problems that are usually generated internally—for example, by logical discrepancies or internal inconsistencies or by anomalous observations that cannot be accounted for within the present intellectual framework. As technologies have become increasingly sophisticated and complex over the past century, the innovation process has become increasingly dependent on the findings and methodology of science, which has been flourishing in the post–World War II era.

Markets are the basic institutional framework within which new technologies are evaluated. Long-term economic growth must, in large measure, be understood in terms of the performance of new technologies within this framework. The functioning of the market has been the specialized concern of the discipline of economics.

Why Should Technologists Be Concerned About Economics?

Just as technological change is related to and operates within the framework of physical science, so the discipline of economics is related to politics. The political sphere establishes the larger societal framework (including the legal structure) within which technological change and economic growth take place. This includes:

1. The macroenvironment flowing from monetary and fiscal policies.

2. The microenvironment resulting from the effects of specific government tax and spending policies, for example.

3. The larger environment established by a changing legal framework; by regulations directed at such problems as health, pollution, and safety; and by foreign trade, antitrust, and other policies.

It is this economic environment, and the political forces that shape it, that in turn determines the effectiveness of the incentives that society provides to the activities of technologists.

The poor performance of the U.S. economy in the past fifteen years or so points forcefully to the limitations of economic knowledge, especially as it pertains to the forces that encourage technological innovation and economic growth. As a result, there are sharp differences within the economics profession over how best to provide a stable environment for continued growth within a framework that simultaneously provides for low levels of inflation and unemployment. It is at least arguable that government policies have, in this period of uncertainty and confusion, exacerbated rather than improved matters. The disagreement among economists inevitably has led to improvisation by politicians conscious of the election cycle, with inadequate regard for the economic consequences of political decisions.

It is therefore time for the intellectual stocktaking that this book represents, by which technologists can be offered guidance on what economists know and on the limits of knowledge on how economic forces shape the environment for technological innovation.

It is important, at the same time, to recognize that the intellectual disarray in economics is only partial. There are broad areas of consensus among economists on matters of vital importance to the ongoing activities of technologists. These need to be identified and emphasized. For example, successful technological innovation always involves more than purely technological considerations. Successful innovation involves the fulfillment of needs as they are expressed in the marketplace, where considerations of cost and adaptation to specific needs and determination of appropriate trade-offs between price and performance are likely to be critical. Thus, from a purely technological point of view, the Concorde was a more spectacular innovation than the Boeing 747. From a commercial point of view, however, the Concorde was a failure, whereas the 747 looks quite different. It is itself an interesting commentary on the commercial uncertainties associated with innovation in some industries that, although the 747 has been in service for more than a decade, it is still hard to judge whether it will be a commercial success.

Thus, successful new product design and manufacture are tightly linked to economic variables. Indeed, good engineering design is close, conceptually, to microeconomics. In both cases a central activity consists of optimizing, subject to certain constraints.

Technologists need to participate more in setting the stage for their own specialized efforts, but in order to do so they must understand better the advice that economists are giving to policymakers and the probable economic consequences of political actions.

Why Should Economists Be Concerned About Technology?

Research in the past thirty years has conclusively established the critical role played by technological change in generating long-term economic growth. While considerable differences persist in attempts to quantify the contribution of technological change to such growth with any real precision (partly because there are basic conceptual problems as well as narrow measurement problems), there is broad agreement to its dominating importance.

Despite such agreement, economists have continued to treat the realm of technology as a "black box." While such treatment may have been understandable in an earlier period when the contributions of technological innovation were less appreciated, this neglect is now much more difficult to justify. It seriously limits improved understanding of both the determinants and the consequences of technological innovation. The limited understanding, in turn, is a serious handicap to the formation of more effective government policies. Better understanding may reasonably be expected to improve the prospects for more effective policymaking, with eventual improvements in economic growth rates and in the competitiveness of U.S. products in world markets.

A consequence of these limitations has been the pursuit of a number of different types of microeconomic interventions by governments in the private sector, where most technological innovation takes place. Some of these interventions may well have slowed the pace of technological innovation in many areas, thus reducing economic growth and impairing the competitiveness of U.S. companies in world markets. Likewise, macroeconomic policies have been proposed or adopted that have unexpected, and sometimes unfavorable, impacts on technological innovation.

Before a better understanding of the determinants of technological innovation can be achieved, it will be necessary for economists to come to understand some of the specific characteristics of technologies. These characteristics differ substantially from one industry to another and, as a result, conditions or policies that contribute to successful innovation in one industry may be much less successful in another. Many issues—such as the role of firm size, the highly skewed distribution of R&D expenditures among industrial sectors, the extremely broad range of activities that fall under the rubric of R&D, differences in the organization of R&D activities, the varying gestation periods and uncertainties of the innovation process, the degree of interdependency between scientific research and the development process—pose problems regarding which a willingness on the part of economists to listen carefully to engineers may improve the economic analysis of the innovation process. We anticipate that technological information of the kind readily handled by engineers can explain much about the generation and diffusion of new technologies that will otherwise remain poorly understood by economists. A carefully structured, selective, and discriminating interchange of information between economists and engineers such as takes place in this volume should, we believe, prove beneficial to both groups and therefore also, ultimately, to policymakers....

22

Capital Formation in the United States and Japan

... The innovation process in its complete form consists of two stages: invention and implementation. The former is usually a function of R&D and experience; the latter is primarily a function of capital investment (which includes the development and design stages) and is the much riskier part of the innovation process. Thus, in examining capital formation and costs in the United States and Japan, this chapter focuses on capital formation in the business sector, which, however, consists of a very wide diversity of companies in various stages of development. Most of the chapter deals with the manufacturing sector, since this sector is the primary component of international trade flows (very few domestic service companies, except those in banking, insurance, and the like, contribute much to imports). Also, ... the manufacturing sector performs the bulk of the R&D undertaken by U.S. companies, hence investment in knowledge and technology.

The Manufacturing Sector

The vital role of manufacturing in the U.S. economy can be seen from the fact that manufacturing accounts for the following:

- About 20 percent of total employment (in Japan it runs close to 25 percent);
- About 23 percent of total output;
- 50 percent of goods output for the economy as a whole; and
- About 60 percent of exports and 75 percent of imports.

With George N. Hatsopoulos. Reprinted with permission from *The Positive Sum Strategy: Harnessing Technology for Economic Growth.* Copyright 1986 by the National Academy of Sciences. Courtesy of the National Academy Press, Washington, D.C.

Moreover, the goods-producing sector has a much greater rate of productivity increase than other sectors of the economy. Total factor productivity in the goods-producing sector, for example, increased 175 percent
between 1960 and 1984, whereas the rate in the service-producing sector
was only about 135 percent.

The average rate of productivity growth over the postwar period in
manufacturing has been 2.8 percent; in services, 2 percent; and in the
overall economy, about 2.5 percent. In constant 1972 dollars, the GNP-
worker ratio in manufacturing is about $20,000, and in all services about
$11,000 (some services, such as banking, are more efficient than the aver-
age). Because of the recent cyclical recovery, manufacturing productivity
increased by 4.5 percent, and services by about 3 percent, over the last two
and a half years. Thus, the manufacturing sector is a vital part of the
productivity growth of the entire economy and is the most robust.[1]

The Japanese have done much better in their manufacturing sector than
has the United States, due to factors beyond the favorable dollar-yen ratio
and the government restrictions placed by the Japanese on imports or
manufacture in Japan by foreigners. They have been investing in their

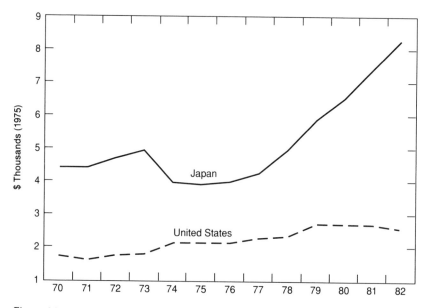

Figure 22.1
Manufacturing fixed investment per year per employee (thousands of 1975 dollars). Source:
Hatsopoulos and Brooks (note 2 in this chapter).

manufacturing sector at rates that are between two and two and a half times the U.S. rate of investment in capital per worker (figure 22.1).[2] It would seem clear, therefore, that the stock of capital is growing more rapidly in Japan than in the United States. Between 1970 and 1981 the rate of growth in constant-dollar gross capital per worker in manufacturing in Japan was 7.1 percent per year, more than twice the 3.5 percent annual rate of gain in the United States. No data are available for gross capital after 1981 for Japan, and none for net capital on a replacement basis. The only data available are for net capital on a historical basis. It is estimated that the net tangible capital per worker among principal manufacturers, on a historical basis, is $48,000 for Japan in 1982, and $32,000 in the United States.

As noted above, it is well supported in the literature that productivity is closely linked to capital-labor ratios. The higher rate of growth of capital per worker in Japan, therefore, has resulted in a higher rate of productivity growth in Japan as compared to the United States (figure 22.2).[3] Whatever the reasons for changes in the rate of productivity growth, ... Japan's advantage in capital investment must be a major factor in its ability to do better than the United States. It becomes important, therefore, to learn more about the quantity and cost of capital in the two countries.

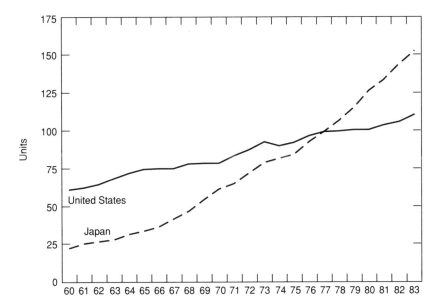

Figure 22.2
Output per hour in manufacturing (1977 = 100). Source: Hatsopoulos and Brooks (see note 2 in this chapter).

Capital Availability

A striking difference between the United States and Japan is the sheer availability of capital. This is due in part to the much higher savings rate in Japan. In the United States, personal savings have averaged about 5 to 8 percent of disposable income over a long period of time, whereas Japan's personal savings rate is in the 17 to 18 percent range (having been above 22 percent before 1975)—almost three times as great. In the United States, overall gross fixed-capital formation, as a percentage of GNP, is in the range of 15 percent, whereas in Japan it is over 30 percent, or nearly twice as much. While savings in the corporate and household sectors vary from one country to the other, the overall effect is clearly that the greater Japanese savings rate contributes to the greater availability of capital for private investment (both governments run roughly comparable deficits as a percentage of GNP).

What causes this greater Japanese savings rate is not easy to determine, even for Japanese economists. There seem to be at least two fundamental factors (before the war the Japanese did *not* have as high a savings rate, so cultural factors are not likely to be the cause):

1. A conscious government policy to increase savings by means of favorable tax policies, control over financial markets, and investment options available to the private saver; and

2. Limitations on social security provisions combined with early retirement (at 55) for employees of large corporations.

John Shoven of Stanford University and Toshiaki Tachibanaki of the Kyoto Institute of Economic Research have made an extensive survey of the tax policies in Japan.[4] Among many favorable features should be listed the absence of a capital gains tax and the existence of a tax-free savings plan that permits an individual to save up to $56,000 in nontaxable form (considerably higher than the average monetary assets per capita). When all the members of a household are included and the widespread evidence of evasion is taken into account, it is clear that households can save large sums tax free. Dividends are taxed at a lower rate than is salary income (the opposite was true in the United States until 1981 when the Economic Recovery Tax Act was adopted, which made the tax on the two forms of income the same, although some states still maintain a differential in favor of earnings as against investment income from interest and dividends). On the other hand, mortgage interest and the like are not deductible from income in Japan, unlike in the United States. Thus, the Japanese tax system,

Shoven and Tachibanaki say, "is responsible for lowering the overall effective tax on income from capital." Hence, they continue, "the Japanese example ... does seem to imply that tax policy can be valuable in promoting a transition to a more capital intensive economy." ...

The fundamental difference between the two economies that arises from this sheer abundance of capital in Japan is that the United States currently imports perhaps $100 billion of capital annually to finance its investments and government deficits, while Japan exports more than $40 billion of capital annually, including, of course, exports to the United States. This performance demonstrates how economic policy is of critical importance in competitiveness. It also demonstrates that the financing of innovation is crucial to economic growth—it is the area in which economics and technology truly intersect.

Types of Companies and Financing Requirement

Not every manufacturing company is of the same size or maturity or has the same financing needs. In the United States, three types of companies are generally recognized: (1) start-up or fledgling, (2) rapidly growing, and (3) mature.

The financial needs and financing methods are different for each type of company.... For [start-up] companies, private capital and venture capital funds provide the necessary finances. Borrowing is generally too risky for both borrower and lender, so the investments are usually in the form of equity purchases. Currently, most young companies, after the infusion of venture capital has run its course, cannot generate enough internal cash flow to fuel the necessary or desired growth. In the event that they remain independent, this means they must go to the equities markets, which leads to an initial public offering (IPO) and subsequent equity issues.... Eventually, borrowing becomes feasible, and the banks and insurance companies are the normal sources of funds. However, because younger and rapidly growing companies are still deemed to be high-risk enterprises by both management and the investors or lenders, these companies retain a high ratio of equity to total capitalization.

In recent years, when venture capital has been abundant and the new public-issues markets strong, many young companies have gone public even before establishing a proven record of profitability. Often they refinance in this way several times. Much depends on the company and the economic climate prevailing at a given time. It was not as hectic a pace in 1985....

However, at about the level of $100 million to $200 million per year in sales, these start-up companies face critical problems. In addition to new management and product-line problems, they must either grow by finding major new sources of capital (as venture capital and the equities markets become unsuited, too expensive, and unavailable) or they must disappear either by failure or absorption (in whole, or in part, by establishing partnerships or joint ventures) into a large company. Of course, it is possible to do neither of these and instead to restrain the growth rate so that the necessary capital can be found in retained earnings alone (Hewlett-Packard followed this practice ...).

The large, mature companies usually have all the borrowing capacity they require.... There is a wide range of permissible debt-equity ratios among companies of various types; recently, the spate of mergers and leveraged buyouts has tended to raise the proportion of debt. Nevertheless, manufacturing companies in the United States, on the whole, have between 60 and 70 percent equity in their total capitalization, as compared with about 30 to 40 percent in Japan (based on inflation-adjusted figures for assets).

In Japan there are few start-up companies and essentially no venture capital.... Large companies often form joint ventures with other large companies, or they form wholly or partially owned subsidiaries designed to undertake special missions or product lines. The many small companies in Japan are basically "mom-and-pop" enterprises incorporated to take advantage of the very favorable tax policies afforded small corporations; they contribute very little to overall growth, productivity, or technology. Probably 1 percent of Japanese companies pay the bulk of the taxes and, since corporate tax is a larger proportion of total revenue in Japan than in the United States (about 28 percent versus 8 percent), this demonstrates the concentration of economic power in the hands of a relatively small number of large Japanese corporations.

As a consequence of the specific Japanese industrial structure, large Japanese corporations that dominate the economy and exports are basically the only ones that need to be studied with regard to their financing needs. As noted above, they are much heavier borrowers than are their American counterparts. This has significance for their capital costs, of course, but it also suggests that Japan, more than the United States, manages to spread the risks at the firm level over society as a whole, and even internationally.

How the Japanese do this is a subject of much study; Aoki (in this volume) and papers by Hodder,[5] Shoven and Tachibanaki,[4] and Hatsopoulos and Brooks[2] describe many of the salient features, such as:

1. Ownership by banks in companies to which they lend (a practice forbidden in the United States by the Glass-Steagall Act).

2. The role of the "main bank" in advising and monitoring company management, with short-term borrowing and rollovers (the fundamental instruments employed) as the means to assure close cooperation and to control the company in the event of business reverses.

3. Stability of government economic policies, which has also led to a high, sustained growth rate.

4. Absence of fear of unfriendly takeovers as a result of ownership of shares by many companies in each other (the *keiretsu*, or affiliate groups, which have taken the place of the old *zaibatsus*).

5. Subcontracting to a much larger extent than American firms do.

6. Conscious diversification into a full line of products, which reduces the risk that downturns in a few products or markets will seriously injure the company. The domination of large companies, compared with the spectrum of sizes in the United States, contributes to the stability of firms and their ability to borrow....

7. Japanese management's view of shareholders as impersonal providers of funds (which are amply available), rather than demanding owners of a company that should consider itself fortunate to receive their resources, as in the United States. Nevertheless, because of their lower costs, the companies' returns are very attractive, and price-earnings multiples are much higher than in the United States (somewhere around 26–28 to 1 versus 10–12 to 1).

8. Close collaboration between government and private companies, with many senior government employees moving to industry after their official careers.

9. Single-party (liberal Democrat) domination since the war and the absence of a credible alternative, leading to freedom from political interference in the private sector.

10. Internationalization of domestic markets and risks by determined export drives coupled with manufacture abroad as circumstances require. Japanese managers recognize the greater political instability in the world today, and always manage foreign operations from Japan so that local and national aspirations do not interfere with the overall Japanese strategy (many American firms are still limited by geographic priorities).

These and other features make the provision of risk premiums in investment decisions much less significant in Japan than in the United States.

While there is employment constraint to some degree as a result of the "lifetime" system of employment in large firms, capital constraints are much less severe and the employment limitations are overcome by retraining, subcontracting, "hiving off" of subsidiaries and joint ventures, and incessant expansion and growth.

This recitation of Japan's capital advantages is indeed a sobering one. The one area in which the United States has a substantial advantage is in the entrepreneurial start-up world and the venture capital and IPO systems that sustain it. This kind of risk taking suits the American culture very well, and derives from its pioneering history. Entrepreneurs start their businesses completely confident of ultimate success, indifferent to the short-term financial picture but determined to make and keep a fortune (based on favorable tax rates) and prepared to work infinitely long hours. They are not true gamblers, since they calculate that the odds are all in their favor—is the entrepreneur not smarter, quicker, harder working, and possessed of superior knowledge than the big companies...? Entrepreneurs strike the best deals they can with venture capitalists (usually giving up 40 to 60 percent of their company), but they do not figure that the money costs them anything, since they cannot get it any other way.[6] However, why does the venture capitalist finance the entrepreneur when the risks of success must be seen objectively as very great?

The secret lies in the portfolio method employed by experienced venture capitalists, much like the product-diversification strategy of a large company. Perhaps only a few of the dozens of companies in any portfolio will hit big and most will be failures, but those few successful ones provide (at low capital-gains tax rates) a fine rate of return for the overall venture capital pool, the rewards thus justifying all the risks taken. The venture capitalists can realize these high returns because they sell their interest in the successful business after a few years through an IPO or to a large company. The large company, on the other hand, in undertaking a project of similar character, must evaluate the potential rate of return over the life of the investment. The venture capitalist earns a substantial multiplier on his investment because the second round of investors (sometimes the third round), anticipating a large future earnings stream after the initial risks have been borne, is now willing to invest in the new business.

The pool of venture capital has risen sharply and is now abundant, led by the 1978 and 1981 reductions in the capital gains tax and the subsequent flow of pension funds into this area. The general surge in the equities markets resulting from these tax actions and the lower inflation rate brought about by monetary policy have sustained the IPO and equities markets.

In this entrepreneurial venture capital area, the United States by far leads the world. It is a tremendous advantage in innovation and technological change. Likewise, ... the large American banks have a major role in the financing of large American and foreign enterprises. The intermediate, growing firms have the greatest problems in financing themselves and in competing with the Japanese, for the reasons cited in this section.

The Cost of Capital

The abundance of capital or lack of it has been described above for the United States and Japan in terms of the different types of organizations and stages in their evolution. Equally important in assessing the competitive situation is the cost of that capital. This is a much more complex subject, and the material in this section is based largely on the work of George Hatsopoulos, as exemplified in his paper with Brooks (see note 2 in this chapter).

Cost of Funds (Cost of Capital)

The AAA corporate bond yield is a measure of the cost of low-risk, long-term debt at fixed interest rate. In recent times, because of the steep yield curves, U.S. corporations have switched to a greater proportion of short-term debt at lower rates; this is the result of the Federal Reserve Board's easing of the monetary policy. However, the recent decline in long-term bond yields is leading corporate treasurers to a renewed interest in such fixed-yield instruments. Hence, even the cost of debt in the United States is now more difficult to track than it used to be.

Debt cost is deductible from gross income by corporations. Moreover, it is the nominal interest cost that is deductible, not the real cost.... Hence, in times of inflation the tax structure favors debt. As an example, consider interest at 12 percent and corporate tax at 50 percent with expected inflation of 5 percent. The net nominal cost to the corporation of the interest is $12 \times 0.5 = 6$ percent. Subtracting the expected inflation yields a net real interest cost of just 1 percent. In the recent past, that cost has been strongly negative because the rate of inflation was higher. If the short-term interest rate is 9 percent, then the real interest cost becomes negative again with 5 percent inflation, as the lender and the government subsidize the borrower. Since corporations have incurred different debt obligations over past years, the average cost of debt requires a historical analysis for each company. However, in computing the marginal cost of debt for a new investment, the calculation will be based on the proposed method of financing.

The cost of equity is a considerably more elusive number. It is not, however, to be equated with the reciprocal of the price-earnings ratio (P/E), that is, the E/P ratio as found on the stock markets. The underlying worth of a corporate share is the discounted present value of the stream of cash flows into the future that is anticipated by the owner. Dividends, capital distributions, and so forth have historically served as proxies for investors' expectations about the future cash flows of the firm. In an efficient stock market, the quoted stock prices will reflect such an underlying value. Each stockholder has his or her own calculation of what such a future cash flow might be and what the appropriate discount rate should be. The net effect of the perceptions of all stockholders results in the market value of the stock. If the stock is unlisted, or private, management would use comparisons with listed stocks of similar companies or would apply discount rates prevailing in the economic climate of the day. Often, management's perceptions of future dividends differ from those of the public, in which case the P/E ratio of the stock market may be low although dividend expectations of management may be high.

Conditions in the stock markets change with general economic conditions, interest rates, supply and demand of equities, and many other factors. Thus, a rise in the market, or in a particular equity, will raise a company's P/E ratio and hence lower the cost of its equity. These changes in market values may occur almost independently of the expected dividends; what changes is the appropriate discount rate. In addition, management's expectations of future dividends may change rather abruptly if new technology becomes available to competitors, or simply new market entrants appear. If this is not realized by the market for some time, the cost of equity of the company is temporarily reduced. Also, the stock market valuation is based on the overall effective tax rate of the corporation, not the marginal rate for a new investment. Hence, past performance and the tax laws affect the marginal cost of equity in an investment. These are examples of the complexity of calculating the cost of equity. Nevertheless, it is possible to study groups of companies in Japan and the United States and to derive reasonable estimates of their cost of equity.

Dividends, of course, are not deductible by American corporations; they are in effect partly deductible in Japan since profits paid out as dividends are taxed at a *lower* rate than retained earnings. In any case, the corporation in each country must earn pretax dollars of sufficient amount to pay the taxes and the dividend: this represents the pretax cost of equity. It will be appreciably higher than the pretax cost of debt (with prevailing corporate tax rates, more than twice for new investments) because it includes, in addition to taxes, a substantial risk premium inherent in equities that are subordinate to debt as to distribution of earnings and security of the assets. On an after-tax basis, therefore, equity is much more expensive in real cost than debt because of the deductibility of the nominal interest cost (shown above). Despite this, well-managed mature organizations use debt within prudent limits only, because of the risk of insolvency or business reverses. In the United States this [debt to equity ratio] generally runs about 1:2. The Japanese, however, because of their unique financial and corporate structure, as described above, have traditionally used much higher leverage; although it is somewhat less so today than in the past, the debt to equity ratio is more like 2:1.

These relationships also help explain why leveraged buyouts, restructuring, takeovers, and acquisitions in the United States often feature a substantial valuation for a company's equity in excess of market. This is not necessarily because the markets are inefficient but because these maneuvers substitute cheaper debt for more expensive equity. It is the tax system that makes corporate takeover specialists like Boone Pickens and Carl Icahn viable, because debt is tax deductible. Of course, the company's risk becomes much greater, too.

Real interest rates in Japan have also been lower than in the United States because of controls on financial markets. Tax rates on corporations in Japan are slightly higher than in the United States, but the effect of this difference is not as great as that of the leveraging and of interest rates.

When a corporation's costs of debt and equity are calculated, the overall cost of funds is obtained by weighting them in the actual pattern. It is, of course, most meaningful if corrected for projected (not current) inflation, to arrive at real costs after taxes.

The nominal after-tax cost of funds is used as a basis in calculating "hurdle" rates by corporations planning a new investment. They would typically add a risk premium, which could be just as much. The resultant sum, which may then be twice the nominal after-tax cost of funds, is the "hurdle" rate, below which a project would not be justified. Then the cash flow after taxes for the new project to the end of its expected useful life is computed, and discounted back to the present using the "hurdle" rate as the discount rate. If the net present value so obtained is equal to or greater than the original total investment, the project is likely to be approved.

Tables 22.1 and 22.2 show calculations of the cost of funds for the United States and Japan, respectively, in the three years 1975, 1981, and 1984. Notable conclusions from these data and the facts underlying them are highlighted below:

Table 22.1
U.S. cost of funds: 1975, 1981, 1984 (percent)

	1975	1981	1984
Marginal tax rate (annual)	52.0	50.3	50.3
Expected inflation	6.5	9.0	4.7
Interest-bearing debt			
Coupon rate (nominal pretax cost)	8.5	13.3	12.0
Real coupon rate	2.0	4.3	7.3
Nominal cost after taxes	4.1	6.6	5.9
Real cost after taxes	−2.4	−2.4	1.2
Equity			
Nominal cost before taxes	33.7	38.8	25.4
Nominal cost after taxes	15.0	17.6	11.9
Real cost after taxes	8.5	8.6	7.1
Funds[a]			
Nominal cost after taxes	11.0	13.1	9.1
Real cost after taxes	4.5	4.1	4.3

Note: All rates are instantaneous, except as noted.
a. Mix of funds: Interest-bearing debt 14.1%
                Interest-free debt 16.7%
                Equity 69.3%
Source: Calculated from methodology of Hatsopoulos and Brooks (note 2 in this chapter).

Table 22.2
Japanese cost of funds: 1975, 1981, 1984 (percent)

	1975	1981	1984
Marginal tax rate (annual)	52.6	54.7	54.7
Expected inflation	10.1	5.4	3.7
Interest-bearing debt			
Coupon rate (nominal pretax cost)	9.2	8.0	7.6
Real coupon rate	−0.9	2.6	3.9
Nominal cost after taxes	4.3	3.6	3.4
Real cost after taxes	−5.7	−1.8	−0.2
Equity			
Nominal cost before taxes	36.6	24.9	20.4
Nominal cost after taxes	16.0	10.7	8.8
Real cost after taxes	5.9	5.3	5.2
Funds[a]			
Nominal cost after taxes	7.0	4.9	4.2
Real cost after taxes	−3.0	−0.4	0.6

Note: All rates are instantaneous, except as noted.
a. Mix of funds: Interest-bearing debt 32.9%
                Interest-free debt 31.9%
                Equity 35.1%
Source: Calculated from methodology of Hatsopoulos and Brooks (note 2 in this chapter).

- Japanese real costs have been and are much below American costs.

- During the period 1975 to 1981, when Japan was engaged in a massive investment program, the actual real cost of funds was negative. Control of interest rates by the government and high leveraging, together with a high corporate statutory rate, produced this remarkable result. Only recently has the real cost of funds become slightly positive.

- Equity costs are lower in Japan, partly because of favorable taxation of income from equities. Not only does a corporation pay less tax on distributed dividends, the shareholder gets a lower tax rate than on earned income, plus valuable exemptions. In addition, corporations are allowed to accumulate substantial tax-free reserves. The Japanese tax structure ... makes equity investment very attractive, particularly in view of the fact that the Japanese have no capital gains tax. They calculate that, from the individual Japanese shareholder's perspective, the effective marginal tax rate in 1980 for all classes of industry and assets (on a weighted basis) was − 1.5 percent versus 37.2 percent in the United States. Even if somewhat different indices of inflation are used, this effective rate lies only in the 7 to 17 percent range. In essence, the marginal investor is slightly subsidized rather than taxed, under the former assumption, or there is nearly an effective expenditure tax in the latter case at the corporate level. The high leveraging of Japanese companies, the special depreciation rules, and the low rate of taxation of interest and dividends at the personal level yield this startling result.

- Under the Japanese system, the low cost of funds is available at the margin only if the company is expanding. If a successful company does not increase its total capital, that is, for expansion, the debt-equity ratio starts to shrink, because the corporation pays off debt (this is cheaper overall than paying dividends beyond those required by the stock market yields, because of the double taxation). At it does so, its reduced leveraging raises its average cost of funds. This is what is now occurring with some successful Japanese companies, such as Toyota, which is faced with export quotas and hence has become cash rich for want of expansion. They, therefore, pay more taxes and help offset the lost tax revenues from rapidly growing companies, which borrow heavily for expansion and obtain all the benefits therefrom at the expense of the tax collector. The successful basic industries keep the cost of capital low for the expanding high-tech companies.

This tax-financial system works differently for companies in the United States, where lower leveraging, lower corporate taxes, and higher equity costs favor companies that are not expanding rapidly. Only incentives such as accelerated depreciation and investment tax credits tend to offset this fact. Lowering the corporate statutory rate further would reduce the cost of equity somewhat for all corporations and reward capital investment already made, but it would also decrease the double taxation of corporate income and therefore tend to reduce expansion in favor of paying out dividends to investors who will be clamoring for them as their marginal rate goes down (a feature of the Treasury tax proposals of May 1985). It is the interplay of a high statutory corporate tax rate (higher for retained profits than for dividends paid out), lower dividend taxation, no capital-gains tax, high leveraging, and a financial-social system that spreads corporate risk that makes the Japanese climate so unique for growth.

• The lower cost of funds in Japan means that Japanese companies can sell products at cost, while their American competitors are losing money. Over a long enough period of time, a determined well-financed Japanese company can drive its competitors out of business. This seems currently to be happening in memory chips. Thus, this study of the cost of capital demonstrates an enormous Japanese advantage. The hard dollar adds insult to injury, and so an American company is crippled when it tries to retaliate in Japan or in other overseas markets.

Cost of Capital Services

Raising money leads to the cost described above. However, the real overall cost of capital depends on how it is used, and here there are different adjustments for inflation, taxation, depreciation, and investment allowances. Thus, for equipment and similar fixed assets, the cost of capital is the cost of funds, plus the cost of depreciation, less the tax benefits from various investment allowances, and less the benefit from inflation (the replacement cost of the assets is appreciating because of inflation).

Land is not depreciated, but appreciates with inflation, and so on. The overall real cost of capital is higher than the real cost of raising the money (cost of funds) because depreciation raises the cost of fixed assets, and the cost of receivables is high because there is no offset for inflation or tax.

All these factors are taken into account when the cost of capital services is computed. This concept was first introduced by Hall and Jorgenson,[7] and developed further by Hatsopoulos and Brooks (note 2) to include inflation, to reflect the timing of tax payments and tax credits, and to include intangible assets, such as the technology resulting from an investment in R&D. Hatsopoulos and Brooks set forth the details of the calculations for the two

Table 22.3
Summary cost of capital calculations for the United States in 1984 (percent)

Concept		Equipment	Structures	10-year R&D ventures
ρ	After-tax cost of funds	0.091	0.091	0.091
π	Expected inflation	0.047	0.047	0.047
ITC	Investment tax credit	0.10	0	0.125[a]
τ	Marginal corporate tax rate	0.503	0.503	0.503
β	Portion of the ITC that reduces the basis of equipment for tax depreciation	0.5	0	0
Z	Present value of depreciation allowance (under ACRS)	0.83	0.63	1.0
δ	Rate of economic decay	0.123	0.066	0.05
d	Utilization delay (years)	0	0	10.0
C	Gross cost of capital	0.169	0.151	0.106

Note: A simplified version of the cost of capital equation is shown below. It ignores the timing of taxes and assumes that magnitudes of the key parameters are relatively small:

$$C = (1 + \rho - \pi)^d \frac{(1 - \text{ITC} - \tau(1 - \beta)Z)(\rho + \delta - \pi)}{1 - \tau}$$

a. Investment tax credit of 0.125 on R&D assumes that only direct costs that constitute one-half of R&D expenditures are allowed under the 25 percent R&D tax credit.

countries. A simple way of expressing it is to see it as equivalent to the fee for which a leasing company would lease a piece of equipment (or a whole plant), over the life of the item involved, including no profit in the fee (that is, at the scrapping of the unit there is nothing left, but the full cost has been retrieved after provision for all the elements described above, including all applicable taxes). This figure, then, is the minimum pretax earning on a new investment that a company could afford to make, assuming no risk involved.

Table 22.3 is a summary of the calculation for the United States in 1984. It uses the cost of funds shown in table 22.1 for that year. These costs of capital services include all the costs associated with the use of an asset: the real cost of debt and equity, costs associated with taxes and credits, and the cost associated with the economic depreciation of the asset. The same calculations can be made for land and inventories, and when weighted appropriately yield the gross cost of capital services for a company, an industry, or a whole sector, as desired. Hatsopoulos and Brooks's methodology ... shows that for the years given in tables 22.1 and 22.2 the comparative weighted results are:

Gross real cost of capital services (cent per year per dollar of capital)

	U.S.	Japan
1975	15.5	3.0
1981	13.6	6.8
1984	13.0	8.2

This again illustrates how the Japanese policymakers kept capital costs low in order to spur the investments they deemed necessary to compete in world markets. They did this despite the sharp increase in inflation in the later 1970s, by controlling interest costs.

Table 22.3 also gives a calculation for the cost of capital of an R&D project that lasts ten years before it can be commercialized; although it can be expensed in the year incurred under tax law, it is still a capital investment and has a cost. In the case shown, that cost is 10.6 percent. As mentioned above, since company balance sheets do not reflect intangible investments in technology, such investments may even be larger than tangible investments, as for example, at IBM.

These basic differences between Japan and the United States are what have permitted the Japanese to invest approximately two and a half times as much in fixed assets per worker as their U.S. competitors, and they lie behind the manufacturing productivity increase in Japan of 6.8 percent per year between 1973 and 1983, compared with the 1.8 percent in the United States disclosed by Jorgenson.... The Japanese thus can compete very effectively in world markets for manufactured goods; the United States is fast losing its competitive position.... It is true that the United States has created many jobs in the service sectors, especially in smaller companies, but except perhaps for a few large financial institutions, the productivity and the competitiveness of the service sectors are far below those of the manufacturing sector.

A further conclusion from the data given above is that the cost of capital differential in Japan's favor would permit a Japanese company to invest in longer-term R&D projects, or to invest much more than its American counterpart. Then, when the fruits of that R&D are to be implemented by physical investment as a completed innovation, the Japanese again enjoy an advantage. This double advantage in the more technologically based manufacturing industries of the future bodes ill for the United States and suggests imminent moves for protectionism and its consequences, such as inflation and loss of markets elsewhere (for example, in agriculture).

One of the important questions raised by these studies is how the costs of capital compare with actual returns. Returns on investments, of course, are not necessarily the "hurdle" rates; they can be higher or lower, depending on the competitive situation, the economic climate, the state of the technology, and other factors. Management seeks the highest return that conditions permit, not just to retrieve the cost of capital. However, good data on actual returns are difficult to obtain, as they must be based on cash flows after tax and not on reported profits. Furthermore, accounting practices do not permit ready calculation of the cash flows of many corporations. It would appear that in recent years many U.S. corporations. had a cost of capital above their returns and the stock market reflected this fact, which explains why market prices may be and often are below book value.[8] This may be due to incompetent management, powerful competition, excessive regulations, obsolete technology, poor labor contracts, or a whole host of possible problems. As mentioned above, this is what attracts leveraged buyouts and acquisitions at seemingly much higher than such market prices. The rise in the market in the last several years suggests that increased corporate cash flow aided by the tax advantages of the 1981 act (Accelerated Cost Recovery System and Investment Tax Credit) and reduced inflation is bringing earnings on new investments into an acceptable range. However, the Japanese are still well ahead, as indicated.

There have been a few other studies of the subject of this chapter, for example, by the Chase Manhattan Bank,[9] the Department of Commerce,[10] and Richard R. Ellsworth.[11] While methodologies differ, the general conclusions do not.

Some Recommendations on Capital Formation and Competitiveness

This is not the place for an extended discussion of tax and other policies required to put American companies into a more competitive position. Both authors of this chapter have written separately on these matters.[12] But a consideration of the studies described herein suggests several very basic conclusions:

1. Interest rates need to be reduced. In view of the low American savings rate in the private sector, dissaving by the government (through its deficit) should be reduced. Permanent reductions will come only by cutting expenditures. This is because the level of spending, to a first approximation, ultimately determines the level of taxation, whether current or future. If inflation is employed by government monetary policy to conceal this effect, it merely substitutes a hidden tax for an overt one. A reduction in the deficit would permit monetary policy to ease and become less volatile.

2. Stability of government policies is essential if America is to remain competitive. Japan has had a long period of relative stability; the United States has had widely varying monetary policies and three major tax bills in four years. To enact another major tax bill incorporating many controversial provisions would be an experiment with unforeseeable results affecting the entire U.S. economy. It is far better to make changes slowly and incrementally.

3. The savings rate in the United States is not likely to increase significantly until the tax system moves toward a consumption tax and away from an income tax. This can be accomplished incrementally, for example, by easing the constraints on Individual Retirement Accounts, by allowing expensing for all capital investments (tangible or intangible) in the year in which they are incurred, and by permitting the issuance of qualified new preferred issues—deductible to the issuing corporation—that are limited to expansion. While an income tax system remains, the incentives for new investment like the Accelerated Cost Recovery System and the Investment Tax Credit are important. Elimination or reduction of capital gains taxes on financial assets, especially on rollovers into other investments, would yield greater market liquidity and risk taking, and would help compensate for the double taxation of corporate investment.

This chapter, then, is an attempt to sharpen understanding of how economics and technology come together in studying the competitiveness of capital formation processes, the financing of innovation, and the technological contribution to economic growth in the United States and Japan. In this critical area can be found one of the major reasons why the Japanese growth rate in GNP is outstripping that of the United States. This is hardly the time for business and politics as usual. The United States has many inherent advantages if its economic policies can be harnessed in a benign way for innovation and investment, leading to a higher sustained growth rate. Americans are good at this, too, as their history proves.

Notes

1. Stephen S. Roach, *Manufacturing, Cyclical Vulnerability and Growth Recession*, Morgan Stanley & Co., June 12, 1985.

2. From G. N. Hatsopoulos and S. H. Brooks. "The gap in the cost of capital: Causes, effects and remedies," in *Technology and Economic Policy*, R. Landau and D. W. Jorgenson, eds. (Cambridge, Mass.: Ballinger, forthcoming).

3. Ibid.

4. John B. Shoven and Toshiaki Tachibanaki, "The Taxation of Income from Capital in Japan," paper presented at Stanford Center for Economic Policy Research Conference on Government Policy Towards Industry in the United States and Japan, May 1985.

5. James L. Hodder, "Investment and Financial Decision Making in Japanese Firms: A Comparison with U.S. Practices," paper presented at a Stanford University-Northeast Asia Forum Conference, Honolulu, January 1985.

6. In strict financial terms it does have a cost. This cost would be measured by the value of the intangible capital the entrepreneur brings to the enterprise. Unfortunately, accounting practices of companies everywhere make no provision for showing intangible capital assets in balance sheets and profit and loss statements, so that using only financial-asset reporting frequently understates a firm's true strengths.

7. R. E. Hall and D. W. Jorgenson, "Tax policy and investment behavior," *American Economic Review* 57 (June 1967):391–414.

8. *Bank Credit Analyst*, May 1985:23ff; C. G. Callard and D. C. Kleinman, *Financial Analysts Journal*, May–June 1985:51.

9. *U.S. and Japanese Semiconductor Industries: A Financial Comparison*. Report prepared by the Chase Manhattan Bank N.A. for the Semiconductor Industry Association, June 9, 1980.

10. U.S. Department of Commerce, International Trade Administration, *A Historical Comparison of the Cost of Financial Capital in France, the Federal Republic of Germany, Japan, and the United States*, April 1983.

11. Richard R. Ellsworth, "Capital markets and competitive decline," *Harvard Business Review*, September-October 1985:171.

12. See *Technology and Economic Policy* (note 2 above).

23 U.S. Economic Growth

Since 1982 the U.S. economy has enjoyed an extended period of expansion. Yet there are abundant signs that all is not well: they include a huge federal deficit, an adverse balance of payments and status as the world's leading debtor. The most telling sign of all is a rate of economic growth lower than that of other industrial nations: since 1979 the annual growth rate of the U.S.'s real gross domestic product has averaged about 2.2 percent while Japan's annual G.D.P. growth rate has averaged 3.8 percent. Although this may not seem like much of a difference, it is actually a matter of grave concern. Only 2.3 percentage points separated the annual average G.D.P. growth rate of the U.S. from that of Great Britain between 1870 and 1913. Indeed, given that the U.S. population increased more rapidly than the population of Great Britain during that period, the difference in per capita G.D.P. growth rate amounted to only one percentage point. Yet that difference was enough to propel the U.S. past the leading industrial power of the 19th century while making it possible for the standard of living to nearly double with each generation. Such is the power of compounding economic growth over long periods of time: a few tenths of a percentage point, which may not appear significant in the short term, reflect an enormous economic and social achievement if sustained over a few decades.

If the rate of U.S. economic growth is not increased soon, the ever greater employment opportunities and ever higher levels of material well-being to which most Americans have grown accustomed will no longer be possible. Is there a way for the U.S. to maintain a high growth rate and thereby ensure for itself both the benefits of growth and a more prominent position of global economic leadership?

Published in *Scientific American* 258, no. 6 (June 1988): 2–10. Reprinted with permission. © 1988 by Scientific American, Inc. All rights reserved. Ralph Landau would like to acknowledge the contributions of Michael Boskin of Stanford, Dale Jorgenson of Harvard, and particularly Nathan Rosenberg of Stanford in the preparation of the article.

My colleagues at the Program in Technology and Economic Growth at Stanford University and the Program in Technology and Economic Policy at Harvard University and I believe the answer is positive. Our reasons for thinking so are based on our examination of the issues from the perspectives of economic theory and our experience in business. Studying the intricate tapestry of the world economy reveals a number of interwoven threads that affect a country's rate of economic growth. One major determinant is the advance of technological knowledge. Equally important is investment in the capital required to apply that knowledge in the manufacture of products or the provision of services. Therefore the development of new technology as well as its diffusion throughout society is influenced by such factors as government policies affecting the money supply, national budgets and taxes. Although a government cannot force innovation, it can nonetheless foster growth by providing the proper economic climate for the private sector to apply the fruits of technological innovation.

In this connection we believe not enough attention has been paid to the role of capital investment in stimulating technological change; specifically the U.S. Government has not provided as advantageous an economic environment for capital formation as the governments of competing countries have. Indeed, in the past few decades its policies have worked against long-term investments in favor of short-term ones. If U.S. competitiveness and economic growth are to be improved, alternative policies that encourage long-range economic planning in the private sector must be favored.

A country's economy can supply more goods and services either by employing more factors of production, such as labor and capital (physical plant and equipment), or by increasing the productivity of such factors: the amount of output per unit of resource input. (The total output of a country's economy is often measured in terms of the country's G.D.P.: the value of all goods and services produced within its territory. G.D.P. differs somewhat from another common measure of economic output, the gross national product, in that it omits international transactions.) Economists for many decades considered the use of additional inputs as the main source of economic growth. Yet the first serious attempts to gauge the importance of additional inputs in economic growth—done in the 1950s—contradicted this view.

Robert M. Solow of the Massachusetts Institute of Technology, among others, formulated the basic relation: An economy's growth is simply the sum of the growths in the inputs of capital and labor, each weighted by a coefficient reflecting its average contribution to the value of products, as well as a third variable that represents the increases in factor productivity

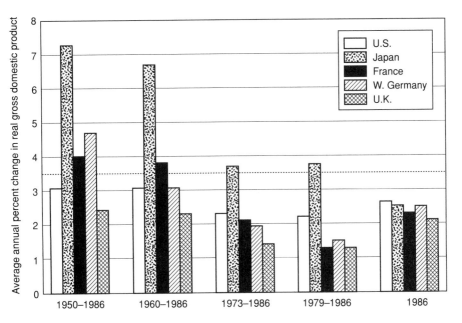

Figure 23.1
International comparison of average annual rates of economic growth shows that the U.S. historically has had lower rates than Japan. The author arguers that the U.S. should aim for an average growth rate of 3.5. percent per year (*dotted line*) in order to ensure long-term economic prosperity. (Gross domestic product is the value of all goods and services produced within a country's borders. It differs slightly from gross national product in that it excludes net international transactions.)

(the combined productivity of capital and labor). At first most economists were satisfied to label the third variable "technological change" and to relate it loosely to scientific and engineering research and development. Nevertheless, it clearly includes other important elements: more efficient resource allocation and economies of scale as well as many social, educational and organizational factors that serve to improve the quality of labor and management.

In the original formulation of the relation the three variables are assumed to be independent, so that increasing the rate of growth of, say, capital does not affect the rate at which productivity increases. The contribution of increases in productivity to economic growth is therefore the difference between the rate of growth of output and the weighted sum of the rates of growth of capital and labor. In this way Solow and others estimated that as much as 85 percent of U.S. economic growth per capita as recorded in historical data seems to be attributable to increases in productivity or technological change....

Moses Abramovitz of Stanford had earlier applied a similar technique and had also found that only about 15 percent of the growth could be traced to the use of more inputs. He was rather circumspect in interpreting the large 85 percent residual, however, calling it "a measure of our ignorance." What seemed to emerge very clearly from those early analyses was that the country's long-term economic growth had until then been overwhelmingly a matter of using capital and labor more efficiently rather than simply increasing those inputs.

Later calculations with data from more recent years presented the matter in a somewhat different light. Whereas the factor productivity of the U.S. economy had increased by an average of 1.19 percent per year between 1913 and 1950, between 1973 and 1984 the factor productivity actually *declined* by about .27 percent per year. Moreover, in contrast to what Solow, Abramovitz and others had deduced from the earlier data, what growth there was in the U.S. G.D.P. during the late 1970s was brought about almost entirely by increases in capital and labor (particularly the latter as the "baby boom" peaked).

Explanations for this striking collapse in factor productivity have varied. A distinctly promising explanation has emerged from recent comparative studies of individual sectors of the Japanese and U.S. economies by Dale W. Jorgenson of Harvard. His work suggests that the productivity of labor is significantly affected by the per-worker rate of capital investment: the amount of money spent in building up the country's capital stock. Jorgenson has also shown that the Japanese factor-productivity growth rates (which between 1973 and 1984 averaged .43 percent per year) were heavily influenced by the high rate of capital investment in a number of industrial sectors. In fact, the rate of Japanese investment was at least twice as high as the rate in many U.S. industries.

Based on recently available data and a more sophisticated methodology that prices capital in relation to its age, Jorgenson states that since World War II capital investment has been responsible for about 40 percent of the growth of the U.S.'s G.D.P., whereas factor productivity accounts for about 30 percent. The remainder can be traced to increases in the quality and quantity of labor. Angus Maddison of the University of Groningen in the Netherlands has recently reviewed a number of studies on economic growth done in the past thirty years and reaches similar conclusions.

Other data also suggest a close correlation between national rates of capital investment and increases in productivity and economic growth. West Germany and France, for example, which have investment rates roughly twice the U.S. rate, also enjoy about twice the growth rate in productivity. (It should be pointed out that measurements of productivity growth usually do not take account of improvements in the quality of goods and services, which are also important.)

How does investment in capital stimulate productivity to cause economic growth? The answer is found in the way technological change is incorporated into capital. Except for a small part devoted to basic science, research and development is seldom undertaken unless its results are expected to be applied in new facilities and superior operating modes that can either increase productivity, reduce costs or raise the quality of goods or services. Hence capital investment embodies technological change and also spurs it, since the availability of superior technology is a major incentive to invest. But a superior technology can only arise from research and development. Capital investment therefore serves as a catalyst that can set off a self-generating "virtuous circle" connecting technological change with research and development, eventually resulting in productivity or quality improvements in goods and services.

Similarly, improvements in labor quality through increases in knowledge and training can be seen as another form of investment (in human "capital") that is both a requirement of and an inducement to technological change. In other words, technological change is incorporated in each of the basic factors of production. This relationship is true to a much greater extent than was ever thought before, although the precise extent is difficult to quantify.

As Michael Boskin of Stanford and others have pointed out, these interactions between technological change, capital and labor quality imply that raising the rate of capital investment can actually increase the rate of economic growth over a longer period of time. This is particularly true in exploiting the results of "breakthrough" research, which requires large capital investments but can create entirely new industries. Unfortunately many managers, government officials and economists still do not understand these critical relationships in growth theory. They often maintain that increasing the rate of capital investment will not substantially accelerate technological change and improvements in labor quality.

Solow has recently joined the ranks of those who criticize this thinking. He has stated he fears that his theory of growth, which downplayed the importance of capital, might have been carried too far, contributing to "a severe underinvestment" in physical capital. Since "you can't take an old plant and teach it very new tricks," he has called for increased spending on behalf of the nation's research-and-development centers and factories— the sources of technological change.

Earlier distinctions between the roles of technological change, capital and labor in economic growth therefore need to be modified in favor of a view that sees them as intertwined parts of the same process. Technological change has been central to U.S. economic growth, both directly (in which case it can be said to account for perhaps 30 percent of economic growth) and through its positive effect on other factors of production (which can be said to account for perhaps another 40 or 50 percent of economic growth). Although scholarly research has not yet provided conclusive evidence, my colleagues and I believe it is in this broad sense that technological innovation is the key to viable strategies for future economic growth: it can raise the factor productivity of the economy at an accelerated rate.

The interactions among technological change, capital investment and labor quality suggest some strategies for U.S. companies to pursue in order to sustain economic growth. Companies in every sector of the economy must adjust to a faster pace of change, insist on continual training and remove obsolete policies that impose unnecessary constraints on technological innovation.

These needs are most acutely felt in the manufacturing sector. It is this sector that currently carries out about 95 percent of private research and development. It provides the major part (about two-thirds) of U.S. merchandise exports. (Indeed, both the bulk of the private research and development and the major part of the exporting is done by only a handful of large manufacturing companies, which also tend to be the ones that invest most in new capital.) The manufacturing sector also buys a large part of the output of the service sector, which in turn helps to improve manufacturing productivity. Finally, manufacturing produces material essential for national security.

Because manufacturing has such a key role in the U.S. economy, no strategy for economic growth that neglects this sector is likely to succeed. One way the sector can attain a capability for quick response to changes in the market is by relying more on the evolving technique of flexible manufacturing: the manufacture of different products by the same capital equipment. Of course, in order for such manufacturing to exploit its advantages fully, product design must be tightly coupled to market needs and be capable of rapid reductions in production costs. As the Japanese have recognized, consumers also demand constantly improving quality and reliability. This means that a company's manufacturing plants need to be in close communication with engineering and marketing staffs. Because they are principal agents of technological change, engineers must understand more than science and engineering; they need to cultivate economic judgment and learn how to use it in the face of technical and commercial risks. Greater worker involvement is also essential; this is a key feature of the successful Japanese manufacturing strategy.

Flexible manufacturing plants integrated on a national scale would allow rapid introduction of new and better products according to market conditions as well as the introduction of new processes that come with growing knowledge and experience. Such improvements in both products and processes need to be made at an increasingly rapid rate to maintain competitiveness. If it is prudently done, the capital investment can be largely recovered before imitation by competitors becomes a threat. U.S. companies that have achieved successes in this way include Allen-Bradley, Caterpillar, Chrysler, John Deere, General Electric, Hewlett-Packard, International Business Machines and Westinghouse.

Even so, U.S. companies that manufacture discrete mechanical goods, such as automobiles, appliances and consumer electronics, have had problems in attempting such integration of design, production and marketing, partly because the companies have been reluctant to adopt a "systems" approach, which includes feedback loops among the company's various departments. The chemical and refining industries of the U.S., in contrast, are in a more receptive frame of mind, owing in large measure to the earlier development of the systems approach of chemical engineering.

Industries that rely heavily on computers, automation and telecommunications are also in a particularly favorable position. They suit American talents, such as the extraordinary ability to establish the entrepreneurial companies that create most new jobs. Although it would seem that commodity industries (such as the petrochemical and steelmaking industries) would be at a disadvantage, some of them can still remain competitive as long as they have a significant advantage in terms of scale, resources or technology. For many commodities, however, the transfer of their manufacture to lower-wage countries is probably inevitable. No one economic strategy fits every company.

The rapid integration of computer-based technologies and transformation of the work force can be exploited by the services sector as well. Even where the bulk of the value added to a product is in marketing, sales and distribution, large amounts of capital are still required, as is immediate feedback to manufacturing. Both sectors can thereby be in a position to add higher value to the products or services they supply. If this turns out to be the case, even high wages would constitute only a small part of the total cost of production, enabling U.S. companies to compete with companies in countries with low wage rates. The key point is that sectors in which the value added per worker is high are the ones that have built up substantial tangible capital (such as physical equipment and machinery) and nontangible capital (such as worker training, developed markets and technical knowledge) per worker.

What has been described so far has to be carried out by the private sector in order to remain competitive in both domestic and international markets. What happens at this microeconomic level, however, ultimately determines long-term growth rates, and it can be affected by such "supply side" factors as government policies regarding taxes, trade, environmental regulation and labor. Yet the private sector must also operate within a macroeconomic environment established primarily by the government's fiscal and monetary policies. These policies, which control the "demand side" of the economy, are generally shaped by political exigencies and by reactions to the many short-term and cyclical problems that beset the economy. As a result these policies have changed frequently.

Such a volatile macroeconomic environment can be inhospitable to major investments in research and development and can therefore hinder prolonged economic growth. Science and technology require distant planning horizons; they are bound to be undervalued if returns on investment in research and development are measured within a short time frame.

An economic climate that puts a premium on quick returns has in fact prevailed in recent years—a result, in large part, of the inflation that took place in the 1970s. Memories of the double-digit percentage increases in prices at that time still linger today, as can be seen in the high real interest rate on long-term bonds. As a consequence managers skilled in financial matters have often been favored over engineers in promotions and salaries, and short-term research-and-development projects have been favored over longer-term work that might produce technological breakthroughs.

Similarly, recent economic "stabilization" policies will adversely affect growth for many years to come. Perhaps the most critical has been the proliferation of debt. Government deficits, which have grown to be in the range of $200 billion per year, are financed to a large extent by borrowing from national savings, reducing the amount of money available for capital investment. At the same time private debt in all sectors has also grown. Total public and private debt in 1986 was more than 200 percent of G.D.P., up from 163 percent in 1975. These heavy debt burdens have resulted in a huge "inflation" of credit that is inherently dangerous, because as soon as there is an economic downturn, servicing the debt squeezes out investment in capital.

As a result a debt-laden company is less likely to accept the risks involved in conducting long-range research and development or in investing in new capital. In fact, the discouragement of long-term capital investment coupled with interest rates that have declined somewhat from their peaks in the early 1980s has prompted investors to move into common stocks, fueling a booming but volatile stock market. In addition investors have turned their attention to higher-yielding, riskier financial instruments, such as the so-called junk bonds.

Some of the debt—particularly, that caused by the sale of junk bonds—has gone into mergers, acquisitions, takeovers, restructurings and leveraged buyouts. In effect debt has been substituted for equity. This tactic is encouraged by tax laws that allow the interest on debt but not dividends to be deducted from corporate income; the U.S. Department of the Treasury, in effect, has become the corporate raider's ally. Because borrowed money thus becomes cheaper, takeovers and leveraged buyouts have become more attractive than productive investments, which require a more judicious mixture of debt and more "expensive" equity.

To be sure, an affected company sometimes becomes more efficient: restructuring has resulted in some gains in productivity and cost control in American manufacturing. More often, however, only the existing shareholders benefit (and only in the short run) and almost everyone else suffers from the constrictions in jobs, money, markets and future-oriented research and development. Moreover, the company (if not dismembered) still has to operate with extraordinarily high debt-equity ratios, a condition that is not conducive to long-term growth.

A prudent macroeconomic strategy for long-term growth would include a tight fiscal policy (aimed at reducing government deficits), a looser monetary policy (aimed at lowering interest rates and stabilizing the value of the U.S. dollar) and a tax system that encourages investment instead of consumption. (Changes in the U.S. regulatory and legal systems to cut down on wasteful lawsuits would also help.) Probably the most important prerequisite is that capital in all its forms, including the capital required for improved education, training and research and development, should be abundant and cheap; it should also incorporate the most efficient technology available. Above all, this means pursuit of policies that encourage high rates of savings, since it is from the savings pool that a nation's money for capital investment is drawn.

Boskin has reported that the savings rate of Japan is from two to nearly three times that of the U.S., depending on how it is measured. A high savings rate allows the Japanese to make heavy long-term domestic and

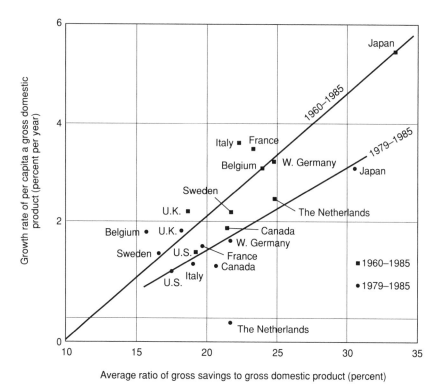

Figure 23.2
National savings rates correlate with per capita growth rates, since a country's aggregate savings account represents a pool of money on which companies can draw for capital formation. As can be seen, the U.S. had one of the lowest savings rates among industrial nations both from 1960 through 1985 ... and from 1979 through 1985.... The flatter slope of the line through the more recent data indicates the fact that growth rates in general have declined throughout the world since 1979.

international investments while still financing government spending. It also explains the fact that the effective cost of Japanese capital has been from a half to a third as great as that of American capital. (Other reasons for the higher cost of American capital include the higher interest rates demanded by cautious investors, who have been hurt by past economic policies of the U.S., and the "second" tax on corporate income entailed by taxing dividends.) Because the future returns on an investment in Japan can be discounted at a half or even a third of the U.S. rate and still cover the cost of the investment, Japanese corporate chiefs have a much longer horizon for decision making. Consequently Japanese can better afford to finance research and development; they can also incur substantial initial losses while establishing markets abroad (as they did with videocassette recorders).

Such activities generally require much longer time horizons than investment in plant and equipment.

Most economists agree that a suitably progressive consumption or excise tax—beginning perhaps with a tax increase on gasoline, tobacco and
alcohol—would favor a higher savings and investment rate, provided it
did not open the door for new spending programs that increase consumption. The U.S. could therefore cut the cost of capital substantially by
relying more on a consumption-tax system and less on its income-tax
system.

In spite of some positive features, the 1986 Tax Reform Act is an example of what not to do: it will probably increase the cost of funds for
investment, considering the loss of the investment tax credits, the changes
in depreciation allowances and the elimination of the capital-gains tax differential. It is curious that although the 1986 act implicitly recognized the
desirability of incentives for more research and development, it ignored
incentives for the necessary downstream capital investment. A further example of the antisavings aspects of the 1986 act can also be found in the
way it has made Individual Retirement Accounts substantially less attractive. David A. Wise of Harvard has recently argued that there was relatively little substitution of IRAs for other forms of savings—they represented a promising new source of net savings.

Compared with such macroeconomic policies, other contributions of
government may be less dramatic, but they are nonetheless important in
smoothing the path to greater long-term growth. These include support of
education in general, funding of research and development, maintenance of
the infrastructure necessary for commerce (such as the national highway
system) and the provision of safety nets for those excluded from the rewards of economic growth.

Of course, there may be valid reasons to enact macroeconomic policies
at home that are at odds with the goal of continued growth. The federal
policies in the past twenty years, for example, have tended to place the
priority of job formation above that of capital formation. Managements of
U.S. companies were in effect induced to substitute cheaper labor for capital
investment, and in fact many jobs were created—far more than in Europe
or Japan. Between 1955 and 1986, 47.4 million new jobs were created in
the U.S., 16.6 [million] were created in Japan and a total of only 5.7 [million]
in the European Economic Community. Indeed, unemployment in Europe
is currently in the double-digit range, whereas in the U.S. it has dropped to
about 5.5 percent. Because high unemployment rates are always a potential
threat to domestic tranquility, the extraordinary success of the U.S. in

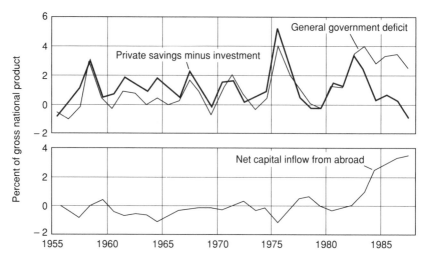

Figure 23.3
Government deficits are usually financed by borrowing from private savings after a country's investment needs have been satisfied. Nevertheless, since 1982 the combined budget of Federal, state and local governments in the U.S. has run sizable deficits, in spite of the fact that there have been few excess funds in savings. The shortfall in domestic savings has been made up by drawing on foreign savings.

creating jobs may well justify in hindsight some of its past economic policies. Nevertheless, such policies have exacted a price in terms of lower productivity growth and a more obsolete capital stock.

All that has been discussed so far is complicated considerably by the inescapable fact that the U.S. economy must operate in the context of a truly global market not only for goods and services but also for technology and money. Goods and services are today bought and sold on a vast scale. Because there is a greater openness to trade, many countries are competing vigorously with the U.S. in the international market—often producing products that are better in quality and lower in price.

New technology is spreading faster than ever before among countries, including many with wage rates a great deal lower than those of the U.S. A century ago transfer of technology from one country to another took place over a number of years, today it may be as short as several months. The causes of this rapid spread include investment abroad (particularly by multinational companies that are moving closer to their markets), international licensing of technology, education of many scientists and engineers in the universities of the West, rapid publication of research and the increasing ease of international travel and communications.

A consequence of the rapid worldwide diffusion of technology is that the country that comes up with a technological innovation is not necessarily the first to commercialize it. Color television, for example, was an American invention superbly perfected and marketed by Japan. In addition other nations have capital-investment rates that are much higher than those in the U.S. Consequently new production technology developed in the U.S. can often be embodied in capital stock sooner in foreign countries than in the U.S. itself. In this way economic competitors of the U.S. can increase the productivity of their workers more rapidly.

The result is that industrial technology has now taken root in many places throughout the world; no longer does the world depend on the manufacturing ability and technical progress of just a few industrialized nations. The sources of supply are nearly global: Malaysian electronic products, Korean automobiles, Swiss pharmaceuticals and Chinese fabrics flood the markets of the U.S. and other nations. It is a historic change, and a permanent one. There is no realistic chance that this situation can be unilaterally changed by the U.S. or any other country, although individual companies have become more conscious of the risks of licensing valuable technology. Governments are also taking more steps to protect the intellectual property of their nationals—a particularly important matter in this day and age, since there are many exciting technologies awaiting exploitation.

Transnational flows of money are now also able to penetrate almost any market in the world instantaneously, exposing a country's policies to strong external market forces. Indeed, trading in financial assets far exceeds trade flows in goods and services, perhaps by as much as a factor of twenty. It would be no exaggeration to say that since about 1979 currency-exchange rates have become an important driving force of the U.S. economy. This situation reflects the fact that money flows in a direction opposite to that of the flow of goods and services. The reason is that whenever the demand for U.S. dollars becomes stronger (as it did in the early 1980s, when high interest rates prevailed in the U.S.), its value in relation to the other currencies increases. Consequently U.S. exports (whose prices are tied to the dollar) become overpriced and imports flood in from many countries. The result is that foreign suppliers gain large domestic-market shares and weaken many U.S. companies, forcing some even into bankruptcy.

This has been the situation until recently, causing the merchandise trade balance (the difference between exports and imports of goods) to plunge to a record $171-billion deficit in 1987. The so-called current-account balance, which in addition takes into consideration the values of such things as payment for international services, repatriated earnings, royalties from abroad and interest on foreign debt, was slightly less: it shows a deficit of $161 billion. As long as exchange rates continue to float, the global financial system will exert a major influence on national economic policies.

Another effect of the tremendous liquidity of borrowed funds in international financial markets has been the startling increase in American debt to other countries. The 1987 Economic Report of the President states that at least 50 percent of net investment in the U.S. came from abroad, mostly because U.S. companies cannot count on domestic savings for investment capital. (Whereas net investment in the U.S. in 1987 was 5.3 percent of the country's GDP net domestic savings was under 2 percent.) At this rate of inflow it will take only a few years for the cost of servicing the foreign debt and the payment of dividends on assets in the U.S. owned by foreigners to become a significant drag on U.S. economic growth. Yet as long as the U.S. savings rate remains unable to cover productive investment in the U.S., the pool of available investment capital will have to be supplemented from abroad (which means higher interest rates). In short, the U.S. has been consuming too much, producing too little and borrowing from abroad to maintain its standard of living.

The negative current account balance of the U.S. (which amounts to about 3.5 percent of the country's GDP) reflects this fundamental imbalance between domestic investment and domestic savings. To remedy the situation either U.S. savings must increase or investment in the U.S. must decrease, which would be catastrophic. Hence the only real choice is to increase savings in a systematic way, by ensuring that the government's spending does not overwhelm Americans' private thrift. (Although the decline in the value of the dollar since 1985 has helped, it certainly will not be enough.) The goal should be to enact policies that regulate consumption so that in a given year it can grow no faster than about 1 percent less than the rate of growth in output, thereby making it possible for net savings rates to increase an average of 1 percent per year more. Over a period of between eight and ten years the net savings rate would move into the double-digit range typical of the U.S.'s international competitors.

Of course, given the size of the U.S. economy, a change in domestic consumption or savings can affect many nations throughout the world, and this has to be taken into consideration when reducing the trade and budget deficits. Indeed, in this sense the country's recent overconsumption and underproduction has actually benefited the world, since it allowed many debt-ridden, less-developed countries to sell their goods and services in the U.S. Nevertheless, it is time for the U.S. to change its priorities and to lay the basis for better long-term growth in a world economy.

The irrevocable changes in the global market I have described pose immense new difficulties particularly for U.S. managers, who gained their experience in the first few decades after the war, when the U.S. dominated world markets and faced little if any competition for domestic markets. International trade has shifted from a situation in which countries could count on long-term stable comparative advantages to a dynamic state in which comparative advantages are constantly being altered. Hence since the 1970s managers everywhere in the industrial world have been compelled to spend a great deal of their time dealing with the consequences of sharp fluctuations in worldwide energy prices, currency-exchange rates and inflation rates. The barrage of external influences has made it difficult even for good U.S. managers to balance short-term exigencies against the longer-term strategic planning that enables a firm to grow and prosper.

Given the current economic situation, there is certainly some room in a general strategy to improve U.S. growth for selective trade actions to meet egregious examples of foreign protectionism. Yet these measures should be applied to open up other nations' markets rather than to close those of the U.S. In fact, the U.S. already has a formidable protectionist arsenal of its own in the form of subsidies, trigger prices, quotas and tariffs. Gary Hufbauer of Georgetown University estimates that protection of some kind covered about 25 percent of U.S. imports by 1986 (it was 8 percent in 1975). Although these measures are considered "temporary," their effect on long-term growth may be much more significant. American companies would lose touch with global technological and economic developments, and the pressure to excel would be reduced.

The true significance of international competitiveness lies in the recognition that it is not an end in itself but a means to raise long-term growth rates so that jobs can be created and the standard of living can be improved. In order to accomplish these goals the U.S. has to restore its long-term real average growth rate of G.D.P. to at least its historic average (between 1870 and 1984) of 3.39 percent per year. Nevertheless, a growth rate of 3.5 percent should be the target for the time being, because it may well take as much as 1 percent of this growth to pay the debts of past profligacy. Taking into account the potential 1 percent penalty for the servicing of foreign capital and a 1 percent increase in the work force in the next decade (down from a peak of 2.9 percent per year between 1976 and 1980), the per capita growth in real G.D.P. would be about 1.5 percent per year.

Although achieving a real per capita G.D.P. growth rate of 1.5 percent will be virtually impossible without some government cooperation, the government must limit itself primarily to establishing the right macroeconomic climate for long-term economic growth. Pervasive government intervention in domestic markets is likely to be counterproductive. Many in government and elsewhere are already using the concept of "competitiveness" as a code word for old-fashioned government manipulation of industry. Yet the government would be overwhelmed in trying to direct the private sector through the rapidly changing conditions imposed by the pace of technological innovation.

Only if we increase investment in both capital and technology in all sectors of the U.S. economy (particularly manufacturing) and improve the quality of labor at all levels can the American standard of living rise at an acceptable rate. In the present highly competitive world market the U.S. has some historically demonstrated advantages, but it must take the longer view and pursue those seemingly trivial increases of a few tenths of a percentage point in growth rate each year.

Capital Investment:
                                      Key to Competitiveness
                                      and Growth

Much is heard about the lack of competitiveness in the United States, but
seldom is that lack defined except in terms of international trade balances
and market shares. In today's global economy, the United States will be
competitive only if it can sustain an acceptable rate of growth in the real
standard of living, with an acceptably fair income distribution, while efficiently providing employment for those who can and want to work. The
country, moreover, must achieve this growth without reducing the potential for growth in the standard of living of future generations, a condition
that constrains borrowing from abroad or incurring excessive future tax
or spending obligations to pay for the current generation's higher living
standards.

   For much of the past century the United States met these conditions.
From 1870 to 1984 real gross domestic product (GDP) grew at an average
of 3.4 percent a year. Real income per capita grew about 2 percent a year,
and standards of living nearly doubled from one generation to the next—
illustrating the great power of compounding even small increments over
long periods of time. In the decades immediately following World War II,
the United States dominated the world economy, relying on domestic
savings to meet domestic capital needs and using macroeconomic policy to
adjust demand to cyclical changes. Supply could—and did—take care of
itself.

   Since 1979, however, growth of real GDP has slowed to an average, but
uneven, rate of 2.75 percent a year, and real income per capita has remained
virtually stagnant. Nor has the United States been able to export enough
to pay for its imports of goods, services, and capital. Even though the
absolute level of U.S. productivity is still the highest in the world, if these
trends are not soon reversed, the United States could find itself yielding its

Published in *The Brookings Review* (Summer 1990): 52–56. Reprinted with permission.

economic and strategic leadership to Japan, whose real growth averaged 6.9 percent a year from 1952 to 1987, and very possibly to the post-1992 European Community, whose economies may be aided by the development of new markets in Eastern Europe.

Economic evidence and experience suggest that the United States must take full advantage of its opportunities if it wants to achieve faster growth. The nation did that in the past both when it invested in great discoveries such as the electric motor, petroleum exploration and refining, machine tools, and semiconductors and when it exploited existing technologies to their fullest potential. Today, the United States must fully capitalize on the promise of many new technologies in computers, telecommunications, biotechnology, robotics, catalysis, pharmaceuticals, materials, and the like. The fastest way to raise the average performance of the economy is to emphasize continuing application of these new technologies to leading-edge industries. But to do that effectively, we must both modify our theories of economic growth and provide a stable environment in which growth can flourish.

The Contribution of Capital

The rate of growth of output, or productivity, of an economy depends on the rates of growth of capital, labor, and technology, Empirically, technological progress accounts for a significant part of the growth in productivity—by some measures as much as 85 percent. The prevailing neoclassical growth theory, developed in the 1950s, holds that in a perfectly competitive economy, in the long-run steady state, the rate of growth is independent of the saving (or equivalently, the investment) rate; in other words, growth is independent of the proportion of output that is reinvested. Recent research, however, has pointed to the significant limitations of this theory, and particularly to its underestimation of the role of capital investment in growth.

Although the classical notion of perfect competition approximates the operation of markets for established goods such as commodities, it is not appropriate for markets that experience continual introduction of new products and rapid technological change. Detailed observation demonstrates that technology is largely a product of traditional economic activity and not exogenous or independent of it, as customarily assumed. Innovation and entrepreneurship have been more powerful forces for growth than the standard neoclassical growth model would recognize.

Particularly in this era of international competition, firms have found that price wars are unattractive and have focused where possible on those forms of competition with the greatest potential for profit—new or improved products, services, and processes. (That is the reason why firms engage in privately financed R&D.) Among the major manufacturing industries, which perform 95 percent of all industrial R&D, companies seek to differentiate themselves by product distinctions, better and lower cost technologies for their production, and more successful financing strategies.

According to detailed measurements made by my colleague Dale Jorgenson and his associates, capital inputs accounted for 44.2 percent of the country's economic growth between 1947 and 1985. Unlike those of earlier researchers, these measurements are wholly consistent internally, although they adhere to the neoclassical assumptions. A detailed explanation of these results is contained in a new book, *Technology and Capital Formation* (Jorgenson and Landau, MIT Press), which deals with the problems of both measurement and composition or aggregation.

Moreover, experience demonstrates that much of the capital spent by companies to maintain or expand their physical facilities incorporates new technology. That is why gross capital additions (and gross output) are the most important numbers to measure in determining the factors of growth. The composition of investment has shifted significantly from longer-lived to shorter-lived assets, such as computers, which depreciate more rapidly. Gross investment data are not affected by such compositional shifts. The substitution of more highly productive capital goods embodying the new technology for goods that are less productive improves the quality of capital. Productivity of the economy thus rises, even if net investment is zero. But traditional measures of the contribution of capital to growth do not take these quality improvements into account. When they are factored in, capital's contribution is much greater than economists and others generally recognize.

One of the disadvantages of the neoclassical growth model of technology, capital, and labor is that it focuses attention only on the relative proportions in which these three inputs are used. It does not emphasize the importance of variation in their common rate of growth. There is no question that relative proportions matter. The experience of the centrally planned economies has clearly demonstrated that massive increases in physical capital without accompanying improvements in technology and the quality of the labor force lead to rapidly diminishing returns, just as the neoclassical model would suggest.

But because it considers improvements in technology and labor quality to be unaffected by public and private decisions, the neoclassical model fails to emphasize that these three inputs are intertwined pieces of the same process—a three-legged stool of human, physical, and intangible capital. The important point here is not to establish exactly how much each of these factors contributes to growth, but to recognize that there are several identifiable ways to improve growth rates over a period of twenty to thirty years—investment in physical capital will pay off, as will improvement in the quality of the labor force and continued technological progress.

Improving the quality of capital obviously requires investment in new fixed assets. Indeed, as important as it is, the emphasis on increasing research and development efforts alone is misplaced, because the physical capital required to realize the R&D results is usually greater than the cost of the R&D involved. And the U.S. economy is not operating everywhere at the technological frontier. Many American industries are far behind those in other nations. Once a company exploits a technological lead with early market penetration, later entrants, even those with better technology, often cannot overcome the first entrant's economies of scale and learning curve improvements. Thus it may take twenty to thirty years of steady investment before existing or potentially important technologies can be fully exploited by American companies.

Martin Baily and Charles Schultze of Brookings, although still adhering to neoclassical theory and some of the earlier methodologies for measurement of growth, nevertheless concur that if an economy is not at the frontier, then additional investment can produce a longer-term increase in productivity growth. What is true for a country is also true for an industry. Jorgenson has shown that the higher productivity growth rates in Japan have been heavily influenced by a much higher rate of capital investment in a number of Japanese industries, which permitted them to adopt the latest technologies rapidly. From now on, comparative advantages of firms or industries in industrial countries will be determined endogenously and result in ever-shifting leads or lags. How competitive an industrialized country is in the world market no longer depends on its relative resource endowments (as Saudi Arabia depends on oil), but on how rapidly the country's industries can develop and adapt innovative technology.

America's failure to recognize fully the contribution capital makes to growth has led to a serious underestimation of the impact of investment in physical capital on growth. This failure is especially serious today, when growing environmental concerns, a deteriorating infrastructure, and a lower growth rate in a work force that needs even more education will require additional capital investments. Few dispute that raising the productive physical investment per worker is beneficial and will raise the *level* of output (and income) per capita; what some do not realize is that greater investment in physical capital offers hope that the *rate* of productivity growth can also be increased. At the same time, government policies in the United States have done too little to improve the climate for such investment. Without a favorable climate, business cannot be held fully accountable for failing to design a successful growth strategy.

The Climate for Growth

Several new studies by my colleagues at Stanford lead to the conclusion that stable government policies (fiscal, monetary, trade, and tax) favoring high rates of investment may be essential for higher levels of economic well-being in both the short and long runs. In fact, that seems to have been the secret behind the remarkable economic recovery both Germany and Japan made from total ruin at the end of World War II.

    After examining business cycles and long-term growth in several major industrial countries, Steven Durlauf has shown that an appropriate stabilization policy is not meaningfully distinct from a high growth policy. High investments in one industry can induce high investments in other industries, resulting in higher growth rates, which allow still more investment even as present consumption increases. Several of my recent studies of the chemical industries illustrate how these spillover effects occur; the petroleum, automobile, apparel, and other industries depended crucially on the growth of the chemical industries, and vice versa. And as *The Economist* has noted, these results also suggest that the lack of investment not only causes a loss of productive capacity in its own right but also hurts the value of investments already made.

    In a study of the economic performance of five industrial countries, Michael Boskin and Lawrence Lau have found that technological progress is capital-augmenting and that the benefits of technological progress are higher when a larger capital stock is deployed per worker. Capital formation and technological progress thus complement each other. Together, they account for about 70 percent of the growth in output in the United States, according to Boskin, who initiated the study while he was at Stanford, and Lau, who completed the work. Theirs is a finding of no small importance, since for the last twenty-five years the United States has invested proportionally less than the other major industrial countries in gross nonresidential physical capital. Furthermore, they concluded, under capital-augmenting technological change, a steady state may not exist even under neoclassical conditions; the limits to growth are expandable....

Why has capital investment lagged in the United States? John Shoven of Stanford and Douglas Bernheim of Northwestern have found that one important factor is the risk premium—the higher average return required by investors on an investment to compensate them for assuming the uncertainty of the outcome of the investment—and that it in turn depends on a country's macroeconomic policies. Frequent changes in those policies, particularly the volatile and unpredictable changes in tax rates, interest rates, and exchange rates (as Ronald McKinnon and David Robinson have found) make the cost of capital more expensive here than elsewhere. The cost of capital for Japanese companies is a third to a half as much as the cost to U.S. companies across a wide range of investments, as confirmed by a major study of the Federal Reserve Bank of New York.

This very expectation of uncertainty has further shortened the time horizons—the discount rates applied to an investment's future returns—of American companies. Yet the gestation period for physical investment is three to five years, while five to ten years may pass before investment in research and development begins to pay off. The return on investment in education and worker training may not be realized for even longer.

Moreover, R&D is only one part of intangible capital, which also includes design engineering, experimental production, worker training, market development, start-up costs, market penetration, insurance, legal precautions, and the like. These operations are generally financed with equity capital or retained earnings, rather than borrowing. According to George Hatsopoulos of Thermoelectron ... the real after-tax cost of equity in the 1980s was two and a half to three times as high as the real long-term, after-tax cost of debt and more than twice the Japanese real after-tax cost of equity. These high costs of equity, combined with the high real interest rates that companies must pay on the money they do borrow, has reduced investments in all kinds of capital by U.S. firms and thus their ability to compete on a long-term basis with high investment countries such as Japan and Germany.

Japan is on a capital spending binge that will surely strengthen its growth and export capability (*figure 24.1*). The recent fall in the Japanese stock market and rising inflation bring to an end the speculative bubble in stock and land prices, raise somewhat the cost of Japanese equity, and herald a reduction in the flood of Japanese capital flowing overseas, especially to the United States. High real interest rates and slow growth may therefore continue here, unless the national savings rate improves, as it has

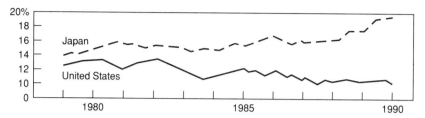

Figure 24.1
Capital formation compared (gross nonresidential capital investment as a percentage of gross national product).

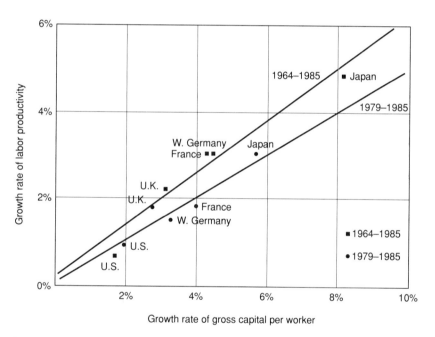

Growth rate of gross capital per worker

Figure 24.2
Labor productivity vs. the capital-labor ratio for five [industrial] countries (average annual growth rates).

recently begun to do. The adaptable Japanese system, however, continues to hold many advantages, and Japan should continue to grow over the longer term at a higher rate than other industrialized countries.

Figure 24.2 clearly shows the correlation of gross investment with growth (on the same basis as Jorgenson's data for the United States cited above) and why the standard growth theory needs modification. The lower curve (1979–85) depicts the relationship when the average level of technology is roughly equal (although the level in individual industries or firms may differ), and the slope of approximately 50 percent is consistent with the findings of Boskin and Lau. New theoretical work by Paul Romer of the University of Chicago, Richard Nelson of Columbia University, and others has shown how the original neoclassical growth models need to be greatly modified to fit actuality. Given imperfect competition, these modified models are the only ones that reflect reality and allow a role for patents and privately financed R&D.

If the United States wants to take advantage of the robust high correlation between capital per worker and growth and raise real living standards, it will need to adopt stable policies favoring long-term investment. The business cycle and long-term growth must be viewed from one overall perspective. Economists may quarrel over whether growth stimulates investment or vice versa, but in practice the order is immaterial. Supply is no longer assured, even if demand is stimulated, because of the long gestation periods now required to adopt technology more efficiently. What matters is that investment in *productive* physical capital can promote growth, as can the proper and stable management of macroeconomic policy by the government and of individual companies by the private sector.

The case for more investment in physical capital, education, and technology is grounded in the economic and technological opportunities facing the United States. The current importance of the great, and only very partially realized, revolution in information technologies means that technical progress is embodied in physical capital to an unprecedented extent. This embodiment links investment in new knowledge for growth with investment in new physical capital. Similarly, opportunities for technological advance are linked with investment in R&D and human capital. These new technologies demand a high mix of skills; here the American higher educational system offers a source of substantial comparative advantage to the United States, if exploited in concept with new investment in physical and intangible capital. But its secondary education system needs major improvement if the advantage is to be sustained for the long term.

What is needed is a policy to stabilize monetary and fiscal policy, increase savings, bring down interest rates, remove tax biases against saving and investment, increase expenditures for research and development, and reduce the inefficiencies in the financial and legal systems that retard investment in the most productive sectors. Without these basic changes, the high cost of capital, greater uncertainty, inadequate savings and investment, increasing reliance on foreign capital in an open world capital market, and short time horizons by corporate managers and public policymakers will continue to gnaw away at the American standard of living. It is time to cast aside the obsolete theories and policies of the past.

Lessons from Life

Ralph Landau views his life in engineering and business as an academy that prepared him for his current studies of technology and economic growth. As a chemical engineer and owner of his own company, he learned to understand the viewpoints of both the technologist and the entrepreneur. His membership on the board of directors of ALCOA gave him an insider's perspective on big business. As both a venture capitalist and a direct investor in several companies, he understands the dilemmas confronting investors generally. These, together with his academic, industry, and professional associations, allow him to speak on issues of technology and economics with an authority that few others can muster. The three papers that follow distill much of what Landau has learned in a lifetime of observing, thinking, and doing.

25

The CEO and the
Technologist

Recently, the Industrial Research Institute participated in a study of the attitudes of top management toward their R&D heads.[1] Surprising to many, it appeared from this survey that a large number of CEOs felt that their R&D managers often failed to understand their problems. Frequently, they stated, projects were brought to management for funding that did not fit the corporation's strategy or resources. This can be a serious situation for the corporation, and needs to be clarified for the research and development community as much as for the CEOs.

Top managements are besieged by advice and information from many sources: business school publications, newspapers, financial newsletters, business and financial organization meetings and discussions, consulting firm publications and reports, academic publications and information, government briefings and interactions, and so forth. Perhaps some technical literature and advice also reaches them, despite the demands on their time.

But do the R&D communities receive similar exposure to the broader problems their managements face, or are they so preoccupied with the accelerating pace of science and technology that it is all they can do to keep up with their own fields of expertise? The question is a critical one, because R&D is not an intrinsically necessary activity. It is justified only if it helps to further the specific needs of the organization of which it is a part.

From my experience, those two worlds and perspectives are often at loggerheads. Even when the CEO is an experienced technologist, which is often the case, he or she must of necessity become increasingly immersed in the kind of business and financial problems reflected in the above categorization.

Published in *Research-Technology Management* 35, no. 3 (May–June 1992): 28–33.

Perhaps, then, because I have been a technologist and a CEO, I can shed some light on both viewpoints. I will briefly cite my own experiences, because I started out as a technologist, and for years technology drove our business. To be sure, we had to solve many business problems, but the 1950s and '60s constituted an era of rapid world and industry growth, and superior technology was indeed in demand. However, as the external environment changed in the 1970s, I was confronted with a new set of problems on the financial side (in which we were not expert) which converted me more fully into a CEO for these times. In an era of capital constraints worldwide, the lessons that I learned then and thereafter as an economist at Stanford may be helpful to the technical community today in understanding some of the key problems posed to technology-based American companies and their managements.

A True Story

As I have described elsewhere, I co-founded Scientific Design Co. Inc. (later Halcon International and Halcon SD Group) in 1946.[2] During our first twenty years, there was no outside founding available. We grew from within, and technology was managed by us for strategic growth. The period 1946–66 could be described as the golden years of America's postwar dominance of the international economy. This led us to form a joint venture (Oxirane) with Atlantic Richfield Co. in 1966 to exploit a major new technology we had developed for the manufacture of propylene oxide.[3] Accordingly, we required a large source of external funds to maintain the rapid growth that our strategy dictated—new technology must be swiftly exploited commercially on as international a scale as possible, so as to gain and hold market share and descend the learning curve of the technology before competitors can make serious inroads.

In a previous article I described the innovative financing arrangement that was worked out by Arco and ourselves to permit a public and private company to work effectively together.[4] This was our introduction to the real world of finance. As a result, the joint venture grew rapidly from 1969–79, to revenues of $1 billion per year from five plants in the United States, one in the Netherlands, one in Spain, and one in Japan. We achieved 50 percent market share in the U.S., developed new related products such as oxygenated gasoline additives, and generated a large cash flow for reinvestment in expansion, and even some dividends for the Halcon stockholders.

This remarkable business and chemical achievement was soon to change abruptly, as the environment external to us changed—an environment we had barely any cognizance of during the preceding years. This was the macroeconomic climate of the country.

The End of America's Dominance

During the late 1960s and the 1970s, we had been aware of changing economic conditions but found it possible to adapt. In the later years of the Vietnam war, Washington imposed capital controls on American investment abroad. We were able to offset this by borrowing from Dutch banks to finance our Rotterdam plant. President Nixon imposed price controls and went off the gold standard in 1971, but we, like others, were able to raise our prices to offset the rising cost of raw materials, brought about especially from the oil shock of 1973. We continued with our expansion by building a large new plant at Channelview, Texas. This entailed borrowing over $230 million from a bank syndicate at prime rate, which was then 11 percent.

For several years, as inflation roared up toward the 13 percent level, the interest levels remained subdued (meaning, of course, a negative real rate of return to the banks). In October 1979, President Carter was forced to apply the brakes by appointing Paul Volcker as chairman of the Federal Reserve Board. Soon thereafter, instead of targeting interest rates, as the Administration and the previous Board had practiced, Volcker targeted and limited the growth in the money supply, which had been growing rapidly and fueling inflation. In effect, the Fed had been inflating the currency by printing money! The prime rate shot up to 21 percent. Suddenly, all our cash flow was going to the banks. Technological strategy was no longer my principal concern—it was sheer survival. Could we meet the next interest payment?

At the same time, we had been involved with Arco in renegotiating some of the terms of our original financing arrangement. I well remember one of their financial executives saying, unimpressed by Oxirane's remarkable previous growth, "I'll teach you the value of money [vs. technology]."

It became clear to me that we could no longer sustain our position as an equal partner in Oxirane; the executive was right. In such unfavorable economic conditions, money (finance) was decisive. I sold our half of the partnership to Arco, which had deep enough pockets to nourish the technology properly. Today Arco Chemicals is a great success story in its own right. We were soon compelled to sell the rest of our business in the recession of 1981–82 that followed Volcker's crushing of the 1970s' inflation. The only positive part of this history was that our stockholders finally cashed in after thirty-six years of patience!

Why did this have to happen to such a technological triumph? I only dimly understood the causes of the traumatic events of the 1970s. For this reason, I decided to become a member of the economics community (at Stanford and Harvard) and study particularly the interaction of technology and economics.[5] I will try to convey in the following some of what I have been learning that may be of general applicability.

The Rise of Financial Dominance

Managing for the long term requires a close understanding of the changing business and technical environment with which CEOs and technologists must contend. Both must understand it. The events of the 1970s and '80s have bred a more stringent financial climate which, understandably, has propelled many financially trained executives to the top of their companies. Understandably also, these executives know comparatively little technology and have less time to devote to keeping up with the technological developments of their more technology-oriented competitors abroad.

This financial orientation seems to the company technologists to lead to a short-term mentality, but even a superficial knowledge of financial theory would suggest that at high interest rates and cost of capital, the benefits of the more distant future earnings gains would be heavily discounted by financial analysts. This condition still does not relieve managements of planning strategically, and many do. But many have not.

One result of this increasing financial orientation among American companies has been that privately owned high-risk startup companies have had no serious problem finding venture capital (unavailable in our earlier years) and planning for a longer horizon than simple financial analysis would seem to justify. In the years they are private, these companies often grow rapidly and are strongly technologically oriented. The problems begin when even more capital is needed fast, and the public markets must be tapped by initial public offerings. The entrepreneurs and venture capitalists who started these companies now cash out handsomely—the real reason why venture capital seems so much more patient than the banks or stock markets. The psychology and motivation of management soon changes, and becomes more like that of companies that have long been publicly held.

During the 1980s we saw some reverse buyouts, in which managements combined with leveraged buyout specialist firms to go private again in order to improve the firm's longer range position, only to go public once more when market conditions permit. Private ownership fosters a longer term technological strategy, but the need for capital to grow or to cash in forces access to public markets in most cases.

When this occurs, we find that increasingly the stocks of large public companies are owned by pension funds and the like. For instance, Alcoa (on whose board I served), a Dow Jones index company, is almost 80 percent owned by such institutions. This leads to a growing separation of ownership and management. Company executives are fiduciaries for their stockholders, who are increasingly pension funds that themselves are managed by fiduciaries. Fiduciaries on fiduciaries—is it any wonder that horizons are short? How else can the performance of professional managements be gauged by their (temporary) owners, the pension funds, than by quarterly financial returns? Business is now so complex that these stockholders cannot readily understand what is happening. Unfortunately, some managements also encourage this behavior by judging their own pension managers strictly on their regular financial returns. Furthermore, some managements, perhaps unwittingly, contribute to the separation problem by rewarding themselves independently of their company's performance.

New Climate for Firms

Of course, many managers who grew up during the halcyon 1950s and '60s found themselves unsuited for the problems of the turbulent 1970s and '80s. This was one of the reasons that technologists and managers seemed to view each other from different perspectives. Although the situation differs widely among firms, most have to contend with completely changed external conditions than heretofore. Let us examine some of these in greater detail:

1. Time horizons have greatly shortened—the well known quarterly financial returns syndrome. Have the genes of managers changed since the earlier period? Most likely not; their circumstances have. Consider:

• *Increased global competition.* We all see this, Japanese, other Asians, and Europeans are in the American market by imports or manufacture, and the U.S. is active in many world markets.

• *Rapidly changing capital markets.* The American financial and securities industries have invented a bewildering array of financial devices: program trading, options markets, hedge funds, asset allocation and mutual funds, American depository receipts for foreign stocks, currency swaps, "junk" bonds, LBOs leveraged buyouts and takeovers, and more. The net result of all these systems is certainly to increase the liquidity of the capital markets and internationalize them. At the same time, however, there has been a great reduction in the number of true long-term individual investors. Rather, the markets are dominated by "bettors" who have no compunction about moving in and out of financial instruments almost instantaneously. Stock prices undergo sharp changes, sometimes overnight. It is an unsettling environment for management, and indeed for many other employers who depend on stock options for added incentives.

• *Higher real cost of capital.* During the 1980s, the financial and economic communities focused on a previously little-noticed phenomenon—the cost of capital. Even the concept, when first introduced by George Hatsopoulos in 1983, seemed foreign.[6] But since then, great strides have been made in several countries to define and measure this concept. The two most recent are those of McCauley and Zimmer[7] and of Bernheim and Shoven.[8] The latter introduced relative-risk premiums into the calculations for the cost of equity. Hatsopoulos has recently measured these numbers also.[9]

The upshot is that the average real risk-free cost of capital to American corporations (debt plus equity) has been up to 5 percent more than that of Japan. Thus, where nominal "hurdle" rates for risk-bearing investment may be 15 percent in the United States, they may be only 5–8 percent in Japan. Part of this differential is also due to the lower risk premiums afforded by the Japanese financial institutions (main banks, *keiretsu*, and the like), although their situation has recently begun to change, and possibly much of the previous differential has dwindled. Obviously, projects that must pass a 15 percent hurdle will have to have a much more rapid payout than those at 5–8 percent, and the latter can justify many more projects that eventually can drive American businesses out of their marketplace or out of existence.

The major reason for this difference is the much greater Japanese savings and investment rate. In Japan, gross domestic savings averaged 28 percent of GNP in the late 1980s, in contrast with only 13–14 percent in the U.S. By the same token, Japanese aggregate domestic investment averaged about 24 percent of its gross national product in the 1980s, compared to 16 percent in the U.S.[10] Therefore, despite its heavy investment rate, which recently surpassed that of the United States in absolute dollars (from a smaller economy), Japan still had surplus capital that it exported to the U.S.

The unfavorable balance of payments for the U.S. was the mirror image of this capital importation—that is, the Japanese obtained their dollars to invest in the U.S. by selling us more than they imported from us. In fact, investment opportunities in the U.S. for them in the recent past were so great that, in addition to this source, they borrowed dollars in the international money markets. Much as we huff and puff about unfair Japanese trade practices (and some are), the root cause of our deficit is the low savings and investment rate in the U.S. Similarly, the root cause of our higher cost of capital can be found in the same place. This very same high cost attracted Japanese investment here, including the buyout of American firms with important technologies. American management must contend with these stark facts, which are largely beyond their control.

Of course, some managements do much better than others in the face of these obstacles. Increasing international competition and the discipline of the financial markets is forcing more restructuring, cost cutting, and attention to the dynamic comparative advantage that strategic management of technology can afford. Managements trained in the easier time of past decades must learn rapidly to adapt. The task is often daunting. Japanese managements, trying to catch up with the United States, and forced to compete earlier in international markets, work very hard to improve their performance and cut their costs. Furthermore, enjoying the advantage of abundant and cheap capital, they are not only better trained, largely technically, but also willing to take the greater long-term risks their economic environment permits.

• *Increased legal liability.* The litigiousness of Americans is by now legendary. The U.S. may well have several-fold more lawyers per capita than any other country, and these lawyers like to eat! Whatever the constitutional and political justification there may have been for our legal system (and Americans have always had a strong sense of justice and fairness), it has now led to an explosion of all kinds of litigation, including stockholder and employee suits against managements, increased regulatory pressures, dishonoring of contractual obligations in certain egregious cases, and many other examples.[11]

• *Changes in accounting standards.* Many forms of investment do not show up on the balance sheets of companies and are, therefore, poorly understood by many financial analysts. Examples of such intangible capital (for they are capital investments despite their being deductible as incurred) include: R&D, advertising, engineering, training, startup losses, organizational development, and customer and supplier relationships, among others.

• In addition, American accounting standards in the era of international markets often discriminate against U.S. firms; for example, there is the provision to, in effect, disallow full deduction of domestically incurred R&D against domestic income, but to specify that it must be allocated among all income (foreign and domestic), where foreign countries have different tax and accounting rules. Such laws force American companies to move more of such activities abroad, to the detriment of American jobs.

• *Volatility in exchange rates.* In the 1980s particularly, as markets became more globalized, the effects of macroeconomic influences on exchange rates became extensive and disturbing. Thus, when the dollar hardened abruptly in the early 1980s as a result of the high real interest rates induced by the Federal Reserve to squelch the inflation of the 1970s, many American exporters suddenly found themselves priced out of the market, and others experienced a flood of low-priced imports. Foreign companies in most cases did not relinquish their increased market share, even when the dollar dropped in the late 1980s, but were willing to accept lower profits in order to do so.

• *Increasing bureaucracy in firms.* The large number of external influences described above have often led to increasing staff requirements to conform to the various requirements of the law and competition. While corporate restructuring has to some extent begun to reduce these layers of management, they are still there in many instances, and inhibit rapid adaptability to a changing environment and new technologies.

• *Frequent and complex tax laws.* There were a number of major tax bills in the 1980s, and there is no end in sight. The 1986 Act was clearly designed to penalize corporations and their investments, and the bills since then have done little to improve matters.

• *More adversarial business-government relationships.* While by no means constant or general, the American government has traditionally been wary of supporting American firms too strongly, particularly in international trade and investment, unlike the governments of our principal competitors.

2. The takeovers and LBOs [leveraged buyouts] of the 1980s have reversed the conglomeration of the 1960s—now easy to recognize as a colossal management mistake made at a time when complacency was endemic owing to lack of competition from abroad. Divestitures have become more frequent, as has corporate leverage, which, while reducing somewhat the cost of capital (because of deductibility of interest, whereas dividends are not) has led to greater risk aversion by management in the face of massive debt repayments and still-high interest rates.

The wave of takeovers and mergers diminished in 1990 and 1991, primarily because of the collapse of the junk bond market and the somewhat unexplained rise in the stock market, which made equities cheaper and takeovers less attractive. These movements in the 1980s made the returns on physical assets (including risk premiums) greater than the returns on financial assets, which appeared to be the goal of financial investors.

3. Technology has become much more sophisticated and difficult to comprehend, even by technically trained CEOs who cannot devote the time to keeping up to date technically in the face of the many other constraints on their actions, described above. This is all the more reason for the trust between managements and their technologists to be nurtured and extended.

4. Finally, a CEO won't hold his or her job long if attention is not paid to all of these factors. While compensation of American chief executives is generally good, the fall from those levels is accordingly very hard indeed. More have been experiencing such shocks recently.

What Is to Be Done?

There is much discussion in the business and academic literature about new ways of managing for the 1990s, in light of all the changes that have taken and are taking place. This is not an appropriate subject for this article. Some companies and some industries won't do well enough in their commercialization of technology even if the external environment were as good as might be desired, and some companies have done well in spite of these difficulties.

But one need seems to be paramount. No company today can afford to neglect its technology, or fail to manage it strategically. Furthermore, no company can generate all its own technology. All must search the world constantly to identify the state-of-the-art technology that suits their needs. For this, newer forms of strategic alliance become essential. One of these is surely an alliance with the energetic entrepreneurial companies I have described above. There should be better ways of funding them without controlling them, and yet make their jobs and future dependent on their own efforts. My relations with Arco are an example of how much this can accomplish for both partners.

Having said all this, I must acknowledge that the direct responsibility for competing successfully is business's. But if business is to be held accountable by the American people, government must aid by better accommodation of the external environment in which businesses operate, especially in

Options for the Future

Good R&D implicitly should position the company for future investment opportunities, directions, alliances, and entry to markets, if and when various contingencies are satisfactorily resolved. R&D portfolios consist of projects that are truly corporate overheads, such as exploratory research. These are knowledge builders, and are generally small in scope and expense. Corporations limit this type of overhead. Another, and much larger part of the R&D portfolio consists of R&D as an investment, such as for development and engineering programs, where the outcome is well enough understood to permit treatment as a capital budgeting exercise by well known financial analysis.

However, there is an intermediate zone, where uncertainty is still substantial, the objective still less sharply defined, and programs only partially focused. This is the area of strategic positioning for the future, yet the R&D costs are too high for overhead, and the uncertainty too great for investments. Such projects are best treated as options, analogous to call options in the financial markets. Here, the price of the option resembles the cost of the R&D, the exercise price resembles the cost of the future investment needed to capitalize on the R&D at a future date, and the value of the stock underlying the call option is like the return the company would get from its future investment.

If the option is never exercised, the lost cost is modest. With great uncertainty, the chance that the ultimate returns could exceed the exercise price *raises* the value of the option. Commitment of investment resources is contingent on the underlying assumptions being realized, and therefore falls under capital budgeting considerations only in the future. Thus, both the technologists and the management can deal with technology as an integral element in the formulation and implementation of strategy.

What are some of these options? One should expect continuing cost reduction and productivity improvement, the protection of existing business, and increasing the barrier to new entry of competitors. More strategic options would deal with better or new products and processes, better packing, storing and distribution, better or different marketing, wider geographical spread, and so on. From these options and their ultimate implementation, further options could emerge from the existing business, or from external sources but contiguous with it, such as new products, new technologies and new markets.

light of the changed international conditions. This would feature a stable, low inflationary fiscal and monetary policy, with relatively stable exchange rates, and a stable tax system that would favor investment and savings. Regulatory policies not only need to be held steady, they must also take account of economic costs as well as benefits.

Meanwhile, many of us are continuing to work to educate government and other institutions about the problems discussed in this article, within the framework of the U.S. competitive position. This involves macroeconomic policies and related actions such as those on taxes, trade, accounting, regulatory, educational, science and technology, and so forth. In addition, in light of recent events and the history recounted above, we must examine our financial and legal institutions critically, in comparison with those of our competitor nations. So much has been ineffectual or counterproductive in these policies during the last two decades that even small changes can bring large improvements. Such changes are much more feasible and fair than micromanagement of companies and industries (mainly declining) by subsidies, protectionism and the like.

In conclusion, therefore, if technologists expect to get understanding and cooperation from their CEOs, they must learn the problems of the CEO's world and convince him or her that they do understand them and take them into account. Much has been written about what technologists must do within their own expertise, but they must broaden their understanding, and offer their managements real strategic options for the future. This is not just a simple apologia. Space does not permit an extensive treatment of this concept, but the box [entitled "Options for the Future"] summarizes some important concepts taken from two recent and penetrating analyses.[12] Technologists can, by using this thinking, help convince their CEOs that R&D is not only a cost, nor even only an investment, but also options for future strategic directions and investments. A useful illustration of this process is contained in Chapter 4 of a recent Arthur D. Little book.[13] Then it will be as it should be, the CEO *and* the technologist, not the CEO *versus* the technologist.

References

1. "Are You Credible With Your CEO?" *Research Technology Management*. Mar.-Apr. 1991, pp. 9–11; B. Uttal, A. Kantrow, L. Linden, and B. Susan Stock, "Building R&D Leadership and Credibility," p. 15 this issue.

2. R. Landau. "Halcon International. Inc.—An Entrepreneurial Chemical Company," The Newcomen Society, Oct. 1978; "Process Innovation." Perkin Medal Address, Society of Chemical Industry, Feb. 13, 1981—published in *Chemistry and Industry*, May 2, 1981;

National Academy of Engineering *The Bridge*, Fall 1981, p. 17; "Harnessing Innovation for Growth," *Chemical Engineering Progress*, July 1988, pp. 31–42.

3. R. Landau, D. Brown, J.L. Russell, J. Kollar, "Epoxidation of Olefins." presented at Symposium on New Concepts and Techniques in Oxidation of Hydrocarbons, 7th World Petroleum Congress, Mexico City, Apr. 1967—in "Proceedings of the Congress." *Petrochemistry*, Elsevier Publishing Co., Ltd., Essex, England, Vol. 5, 1967, pp. 66–72.

4. R. Landau, "Corporate Partnering Can Spur Innovation," *Research Management*. Vol. XXX, No. 3, May-June 1987, pp. 21–26.

5. R. Landau, "How Competitiveness Can Be Achieved," in *Technology & Economics*, National Academy Press, Washington, DC. 1991, pp. 3—16; "Capital Investment: Key to Competitiveness and Growth," *The Brookings Review*, Summer 1990, pp. 52–56; *The Positive Sum Strategy*, R. Landau, N. Rosenberg. Eds., National Academy Press, Washington, DC, 1986.

6. G. N. Hatsopoulos, "High Cost of Capital: Handicap of American Industry," paper presented at American Businerss Conference and Thermo Electron Corporation, Apr. 26, 1983.

7. R. McCauley, S. Zimmer, "Explanations for International Differences in the Cost of Capital," Federal Reserve Bank of New York, *Quarterly Review*, Summer 1989.

8. R. D. Bernheim, J. Shoven, "Comparison of the Cost of Capital in the U.S. and Japan: The Roles of Risk and Taxes," in *Technology and the Wealth of Nations*, N. Rosenberg, R. Landau, D. Mowery, Eds., Stanford University Press (forthcoming).

9. G. N. Hatsopoulos, "Technology and the Cost of Capital," in *Technology & Economics*, National Academy Press, Washington, DC, 1991.

10. C. Wolf, Jr., "Demystifying the Japanese Mystique." *The New York Times*. May 26, 1991, p. F11.

11. W. K. Olson, *The Litigation Explosion*, Dutton, New York, 1991; P. W. Huber and R. E. Litan, *The Liability Maze*. The Brookings Institution, Washington, DC, 1991.

12. R. Malpas, "Marketing the Future," Duncan Davies Memorial Medal Lecture, The Research and Development Society, London, 3 Apr. 1990; W. F. Hamilton, G. R. Mitchell, "What is Your R&D Worth?," *The McKinsey Quarterly*, No. 3. 1990, pp. 150–160; R. Malpas and S. J. S. Watson, "Technology and Wealth Creation," Lecture, British Association for the Advancement of Science, London, Aug. 29, 1991.

13. P. A. Roussel, K. N. Saad. T.J. Erickson (Arthur D. Little, Inc.), *Third Generation R&D: Managing the Link to Corporate Strategy*, Harvard Business School Press, Boston, MA, 1991.

26

Risk-Taking and Entrepreneurship

Why are risk-taking and entrepreneurship important? They relate to two basic forces of the economy:

1. Growth (which means productivity)
2. Jobs

Everyone now talks of the need for greater economic growth. Everyone talks about the decline in growth of labor productivity, and stagnating per capita income, and everyone worries about rising unemployment. But how can we reconcile these? After all, if productivity per worker is to increase, some jobs are lost. That happened first at the beginning of the 1980s in manufacturing, and now it is beginning to happen in the 70 percent plus of the economy which is labeled service industries. Steven Roach of Morgan Stanley and Lester Thurow of MIT and others have been complaining for years that the huge investment by the service sector in information equipment has not resulted in a corresponding rise in productivity. Hence, as jobs were lost in manufacturing, employment was found in services by a burst of entrepreneurial energy and a flexible labor market, but the economy grew very slowly while unemployment stayed low.

No longer. Unemployment is rising while growth is still low. Since the later 1980s, the major companies have been restructuring and downsizing, but have *not* created any net new jobs. They must create wealth and stay competitive, but they don't produce jobs. Between 1979–89, twenty million new jobs were created in the U.S.—but employment in the Fortune 500 largest firms (which have total sales equivalent to 40 percent of GNP) fell from 16.2 to 12.5 million.... Their share of total non-farm employment fell from a high of 20.6 percent to 17.1 percent in 1981, and then steadily until

Comments on a paper by James Poterba, presented at the fourth Stanford-Harvard Workshop on Tax Policy, July 1992, Washington, D.C.

10.9 percent in 1991. From 1988–90 businesses with less than twenty employees added four million new jobs. Especially in bad times, only the smaller businesses and entrepreneurial firms (mostly non-technical) can create jobs—lots of them. In good times, both expand, but the larger companies generate more jobs. The shares between small and large company job creation over time are shown in ... table 26.1

Smaller companies are more flexible and have more focus, and they also are important providers of new technologies, new products and new services. This entrepreneurial sector is America's unique comparative advantage. Other countries envy us in our honoring of the entrepreneur and seek to emulate our success, with so far meager results. You cannot look at growth solely from the aggregate level. You must understand the structure and function of firms and industries.

But at the same time, public policy is tending to do great harm to the small business and entrepreneurial sector of our economy. Risk-taking is increasingly discouraged in a country that loads more and more regulations, mandates, liabilities, and responsibilities on such firms—even the very small ones. We do it also to larger firms, but they have the resources and scale to provide staff and political clout to take care of themselves. Even so, more and more large firms are restricting their hiring of new employees because of the high cost of social benefits; they prefer to employ part-time or independent contractors who do not require such benefits. The smaller and younger firms cannot afford much of this, and are often ignorant of their requirements. If they focus on these, it distracts them from the back-breaking job of building the business or the tech-

Table 26.1
Where the jobs are: Net job growth in the small companies (under 500 employees) and large companies (500 + employees)

Time period	Total net employment growth	Percentage share in	
		Small companies	Large companies
1976–1978	6,062,000	72.2	27.3
1978–1980	5,777,000	45.1	54.9
1980–1982	1,542,000	95.5	4.5
1982–1984	4,318,000	76.7	23.3
1984–1986	4,611,000	52.3	47.7
1986–1988	6,169,000	44.9	55.1

Source: *Wall Street Journal*, February 14, 1992, p. B1.

nology. One lawsuit will do it—just one. The recent Americans-with-Disabilities Act, admirable as its intentions are, is a good example. It applies to a firm with only ten employees. It covers a lot more than access ramps for wheelchairs. An even more egregious example will be found in some of the mandated health plans and other safety nets and regulations being proposed by politicians these days, which simply would be beyond the capability of many smaller firms to cope with or afford. If they cannot do so, we cannot return to a satisfactory rate of employment.

Then, having created such a restraining climate for our entrepreneurial businesses, we have made their access to and cost of capital even worse than before. Most of these are not public companies—they depend on financing from friends, relatives, personal savings, and in some cases venture capital. The informal venture capital market is estimated to be not far from $60 billion/yr., vs. the less than $1.5 billion/yr. in the organized venture capital market (down from about $4.0 billion in the mid-1980s).

These are not cheap capital sources, such as a public company's high P/E multiple signifies. An investor of these kinds must be patient, and expect no return for years. When (and if) he (or she) does, he (or she) is taxed as if the income (and gain) were current earnings at top marginal rate, without correcting for intervening inflation or lack of current returns. An alternative investment in tax-exempt municipal bonds, for example, which yield regular income, will often look more attractive. This real opportunity cost of patient money is often overlooked by tax experts who claim the tax deferral features of capital gains taxes ... mean a benefit in the form of a lower tax rate. This is part of the reason the new investment in recognized venture capital organizations has fallen. Now the IPO [initial public offering] market has faltered, which traditionally provides a way for long patient investors to get liquid. Investors in IPOs themselves are risk-takers. In fact, in the recent past the IPO market has functioned as a gigantic venture capital market. The recent experience with biotechnology stocks exemplifies this. Yet the funds that were obtained by such companies earlier have been vital for their continuing development. Failing such resources, large companies may become the financiers, many foreign. This is not necessarily good. Some of us think American ownership of advanced technology matters for future growth. Markets for small company stocks that involve fewer registration requirements are not robust.

Furthermore, lending by the banking system today, in view of tighter government regulations, has declined the most for smaller companies. Even though initially they require equity capital, ultimately they expand by borrowing money.

If we are to encourage job formation, the creation of new technologies, and the foundation for future large companies, we must make a special effort to relieve the burdens on the new companies and on their investors. Of course, jobs can also be created by public works "infrastructure." The skill levels for these jobs are lower. But the money to pay for them must come from the private sector's increasing wealth. Physical capital investment (including R&D) is the major driving force for this. The research we have been doing at Stanford in recent years on the causes of postwar growth of the major industrial countries unequivocally identified capital investment as "by far the most important source of postwar economic growth in the Group-of-Five [industrial] countries," in the words of Professor Lawrence Lau. He goes on to say in his latest paper, "Given the complementarity between capital and technical progress, a pro-investment policy should go hand-in-hand with a pro-technology policy." Work at Harvard by Brad DeLong and Larry Summers finds similar results for investment in machinery and equipment.

It is even becoming apparent that larger companies are seeking "entrepreneur-type" managers—creative, innovative, internationally oriented managers. The younger company can continue to breed such people for the larger ones; they cannot be taught in business school.

Some small companies do not have valuable technology or great potential to grow—but they do provide jobs, sometimes also for unskilled or semi-skilled labor. The smaller business sector is one which deserves much more attention. Tax policy can play a large role in encouraging it. Rewards for risky and/or patient investments of this kind must be large.

But what should such a policy be? All three presidential candidates [in 1992] have agreed that some form of a capital gains tax differential should be strengthened as it has been for most of the postwar era. The 1986 Tax Reform Act was passed in a major effort to remove biases and misallocations in capital markets, and improve neutrality among classes of assets. With all its blemishes, this is still a great step forward in tax policy (and I have seen many in forty-six years!). But it still has some biases or asymmetries . . . : home ownership vs. productive investment (i.e., debt vs. equity taxation); double-taxation of corporate income; tangible vs. intangible investment. One not mentioned is the strong bias in favor of tax-exempt institutions, which own more or less 50 percent of large company stocks and contribute more or less the same percentage of formal venture capital funds. In effect, they can accept a lower overall rate of return on their pre-tax investments because they are also their after-tax yield. Not so for the taxable investor, who needs a substantially higher after-tax return for investing patiently in risky investments, especially considering the opportunity cost from safer investments. Thus, the 1986 Act thrust toward neutrality needs to be corrected for this asymmetry.

The best solution in theory would be the abolition of all taxes on income by replacing the income tax with a consumption tax. A near approximation is Bob Hall's flat tax. With Jerry Brown's defeat, this idea has faded. Nevertheless, it is an idea that could be resurrected and improved under the right circumstances....

So we are left with some form of incentive via the tax code. It need not be a capital gains tax differential. It could be:

1) Indexation for inflation (not very good in a low inflation era).

2) Full deductibility of capital losses against capital gains.

3) An investment tax credit for investors in start-up companies (useful in shielding income from other sources). Whereas an ITC for corporate investments requires that companies must first have profits (often not true for young companies), this would not be the case for an ITC to an individual investor.

4) A capital gains tax differential. If this is to be the preferred solution, ... then it must be carefully structured.

a. Prospective only. Don't reward investments in place. But, in view of the off-again, on-again history of this tax, legislation must guarantee at least ten year validity for such an incentive by "grandfathering."

b. Targeted toward sales of equities in productive companies. IPOs can not be the end point, because after-markets are also important for the start-up investors. Furthermore, it would raise P/E multiples for smaller public companies, which lowers their cost of capital.

c. Sliding scale with length of holding, down to zero percent in perhaps three years (this then adjusts for the asymmetry with tax-exempt institutions). It also largely eliminates the trading patterns of large tax-exempt institutions.

d. Do not limit solely to technical companies, but do exclude real estate and predominantly professional firms [such as doctors and lawyers].

The code still retains the capital gains differential, tiny though it is. It could be amended along these lines. Which alternative is picked is a political decision.

27   Economic Growth and
                                     the Chemical Industry

Now that the cold war has ended, and markets are increasingly global, renewed attention is being given to the manner in which the wealth of nations can be increased.[1] Long-term growth and development are once more on governments' and economists' priority lists. As Adam Smith emphasized, the wealth of nations is properly measured by the standard of living of the population. David Ricardo's principle of comparative advantage further amplified this concept by expressing the benefits that trade with other nations would offer. However, in the examples he used, such advantages of a country were static, determined by nature or geography. Nevertheless, it was an early expression of the idea of national competitiveness. Recent experiences have shown that ... international comparative advantage in growth is a dynamic process.

What path should government and industry follow to create a dynamic comparative advantage? This paper tackles that question by first discussing some connections between economic growth, competitiveness, and trade, as discussed in recent economic research on the experiences of the leading industrial countries. It then describes how comparative advantage has evolved in the world chemical industry during the past 150 years. Chemicals were the first science-based industry, and the more familiar high-tech industries of the post–World War II era are essentially similar to it in their dependence on innovative science and the commercialization of technology. Lessons gleaned from the development of the chemical industry are broadly applicable in considering policies that will nurture the long-term health of the U.S. economy.

The key analytical insight here is that international advantages in productivity can be created. This dynamic comparative advantage offers an image where industries and firms, aided by a government-sustained busi-

Forthcoming in *Research Policy*.

ness climate favoring innovation and commercialization of new technology, search continually for new and improved products and services to customers. The case of Japan is especially revealing here: a country without much arable land, and few resources except the skill, determination, and hard work of its people, has become the second-largest industrial country in barely two generations! Just as such an advantage can be created in a surprisingly short period of time, it may disappear or diminish as new competitors appear, unless continually pursued.

Growth and Competitiveness

Accordingly, when economists nowadays discuss "competitiveness," they typically mean a nation's ability to sustain an acceptable rate of growth in the real standard of living of the population, while avoiding social costs like high unemployment, environmental damage, or an excessively uneven distribution of income. Furthermore, this must be done without reducing the growth potential in the standard of living of future generations. This last condition constrains borrowing from abroad, or incurring excessive future tax or spending obligations, to pay for the present generation's higher living standard. From this approach, the most promising way to increase the U.S. (or any other developed nation's) standard of living is a healthy annual increase in the productivity of labor. Although U.S. workers remain the most productive in the industrialized world, ... their lead over foreign competitors has diminished in the last few decades (figure 27.1).

In contrast with the way economists use the term, the popular meaning of "competitiveness" often seems wrapped up in the size of trade balances and capital flows. As will be explained below, this view has only a modest portion of the truth. But before criticizing it, it is worth noting that those who believe that annual trade balances offer an appropriate measure of U.S. competitiveness should be bullish on the U.S. economy! The most commonly cited trade figure is the U.S. imbalance in merchandise trade—that is, the excess of imports over exports—which rose from $9.5 billion in 1976 to a peak of $160 billion in 1987. However, the deficit in merchandise trade has since fallen to $74 billion in 1991, and approximately $96 billion in 1992. On this basis alone, one would think the worst is over, despite the slight uptick last year.

Other trade figures are encouraging as well. The broadest definition of a nation's international balances is the current account balance, which includes not only imports and exports of merchandise, but also sales and purchases of services and net returns on investments abroad. Because of

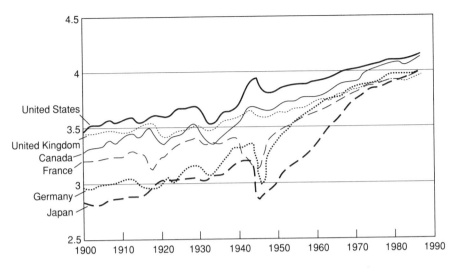

Figure 27.1
Per capita income, logs. Source: Steven N. Durlauf, University of Wisconsin.

comparatively strong U.S. services industries, and extensive U.S. investments abroad (many made in the decades after World War II), the U.S. trade position looks better on this measure. The service sectors, including the military, had a favorable balance of $45 billion in 1991 and $55 billion in 1992. In addition, there was a surplus of net income on investments from abroad of $16 billion in 1991 and $10 billion in 1992, despite the increased cost of servicing a foreign debt currently estimated at about $420 billion. The decline in U.S. interest rates in 1992 offset the increase in foreign holdings, and payments to them were virtually unchanged over the previous year. The U.S. current account imbalance deteriorated sharply during the early and mid-1980s, falling from a surplus of $6.9 billion in 1981 to a deficit of $160 billion in 1987. However, by 1991, the current account deficit was only $4 billion, due to reimbursements of $42.4 billion by foreigners for the Gulf War. This reimbursement was not present in 1992, and the current account deficit was $62 billion.

Those still looking for bad news in the trade statistics often focus on Japan, and while the U.S. merchandise trade deficit with Japan has declined by one-fourth since 1987, it remained at $44.3 billion in 1991 and $50 billion in 1992. Japan has maintained this balance by developing products, such as cars and electronic devices, of such quality and price that Americans and other consumers often prefer them above those of domestic manufacture. Such quality competition forces domestic producers to become more efficient, which is of course one of the primary benefits from international trade and competition. Moreover, since international competition helps to hold down prices and reduce the risk of inflation, it allows monetary policy to permit lower interest rates. The U.S. has also benefited from its growing export capability. Half of U.S. growth since 1987 has come from exports.

However, an isolated focus on trade with Japan is inherently misleading. A trade deficit with any single country tells literally nothing about a nation's global competitiveness. Even if the U.S. ran a trade deficit of zero with the world as a whole, it could (and probably would) still run a deficit with Japan, since Japan must sell in the U.S. and Europe to earn funds for importing raw materials, like oil.

A country's international trade deficits indicate only the the nation is consuming more than it is producing in goods and services. The only way that these deficits can be financed is by borrowing. Conversely, a surplus is one where a nation is exporting capital because it is producing more than it is consuming. Thus, the high trade deficits of the 1980s meant, by definition, an inflow of foreign investment into the United States, to counterbalance the deficiency of domestic savings over domestic investments. So, does the decline in these trade deficits since the mid-1980s—and thus in the amount of foreign investment—signify that U.S. competitiveness is also improving? Not necessarily. One reason that U.S. imports grew more slowly than exports in 1990–91 was that the U.S. economy was in recession, reducing its demand for imports, while overseas consumers of U.S. products were not. During the slow recovery of 1992, America's foreign industrial customers themselves fell into recession and reduced purchases of American exports.

Moreover, the reduction in foreign capital from abroad—which is, remember, the same as a reduction in the current account deficit—means less capital invested in the United States. Since U.S. national savings, both personal and government, have been very low in the late 1980s, overall investment has been decreasing. This bad news is illustrated in figure 27.2. Rather than a declining current account imbalance signaling improved prospects for competitiveness, the reverse may actually be the case. Of course, some of this reduced investment has been in areas like commercial and residential real estate, which do not contribute as much to productivity growth as does investment in industrial plant and equipment. However, despite the growing importance of global capital markets, detailed studies by George Hatsopoulos of Thermoelectron and James Poterba of M.I.T. (1993) show that for the more risky equity investments, domestic savings are the primary source. Those who are forced to seek foreign financing

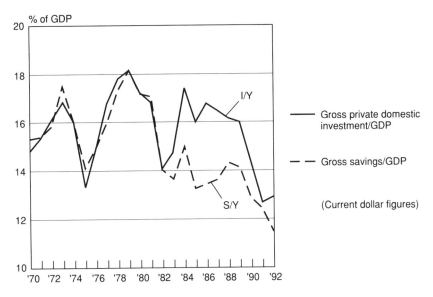

Figure 27.2
The savings gap. Source: Survey of Current Business, U.S. Dept. of Commerce.

usually pay a higher price for it. To be sure, foreign direct purchases of companies or assets are different and pose other questions.

This situation demonstrates a broader point: running a trade deficit and borrowing from abroad can benefit economic growth or hurt it, depending on whether the money is spent productively. When the United States borrowed from abroad during the nineteenth century to build its railroads, or when South Korea borrowed for industrialization in the 1960s and 1970s, the inflow of capital helped long-run growth. However, a sizeable proportion of the funds borrowed from abroad by the U.S. during the 1980s was used for consumption, not investment.

The concern for the United States during the 1980s is that its surge of borrowing from abroad was not accompanied by an increase in labor productivity, which as earlier noted is the root source of growth in the overall standard of living. In the 1960s, the annual growth in productivity averaged 2.4 percent; it was 1.3 percent in the 1970s, and 0.8 percent in the 1980s. During this period, the rate of increase of private capital formation per employee dropped from 2.6 percent per year to 0.6 percent per year; as shown later, this had a depressing effect on output and real hourly earnings. In the last two decades, most of the increase in the standard of living of families has been due to having more two-earner couples and working longer hours. While these changes raise national output, they do not raise the standard of living that can be earned by a person working a standard work week, and it clearly makes little sense for a nation to seek to purchase higher competitiveness with longer hours and declining or stagnant real wages. In manufacturing industries, labor productivity growth did rebound to about 2.5 percent per year toward the end of the 1980s. But the overall increase in labor productivity was only 0.3 percent in 1991, rebounding to 2.9 percent in 1992 as recovery began (it has slipped again in the first half of 1993). Productivity often suffers during a time of recession, but the 1991 increase is nonetheless depressingly low. Such considerations make it clear that trade imbalances have important effects on productivity growth, but the size and direction of such effects is murkier than might at first have been imagined.

The modern study of the sources of economic growth dates from the late 1950s and early 1960s, when Robert Solow of M.I.T. (1957), Moses Abramovitz of Stanford (1956), and Dale Jorgenson of Harvard (1987) identified the basic inputs to a growing economy as land, labor, capital, and technology. In their studies, they demonstrated that most aggregate steady state growth of the economy could not be explained by increases in the amounts of the first three of these basic inputs alone. Some other factor, which they labeled "technology," was responsible for up to three-quarters of all growth. Since "technology" in these studies covered whatever could not be explained by the first three factors, Abramovitz called it "the measure of our ignorance."

A number of strong mathematical assumptions were then needed to build a manageable methodological growth model upon this idea of technology. For example, the early models used the neoclassical economic assumption that markets are perfectly competitive and that all firms maximize their profits, given their particular endowments of resources. Moreover, the models of economic growth formulated by Solow at that time postulated that this growth in technology was exogenous; in other words, it came as "manna from heaven," not from within the system of economic activity. Paul Romer of the University of California at Berkeley (1990) stated the resulting dilemma of this growth theory as follows: "The [neoclassical] assumptions of [diminishing returns to increasing investment] and perfect competition placed the accumulation of new technologies at the center of the growth process and simultaneously denied the possibility that economic analysis could have anything to say about this process." There is no room in this theory for the inventions and innovations that produce new and improved products, processes, and services.

Nonetheless, these early neoclassical models helped clarify the major causes of long-term steady state growth. They permitted economists to examine what was happening in the overall economy, the "big picture," without being confused by a myriad of obscure details which they could not measure or model. In so doing, they showed that technology had been the dynamic force of growth in the United States since the Civil War.

A simple analogy to this methodological approach may be found in the physics of gases. Scientists have long known that gases contain very large numbers of molecules in random but constant motion against each other and the walls of their containers. A useful simplification for predicting the behavior of gases was that they obeyed the perfect gas laws. This permitted the observer to calculate the pressure of a gas if he knew the temperature and the amount of gas. In effect, in this model the molecules did not react with one another, but bounced off each other like billiard balls. In reality, though this rule serves for many cases, it was soon observed that for heavier or more complex molecules, there was a tendency for them not to bounce away from an encounter, but to adhere, or cluster, at least for a while. These interactions would result in imperfections, or deviations from the perfect gas laws. As the complexity of the gas and the severity of the conditions increased, it became necessary to develop tables of deviations for use by engineers in designing their gas handling equipment. In many instances, these deviations were substantial, even involving a chemical reaction that changed the nature of the system itself. Increasingly, with more refined analytical tools, scientists were able to examine directly the interacting molecules and clusters. Although economic systems are far more complex than gases, events at the microeconomic level likewise affect the macroeconomic system.[2]

Only in the last few years have mathematical modeling techniques and richer data on a number of industrial countries accumulated to the point where many of the strong assumptions of the early Solow-style growth theory could be relaxed, and additional understanding gained from more realistic models. Instead of viewing technology as a sort of manna from heaven, this work explored the actual causes of productivity growth.

For example, firms in early growth theory are largely undifferentiated, like the billiard-ball molecules. The emphasis was on aggregate macroeconomic causes, not at the level of the individual company. How firms learn from experience, how good management differs from bad, how firms differ in access to and transmittal of information internally, how some firms compete successfully in international markets and others do not; these issues do not arise in the early models. But the empirical evidence, indeed the entire business literature, suggests that firms do differ in their characteristics, behavior, performance, and problem-solving abilities and strategies, and moreover that what firms do vis-a-vis their competitors is where dynamic comparative advantage really occurs. Michael Porter of Harvard University (1990) has contributed greatly to the understanding of what makes for competitive advantage at the level of the firm.

A second area where the early growth theory conflicts with everyday experience is its description of technology as an exogenous process. If technology was completely available from outside sources, firms would never justify doing research and development. There would be no point to it if technology was available to all; moreover, the assumption of perfect competition in the model means that successful innovations would be immediately copied, and no firm could ever recoup its R&D costs. But every observation of the business world tells us that new technology is generated by human ingenuity and effort—in research and development, in learning by doing and producing, in design and invention—in short, by endogenous activity within the economic system. Moreover, real companies do R&D for proprietary purposes to gain advantage and to earn profits by selling at high prices for as long as possible before the competition catches up. The neoclassical assumption of perfect competition would imply that no firm has any market power. Today's growth economists have been exploring the roots of this economic behavior.

A third extension of the early theory came from its implications that since the secrets of technical progress are available to all and therefore common to all, then countries' growth rates must converge, eventually, to the same level. But the world around us demonstrates that such convergence need not occur. As Robert Lucas of the University of Chicago has written (1990), India's standard of living is *not* converging on that of the U.S., despite the availability of most of the latest technology. The collapse of the Soviet Union despite very high capital investment rates shows that much more is involved in growth than pouring money into obsolete plants run by unmotivated workers in the absence of market competition. Why are some countries or areas more economically successful than others? Clearly national, organizational, and firm efficiencies vary greatly among nations. These and other difficult-to-measure factors probably account for a large part of productivity growth of nations, and technology itself may well be only a minor fraction of the total.

A fourth unstated implication of the early growth models was that since all firms were undifferentiated, all industries were equally important. The traditional description of a market economy, as summarized by Adam

Smith's metaphor of an "invisible hand," is that the market coordinates the decentralized behavior of firms and individuals, providing all the required information for optimal and coordinated decision making. Government intervention in the private sector, in the modern purists' view, is either unnecessary or counterproductive. But at a gut level, few are willing to accept the neoclassical implication flowing from this conception, that $100 worth of potato chip is worth the same as $100 worth of semiconductor chips. It seems clear that some industries are more important to long-run productivity growth than others; in economists' terms, investing in some industries (whether in physical capital, knowledge, labor skills, or some other way) offers a broader social return which will not be captured by the private investor. An industry like computers, which generates many spill-over effects to a host of other industries, and contributes significantly to the productivity growth of the economy, may well be more important to the nation's productivity growth than others that have fewer such externalities as, for instance, office buildings. Other industries may offer the possibility of increasing returns to scale; in the chemical industry, for example, it is well known that doubling the capacity of a plant can be achieved by only a 60 percent increase in capital. Some industries may be more important to international trade. Others may be key to job formation, or to encouraging investment by other firms. Jorgenson (1990) has studied such interindustry differences among several countries. None of this is contained in the early Solow model.

A fifth counterintuitive implication of the early views of growth was that the long-term, *steady state* rate of growth was independent of the rate of savings and investment. In Solow's early theory, technology was considered to be *labor augmenting*, which means it applies solely to improving the efficiency of labor. Steps to improve the quality (efficiency) and quantity of labor could increase the long-term rate of economic growth. But while an increase in savings and investment could provide a boost in economic productivity, the economy would then revert (in these models) to the rate of growth determined by the exogenous rise in the quality and quantity of labor.

But since Adam Smith, economists have argued that the process of capital accumulation and investment was a fundamental force that leads to productivity growth. Indeed, Solow has also advocated higher rates of saving and investment (Landau 1991). In very recent studies, Michael Boskin and Lawrence Lau of Stanford University (1992) show by cross-country comparisons in the postwar era that technology is *capital augmenting*, which means the higher the capital stock, the more technology can increase productivity. In this case, it is no longer true that a higher savings rate provides only a one-time boost to productivity. Instead, a higher rate of capital investment increases the rate at which productivity rises. *There is no steady state of growth.* Economies are always in a transitional and dis-equilibrium condition, except perhaps from an extremely long-run perspec-tive, especially in today's world of accelerating technological change. U.S. policymakers and economists also have become increasingly concerned with fostering economic growth for periods much longer than the usual business cycle, say, over a generation. The key inputs of growth—more and more skilled labor, more and more sophisticated capital, other forms of technology—are not independent of each other, but are positively interde-pendent.[3] The steady state Solow model has given way to the dynamics of growth, in which technology and its embodiments are the engines.

The recent evolution in the study of economic growth can be summa-rized in this way. The early view of growth was macroeconomic in nature, focused on the broadest concept of improving labor productivity and capi-tal investment. In this view, the main economic growth policy of govern-ment should be to influence the overall direction of the economy and to keep trade deficits within desirable bounds. This would be accomplished by addressing the difference between savings and investment. Get this right, and the current account balance, by an accounting identity, must be at the desired level. What happens in the microeconomy is not relevant. Of course, this pure laissez-faire macroeconomics has never been practiced—witness import quotas, trigger prices, government subsidies, and the like. Those who emphasize a view of competitiveness based on aggregate inter-national trade statistics are going back even earlier to the mercantilist tradition. The neoclassical view would accordingly be that some products and services will gain, some will lose, and overall, the result at the macro level will meet the requirements of the system. Not only is this indifference to events at the micro level refuted by experience, but in fact resulting changes in the microeconomy (where the real growth originates) may well have real macroeconomic consequences, by a feedback mechanism, as the gas physics example showed, and as will be discussed further below.

The more recent study of growth thus recognizes the importance of improving macroeconomic variables like saving and investment ..., but it also focuses on microeconomic issues of firms and industries. From this perspective, savings and investment in different industries may have differ-ent importance to long-run growth, and a variety of issues arise which the overall macroeconomic view does not address. For example, what should be done about seemingly important firms or industries that face international competition from firms that either seem to or do receive favored treatment by their governments? When should the U.S. government step in?

Empirical and theoretical work by Romer (1986), Joseph Stiglitz (1993), and Steven Durlauf (1992) of Stanford, Robert Barro (1991) and Jorgenson (1987) of Harvard, Ishaq Nadiri (1988) of New York University, and others also shows, by cross-country comparisons over time, that these microeconomic differences leave a legacy. The rate of growth in the future depends somewhat on the rate of growth in the present, which in turn depends on decisions made in the past. History matters. Internal behavior and structures matter. Firm and individual differences matter. Which industries or firms survive in world competition matters. Countries, industries, and firms that apply these lessons properly can consistently do better than others.[4]

These developments in economic theory hold both a promise and a warning. The promise is that the existence of investment (in physical, intangible, and human capital) that stimulates other investment can lead— at least in theoretical models—to a sort of virtuous circle of feedbacks to yield increased productivity growth. Economic growth need not diminish or die down over time. Competitiveness may now be viewed as achieving or sustaining a comparative advantage for a sufficient number of local industries and firms for the country to prosper in a global marketplace. The corresponding warning is that the policies for achieving this continuing increase in the standard of living are not obvious. Some advocates of "industrial policy" speak as if government can guarantee future prosperity by showering favors on private industry, without regard for the critical importance of the macroeconomic climate within which all business must work. Without an appropriate blend of macroeconomic and microeconomic insight, there is no guarantee that the United States can keep its lead as the nation with the highest standard of living in the world.

The Nature of the Chemical Industry

The history of the chemical industry since the 1840s offers clear illustrations of the interdependence between the government-created policy environment and the actions of individual firms. By relating that history, one can seek to draw out lessons for policies that could be adopted to improve the rate of productivity growth.

By the standard definitions of what constitutes high technology industry, the chemical industry certainly qualifies. The most common criterion

Table 27.1
The major R&D investment industries 1989 & 1990 R&D expenditures (in bil. $)

Industry	1989	1990	Privately financed	Percentage privately financed
1. Aerospace	25.64	25.36	10.59	42
2. Electrical Machinery & Communications	16.93	17.40	11.77	68
3. Machinery	14.64	14.70	13.80	94
4. Chemicals	11.47	12.57	12.50	99
5. Autos, Trucks, Transportation	11.20	10.54	4.40	42
6. Professional & Scientific Instruments	5.74	6.16	6.06	98
7. Computer Software & Services	3.78	4.19	2.73	65
8. Petroleum	2.07	2.10	2.08	99
TOTAL	91.47	93.02	63.93	

Total R&D estimated (by Battelle Memorial Institute) at $145.5 bil. for 1990, of which industrial R&D was $104.2 bil. so that the above are the bulk of investors in R&D.
Source: National Science Foundation.

for "high tech" is an industry's expenditure upon research and development. Chemicals and Allied Products (Standard Industrial Classification No. 28, according to the Commerce Department) is near the top of the list when industries are ranked in terms of the total amount of industry funds spent on R&D and virtually at the top in terms of the share of total R&D that is financed by private funds (table 27.1).

The chemical industry is useful to consider for two other reasons, as well. First, chemical processing has played a central role in generating technological innovations for other industries. In this regard, it is illustrative of the more general fact that the benefits of internationally competitive industries spill over to other industries, contrary to the neoclassical view. Second, the chemical industry is a U.S. success story. Chemicals are one of only two major high-tech industries (aerospace is the other) where the U.S. has maintained its competitive lead in international trade, and the industry growth rate has exceeded that of the economy since the World War II.

Nineteenth Century Origins

Britain achieved an initial dominance in the chemical industry in the nineteenth century, because of its early entrance into textiles, but later began to flag. Part of the reason may have been that industrialization had come about fifty years earlier in that country, and hence more capital had been sunk in plants embodying old technology. But that simply raises the question of why British plants were not updated.

One important reason is that technical education and scientific research were not accorded the status and government promotion in Britain that applied in Europe, particularly in Germany. As early as the 1850s, most important chemical research and education was done on the continent. This was particularly evident in the evolution of the synthetic organics industry based on coal tar which revolutionized dyestuffs and eventually opened the road to plastics, synthetic fibers, and modern pharmaceuticals. The Germans were particularly skilled in applied scientific research. Close relations were fostered between industry and the universities, and industrialists sent their children to study science in the universities far more frequently than did their British counterparts. German industry in the latter part of the nineteenth century established research laboratories to complement academic research, whereas no such laboratories seem to have existed in Britain until the First World War.

Another reason why British plants remained relatively stagnant may have been that British investors (aided by the greatest free financial market of the time) found opportunities for lower risk and higher financial returns overseas in the rest of the British empire, as well as in the more traditional fields of iron, coal, steel, and textiles. The British banking system encouraged growth in commerce and trade. By contrast, German investors were latecomers on the industrial scene, forcing them to look for new opportunities, which they found in exports and in domestic industries based more heavily on scientific research and newer technologies (including a drive for military self-sufficiency). Shut out of the easy opportunities for short-term profit, the Germans appear to have adopted longer time horizons than the British in their industrial undertakings.

A thumbnail history of the first dye—mauve—illustrates many of these points. It was discovered in England by William Henry Perkin in 1856, a student of a famous German chemist, August Wilhelm Von Hofmann. At the time Hofmann arrived in England (1845), English students who wanted training in chemistry had to go to Germany. Their enthusiasm for the German methods of teaching chemistry led them, upon their return, to wish to establish educational facilities modeled on German universities. However, the attempts to found the Royal College of Chemistry proved unsuccessful. Oxford and Cambridge neglected science education in favor of the classics, languages, religion, and literature. Students went into the armed forces, the foreign and civil service, law, politics, the clergy, and medicine; even sons of industrialists neglected science and shunned industry. J. D. Bernal (1939, p. 96) observed that the nineteenth century scientist deliberately distanced himself from the industrial application of any discoveries, a self-removal which Bernal described as a "sign of a scientist aping the don and the gentleman." By 1865, Hofmann received an attractive offer to return to Germany. He had become disappointed with the unprogressiveness of the British dye industry, the backward state of organic chemical education, and the lack of sympathy on the part of business, the government, and the conservative banks.

In Germany, a different atmosphere prevailed. The Germany that was united by Otto von Bismarck in 1871 was dominated by the landed aristocracy of Prussia—the Junkers. But while the Junkers were militaristic and autocratic, learning and scholarship were nevertheless respected and received high social status. The unification of Germany resulted in the elimination of all internal tariff and customs barriers. Furthermore, victory in the Franco Prussian War produced war reparations. An economic boom resulted, which ended in a speculative mania. However, because of their continuing heavy emphasis on research and the application of the latest science, the young German chemical companies survived the boom and then the collapse into the great depression of 1873 to 1879. This was in striking contrast to their French and British competitors.

As the German government thus became increasingly involved in the economy and concerned for national security, it imposed protective tariffs to encourage domestic industrialization, including the chemical industry. In addition, the German government passed important patent legislation to protect intellectual property. Before the end of the century, it even legalized cartels (just before America's trustbusting era and legislation). By contrast, the British government took no particular initiative to strengthen its infrastructure or its industry, whether in general or in the specific case of chemicals. It practiced more of the laissez-faire approach, letting some industries gain and some lose. Many economists then and now feel that this policy, which was not basically concerned with war preparation, had a positive effect on British growth. Nevertheless, the rate of growth per capita was declining. From 1870 to 1913, the German rate was 1.8 percent per year, that of the U.S. 2.2 percent, and the UK's only 1.3 percent. Compounded over another fifty years, differences of this magnitude have reduced Britain's standard of living to a mediocre position in Europe.

Whatever the overall advantages of Britain's policies were, they did not specifically help the chemical industry. In the 1860s and 1870s Britain had a *comparative advantage* in the new chemical industry. It had the largest supplies of high quality coal in Europe, and the largest and most successful textile industry. It knew how to make dyes. It was rich. But it let its advantages slip away. By the end of the 1880s, the large German plants were producing more than 500 different dyes and pharmaceuticals at unit costs far below those of smaller competitors. Although Britain continued to manufacture dyestuffs, it never regained its earlier prominence. Thus, the Germans came to excel in synthetic organic chemistry, based on coal tar and its derivatives. By 1913, German companies produced 140,000 tons of dyes, while 10,000 tons were produced in Switzerland, and only 4,400 tons in Britain.

Domination of dyestuffs helped to create the wealth which propelled Germany into the position of strongest continental industrial power. Her banking system was strong, and had already assumed the major role in domestic industry which it possesses today. It worked very closely with the government to further Germany's imperial interests.

American Chemical Industries Early in the Twentieth Century

By the time of the First World War, America's chemical industry was already roughly as large as Germany's. But the war cut off American imports of German chemicals, forcing the U.S. companies to accelerate development of their own organic chemical industry.

The combination of new large-scale production techniques for new chemical was greatly assisted by the development of a new academic discipline: chemical engineering. Although Germany had, in the late nineteenth century, established a strong tradition of chemical research at universities, the findings of the chemist were subsequently more or less handed over to mechanical engineers at individual companies. But the mechanical engineers had little understanding of chemical transformations, and were ill-equipped to evaluate the inherent trade-offs involved in designing new chemical processing equipment.

In America, under the leadership of the Massachusetts Institute of Technology, these separate roles of chemist and engineer were fused. Historically, success in the commercialization of new chemical technologies has turned upon the ability to make the transition from small-scale, batch production to large-scale plants. The emergence of the distinctly American discipline of chemical engineering, supported by a university system that was highly accommodating to the needs of a newly emerging industry, made an enormous difference to the chemical industry. By contrast, there were no departments of chemical engineering—or even extensive curricula in chemical engineering—outside of the U.S. before the Second World War, except for two that appeared in the 1930s in Britain.[5]

A final boost for the U.S. chemical industry came from a happy convergence with regard to petroleum. Thanks to Henry Ford, the automobile spread through America after World War I, necessitating a rise in the petroleum refining industry. At the same time, the basic feedstock for organic chemicals was in the process of shifting, on a worldwide basis, from coal to oil (although the shift was not complete until after World War II). The U.S., as it happened, had vast oil and gas resources, and the American chemical engineering discipline had matured in a direction that was distinctly well-suited to developing a large-scale petrochemical manufacturing technology that was appropriate to the new feedstock.

The German Chemical Industry in the Interwar Years

The loss of World War I weakened the German chemical industry tremendously, although it did manage after the war to keep many of its technical secrets concealed from the Allied investigating teams. The German edge in chemical technology had been based on using coal as a feedstock, which largely involved aromatic chemicals. In the interwar years, however, it became apparent that the cheapest feedstocks would come from petroleum and natural gas. When these materials became abundantly available in the United States, coal and alcohol chemistry were not economic for producing commodity organic chemicals (the building blocks of the modern chemical industry). As American oil and chemical companies recognized the value of petroleum hydrocarbons, they not only came up with a number of industrially significant processes for aliphatic chemicals, but also discovered ways to make the original chemicals derived from coal tar more inexpensively and in much larger quantities.

The early German domination of the dyestuffs industry locked the German industry into certain methods and approaches that were far less suited for other branches of the chemical industry. One major problem was that many dyestuffs are specialty products typically manufactured by batch processes. Thus, German manufacturers were not especially well-prepared for the shift to large-scale, continuous, petroleum-based manufacturing.

Finally, Germany continued to have a strong educational system, and to hold technically trained people in high esteem. However, the German universities continued to produce students who were very capable research chemists but who could not design systems for manufacturing the products that they invented. Mechanical engineering was not taught at all in universities, but in technical high schools and trade schools, and was not held in as high esteem in the social hierarchy. The German ... reluctance to make chemists less predominant and to create space for the chemical engineer until well after World War II undoubtedly played a large role in the decline of earlier unquestioned German leadership in the chemical industry.

With the deep recession of 1920–21, many German chemical firms found themselves with severe overcapacity. Moreover, the government owed considerable amounts in war reparation payments. Even more significantly, the recession was followed by one of the world's greatest hyper-inflations, which threatened the very existence of even the major surviving companies. Only in this environment did it become possible, and indeed urgent, for the government to encourage the major German chemical companies to merge together and form the famous I. G. Farben Industrie, and again to focus on exporting heavily. A European cartel emerged.

The Rise of American Chemical Firms after World War II

The period immediately after World War II was a time of resurgence for the American chemical industry. The early phases of the innovation cycle in many chemical and petroleum-based products and processes had already begun during the interwar years. But after the war, demand for relatively homogeneous petrochemical products grew explosively, which created opportunities for scaling up chemical production processes to levels far higher than those of the prewar period. The European chemical industry had been disrupted by the war, whereas the American industry had emerged unscathed, and was well-positioned to take advantage of the evolution of the chemical industry.

Although America had been a latecomer to the chemicals scene, its abundance of petroleum (and natural gas) deposits and the experience that it gained in continuous processing methods in exploiting these deposits, opened up a development path that provided an excellent entry into the continuous processing technologies that became central as the industry moved to a petrochemical feedstock base. Moreover, while the German cartel arrangements had worked well for that industry in some ways, they had also hindered innovation among its members. The U.S. companies, operating under American law, were less inhibited. The national wartime effort had inspired crash programs involving new technologies and expanded facilities for such things as synthetic rubber, petroleum refining, chemicals, munitions, light metals, and so on. There was a tremendous burst of innovation between 1935 and 1950, which came from the loosening of the cartel bonds and the demands of the war.

The opportunities for gaining efficiency with larger plants—and more generally, for cutting costs through more efficient production processes— induced chemical producers to focus attention on the production process. Many set up internal departments aimed at designing and engineering new and improved manufacturing processes. However, since process development for the new high-volume products could be undertaken without simultaneously investing substantial funds in research and development for new products, there was a place for specialized contractors to design and engineer chemical production processes for the major chemical producers. Indeed, chemical firms increasingly relied upon specialized engineering firms (or SEFs) to design, engineer, and develop their manufacturing installations. Most of the early specialized engineering firms were American. By the 1960s, nearly three-quarters of the major new plants were engineered, procured, and constructed by specialist plant contractors.

Specialized engineering firms were the channel by which the American expertise in large-scale continuous processes, developed in the petroleum processing and refining industry, found its way into the world chemical industry. The existence of the specialized engineering firms permitted many new entrants into the industry from petroleum, paper, food, metals, and the like. Vigorous competition ensued, both domestic and international, and continues today.

The Chemical Industry since the 1970s

During the past twenty years or so, the growth rate of the chemical industry has declined substantially, and the focus of the market has shifted again. After the oil shock of 1973, the rising inflation and interest rates, and extreme volatility of macroeconomic policy, the annual growth rate of the industry went from a double digit figure to about 5 percent. The production of large volumes of homogeneous chemicals has declined as well, as many companies have tended to place greater emphasis on the production of heterogeneous specialty chemicals. Emphasis in the modern chemical industry has shifted toward product innovation, and to the interactions between product innovation and marketing. In many of the best companies, "technology push" receives as much attention as "product pull." The discipline of chemical engineering has shifted as well, toward including the skills needed for producing the newer specialty products.

With the help of specialized engineering firms and much licensing, a powerful European chemical industry has been reborn, providing strong competitive pressure for American firms. In addition, firms from other industries also entered into chemical manufacturing. By grafting the strengths of the American approach on to their traditionally strong chemical research, and aided by a favorable macroeconomic climate for industry (Ludwig Erhard's *Wirtschaftswunder*), German firms have once again become a major factor in the world chemical industry. In fact, three of the world's top ten chemical companies are in Germany, and three more are in the United States.

Global competition in the chemical industry is very tough. The top ten chemical companies account for less than 20 percent of the industry's worldwide sales; by comparison, the top ten auto companies command approximately 60 percent of the global market. The English, French, Italians, Dutch, and Swiss have carved out very competitive niches of their own in the chemical industry in recent years. The Japanese chemical companies are only one-third to one-tenth the size of the large western companies, because Japan tended to build relatively small plants to serve individual *keiretsus* (which were groups of related companies organized around a main bank, usually with cross-ownership). But even though the lack of economies of scale has seriously hampered its effort to become a major force outside Japan, the Japanese chemical industry is the second largest in the world, due to the rapid growth of the Japanese economy. U.S. chemical firms remain the world leaders, but the competition is not far behind. Today, this industry is an important source of growth in many countries (it is the largest industry in the European Common Market), and, while no country is as clearly dominant as Germany once was, everyone can be a winner in this competition. After all, prosperity is a positive sum game.

Lessons of General Significance

By focusing on the particulars of the chemical industry, the preceding discussion runs the risk of neglecting the importance of macroeconomic financial considerations. This industry has been one that survived better than many others the volatile and often unfavorable government policies of the past, for reasons that have been depicted in this account. While some broader issues are revisited in the concluding observations, it seems appropriate at this point to draw out some particular lessons from the history of the chemical industry that are of more general significance.

1. Comparative advantage is rightly seen as dynamic and ever-changing. In the chemical industry, the advantage has shifted from Britain to Germany to the United States, and now to a more diffuse group. Nor are such shifts a zero-sum game—over time, all countries can benefit, even if advantage shifts from time to time, from place to place, and from industry to industry. For better or for worse, a nation's economic fate is in its own hands to shape.

2. Unlike many other American industries, the chemical industry has fused the ideas of product and process innovation. Science and new innovations are vital from beginning to end in the chemical industry, both for the relatively small number of major breakthroughs, and the relatively large number of incremental improvements. The Japanese employ this system in some of their other high-tech industries, and other U.S. industries might wish to consider it as a model. For example, it is tempting to ask what a new engineering discipline for manufacturing of discrete objects would look like, by analogy with the historic systems design role played by chemical engineering.

3. The university-industry linkage is a profound factor in the growth of high-tech industries, as shown in the development of the chemical industry in both Germany and the United States, and the decline of the industry in Great Britain.

4. The link between new technology and the commercial capabilities of firms is critical, and studies of how to facilitate this link should be a high priority. The history of the chemical industry offers a hint: German and U.S. chemical companies have long had their managements and operations in the hands of scientifically trained or oriented people. These in turn have always emphasized a strong research and development activity. On the other hand, the systems of corporate governance in the two countries are very different. This is now changing as financial and legal considerations become even more critical in a world of low savings. In the last few years, the external pressures on the German industry (such as very generous social policies and the high costs of reunification) have brought non-technologists to the top managements of all three large German chemical companies for the first time.

5. Some industries are more important for growth than others, either because they offer especially good opportunities for growth, or because their success spills over to the economy as a whole. The chemical industry presents a vivid picture of an industry where productivity could increase both through economies of scale, and through the experience of learning

to use new technologies. There are many externalities and spillovers which characterize this and other industries, especially the high technology industries.

6. Wars have often had decisive effects in shaping the direction of technological development. In the chemical industry, national security concerns influenced both the rise of the German industry in the later nineteenth century and its decline after World War I. A challenge for the end of the cold war is to focus on peacetime development.

7. The appropriate role for government "industrial policy"—taken here to mean more direct government intervention in or support of certain industries—is not very clear. On one side, the German government has played a prominent role in the emergence of a world-class chemical industry. On the other side, the American chemical industry has had very little direct support or influence by government, and this is one of its secrets of success. Although the issue is hotly debated, the recent research leads strongly to the belief that broad government policies like support of education, capital formation, research and development, provision of infrastructure, restraint on pollution, and open markets are more important to industrial success than incentives targeted to a particular industry or a particular technology. Indeed, the American government structure of separation of powers, weak bureaucracy, strong interest groups, and extensive litigiousness makes such direct intervention particularly likely to prove inefficient or counterproductive, especially in an age of rapid technological developments which those directly involved in the marketplace are best able to respond to with their own investments. As Kevin Phillips (1992) has predicted, the political process may well yield to the many powerful special interests, resulting in an "incoherent and ineffective industrial policy." From the historical record of the chemical industry, it seems clear that competitive pressure, complemented by effective macroeconomic and educational policies, is the surest way to push rapid commercialization and economic growth.

8. The chemical industry everywhere has been one of the very first to encounter environmental restraints and challenges to its activities. Before Perkin's efforts in the 1850s, for example, the sheer volume of waste products from the textile industry, and the resulting lawsuits, forced scientists to look for ways to utilize the by-products of industry more constructively. Today, Germany's severe environmental and other regulations have combined to force serious consideration of the possible emigration of the German chemical companies. This illustrates the negative potential of a close government-industry alliance as compared with the more distant relationships in the U.S. (where, however, there are also environmental pressures).

These problems have continued right up to today, but this industry has now been joined by many other industries. Technology will also be the solution to the growing concern for sustainable growth. Preserving growth with a sustainable environment constitutes the next great issue facing the world chemical industry, and indeed for industrialized societies more generally.

Creating a Climate for Commercialization

The United States should seek to raise its annual rate of productivity growth to 3–3 1/2 percent from what seems to be the current maximum of 2 to 2 1/2 percent ... (Landau 1988).

What is to be done to raise the U.S. growth rate? The problem is a *lack of commercialization*, the process whereby technology is converted into commercially saleable products and services. Much of recent research has focused on how the government can create a regime favorable to this sort of commercialization and high productivity growth. Such a growth strategy by government is a necessary precondition for successful commercialization of technology by the private sector.

Specifying the elements of such a policy both relies on the experience of the chemical industry and to some extent reaches beyond the experience of that particular industry. In the current research, it has also involved an examination of what has worked well for Germany and Japan, two economic success stories of recent decades. The elements of the emerging plan for growth involve creating a stable backdrop for businesses to plan, the right incentives to invest, a supply of capital and skilled labor, and the opportunity to compete worldwide.

Germany and Japan have largely managed in the postwar era to keep inflation low, with a less volatile macroeconomic policy, and thus to reduce the need for business to worry either about the financial risks of inflation or the chance of a high interest-rate policy to fight that inflation. This stable pro-investment macroeconomic background by government is essential if business is to focus all of its attention on commercializing new technology and be held accountable to society for its performance.

New technology requires new ideas, and economists have long argued that in perfectly free markets, companies will tend to underinvest in research and development, because it will be hard to recoup such investments. When government subsidizes research and development through tax credits to private industry and direct support, society as a whole reaps benefits. But the current R&D tax credit has been allowed to expire over and over during the last five years, before receiving temporary renewals—hardly a policy that leads business to base long-term plans on the existence of the credit. Yet the importance of sustained substantial industrial research has been amply demonstrated by this industry. In addition, the federal R&D budget is overdue for a shift from defense-driven to civilian-driven research projects.

Finding these new ideas, and making use of them, will require a skilled work force, which calls for efforts at all levels. The education of youth from kindergarten to twelfth grade requires continuing improvement. The German emphasis on education, including ... apprentice schools, has paid rich rewards. While the U.S. research universities remain supreme in the world, it is also true that a declining proportion of U.S. citizens are receiving engineering degrees at U.S. universities, leading to fears of a shortfall of skilled personnel.

If skilled workers and managers are to put their ideas into effect, they will require sufficient and low cost capital, and capital comes from maintaining a high savings economy, as Germany and Japan have done in recent decades. Remember that recent research has shown technology and capital investment to be mutually reinforcing: they are not independent inputs to growth, as earlier growth models have assumed. Technology works better with more investment; more investment facilitates more rapid technology improvements. The recent research of Lau (1992) has found that more than 50 percent of the measured technical change in the postwar era is embodied in physical capital (and it would be an even higher percentage in the machinery and equipment component). The increase in national savings should come from all available sources: government, households, and industry. This saving must be allocated to the investors by an efficient financial system in which incentives for both lenders and users favor longer term investments for greater growth.

The interlocking systems of tax policy, regulation, and law need to be examined to assure that they encourage commercialization of new technology. In the past, tax incentives for investors in young and growing firms, where most new jobs are created, or for encouraging more risky investment, have filled this role. It may be especially important to offer a higher return to those who hold an equity investment for a relatively long time: the German and Japanese systems use strong bank ownership of individual firms to encourage more patient investment. A certain number of environmental and other regulations are inevitable, even welcome, but they should be examined to be sure that the costs they inflict on business are as light as possible, given society's goals.

Finally, postwar economic history does show that trade promotes growth. No country has completely free trade, but increasing the freedom to buy and to sell abroad is tremendously important to growth of the U.S. economy.

Notes

1. I owe an enormous debt to Nathan Rosenberg, my close collaborator and friend for ten years, for my education in so many matters, great and small, including much of the material in this paper. We have published much on many subjects, starting with the first real look at what truly makes for a nation's competitiveness in *The Positive Sum Strategy* (National Academy Press 1986) and most recently in our new book (with David Mowery), *Technology and the Wealth of Nations* (Stanford Press 1992), which contains a longer study by us on the chemical industry—an industry in which I was an active contributor and participant for nearly forty years. I am also indebted for useful comments to Edward Steinmueller, Lawrence Lau, Timothy Taylor, and the anonymous referees. All remaining failings are mine, however.

2. In the early 1960s and subsequently into the 1970s, the inflationary shocks to the macroeconomy soon focused the attention of mainstream economists on the short-run (perhaps only a few years) stabilization of volatile economic cycles, employing general equilibrium macroeconomics, and the study of long-term growth was largely relegated to a few specialists.

3. The Soviet collapse underlines this point also. As Solow's model, quite correctly within its assumptions, shows, the rate of Soviet capital investment, by itself and without the other complementary investments and organizational structures should have had no important effect on the rate of growth of economy. This finding has been fortified by empirical work of Durlauf of Stanford (1992), J. Bradford deLong and Lawrence Summers of Harvard (1991) (who especially emphasized the importance to growth of investment in machinery and equipment), and Edwin Wolff of New York University (1992).

4. In addressing questions like these, the macroeconomic theory of growth begins to approach the extensive findings of the microeconomists of technical change, such as Nathan Rosenberg of Stanford (1986), and Richard Nelson of Columbia (1982), among others, who long age identified these interactive effects.

5. The story of the American invention of chemical engineering has been told by Landau and Rosenberg in *Invention and Technology* for Fall 1990 and in Landau and Rosenberg (1992)

References

Abramovitz, M. 1956. "Resource and Output Trends in the United States since 1870." *American Economic Review* 46 (May): 5–23.

Barro, R. J. 1991. "Economic Growth in a Cross Section of Countries." *Quarterly Journal of Economics* 106:407–43; and with Xavier Sala-i-Martin. 1992. "Convergence." *Journal of Political Economy* 100:223–51.

Bernal, J. D. 1939. *The Social Function of Science.* Cambridge: MIT Press.

Bernstein, J. I., and M. I. Nadiri. 1988. "Interindustry R&D Spillovers, Rates of Return, and Production in High-Tech Industries." *American Economic Review* (May): 429–34. Also 1989. "Research and Development and Intra-Industry Spillovers: An Empirical Application of Dynamic Duality." *Review of Economic Studies* 56 (April): 249–67.

Boskin, M., and L. J. Lau. 1992. "Capital, Technology, and Economic Growth." In *Technology and the Wealth of Nations*, edited by N. Rosenberg, R. Landau, and D. Mowery. Stanford: Stanford University Press.

DeLong J. B., and L. H. Summers. 1991. "Equipment Investment and Economic Growth." *Quarterly Journal of Economics* 106:445–502.

Durlauf, S. N. 1992. "International Differences in Economic Fluctuations." In *Technology and the Wealth of Nations*, edited by N. Rosenberg, R. Landau, and D. Mowery. Stanford: Stanford University Press.

Hatsopoulos, G. N., and J. M. Poterba. 1993. "America's Investment Shortfall: Probable Causes and Possible Fixes." Report to the Board on Science, Technology, and Economic Policy, National Research Council, Washington, D.C.

Jorgenson, D. W., F. Gollop, and B. Fraumeni. 1987. *Productivity and U.S. Economic Growth*. Cambridge: Harvard University Press.

Jorgenson, D. W., H. Sukuramoto, K. Yoshida, and M. Kuroda. 1990. "Bilateral Models of Production for Japanese and U.S. Industries." In *Productivity in the U.S. and Japan: Studies in Income and Wealth*, edited by C. R. Hulten. vol. 5. Chicago: University of Chicago.

Kim, J. I., and L. J. Lau. 1992. "Human Capital and Aggregate Productivity: Some Empirical Evidence from the Group-of-Five Countries." Working paper 318. Center for Economic Policy Research, Stanford University, Stanford, California.

Landau, R. 1988. "U.S. Economic Growth." *Scientific American* 258, no. 6 (June): 44–52.

Landau, R. 1991. "How Competitiveness Can Be Achieved." In *Technology and Economics*. Washington, D.C.: National Academy Press.

Landau, R., and N. Rosenberg. 1992. "Successful Commercialization in the Chemical Process Industries." In *Technology and the Wealth of Nations*, edited by N. Rosenberg, R. Landau, and D. Mowery. Stanford: Stanford University Press.

Lucas, R., Jr. 1988. "On the Mechanics of Economic Development." *Journal of Monetary Economics* 17:3–42; Also 1990. "Why Doesn't Capital Flow from Rich to Poor Countries?" *American Economic Review* 90, no. 2: 92–96.

Nelson, R., and S. G. Winter. 1982. *An Evolutionary Theory of Economic Change*. Cambridge: Harvard University Press.

Phillips, K. 1992. *Harvard Business Review* (July-August).

Porter, M. E. 1990. *The Competitive Advantage of Nations*. New York: The Free Press.

Romer, P. 1986. "Increasing Returns and Long-Run Growth." *Journal of Political Economy* 94: 1002–37.

Romer, P. 1990. "Endogenous Technical Change." *Journal of Political Economy* 98:S71–S102.

Rosenberg, N. 1986. "The Impact of Technological Innovation." In *The Positive Sum Strategy*, edited by R. Landau and N. Rosenberg. Washington, D.C.: National Academy Press.

Solow, R. 1957. "Technical Change and the Aggregate Production Function." *Review of Economics and Statistics* 39 (August): 312–20.

Stiglitz, J. E. 1993. "Endogenous Growth and Cycles." Working Paper 4286. Cambridge, Massachusetts: National Bureau of Economic Research.

Wolff, E. N. 1992. "Capital Formation and Productivity Growth in the 1970s and 1980s: A Comparative Look at OECD Countries." In *Tools for American Workers: The Role of Machinery and Equipment in Economic Growth.* American Council for Capital Formation, Center for Policy Research, Washington, D.C.

Appendix

Papers and Patents of
Ralph Landau

A. Papers

1. "The Use of Electron Diffraction in Studying Corrosion." *Metals & Alloys* 9 (March 1938): 73–77; (April 1938): 100–103

2. "Corrosion of Binary Alloys" (With Carl S. Oldach). Paper presented at the eighty-first general meeting of the Electrochemical Society, Nashville, Tennessee, April 15–18, 1942. Printed in *Transactions* of the Society, 81 (1942): 521–558.

3. "Some Mechanisms of Alloy Corrosion." Paper presented at the eighty-first general meeting of the Electrochemical Society, Nashville, Tennessee, April 15–18, 1942. Printed in *Transactions* of the Society 81 (1942): 559–571.

4. "Cobalt Electrolytically Refined" (with Carl S. Oldach). *Metals & Alloys* 17 (May 1943): 967–968.

5. "Industrial Handling of Fluorine" (with Raphael Rosen). *Industrial and Engineering Chemistry* 39 (March 1947): 281–286.

6. "Fluorine Disposal —Continuous Process" (with Raphael Rosen). *Industrial and Engineering Chemistry* 40 (August 1948): 1389–1393.

7. "Absorption in a High-Molecular Weight, Non-Aqueous System— Uranium Hexafluoride in Heavy Oil" (with C. E. Birchenall, George G. Joris, and Joseph C. Elgin). In *Engineering Developments in the Gaseous Diffusion Process*, edited by Manson Benedict and Clarke Williams. New York: McGraw-Hill, 1949.

8. "Corrosion by Fluorine and Fluorine Compounds." Paper presented before the eighth annual conference of the National Association of Corrosion Engineers, Galveston, Texas, March 10–14, 1952. Printed in *Corrosion* 8 (August 1952): 283–288.

9. "Ethylene Oxide by Direct Oxidation." *Petroleum Refiner* 32, 9 (September 1953): 146–151.

9a. "Direct Oxidation of Ethylene to Ethylene Oxide." *The Industrial Chemist* (May 1955); *The Petroleum Engineer* (May 1955).

10. "Aromatic Oxidation." Paper presented before a meeting of the Organic Synthetic Chemical Society of Japan, Tokyo, Japan, July 4, 1956. Published in the *Yuki Gosei Kagaku Kyokai Shi* 14, 10 (1956): 629–630.

11. "Europe's Chemical Industry Shows Renewed Vigor." *Chemical & Engineering News* 35 (February 25, 1957): 16–21.

12. "International Collaboration in the Chemical Industries." *Chemical Engineering Progress* 53, 11 (November 1957): 531–536.

13. "Expansion by Acquiring Foreign Know-How" (with Thomas P. Brown). Paper presented before the Chemical Market Research Association, New York, May 21, 1958. Printed in *Chemical Processing* (December, 1958): 27–28, 87–88.

14. "Chemical Engineering in West Germany." *Chemical Engineering Progress* 54, 7 (July 1958): 64–68, 115.

14a. "American Chemical Engineer's View of the European Congress of Chemical Engineering 1958 Meetings." *Chemical Engineering Progress* (August 1958).

15. "A Critical Look at Scientist-Management Relations in the C.P.I." Paper presented at American Institute of Chemical Engineers meeting, New York Section, September 1958.

16. "Estimating Costs of Foreign Plant Construction." Paper presented before the Northeast Ohio Section of the American Association of Cost Engineers, April 1959.

17. "Research and Management in the Chemical Process Industries." *Industrial and Engineering Chemistry* 51, 7 (July 1959): 47A–52A.

18. "Current Developments in the European Chemical Industry." Paper presented before the International Executives Association, Inc., New York, May 24, 1960.

19. "Package Plants for the Latin American Petrochemical Industry." Paper presented before the International Congress of Chemical Engineering—joint meeting of Instituto Mexicano de Ingenieros Quimicos and the American Institute of Chemical Engineers, Mexico City, Mexico, June 19–22, 1960.

20. "Recent Developments in Aromatic Chemicals." Paper presented before the Petrochemical Symposium, American Institute of Chemical Engineers, Tulsa, Oklahoma, September 27, 1960.

21. "Role of American Engineering Design Companies in the Chemical Process Industry." Paper presented before the thirty-second International Congress of Chemical Industry, Barcelona, Spain, October 25, 1960. Printed in *Chemical Age of India* 13, 1 (January-February 1962): 9–15.

22. "Industrial Package Plants at Home and Abroad." *Industrial and Engineering Chemistry* 53, 2 (February 1961): 34A–41A.

23. "Phthalic Anhydride" (with Hugh Harper). Paper presented before a symposium on Organic Intermediates in the 1960s, organized by the Manchester Section of the Society of Chemical Industry, Continental European Section, and the Paper and Textile Chemicals Group, Manchester, England, March 24, 1961. Printed in *Chemistry and Industry* (July 29, 1961): 1143–1152; *Chemical Age of India* 13, 2 (March-April 1962): 97–105.

24. "Recent Trends in Aromatic Chemicals from Petroleum." *World Petroleum* 32, 4 (April 1961): 56, 58–60, 62, 64, 80.

25. "Recent Developments in Aromatic Oxidation" (with Robert W. Simon). Paper presented at the American Institute of Chemical Engineers meeting, Cleveland, Ohio, May 8, 1961; Symposium of the London Section of the Society of Chemical Industry on "Oxidation Processes in Chemical Manufacture," September 29, 1961; American Institute of Chemical Engineers meeting, Philadelphia, Pennsylvania, October 23, 1961. Printed in *Chemistry and Industry*, No. 2 (January 13, 1962): 70–75; *Industrial and Engineering Chemistry* 53, 10 (October 1961): 32A–41A.

26. "Production of Phthalic Anhydride" (with David Brown). Paper presented at the First Tri-Section Symposium of the American Institute of Chemical Engineers, Newark, New Jersey, May 9, 1961.

27. "Expanding Through Creative Research, Development, and Engineering." Paper presented at American Institute of Chemical Engineers meeting, Lake Placid, New York, September 24–27, 1961; Symposium on Petrochemicals, University of California, Los Angeles, May 1962.

28. "Isoprene from Refinery Propylene: The Lowest Cost Route to Synthetic Natural Rubber" (with Robert W. Simon and G.S. Schaffel). Paper presented at XXXIIIe Congres Internationale de Chimie Industrielle, Bordeaux, France, October 2, 1961. Printed in *Chimie et Industrie* 90, 1 (July 1963): 37–43.

29. "Comparative Postwar Evolution of the West European and American Chemical Process Industries." Paper presented at the American Institute of Chemical Engineers symposium on Competition of the U.S. Chemical Industry in World Markets, New York, December, 1960. Published in *Dechema-Monographien, Deutsche Geselschaft fur Chemisches Apparatewesen C.V.* 41 (Frankfurt, 1962): 243–247.

30. "Changes Are Coming Everywhere." *Chemical Engineering Progress* (February 1962): 27.

31. "Recent Advances in the Oxidation of Olefins." Paper presented before the Bombay Chapter of the Indian Institute of Chemical Engineers, Bombay, India, February 9, 1962.

32. "Intermediates for Synthetic Fibers." Paper presented before the Indian Institute of Chemical Engineering, Calcutta Regional Center, Calcutta, India, February 16, 1962. Printed in *Indian Chemical Engineer* (July 1962): 126–132.

33. "Chlorinated Methanes" (with Sherwood N. Fox). Chap. 12 of *Chlorine —Its Manufacture, Properties, and Uses*, American Chemical Society Chlorine Monograph 154. New York: Reinhold Publishing Corp., 1962.

34. "The Newer Synthetic Rubbers" (with Alfred R. Smith). *Indian Chemical Engineer* (April 1962): 81–86, 100.

35. "Growth of Chemical Processing in Western Europe and the USA." *World Petroleum* (August 1962): 48–51.

36. "The Goodyear-SD Process, and the Newer Synthetic Rubbers" (with G. S. Schaffel and A.D. Deprez). Paper presented before Deutsche Geselschaft fur Mineralwissenschaft und Kohlechemie E.V., Karlsruhe, Germany, October 1962. Printed in *Erdol und Kohle Erdgas Petrochemie* 7, 2 (July 1963): 754–759.

37. "Adipic Acid and Other Cyclohexane Derivatives—Their Role in Nylon Production" (with David Brown). Paper presented before a symposium of the American Institute of Chemical Engineers, New Orleans, March 10–13, 1963.

38. "Comparison de l'evolution de l'industrie Chimique Europeenne et Americaine Depuis la Derniere Guerre Mondiale." *Chimie & Industrie* 89, 4 (April 1963): 357–368.

39. "Japan—The Never-Easy Struggle toward the Top" (with T. P. Brown and G. S. Schaffel). *Chemical & Engineering News* (July 1, 1963): 68–82.

40. "The Scientific Design Phenol Process" (with David Brown). Paper

presented before the Institute of Chemical Engineers, Northwestern Branch Symposium on Alternative Routes to Synthetic Phenol, Manchester, England, November 1963.

41. "Chemical Engineering Abroad." Paper presented at a meeting of the North Jersey Section of the American Institute of Chemical Engineers, East Rutherford, New Jersey, February 11, 1964.

42. "West Europe, Japan Narrow U.S. Lead in Petrochemicals" (with Peter H. Spitz). *Oil and Gas Journal* (September 7, 1964): 92–96.

43. "Technology and Obsolescence in the Petrochemical Industries for Developing Countries." Paper presented before the United Nations Inter-Regional Conference on the Development of Petrochemical Industries in Developing Countries, Teheran, Iran, November 16–30, 1964. Published in *Proceedings of the Inter-Regional Conference*, 1965; printed in *Chemical Age of India* 16, 3 (March 1965): 213–225.

44. "How Industry Looks at Society Activities in International Sphere." Paper presented before a symposium of the Engineers Joint Council on Relationships between Engineering Societies and Industry, New York, January 18–19, 1965. Excerpted and printed under the title "American Success Brings Problems." By the Engineers Joint Council, New York, 1965, pp. 37–41.

45. "Procurement of Completely Developed Processes from the Engineering Construction Industry." Paper presented before the fifty-fifth National Meeting of the American Institute of Chemical Engineers, Houston, Texas, February 8, 1965.

46. "The Impact of Technology on the International Operations of the Chemical Industry." Paper presented before a symposium of the Midland Section of American Institute of Chemical Engineers on the Economic Impact of International Operations on the Chemical Industry, Midland, Michigan, April 24, 1965.

47. "Recent Developments in the Chemical Industries of Europe and East Asia." Paper presented before the Northeastern New York Section of American Institute of Chemical Engineers, Albany, New York, May 11, 1965.

48. "Making Research Pay" (with David Brown). *Symposium Series No. 7.* London: Institution of Chemical Engineers, 1965: 7:35–7:43.

49. "European Technology Today." Paper presented before the Chemical Marketing and Economics Division of the American Chemical Society, New York Section, November 1965.

50. "Foreign Chemical Technology in the U.S." Paper presented at the International Business Symposium on Foreign Competition in the U.S.A., sponsored by the American Institute of Chemical Engineers, Atlantic City, New Jersey, September 21, 1966. Printed in *International Business* (1967): 82–89.

51. "The Development and Licensing of New Processes" (with David Brown and Hugh Harper). Paper presented before the annual symposium of the Graduates and Students Section of the Institution of Chemical Engineers on Advances in Chemical Process Engineering, London, October 6–7, 1966.

52. *The Chemical Plant, From Process Selection to Commercial Operation* (Ralph Landau and others). New York: Reinhold Publishing Co., 1966.

53. "Recent Developments in Oxidation Technology" (with Joseph E. Jewett). Paper presented before the American Institute of Chemical Engineers, Houston, Texas, February 22, 1967.

54. "Epoxidation of Olefins" (with David Brown, J. L. Russell, and J. Kollar). Paper presented at symposium on New Concepts and Techniques in Oxidation of Hydrocarbons, Seventh World Petroleum Congress, Mexico City, April, 1967. Printed in *Proceedings of the Congress, Petrochemistry* (Essex, England: Elsevier Publishing Co., 1967) 5: 67–72.

55. "Ethylene Oxide Economics: The Impact of New Technologies" (with David Brown, A. Saffer, and J. V. Porcelli, Jr.). Paper presented at the sixtieth annual meeting of American Institute of Chemical Engineers, New York, December, 1967. Printed in *Chemical Engineering Progress* (March 1968): 27–34.

56. "Oxidation of Aromatic Hydrocarbons—Development of the M-C Process" (with Alfred Saffer). Paper presented at the Modern Chemistry Symposium sponsored by *Modern Chemistry in Industry*, Eastbourne, England, March 11–14, 1968.

57. "Development of the M-C Process" (with Alfred Saffer). *Chemical Engineering Progress* 64, 10 (October 1968): 20–26.

58. "Ethylene Oxide" (with Rex E. Lidov). In *Ethylene and its Industrial Derivatives*, edited by S.A. Miller. London: Ernest Benn, 1969.

59. "Boron-Promoted Oxidation of Paraffins and Cycloparaffins" (with David Brown and J. L. Russell). Paper presented before the 158th national meeting of the American Chemical Society, New York, September 7–12, 1969.

60. "Ethylene and Propylene Oxides and Their Derivatives" (with Andre C. Deprez). In *Petrochemicals and Their Raw Materials in Europe*. Proceedings of the Fourth International Conference of the European Chemical Marketing Research Association, Budapest, Hungary, October 13–15, 1970.

61. "Recent Developments in Ethylene Chemistry" (with G. S. Schaffel). *Origin and Refining of Petroleum*. Advances in Chemistry Series no. 103 (1971): 150–157.

62. "The Chemical Engineer—Today and Tomorrow." Paper presented before the American Institute of Chemical Engineers, Dallas, Texas, February 21, 1972. Printed in *Chemical Engineering Progress* 68, 6 (June 9, 1972): 9–19.

63. "Industrial Innovation: Yesterday and Today." Chemical Industry Medal Address to the American Section of the Society of Chemical Industry, New York, October 3, 1973. printed in *Chemistry and Industry*, no. 3 (February 2, 1974): 96–100.

64. "Financial and Capacity Needs." Testimony before the Joint Economic Committee, Congress of the United States, 93rd Congress, 2nd Session, October 1, 1974, pp. 112–133.

65. "The Chemical Process Industries in International Investment and Trade." In *U.S. Technology and International Trade: Proceedings of the Technical Session at the Eleventh Annual Meeting of the National Academy of Engineering*, April 23–24, 1975.

66. "Ethylbenzene, Styrene, and the Styrene Polymers" (with Rex E. Lidov, J. Habeshaw, and A. N. Roper). In *Benzene and Its Industrial Derivatives* edited by E. S. Hancock. New York: John Wiley, 1975.

67. "An American View of Chemical Investment Patterns in the Era of High Energy Costs" (with Arthur I. Mendolia). Paper presented before the annual meeting of the Continental European Section, Society of Chemical Industry, Sicily, Italy, October 18, 1975. Printed in *Chemistry and Industry* (December 6, 1975): 1009–1014.

68. "The Enduring Need for Entrepreneurship." *Pennsylvania Triangle* (Spring, 1976): 42–43; *Chemtech* (June 1976): 347–348.

69. "From Chemical Engineering to Moral Philosophy." Address on the occasion of the dedication of the Landau Chemical Engineering Building, Massachusetts Institute of Technology, March 5, 1976.

70. "The Chemical Engineering Trilemma." Paper presented before a seminar on the Future of Chemical Engineering at the Massachusetts Institute

of Technology, April 4, 1976. Printed in *Chemical Engineering Progress* 72, 8 (August 1976): 13–16.

71. "Technology, Trade, and the U. S. Economy." Paper presented before the Workshop on Technological Factors Contributing to the Nation's Foreign Trade, Woods Hole, Massachusetts, August 22–31, 1976. Report published by the National Academy of Sciences, Washington, D.C., 1978.

72. "The Role of R&D in the Development of Brazilian Technology" (with Arthur I. Mendolia). Paper presented before the first Brazilian Petrochemical Congress, Rio de Janeiro, Brazil, November 8–12, 1976. Printed in the *Proceedings* of the Congress, published by the Brazilian Institute of Petroleum.

73. "Development of Japan's Petrochemical Industry." Paper presented before the Japan-American Chamber of Commerce, Tokyo, Japan, December 3, 1976. Published in *Hydrocarbon Processing* (June 1977): 56I–56Q.

74. "The Joys of Entrepreneurship." Address upon receiving the Winthrop-Sears Medal for Chemical Entrepreneurship, delivered before the Chemical Industry Association, New York, April 5, 1977.

75. "International Chemical Investment Patterns Reviewed" (with Arthur I. Mendolia). Paper presented before the annual meeting of the Continental European Section of the Society of Chemical Industry, Vienna, Austria, October 16–18, 1977. Printed in *Chemistry and Industry* (November 19, 1977): 902–910.

76. "Entrepreneurship in the Chemical Industry and in the United States." Paper presented at a symposium on Innovators and Entrepreneurs—An Endangered Species? at the thirteenth annual meeting of the National Academy of Engineering, Washington, D. C., November 10, 1977. Published by the National Academy of Engineering, Washington, D. C., April 1978.

77. "Trans-National Investment and Technology Transfer." Paper presented before the American Institute of Chemical Engineers, New York, November, 1977. Printed in *Chemical Engineering Progress* (February 1978): 21–26.

78. "Innovation and Entrepreneurs." Hearings before the Committee on Ways and Means, U.S. House of Representatives, 95th Congress, 2nd Session, on the President's 1978 tax program, Washington, D.C., March 10, 13, 1978, pp. 3026–3058.

79. "The Chemical Industry, 2000 A.D. (with David Brown). Paper presented before the American Institute of Chemical Engineers, Philadelphia,

Pennsylvania, April 1978. Printed in *Chemical Engineering Progress* (October 1978): 27–31.

80. "Halcon International, Inc.—An Entrepreneurial Chemical Company." Paper presented before the New York dinner meeting of The Newcomen Society in honor of Halcon International, Inc., June 21, 1978. Published by The Newcomen Society, October 1978.

81. "Entrepreneurship in Today's Environment." *Experimental Mechanics* (August 1978): 3N.

82. "The Inventor and the Entrepreneur." Introduction to the General Electric Centennial Symposium on Science, Invention, and Social Change, Schenectady, New York, September 20–21, 1978. Published under the title of "Innovation for Fun and Profit," CHEMTECH 9, 1 (January 1979): 22–24.

83. "Technology Transfer: Some Case Histories and Observations." Distinguished Award for Industrial Technology Address delivered before the fiftieth Anniversary Dinner Meeting of the Association of Consulting Chemists and Chemical Engineers, New York, October 24, 1978.

83a. "Presentation before Academy Forum, National Academy of Sciences, Washington, D.C. Printed in a booklet entitled *Technological Innovation and the U.S. Economy* (November 14, 1978): 26–35.

84. "Production of Propylene Oxide via Co-Product Processes" (with David Brown and G. Allan Sullivan). Paper presented before the symposium of the American Chemical Society and the Chemical Society of Japan on Worldwide Progress of the Petrochemical, Organic, and Polymer Industries, Honolulu, Hawaii, April 1–6, 1979. Published in CHEMTECH (October 1979): 602–607.

85. "Chemical Industry Research and Innovation." Paper presented before the symposium on Innovation and U.S. Research: Problems and Recommendations, cosponsored by the Industrial Research Institute and the American Chemical Society, Washington, D.C., September 10, 1979. Published as a part of a volume in the ACS *Symposium Series* 129 (1980): 19–50.

86. "Innovation in the Chemical Processing Industry." Warren K. Lewis Lecture in Chemical Engineering at the Chemical Engineering Department, Massachusetts Institute of Technology, Cambridge October 12, 1979.

87. "Technology" (with David Brown). Published as part of a special report on "Chemistry in the 1980s," *Chemical & Engineering News* 57 (November 26, 1979): 34–40.

88. "Taxes—Their Impact on Innovation Decision-Making." Paper presented before the National Manufacturers Association, Washington, D.C., March 21, 1980.

89. "The Innovative Millieu." Paper presented before a symposium of the Aspen Institute for Humanistic Studies, Wye, Maryland, November 7–9, 1980. Published in *Managing Innovation*, edited by Sven B. Lundstedt and E. William Colglazier, Jr. Oxford: Pergamon Press, 1982.

90. "Recent Technological Developments and Their Influence on the Future of the Japanese Chemical Industry." Paper presented before the Chemical Society of Japan, Tokyo, June 25, 1981. Published in *Chemical Economy & Engineering Review* (October 1981).

91. "Process Innovation." Perkin Medal Address delivered at the seventy-fifth Perkin Medal Award Dinner of the American Section, Society of Chemical Industry, New York, February 13, 1981. Published in *Chemistry and Industry* (May 2, 1981); *The Bridge* 11 (Fall 1981): 17.

92. "Taxation, Technology, and the U.S. Economy." *Technology in Society* 3, 1–2 (1981). A special issue edited by Ralph Landau and N. Bruce Hannay; reprinted in book form (Oxford: Pergamon Press, 1981).

93. "Statement of Dr. Ralph Landau before the Committee on Finance, U.S. Senate, June 12, 1981."

94. "Chemical Process Innovation." Chemical Pioneer Award Address. Printed in *The Chemist* (January 1982).

95. "Technology, Economics, and Politics—Observations of an Entrepreneur." National Academy of Engineering, July 1982.

96. "The U.S. Position in World Markets—The Effect of Technology on Selected Industries," Adapted from a keynote address at the fiftieth anniversary meeting of the Accreditation Board for Engineering and Technology, Colorado Springs, Colorado, October 28, 1982; printed in the proceedings of the meeting.

97. "Technology, Economics, and Public Policy." Keynote address delivered to Engineering Dean's Institute Annual Meeting at Hilton Head, South Carolina, March 28, 1983.

98. "Tribute to Courtland D. Perkins." Remarks on the occasion of the Commemoration Program for Courtland D. Perkins, former President, National Academy of Engineering, Washington, D.C., June 30, 1983. Published in *The Bridge* 13 (Summer 1983): 20–22.

99. "Technology, Economics, and Public Policy." *The Bridge* 13, 3 (Fall 1983): 17–21.

100. "Technology, Economics, and Public Policy." Paper presented at the New York Seventy-fifth Diamond Jubilee Luncheon of the American Institute of Chemical Engineers, November 15, 1983.

101. "Technology, Economics, and Public Policy in the U.S.A.." Paper presented at Texas A&M University, September 23, 1983. Published by Texas A&M University in the *1983–84 University Lecture series*, April 1984.

102. "Ethylene Glycol" (with Brian J. Ozero). In *Encyclopedia of Chemical Processing and Design*, vol. 20. New York: Marcel Dekker, 1984.

103. "Corporate Partnerships with Entrepreneurs." *The MIT Report* (September 1985).

104. "Understanding Innovation and Growth." CHEMTECH (January 1986): 14–15.

105. "*The Positive Sum Strategy: Harnessing Technology for Economic Growth*, edited with Nathan Rosenberg. Washington, D.C.: National Academy Press; 1986. Proceedings of the Symposium on Economics and Technology held at Stanford University, March 17–19, 1985.

106. "Introduction" (with Nathan Roseberg). In *The Positive Sum Strategy: Harnessing Technology for Economic Growth.*

107. "Editors' Overview" (with Nathan Rosenberg). In *The Positive Sum Strategy: Harnessing Technology for Economic Growth.*

108. "Capital Formation in the United States and Japan" (with George Hatsopoulos). In *The Positive Sum Stategy: Harnessing Technology for Economic Growth.*

109. "*Technology and Economic Policy*, edited with Dale Jorgenson. Cambridge, Mass.: Balinger, 1986. Proceedings of the Conference on Technology and Economic Policy, Harvard University, held at the National Academy of Sciences, February 4–5, 1985.

110. "Technology, Economics, and Public Policy." In *Technology and Economic Policy.*

111. "The Chemical Industry in the 90's." *The Chemist* (November 1986).

112. "Corporate Partnering Can Spur Innovation." *Research Management* 30, 3 (May–June 1987): 21–26.

113. "Investing in the Nation's Technological Future." Remarks made at National Academy of Engineering Annual Meeting, October 13, 1987. Printed in *The Bridge* (Winter 1987).

114. "Rebuild America (A Non-Partisan Strategy)." Excerpted from a speech given at the conference Invest in America: From Stock Shocks to

Investment Economics, February 26, 1988, Los Angeles, California; printed in *Rebuild America* (March/April 1988): 8.

115. "What Do We Really Mean By Competitiveness." *The MIT Report* 16, 4 (May 1988).

116. "U.S. Economic Growth." *Scientific American* 258, no. 6 (June 1988): 44–52.

117. "Technology, Capital Formation, and the Twin Deficits." The Bray Lecture, California Institute of Technology, April 14, 1988. Printed in *Engineering & Science* 51, no. 4 (Summer 1988).

118. "Strategies for U.S. Economic Growth" (with Nathan Rosenberg). Paper presented at the sixth Convocation of Academies of Engineering and Technological Sciences, March 30–April 1, 1987. Printed in the proceedings volume, *Globalization of Technology: International Perspectives*. Washington, D.C.: National Academy Press, 1988.

119. "Harnessing Innovation for Growth." *Chemical Engineering Progress* (August 1988).

120. "Competitiveness Linked to Higher Investment." Remarks presented at the March 23, 1989, meeting of the New York Academy of Sciences' Science Policy Association. Printed in the Academy's newsletter *Science Focus* (July 1989).

121. "*Technology and Capital Formation*, edited with Dale Jorgenson. Cambridge, Massachusetts. The MIT Press, 1989. Proceedings of the Conference on Technology and Capital Formation, Harvard University, November 7–9, 1985.

122. "Technology and Capital Formation." In *Technology and Capital Formation.*

123. "The Chemical Engineer and the CPI: Reading the Future From the Past." Adaptation of a presentation at the Centennial Celebration of Chemical Engineering Department, Massachusetts Institute of Technology, October 8, 1988. Printed in *Chemical Engineering Progress* (September 1989).

124. "Agriculture at the Crossroads." Adaptation of a presentation at the Conference on Technology and Agricultural Policy, Harvard University, December 11–13, 1986. Printed in the proceedings volume, *Technology and Agricultural Policy*. Washington, D.C.: National Academy Press, 1990.

125. "Chemical Engineering: Key to the Growth of the Chemical Process Industries." *A.I.Ch.E. Symposium Series* 86, 274 (1990).

126. "Capital Investment: Key to Competitiveness and Growth." *The Brookings Review* (Summer 1990).

127. "Business Taxes, Capital Costs, and Competitiveness" (Ralph Landau and others). Commentary given at ACCF, Center for Policy Research Symposium, May 1, 1990. Printed in Monograph Series on *Tax and Environmental Policies & U.S. Capital Costs* (July 1990).

128. "America's High-Tech Triumph" (with Nathan Rosenberg). *American Heritage of Invention & Technology* 6, 2 (Fall 1990).

129. "How Competitiveness Can Be Achieved: Fostering Economic Growth and Productivity." Written for the National Academy of Engineering Symposium on Technology and Economics, April 4–5. 1990, in honor of outgoing Vice President Ralph Landau. Printed in the proceedings volume, *Technology and Economics*. Washington, D.C.: National Academy Press, 1991.

130. "Innovation in Chemical Processing Industries" (with Nathan Rosenberg). Written for the National Academy of Engineering Symposium on Technology and Economics, April 4–5, 1990, in honor of outgoing Vice President Ralph Landau. Printed in the proceedings volume, *Technology and Economics*. Washington, D.C.: National Academy Press, 1991.

131. "Academic-Industrial Interaction in the Early Development of Chemical Engineering." In *Intellectual Foundations of Chemical Engineering*, edited by Clark Colton. New York: Academic Press, 1991.

132. "Technology, Capital Formation, and U.S. Competitiveness." In *International Productivity and Competitiveness*, edited by Bert G. Hickman. New York: Oxford University Press, 1992.

133. "The CEO and the Technologist." *Research-Technology Management* (May–June 1992).

134. *Technology and the Wealth of Nations*, edited by Ralph Landau, David C. Mowery, and Nathan Rosenberg. Stanford: Stanford University Press, 1992. Adaptations of papers presented at the Conference on Economic Growth and the Commercialization of New Technologies, Stanford University, September 11–12, 1989.

135. "Introduction" (with Nathan Rosenberg and David Mowery). In *Technology and the Wealth of Nations*.

136. "Successful Commercialization in the Chemical Process Industries" (with Nathan Rosenberg). In *Technology and the Wealth of Nations*.

137. *Tax Reform and the Cost of Capital: An International Comparison*, edited by Dale W. Jorgenson and Ralph Landau. Washington, D.C.: The Brookings Institution, 1993. Adaptation of papers presented at the International

Conference on the Cost of Capital, held at the Kennedy School of Government, Harvard University, Cambridge, Massachusetts, November 19–21, 1987.

138. *Risk-Taking and Entrepreneurship: A Perspective from 46 years of Experience and Articulation. Commentary on a Paper by James Poterba.* Presented at the fourth Stanford-Harvard Workshop on Tax Policy, Washington, D.C., July 1992.

139. *Economic Growth and the Chemical Industry.* Paper presented at a conference in honor of Nathan Rosenberg, Stanford University, November, 1992. Forthcoming in *Research Policy.*

B. Patents

Oxidation of ethylene. U.S. 2,752,362. June 1956.

Ethylene oxide. U.S. 2,766,261. October 1956.

Recovery of maleic acid and phthalic acid anhydrides. British 763,339. December 1956.

Recovery of dicarboxylic acid anhydrides. British 768,551. February 1957.

Preparation of ethylene oxide using alkyl silicones and silanes as carbon dioxide repressant. U.S. 2,785,186. March 1957.

Terephthalic acid (with David Brown and Alfred Saffer). German 1,004,159. March 1957.

Ethylene oxide (with Alfred Saffer). U.S. 2,814,628. November 1957.

Triisopropylbenzene. U.S. 2,814,652. November 1957.

Alkaryl compounds (with Robert B. Egbert and Alfred Saffer). Israeli 10,474. December 1957.

Triisopropylbenzene. British 789, 366. January 1958.

Terephthalic acid (with Robert B. Egbert and Alfred Saffer). Israeli 10,473. January 1958.

Terephthalic acid (with Alfred Saffer). U.S. 2,833,818. May 1958.

Diisopropylbenzene (with Robert B. Egbert and Alfred Saffer). U.S. 2,855,430. October 1958.

Phthalic acids (with Robert B. Egbert and Alfred Saffer). U.S. 2,858,334. October 1958.

Terephthalic acid (with Robert Baldwin and Alfred Saffer). German 1,060,378. July 1959.

Isopropylbenzenes (with Robert B. Egbert and Alfred Saffer). U.S. 2,920,118. January 1960.

Ethyltoluene and terephthalic acid (with Robert B. Egbert and Alfred Saffer). U.S. 2,920,118. January 1960.

p-Diisopropylbenzene (with Robert B. Egbert and Alfred Saffer). British 841,424. July 1960.

Terephthalic acid (noncondensed aromatic compounds) (with Robert B. Egbert and Alfred Saffer). German 1,112,972. March 1962.

Isophthalic acid (with David Brown and Alfred Saffer). German 1,131,201. June 1962.

Process of separating lactams from Beckmann rearrangement reaction mixture. U.S. 3,127,305. March 1964.

Phthalic anhydride. U.S. 3,201,423. August 1965.

Phthalic anhydride. British 1,074,316. July 1967.

p-Diisopropylbenzene from benzenes and propene (with Robert B. Egbert and Alfred Saffer). German 1,268,125. May 1968.

Brevet d'invention. Procédé de préparation de résines polyesters. French 1,566,913. 1969.

Index